Revised Edition

Relationships
A Study in Human Behavior

Helen Gum Westlake
Department Chairperson
York Community High School
Elmhurst, Illinois

GINN
AND
COM-
PANY

FOUNDED IN 1867

Ginn and Company

Dedication

To my husband, Don, our daughter, Dawn,
my mother, Helen McNair Gum,
and to the memory of my father, Cecil L. Gum.

Acknowledgements

I would like to thank my husband, Don, for his constant encouragement and for his photographs which appear in the book. Our daughter, Dawn, contributed by her faith in me and by her willingness to leave me alone to write when she would have enjoyed my companionship. Dawn's humor provided both diversion and insight into the current concerns of young people. Many pictures of Dawn appear in the book and her experiences help to illustrate the manuscript.

I am grateful for the students who have shared their problems, goals, and dreams with me over the years. I sincerely hope that they learned from me as much as I learned from them.

Helen Gum Westlake

Preface

Relationships: A Study in Human Behavior has been written to help students understand their behavior and the behavior of others. The book is divided into four main units. The four units are Understanding Ourselves, Understanding Others, Understanding Marriage, and Understanding Parenthood. Most people during their life span move from individualhood, to couplehood, to parenthood. This progression is helped by a study of self and of self in relation to others.

This book is designed to give students facts on both sides of a question. It is written from study of the many disciplines that research human behavior. The fields of psychology, sociology, anthropology, biology, physiology, philosophy, religion, and education must be studied for essential principles. Some of the authorities in the various fields are quoted and their theories are described to help the students understand themselves and their relationships.

The book is written to encourage and to challenge students. It is designed to encourage students to follow those behaviors which strengthen individuals and families. It is also designed to challenge students to oppose those behaviors which tend to weaken individuals and families.

Contents

Understanding Ourselves

Chapter 1

Our basic needs

In order to understand ourselves and others, we must first understand our basic needs. However, many times we think we need what other people have. Once we get it, we wonder if it is what we want.

THE RYATTS

THE RYATTS by Jack Elrod.
© Field Enterprises, Inc., 1977. Courtesy of Field Newspaper Syndicate.

Physical and psychological needs

Basic needs are divided into physical needs and psychological needs. The *physical needs* are satisfaction of hunger and thirst; shelter from the elements in order to maintain a comfortable body temperature; rest when tired; exercise or activity when rested; satisfaction or sublimation of sexual drives when sexually mature. Physical needs can also be called life-maintaining needs, or biological needs. These needs must be satisfied if one is to live.

The *psychological needs* come from the requirements for love, esteem, sense of worth, recognition, status, new experience, and approval. The psychological needs are often products of society, the culture, the environment, and the reward and punishment system of one's home and community. The psychological needs vary more widely from person to person than do physical needs.

The physical and psychological needs are basic in a person's total makeup. But their expression and satisfaction develop many complicated patterns of behavior. Survival is probably the most basic of all human needs. When life is threatened, a person usually forgets all other considerations. The person who believes his or her life is in danger will do almost anything, including break laws, kill others, or sacrifice wealth in order to eliminate the threat. However, people vary in what threatens them. One person may feel that he or she can't survive if certain freedoms are lost. He or she will lose life rather than suffer life without freedom. Another would prefer any kind of life rather than to lose life itself. Certainly the basic physical needs such as food, drink, shelter, and relief from pain and discomfort are powerful determiners of everyday behavior. When there is a threat to supplies of food or shelter, one will do anything and everything to secure them.

Need and love

In order to function as a social and human being, one needs to be or have been loved by others. When a person feels unloved, the quest for love from others may become the main goal. The quest for sexual gratification is frequently confused with the search for love. One of the human developmental tasks is to reconcile sexual needs and love needs.

Need and status

People need to feel recognized, respected, and approved by others. Without such recognition, they tend to feel worthless, alone, or inferior. The search for wealth, power, prestige, and other symbols of status is common in all societies. The ways to attain such status and the symbols of its attainment differ widely from person to person. They also differ from social group to social group, as well as from time to time.

Need and challenge

Another basic human need may be called the need for challenge. This need becomes more visible when one has been able to fulfill needs for food, shelter, status, love, sex and finds only boredom from the sameness of life. Under these conditions, the boredom serves as a prod causing one to seek excitement, a new experience, or a more challenging goal. This challenge may also come from other people, catastrophes, problems, or one's religious background. We need variety in stimulation, not just to avoid boredom, but actually to preserve our ability to perceive the world.

Maslow's hierarchy

A. H. Maslow (1908–1970) has developed a needs structure. He has placed human needs into groups. The first group consists of those needs that are most basic. If these needs are not met to some degree, the individual cannot move to the next group of needs. Maslow's five categories of needs follow.[1]

1. A. H. Maslow, "A Theory of Human Motivation," *Psychological Review,* Vol. 50 (1943), pp. 370–396.

Physical needs.   These are the need for food when hungry, the need for something to drink when thirsty, the need for rest when tired, the need for exercise when rested, the need to maintain a comfortable body temperature, and the need for shelter and clothing.

Safety needs.   These are the need to have protection from physical harm or injury, the need for fire protection, police protection, laws that say that one person does not have the right to take another person's property or life, the need for insurance to replace property lost through theft, fire, floods, and other disasters.

Love needs.   These are the need to be wanted by another person, to feel warmth, to have a sense of belonging, to be able to give and take affection from another person, and the need to be loved by another and to return that love.

Esteem needs.   These are the need to be proud of one's self, to respect one's self and others, the need for approval, the need for status, and the need to be important for what one does, for who one is or for what one knows.

Self-actualization.   This is the need to achieve one's full potential. The need to be one's own self, working and behaving so that you are aware of others and alive to their needs.   The self-actualized person has succeeded in meeting his or her own basic needs and is able to help other people develop.   The self-actualized person goes beyond self.   He or she achieves a loss of self-awareness which is the ultimate expression of real self.   For example, Sister Candida Lund, of Rosary College in River Forest, Illinois, expressed this stage when she says, "I am so strongly linked with the college."   "It's hard to separate my ambitions from its ambitions."[2]

When needs are met

Until physical needs have been satisfied or reduced to a reasonable level, a person's behavior will be concerned only with those needs. For example, if a person is very, very hungry, he or she will sacrifice safety needs, love needs, esteem needs, and self-actualization in order to satisfy the urgent physical need of hunger.   To talk to hungry people about self-respect, love of people, and democracy is futile until their stomachs are full.

2. *Chicago Daily News,* Suburban Week, 1 and 2 October 1977.

After physical needs are met, a person begins to think about keeping the protection of food supply, the house, and his or her physical being safe. Only after a person feels safe, and safe in another's presence, can that person begin to think of love needs. Now, safe and secure in the presence of another, freed from outside fears, he or she can experience warmth, affection, and love. With the fulfillment of these love needs, one is able to go on to accomplish social approval, status, and self-respect. Only when esteem needs are met can one go on to become one's own best self or work toward the actualized self.

When needs are not met

Movement on Maslow's hierarchy, however, is not always upward. Sometimes people stay at a stage and work to enhance it. For example, in stage one, one has basic food needs, but now one wants fancier food. One has a house for shelter, but now needs four bedrooms, two baths, and a two-car garage. In stage two, one has basic safety needs met but now needs more insurance because he or she has more property. One needs more insurance because his or her possessions are more desired by others. In stage three, one has basic love needs met, but now wants to explore new love techniques, greater love satisfaction. One wants to test and strengthen his or her sense of belonging. One feels the need to improve communication skills to become more aware of the love needs of oneself and others.

One gains status and is well thought of as a person who represents a particular vocational choice. One now wants to be named man or woman of the year, outstanding worker, or some other proof of importance. Instead of going forward on the Maslow hierarchy, a person stops at one stage, gaining more and more that is possible within that stage.

For all people self-preservation is basic, but life at what cost? Will a person risk life if he or she sees a loved one in danger? Will one risk life to gather food for his or her starving children? These questions cause us to realize that all people have the same basic needs. How these needs are expressed and satisfied varies.

Needs and self

Each person ranks needs in his or her own ways after the minimal requirements are reached. This ranking determines his or her behavior. It is difficult to understand other people's ways of behavior.

It is also very difficult to understand our own actions. This is because our needs vary from time to time as our desires and ambitions change. A particular combination of needs may collect to reach a goal. Let's look at an example of the collection of needs as they affected the life of Mary T. Mary's mother was a happy, easygoing person who liked people as they are. Mary was put in the custody of her grandmother who was very strict and very concerned with status. Mary missed the gaiety, love, and approval of her mother. She needed approval, love, and a sense of security. The only way she could gain approval from her grandmother was to follow her rules and succeed. As a result Mary studied to the exclusion of all other school activities. She graduated valedictorian of her class. Her constant study and success pleased her grandmother. This substitution of needs helped her reach an academic goal. But the real goal she pursued was acceptance and approval of her grandmother.

Needs change as goals change

A goal that may motivate us when we are young may have very little value for us when we are older. For example, a junior high girl may practice long hours to learn to be a cheerleader. Fifteen years later she may be completely disgusted with anyone who would waste time on such an unimportant goal. As needs are met, our goals change.

Needs are internal tensions

Needs are internal tensions that we seek to resolve. The behavior sequences that they initiate end when the needs are satisfied or reduced. In many cases, the sequence from need to need-reduction is clearly understood. We are hungry, we eat, we are no longer hungry. After a certain length of time, the need will reappear. We shall probably use the same behavior to satisfy it. However, in other cases, a person may not be so certain of the way to meet needs. He or she may be aware only of a certain restlessness that drives him or her into trial and error behavior. One way of behaving may reduce tensions. Then he or she is likely to repeat that behavior if the restlessness recurs. This is the case with a child who needs love but is unaware of the need or of ways to satisfy it. He or she may resort to attention-getting behavior that only invites further rejection rather than the love so badly needed.

Goals alter needs

Goals can alter a person's response to basic needs. For example, young wrestlers may delay eating or eat only low calorie foods in order to weigh in at a certain weight before a wrestling match. The young gymnasts must put in many years of exercise, practice, and training before becoming capable of performing on the high school team or in the Olympic tryouts. If they see themselves passing various tests, winning medals, and receiving public notice, they can bear to continue the difficult exercise and self-discipline. However, if they are unsuccessful, and cannot accomplish the gymnastic stunts to the coach's satisfaction, they either change goals or use their gymnastic talents in another way or they become frustrated.

Culture affects needs

In addition to our universal human needs, each culture has created individual cultural needs. In China, a society dedicated to developing group-oriented people, there is no "star" concept in sports. Emphasis is on the slogan appearing in each school, "Friendship First, Competition Second." All children are expected to help others. Preschoolers take turns sweeping. They help each other with clothing problems. Buttons are on the backs of shirts so children can help each other with buttoning.

Group dramatizations, dance performances, stories, and songs in which the group helps the individual and individuals help each other are an important part of the educational program at all age levels.

In our culture, the value of individualism is assumed. We feel that a child must have his or her own distinct identity, his or her own toys, and his or her own room. Anyone observing a two- or three-year-old child quickly recognizes that his or her need is culturally imposed and not basic. The toddler wants to be where family members are. No matter how well decorated his or her own room is he or she prefers the area around the mother's feet. The mother has the cultural need for privacy so she rewards the child for putting away his or her own toys and staying in his or her own room. She scolds when the child encroaches on her time, friends, or possessions. Now the

Reprinted from *The Saturday Evening Post.*
© 1966 The Curtis Publishing Company.
Courtesy of *The Saturday Evening Post* and John Gallagher.

child grows up needing time alone, a room of his or her own, freedom of choice, freedom to plan his or her own time and his or her own life.

The culture influences basic needs in many ways. What stimulates or destroys appetite depends on culture more than on physiology. Swallow nest soup, ancient eggs, grasshoppers, and termites are all considered delicacies by some. Yet none of these foods is apt to arouse many American appetites. Anger and fright are inborn emotional states. But what angers and what frightens vary greatly.

Life situations affect needs

The ways to react to life situations vary a great deal and affect the actions of people. The Hopi Indians, for example, believe that thinking and concentrating cause something to happen. Relatives and friends beg a sick person to forgive any slights they may have done without knowing, to have positive thoughts about living, to wish to live for their sakes. They seek to save the life by having affectionate thoughts about the person and by collectively wishing for his or her recovery.

Needs interaction

The shaded area in the diagram below indicates the individual in society. The individual has many basic needs, both physiological and psychological, interacting within. Also piercing his or her person are the demands of age and stage of development which are indicated by the arrows. The demands of the culture, conditioning, family, society, and personal aspirations are also piercing and urging the person into action. At no time does any basic need react alone. Basic needs must react together with social needs, the needs defined by personal standards, goals, and values. Interaction means the mutual action or influences that the many factors in the shaded area have upon each other.

This needs interaction happens if a person's personal goals reinforce cultural, professional, and social class goals. We see this in young people who may delay close personal attachments or marriage and in young people who may live on a substandard economic

INTERACTION

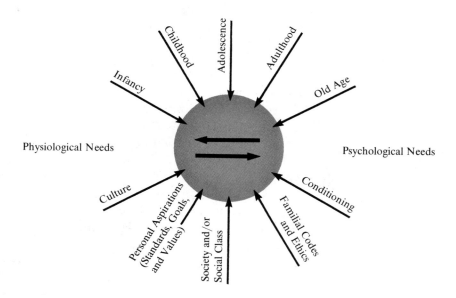

level in order to reach a long-term goal. The young scientist, for example, must put in many years of study and work to become capable of doing basic research. Getting the doctor of philosophy degree may involve prolonged frustration. This may be relieved by a succession of subgoals, such as passing a series of courses to fulfill other necessary requirements. If we can see ourselves making progress toward a goal, we can bear waiting to achieve it. In other cases, one may be consistently prevented from reaching a distant goal, no matter how hard he or she works toward it. This frustration may result in strong emotional disturbances. At times, these disturbances may be so severe that they affect one's physical health. This emphasizes the interaction between physical and psychological needs.

Basic principles of human behavior

Here, in summary, are some principles of human behavior. They will provide guidance as we search to understand our basic needs and ourselves. The ideas here will appear again and again throughout this book.

1. All human behavior is motivated by needs. We behave in order to adjust to these needs or to remove or satisfy them.

2. Rarely are these needs easily satisfied or thoroughly acceptable to us. Rather they are frustrated by conditions in our environment or in our minds which block our satisfaction. In other words, conflict is inevitable.

3. When conflicts occur, the behavior that involves the least resistance from any source, be it personal, family, friends, or society, is often selected. This selection is made whether it is appropriate for our overall and long-term development or not.

4. The way we see our needs or motives and the situations that satisfy or fail to satisfy them are related to parts of our total experience, past and present.

5. Behavior will vary depending on the strength and intensity of the needs, the nature of the goals, and the availability of socially approved outlets for satisfying needs.

6. Behavior patterns in satisfying our basic needs are culturally determined, socially directed, and goal oriented.

7. Behavior is directed by intelligence, emotion, and age, plus learned responses and conditioning.

By our behavior, we seek not merely to maintain the self but to develop an adequate self. We seek a self that is capable of dealing effectively and efficiently with the demands, needs, and wishes of life, both now and later. To achieve this self-adequacy, we must keep our existing organization. We must also make more adequate the self of which each of us is aware. We must seek to maintain and to enhance our perceived self. We can define one's basic need, then, as a need for adequacy. By the need for adequacy, we mean that great driving, striving force in each of us by which we seek to make ourselves more capable to cope with life.

Questions

1. How does early childhood training affect our needs?

2. We often have conflicting needs. What are the need conflicts in the following situations?

   a. wearing a tuxedo to the dance on a very hot evening

   b. wanting to eat immediately but waiting until guests have arrived

   c. wanting to tell someone to shut up

   d. being disturbed because the doorbell rings but smiling at the guests and welcoming them

3. List the five stages of Maslow's Hierarchy.

4. There are a number of conditions that people in our society try to avoid because they are in direct conflict with needs. Identify the needs which are involved in avoiding the following: (a) loneliness; (b) poverty and want; (c) threatening situations; (d) feelings of inferiority.

5. What basic psychological needs are expressed in the following quote from Addison, "The grand essentials to happiness in this life are something to do, something to love, and something to hope for"?

Further reading

Johnson, David W. *Reaching Out: Interpersonal Effectiveness and Self-Awareness.* Englewood Cliffs, NJ: Prentice-Hall, Inc., 1972.

Lee, Dorothy. *Freedom and Culture.* Englewood Cliffs, NJ: Prentice-Hall, Inc., 1959.

Maslow, A.H. *The Farther Reaches of Human Nature.* New York: The Viking Press, 1971.

Maslow, A.H. *Toward a Psychology of Being.* New York: D. Van Nostrand Company, 1968.

Platt, Robert M. *About Us: An Introduction to Psychology.* San Francisco: Boyd and Fraser, 1972.

Tussing, Lyle. *Psychology for Better Living.* New York: John Wiley & Sons, Inc., 1959.

Wrenn, R. L., and Mencke, R. A. *Being: A Psychology of Self.* Chicago: Science Research Associates, 1975.

Chapter 2

Our character growth

Character is what one is.   Character is bringing into harmony one's own demands and the demands of the outside world.   Character is the tendency of one's behavior to be consistent with values.

Character includes both one's habit and tendency to make choices in line with one's values. It includes being able to work toward long-range goals. It means avoiding being diverted by obstacles or by more immediate goals of lesser worth. Character is a part of personality.

Patterns of character

The major patterns of character seem to be formed in the first years of life. However, values are learned and changed throughout life. *Young children gain character values from their parents.* The parents' "yes" or "no," smile or frown, pat or slap carry the message of "good" or "bad" to the child. Children's reactions to messages determine which values will be learned and which values will be accepted. If children mistrust their parents, they will reject parental values. However, if they trust their parents, children will probably accept the value. Through reward and punishment, children learn first to comply with a value in the presence of an authority figure. Later, when they are away from the authority figure, and conform with the parental value, the child is said to have introjected the value. That is to say, they have taken the value "inside" and have behaved accordingly. This is called *introjection.*

Reprinted by permission of Clem Scalzitti.
From *Saturday Review,* © 1978 by Saturday Review Magazine Corp.

Character develops
each day.

The formulation of character in childhood is not always a conscious process. *Many values are learned in early childhood through conditioning.* If parents respond in a consistent, positive manner to children's behavior, the children behave more often in this way. Children come to feel that this is a "right" way to behave because it "feels good" when they behave this way. This can be described as the learning of a value which then becomes part of the person's character. Neither parents nor children may have been conscious of the learning that took place. The same kind of unconscious learning can take place with negative values.

At first culture influences children only through their parents. However, as a child moves out of a family into more contact with neighborhood, school, and religious groups, his or her character is directly influenced by a variety of social factors. These may be class values, ethnic values, and later on the values of a business organization or a chosen professional group.

Character development includes what you are and the influences of forces both internal and external, conscious and unconscious.

Character development

In order to understand the development of character, a set of five character types has been defined by Robert Havighurst and Robert Peck.[1]

1. From page 3 of *The Psychology of Character Development* by Robert F. Peck and Robert J. Havighurst. Published by John Wiley and Sons, Inc., 1960. Used by permission of Robert F. Peck.

These types are representative of a successive stage in the psycho-social (psychological and social) development of a person.

Age in Years	Developmental State	Character Type
0–2	Infancy	Amoral
2–7	Early Childhood	Expedient
7–14	Later Childhood	Conforming Irrational-conscientious
14–on	Adolescent and Adult	Irrational-conscientious
21–on	Adult	Rational-altruistic

Amoral character type. Amoral is an adjective that means without a sense of moral responsibility. Amoral character types, characteristic of infants, want what they want when they want it. Infants are not concerned that it is 2:00 A.M. and that parents are tired. They are hungry and want to eat, so they cry until food is given and their hunger need is satisfied. Infants cannot be reasoned with. They must have their basic needs fulfilled immediately. They react on impulse according to physical or psychological needs. When one is in infancy we expect amoral behavior.

Expedient character type. The word expedient means that which is immediately advantageous without regard for ethics or concern with consistent principles. The expedient character type develops in early childhood. Children find that needs are better satisfied if they learn to react with other people. For example, the toddler may try to take a toy from another toddler. The child refuses to give up the toy, however. A tug-of-war begins. The first child may learn that if he or she offers to trade an old truck for the toy airplane that is wanted, the other child may give up the plane without a struggle. Parents of very young children often use this stage of development to advantage. For example, a young child insists upon trying to touch an expensive vase. The parent may distract him or her by offering a suitable toy, praising its merits and causing the child to leave the vase alone. This resolves the actions of the child for the moment.

Conforming character type. The conforming stage develops in later childhood when children want to be like everyone else. Visit a fifth grade classroom and notice the dress of the students. If it is a school where boys wear blue jeans and plaid shirts, all boys wear this outfit as if it were a uniform. Youngsters in this age group need the security of conformity. They are beginning to be independent.

They can go to club meetings, athletics practice, and other events alone. To take this new step toward independence, they need the security of the group. They thrive on conformity in dress, activity, speech, and habits. Adults often object to this stage. They object particularly if they feel that their child is conforming to the standards of friends whom they consider to be intellectually or socially inferior. At this stage of development, the environment or neighborhood in which a child lives has great influence. Children will probably use the same speech, dress, values, and habits as those of their own age and position.

Irrational-conscientious type. From the conforming period, the character grows into the irrational-conscientious stage. In this stage of development, conformity to the group code is not the issue. Rather, it is conformity to a code the individual child has internalized and believes in. For example, children who have been brought up to attend church every Sunday may make this idea a personal belief. They may believe that all people are good who attend church every Sunday. All those who do not attend church are bad. They judge whole groups of people on one act which they have evaluated according to their own standards of right and wrong.

The irrational part, without reason or understanding, is the person's application of self-made rules. An act is "good" or "bad" because he or she labels it as such. Not necessarily because it has positive or negative effects on others.

Rational-altruistic character type. The rational-altruistic type describes the highest level of moral maturity. Persons of this type think of assuring the welfare of others as well as assuring their own welfare. These persons have a reasonable regard for others. For example, one might picture several high-school seniors who are attending a tournament. They want their team to win very much because winning the championship will mean that their school has the best team in the district. However, although they cheer their team wholeheartedly, the students do not boo the referees when they make a judgment against their team. They say or do nothing against the members of the opposing team. They do not abuse the members of the opposing team in deed or word because they have no need or wish to do so. In other words, rational-altruistic persons react with emotion appropriate to the occasion. This does not mean that they are unemotional. For they are enthusiastic about promoting what is good and, on the other hand, aroused to prevent what is bad. These high-school students know themselves and face their own reactions honestly. They do what is morally right because they want to, not because it is "the thing to do."

These students are as friendly and respectful to the custodian of the building as they are to their friends and to their teachers. They try to be honest and kind to all and to respect the integrity of every human being. Further, they accept responsibility for their own acts and accept blame when it is deserved. They judge other people's individual actions without making blanket approval or disapproval of people as a whole.

Fortunately for them, their public and private values are just about identical. They see themselves as they are, work for deeper perception and understanding, and respect their own capacities as they do those of others. They feel no unreasonable anxiety or guilt. If they err, they feel guilty. But their response is to take steps to correct the error. When they succeed, they no longer feel guilty.

At this time in their lives their moral horizons take in all people, as their behavior shows. It is probable that as adults they will assume an appropriate share of responsibility in their families, communities, and among people.

This picture of the rational-altruistic person represents an ideal goal. A goal to be sought as one moves toward adulthood, but probably never to be perfectly achieved and maintained. Maturity is a process which goes on indefinitely.

Character traits and developmental stages

If all conditions for character growth were ideal, one would go through the normal stages of development. That is, one would go from amoral through expedient behavior, conformity, and irrational-conscientious to a rational-altruistic behavior. All adults would then be in the rational-altruistic stage of development. If this were true, all adolescents and adults would be described in these terms. They would be honest, kind, and willing to take responsibility for themselves and others. They would be unselfish, self-sacrificing, willing to work constructively in some area, and producing results useful to everyone. Wouldn't it be a wonderful world if this were true?

Unfortunately, character growth does not always go through each stage. It may become blocked, stalled, or stymied at a particular stage for the rest of a person's life.

Examples of the amoral character types. Harry W. is a boy of 18 whom we like very much. He's charming but irresponsible. Although he is bright, he is not able to concentrate on studying. He is distracted constantly by short-term pleasures. Rather than planning his assignments carefully in advance, he prefers to delay writing his papers until the night before they are due. Even though Harry can write well, his reports are not good enough to deserve passing grades. They are hastily and carelessly written. Although he wants to go to college, he won't be able to pass the necessary exams.

In his social relationships Harry doesn't do much better. One day, for example, he was invited to go on a picnic. On the day of the outing, everyone but Harry met at the appointed place. After the group had waited for over 25 minutes, a call was made to Harry's house. Harry's mother said that Harry had decided to go swimming. He had kept everyone waiting while he followed an impulse to go to the lake.

Another kind of amoral boy is Karl, whom few persons like because he's always hostile and belligerent. Tales are told about his behavior behind the steering wheel of his car. He swerves out to pass all cars in his way without regard for other drivers. He toots his horn and swears at others who don't spin their wheels as soon as the stoplight turns green. When his driver's license was revoked, Karl was very upset.

Amoral people follow whims and impulses without regard to the effect these may have on other people. They consider themselves the center of the universe and see other people or objects only as means of their self-gratification. If they have a positive view of others, they are more apt to be known as "charming but irresponsible." They may form temporary alliances with others, but abandon them the minute they see a better source of gratification. If, however, their basic emotional attitudes are hostile, they are apt to be found committing delinquent or criminal acts.

In a way, this is a picture of an infant in its first year. Adults who have such a pattern are said to be arrested at an infantile level.

Examples of the expedient character types. Sara is a college girl. She has seldom completed an assignment. She copies the reports from her roommate and her friends. She cheats on exams. Her social behavior is expedient. She is particularly friendly with girls who have good-looking brothers. She does not hesitate to break a date if a more interesting person comes along.

Sara is a restless, lonely girl. Since she hates to stay in her room alone, she is always going into someone else's room looking for company. She goes not only to copy notes but also to be with someone. In order to attract attention she knows just what to do and does it when she thinks people will notice.

Expedient persons tend to get what they want with a minimum of giving in return. They behave in ways that society defines as moral only so long as it suits their purpose. For instance, these persons may act in "honest" ways to keep an advantageous reputation. If they can gain more by being dishonest, particularly if they can avoid detection and censure, they do so. They are not particularly concerned with other people's welfare, except when they show concern in order to obtain approval.

The motivation-behavior pattern of the expedient person is characteristic of many very young children. They have learned to respect the reward-punishment power of adults. They, therefore, behave correctly whenever an adult is around. Without such control they immediately go back to doing as they please. This happens even if it means that they shove other people around, to take what they want or to otherwise gratify their self-centered desires.

Examples of the conforming character type. The adolescent or adult who stays in the conforming stage of development is the person who has one general, internalized principle. This principle is to do what others do and what they say one "should" do. His or her only anxiety is from disapproval.

Jessie is an example of a person who has a need to conform. Jessie used to help in a Girl Scout troop as a program aide. She checked what the troop members had done to meet requirements for badges. Then it was noticed how severe she was in her checking. Every rule had to be followed to the letter. For instance, if there was something that made it impossible for a youngster to tie a muzzle on a dog, she wouldn't allow the child to tie the muzzle on a cat. It had to be on a dog. Often the troop went camping. Instead of letting everyone have fun and work in ways agreeable to all, Jessie would insist that the right persons do the right jobs in exactly the right ways.

A rather easy way to distinguish the conforming type may be to ask whether the person feels badly because of fear of disapproval by others or guilt when he or she breaks a rule. Persons who act morally because they would be ashamed if others found them violating the moral rules are controlling themselves according to external sanctions. The violation is not wrong in itself, not because of its effects, but because other people say it is wrong and their approval is at stake.

We can also see conforming adults when we drive through the suburbs. As the people get off the train, they may be uniformly dressed. The neighborhoods are similar. The automobiles are in the same price bracket. The people tend to belong to the same social groups. A degree of conformity is necessary in our world. However, one's character hasn't developed if this conformity of dress and appearance carries over into thought, deeds, and actions. If one must do exactly as others do because one is afraid to think for oneself, then one's character growth is stopped at the conforming stage. The one redeeming fact is that this group is in the third stage rather than being in the first (amoral) or the second (expedient) stage.

Examples of the irrational-conscientious character type. John has a very strong conscience. He holds firmly to a set of moral values. He believes that his religious faith is the only acceptable faith. He insists that his moral rules are the only ones to be followed by all people.

When John meets persons of another faith, he tries to encourage them to follow his beliefs. He privately, if not publicly, discredits the particular values, beliefs or ideas that others may hold.

The irrational-conscientious character type is toward the top in level of maturity. Irrational-conscientious character types have altered the course of history. These alterations have many times been in a positive direction, but they have also been negative.

More than by any other consideration, the irrational-conscientious type is ruled by the dictates of a conscience which acts from a firm, well-integrated body of moral rules. These rules, followed faithfully, are much stronger than the person's ability to judge present reality and figure out logical ways to behave morally. In fact, this person's weak-to-moderate ego strength (see Chapter 3) is not enough to enable him or her to test or question the rules that have been accepted without question or critical thought.

These persons automatically behave in responsible, loyal, honest, kind ways. But it is more from force of habit than from personal intent. They demand as much of others as of themselves but in the way of conventional morality. Nevertheless, they lack any strong, positive concern for others as persons. Their repressed hostility makes them far too literal-minded and rigid in their righteousness to be very easy to live with. In fact, they do not begin to approach the spontaneous, sincerely considerate behavior which marks the highest level of maturity. They may be prominent in the community. They often seem cold and unfeeling.

Irrational-conscientious persons usually do not really like people. They find it hard to accept others' faults. They usually do not have positive or warm self-acceptance. Others may respect them, but not necessarily like them.

Examples of rational-altruistic character types. The rational-altruistic persons have firm, moral principles. They act on rational, moral principles rather than on "absolute" rules because they have a high regard for people and for themselves.

Margaret is a rational-altruistic person. Everybody likes her. Although she is not beautiful, she was made prom queen because of her personality. She was also valedictorian, although she was not the brightest student in the class. These honors pleased her very much. But she had the extra pleasure of knowing that everybody was sincerely happy for her.

Margaret is well-liked because of the beliefs she holds and the qualities she displays to others. When she talks to a friend, she truly thinks about the person and his or her ideas, problems, and joys. At a party for boys and girls she talked with everyone there, even though her best boy friend was with her. When one of her classes went to a mental hospital to give a party for the people there, she did her best to make the party a success. This included thinking about the people and helping to decide what would be best for them. Margaret was concerned that the people to be entertained would have a pleasant time. Some of her classmates were afraid and uneasy about the trip. However, Margaret was so busy thinking about the people and their party that she didn't think about herself. So she was not afraid.

Margaret has not achieved perfection. However, although she is not entirely grown-up, she has the rare quality of being open to growth. She is already as mature, emotionally and socially, as a person of her years can be. It is within her to look at life, to know it, and to live by the principles that will bring the greatest good to herself and to others. She will continue to develop in wisdom, consideration, and knowledge of self and others.

Family influence on character development

What are the family environments that produce children who can develop their characters to their greatest potential? This was one of the concerns of Havighurst and Peck's[2] study of character development. The most striking feature of the parents of amoral children is that, without exception, they are markedly inconsistent. They are highly mistrustful and disapproving of their children. Havighurst and Peck found that these boys and girls grow up knowing very little love, little emotional security, and little, if any, consistent discipline.

2. Ibid., pp. 176–182.

The typical amoral subject is a rejected child. The parents of an amoral child generally disapprove of him or her. The feelings of success that the child can find through them are very few. At the same time parental control is extremely inconsistent, though it may or may not be severe. In the family environment, children can never get a clear idea, or pattern, of moral principles, because the parents show inconsistency. They also give reason to make children feel that they cannot please their parents no matter how hard they try.

The typical background of children of mainly expedient character might be summed up as laissez-faire homes. These are homes where the parents give children indiscriminate freedom to make their own decisions. They approve of children and are very lenient in their discipline. But the parents are also inconsistent in the moral and social pattern which they set.

The typical conforming person comes from a family which is regular in its rules and its way of life. It is authoritarian and all-severe to extremely severe. Authoritarian is used here to mean that children must obey the rules and wishes of the parents. Such strictness provides children with stable moral patterns, but ones to be adopted without thinking. These children are trained to "do as others do" without asking questions. This pattern is followed as long as others are conventionally respectable people like the parents.

The families of irrational-conscientious children are usually all-severe to extremely severe in their discipline. They, however, show mild mutual trust, approval, and confidence.

In view of the importance of the most mature kind of moral character as an ideal to aim for, it is worthwhile to look at the families of the rational-altruistic children in more detail. The parents of these families trust their children. The homes are democratic ones in which leniency prevails over severity. The children are able to develop their emotional and social selves in an atmosphere of acceptance. As they become increasingly able to reason, they confide openly to their parents. They discuss problems with them and share in family decisions. Since there is no harsh enforcement of rules, the children's moral code has the possibility of being appropriate to the occasion in a rational way.

Thus the rational-altruistic children go out into the world with the experience of social success in their families behind them. They can participate with other people without much personal anxiety. These children's parents approve of their moving out into the world. Because their internalized morality is one that society approves and rewards, they receive even more success. Accordingly, positive concern for people, in general, becomes a realistic possibility.

This chapter has discussed character typing and some of the environmental factors that influence character. Character growth is uneven. Not all people progress through all stages. Some stop growing at a very early stage. Others develop a character type that helps them achieve good relationships with themselves and others.

Questions

1. Define the following terms:

   character   conformity   altruistic
   amoral   expedient   introjection

2. When and how is character developed?

3. Is the formation of character always a conscious process? Explain your answer.

4. How does family environment affect character development?

5. Is a degree of conformity necessary in our culture? If so, why? If not, why not?

Further reading

Deutsh, Albert, ed. *Encyclopedia of Mental Health.* Volumes 1, 3, 4, 5. New York: Franklin Watts, Inc., 1970.

Duvall, Sylvanus M. *The Art and Skill of Getting Along With People.* Englewood Cliffs, NJ: Prentice-Hall, Inc., 1961.

Emery, Stewart. *Actualization: How to Communicate and Make Your Relationships Work.* Garden City, NY: Doubleday and Co., Inc., 1978.

Flugel, J. C. *Man, Morals and Society.* New York: The Viking Press, 1970.

Fromm, Erich. *Man for Himself.* New York: Holt, Rinehart & Winston, 1947.

Fromme, Allan. *The Ability to Love.* New York: Farrar, Straus & Giroux, Inc., 1965.

Reich, Wilhelm. *Character Analysis.* Beaverton, OR: The Touchstone Press, 1974.

Thigpen, Corbett Helsman, and Cleckley, H. M. *Three Faces of Eve.* New York: Popular Library, 1974.

Stutz, Robert M. *Exploring Behavior and Experience Readings in General Psychology.* Englewood Cliffs, NJ: Prentice-Hall, Inc., 1971.

Chapter 3

Our personality development

For when someone says that they have a personality problem, I'm not sure whether to say "Good" or "I'm sorry." It depends on the reasons why one has the problem. One can do the popular thing and at the same time destroy one's health or reputation.

Reprinted by permission of Richard McCallister.
From *Saturday Review/World*, © 1974.

"Who's the clown going 'beep beep'?   Doesn't he know we're honkers?"

Definition of personality

Personality is the sum of what a person has been, is, and predicts what he or she will become. It is the combination of body type, traits, habits, dreams, interests, hopes, experiences, perceptions, and talents that makes each person unique. Personality really means everything about a person—cheerfulness or grumpiness, kindness or thoughtlessness, likes and dislikes, ability and inability. It means accomplishment and lack of accomplishment, popularity with people, and inability to get along with others.

Personality make-up

Three main mechanisms make up personality. They are identification, introjection, and sublimation. One's personality is forever changing and growing because these mechanisms are always exerting their influence.

Identification. Identification is a device whereby you automatically imitate people whom you admire. Little girls imitate their mothers in the treatment of their dolls as children. Little boys imitate their dads. It is natural to imitate those around you. For it is from these persons that you learn how to do many things. It is not just that a boy is his father's son that he walks or acts like his father. He is automatically imitating his father's mannerisms and behavior as well as absorbing his father's attitudes and ideals.

We imitate behaviors that seem to work for others. If we notice that those who show tempers seem to get their way, then we may also use temper tantrums. If they work then we identify with that kind of behavior. Often, people speak of a child as inheriting the family temper. The child was not born with the temper but copied it from the other family members. The child who sees adults or other children reading, using good manners and habits will identify with these as the way to behave. This behavior becomes a part of his or her personality.

Identification goes on through life. When we fall in love with somebody we find ourselves behaving and believing as they do. When we join a group we want to be like the others in that group. As we grow through the various stages of the life cycle, we have various roles to play. We play the role according to our identification of that particular age. For example, if we see the role of a high school student to be one of assuming responsibility, being active in school organizations, running for offices, paying attention in class, and following the teachers' requests, we have identified with the student role in one way. If, on the other hand, we identify with those who cut class, talk back to authority figures, never attend school functions, and strive to see how much they can drink and how fast they can drive, we play the student role differently. How the roles in life are played during each stage of the life cycle determines the personality identity, the behavior, and the outcomes during that particular stage of life.

The language that we speak, the way we speak it, the clothes that we wear, the kinds of housing where we feel most comfortable, the initial habits that we acquire are all based on the identification mechanisms. Children who copy behaviors, mannerisms, and language skills that are of high quality are fortunate. Children who copy or imitate negative behaviors, mannerisms, and language skills have to change their initial identifications in order to succeed in society. This is very difficult to do and often impossible. William Wordsworth stated this situation in a phrase when he said, "The child is father to the man."[1]

---

1. Wordsworth in "My Heart Leaps Up When I Behold."

Introjection. *Introjection is the mechanism by which persons unconsciously absorb ideas, emotional attitudes, standards, and ideals from the people around them.* Even as a very small child you absorbed attitudes and ideas. This is one of the ways in which your conscience was formed. Even though you do not remember the time when you did not have one. Your ideals and your present standards of behavior did not start with you. The beliefs of your parents or caretakers regarding morals, education, or working conditions automatically became your beliefs. Although these beliefs may have changed to some degree as you have had more education and have gained experience, even these changes were absorbed mainly from people around you.

Everyone gets most of their ideas from someone else. You are a Republican or a Democrat probably because someone you admire is. The following situation illustrates this point. A high school class was observing a nursery school class in order to better understand children of four years of age. It was during a presidential election and, with introjection in mind, the high school students asked the children if they were Republicans or Democrats. The children replied with very definite responses, Democrat, Republican, and so on, when suddenly a little boy said "Methodist."

The four-year-olds were allied to the big word they had heard most often. The little boy who replied "Methodist" had heard that word more often than either Democrat of Republican, so he replied accordingly. How often have you argued a point about which you feel very strongly? Then, when you were told to give the source of your information, you realized that your older brother at the age of nine told you that when you were only six. You automatically absorbed it and never questioned its validity.

Sometimes, however, resentment toward parents causes children to take the opposite stand on various subjects. A great many young people have periods when they defy their parents and hold a different point of view taken from their peers. This can be a painful period because the young people are rebelling not only against parents but also against a part of themselves.

You introject in many ways. You absorb the spirit of a party. If it's a good party, you have a good time. If you are with someone you like, you usually accept his or her ideas. If you live in an environment where there is prejudice against people of a different color or religion, you are likely to be prejudiced in the same way as others around you. Because the process of introjection is automatic, you may not recognize it.

Sublimation.   Sublimation is a mechanism by which your energy is directed into society approved activities. Every one of us has two psychological drives which seek expression in one way or another. One drive is toward loving. It expresses itself in thoughts and acts that are creative, constructive, healthful, and generous. The other drive is toward hating. It expresses itself in thoughts and acts that are mean, destructive, and hostile. To live according to the laws, customs, and morals of the people around you, you must "sublimate" many of the impulses connected with your drives. In other words, things that you would like to do and attitudes that are socially or personally disapproved of must be changed into acceptable activities and attitudes.

If you stop to think of it, you can find illustrations of sublimation at work every day. If you are feeding a ten-month-old baby and spill applesauce on the high chair tray, the child will immediately play in it. If you set the dish of food down, the child will smear the food all over the tray. As the child grows older, however, he or she is taught to sublimate this desire. He or she is allowed to sublimate this desire by mixing up pie dough and making a pie since that is an acceptable activity. He or she therefore has the opportunity to play in the shortening, flour, and water mixture while forming the dough.

Other sublimations of this desire to smear are painting, clay modeling, stirring up a batch of cookies, or mixing concrete. In this way, the same energy is put to work in a socially useful or acceptable way. Hence, substituting adult interest for infantile desires is sublimation.

Most of your everyday activities involve sublimation. Instead of saying the first thing that comes to mind during a conversation, you consider the position of the other person, his or her feelings, and his or her associations. You say what you mean but with tact and consideration. Instead of buying worthless trinkets as you did as a child, you may collect coins, stamps, or records which are of more interest and usually have real value.

Theories of personality

Kurt Lewin, an American behaviorist (1890–1947), developed and researched the self theory. His theory concerns the three parts of the self. These are the personal self, the social self, and the ideal self.

The self includes not only the person's beliefs about his or her own characteristics. It also includes what one wishes to present of oneself to others and what one believes one should be. We will consider these interrelated subselves as the personal self, the social self, and the ideal self. The personal self is the image the person has of himself or herself as a physical and social being. As a result of one's developmental experiences, the personal self becomes a highly organized system. It includes attitudes, beliefs, impressions, habits, and values. The social self is not identical with either the social stimulus value which a person has or the sum total of his or her social skills. Rather, it represents his or her perception, attitudes, and feelings about self in relation to other persons. The ideal self is the image the person has of what he or she wishes to become. See the illustration below.

In order for a person to adjust and be stable, it is necessary for these three selves to be pulled together and superimposed upon each other. If this type of closeness and integration can be maintained within a person, he or she becomes adjusted. He or she is satisfied with the total self.

The case of Carolyn A. illustrates a person whose personal self, ideal self, and social self are pulling against each other. Carolyn's standards are kept in a logic-tight compartment that makes up her ideal self. When crises arise in Carolyn's relations with other people, her social self cannot use these moral standards because she hasn't translated them into operation. Her standards are idealistic and relatively rigid. Her ideal self is in great conflict with her personal and social selves.

Carolyn is the youngest and the only girl in a family of good, solid reputation. She is very close to her father who is a minister. Discovering early in life that it was not difficult to secure his favor, special attention, and privileges, Carolyn accepted all her father's standards without question. Following her father's wishes, she readily accepted religious instruction. Her religious experiences in both childhood and adolescence were genuine.

Even though she was the favorite of the children in the home, she became a hanger-on in the neighborhood group. She developed the habits and attitudes of the group, which were not in keeping with some of her training. The two patterns of behavior were never compared. When she was with the gang, she lost herself in the group's pranks, but when she was with her father, she was his "good little girl." It was not until college that she became conscious of how strong her tendencies were to violate the standards of sexual behavior indicated at home. She noticed how weak her efforts seemed to be to live up to what she thought was right. It was puzzling to her that moral standards could be so clearly defined when she considered them at home. Yet they were so vague and ineffectual when she was with people whom she considered immoral.

Never did Carolyn think through the whole problem. She thought that since she paid allegiance to morals and ethics, they should function at all times. Religion to her was like a rabbit's foot or talisman that worked automatically. She didn't realize that in order for a code to work, it must dominate attitudes and behavior. She often became depressed, especially when she was unable to forget her shortcomings and failures.

Carolyn had not been able to correlate her three selves. She had been sheltered all her life and allowed to follow her own pleasures in the family. She had accepted certain standards without actually internalizing them. Furthermore, she carried this same behavior to her other relationships outside the family. The moral standards of her ideal self were mainly verbal. They were never associated in thought or action with events in her daily life. Yet her social behavior was influenced by her associates of any given moment. Her personal self struggled between her social and ideal selves. She began to dislike her misbehavior. Eventually she disliked anyone who misbehaved in the same way. After misbehavior, she plunged into her moralistic rituals. This was obviously a means of escape from guilt. She made no attempt to discover and understand the source of or motivation for her behavior. Nor did she accept it as a vital part of her personality with which she must deal. Rather Carolyn thought that if she denied and repressed it, her misbehavior would cease to be. She certainly did not question the standards of her father or her ability to live up to them. Carolyn was a person divided into three selves torn by both her father's immovable standards and her own emotions.

Sigmund Freud, an Austrian psychiatrist (1856–1939), did work which led to the theory and techniques of psychoanalysis. It is a scientific method of observing certain mental and emotional conditions. On the basis of observations made in psychoanalysis, a body of knowledge has been collected that helps explain personality development.

The following five points define some of Freud's major contributions relative to the development of personality.

1. Early childhood experiences influence psychological development. Freud pointed out that the experiences of the child during infancy and early childhood have a significant effect upon psychological development. He provided a technique whereby experiences of the early years, which seemingly have been forgotten, can be recalled.

2. Human behavior is influenced by irrational or unreasonable motives as well as rational or reasonable ones.

3. Behavior is multidetermined. This suggests that any specific behavior may be explained by a number of different combinations of motives and causes.

4. There are different levels of conscious awareness. In light of this, Freud pointed out that people may be quite unaware of the origins of their behavior. He introduced the term "unconscious" to account for a person's lacking awareness or forgetting experiences that may continue to affect behavior.

5. Psychological equilibrium is maintained through the use of the mechanisms of defense. Trying to keep a state of little conflict and to minimize anxiety, the personality uses certain protective and defensive techniques. These mechanisms of defense are also called mental dynamisms. Some of the common mental mechanisms such as compensation, conversion, displacement, idealization, identification, rationalization, and projection will be discussed in Chapter 6.

These five points are accepted within the fields of psychiatry and psychology with little controversy.

In the development of the ego concept of self, Freud felt that a person acts in two ways. He or she acts in relation to the environment and in relation to the self in satisfying basic needs. Freud then departmentalized the individual's thinking into three parts: the *id,* the *superego,* and the *ego.* The concepts of the id, ego, and superego are generally recognized as having value in describing complex psychological processes.

The *id* became the generating source and reservoir for satisfying infantile, instinctual, basic wants. It created the desire within the person to have food, sex, and bodily needs satisfied immediately. This creates a tremendous power within a human being. When the basic needs cannot be expressed, tension is created.

Freud described the *superego* as the internal watchdog or the conscience of the individual. This force is forever exerting pressure to uphold the values learned early in the childhood from parents and teachers. These are the social values and the rights and wrongs developed from the relationship of a person to his or her environment. The superego tries to make the person conform to the cultural pattern with its mores and regulations so that punishment will not result from his or her actions. The superego controls behavior by making the person prejudge his or her behavior.

The *ego* was considered by Freud to be an integrating mechanism within a person. A mechanism that accepts the instinctual demands of the id on the one hand and the culturally and conscientiously accepted regulations of the superego on the other. The ego is in constant contact with the real world. Thus, it takes on an even greater function because it is regulating the forces between the id and the superego. It is also regulating the relationship of these two forces to the external conditions. Actually, the ego acts as a judge which determines how the personality can best survive.

Suppose a person is watching a child walking down the street holding an ice cream cone. The id might say to the person, "You're hungry. You would like to have the ice cream cone. Take it away from the kid. You're bigger."

But the superego would say, "No, maybe the child's mother will come along and call a police officer. You'll get into trouble. You will be punished if you do this."

The ego stands between the id and the superego. It will try to resolve this conflict of getting something to satisfy the body while not getting into trouble with the outside environment. It does fairly well under certain circumstances. For example, in this case it might say, "Well, I could satisfy this desire to eat by taking fifty cents from my pocket and buying an ice cream cone. I (the ego) will satisfy the id.

I will also satisfy the superego by not being punished or getting into trouble."

The id represents the basic drives of people. These are the striving within for protection, pleasure, and comfort. They fulfill wants without considering how they may be obtained or restrained from the outside.

The superego is the result of the restraints that are put on the desire to be accepted by others, to gain the approval of others through one's actions, and to attain recognition and status in society. The superego is also the result of the moral teachings and the fundamental religious and philosophical doctrines thoroughly instilled in a person. Only by following the rules and regulations that society, culture, and conscience have imposed can a person gain these desired results in life.

The ego evaluates behavior. If one becomes too concerned in satisfying the id, one becomes self-centered and selfish with little concern for others. On the other hand, if one acts only to satisfy the superego, one lives in a state of anxiety or tenseness because one fears being unable to satisfy cultural standards or others' ideals which may be varied and inconsistent. The ego is the equalizer which helps the person avoid extremes. The ideal personality maintains a balance between the id, the ego, and the superego.

W. H. Sheldon (1889–1963), an American researcher, has developed a personality theory based on body types. He has classified man into three distinct types: *endomorphic, mesomorphic,* and *ectomorphic.* A study was made from measurements of thousands of photographs of male bodies. Sheldon concluded that the physique could be identified through three main body components: the fatty, visceral component, endomorphy; the muscular and body component, mesomorphy; the skin and nerves component, ectomorphy.

Although Sheldon's studies showed a high correlation between body build and temperament, other critics were not able to establish as high a correlation. They presented evidence to show that nutritional differences, ill health, and dietary factors can make changes in physical types. Sheldon then modified his concept to allow for these changes. Since the value of this type of classification is that it is a simple method of finding a clue to a person's personality, these modifications limit its usefulness.

We have said that physical factors are not, in themselves, an index of behavior. However, there are some physical characteristics that do promote certain types of behavior. For example, a fat man may have established patterns of behavior that do not require quick movement of which he is incapable. A threatening situation like a fist fight may be resolved more successfully if the fat man treats it humorously or ignores it. Thus, the physical limitation that involves the lack of mobility of large bulk and slow physical response may produce an easygoing good humor as the best defense.

The deer runs when in danger. The turtle pulls in its head because it cannot run. The chameleon changes its color to match its environment. Their defense patterns are developed according to the circumstances in the environment. Consequently, certain personality traits are shown not only under threatening circumstances, but also as expected behavior.

Carl G. Jung (1865–1961), Swiss psychologist, believed that all people can be divided into two types, the *extrovert* and the *introvert. Extrovert means to turn outward. Introvert means to turn inward.* Jung believed that each of us has both tendencies but that in each of us one tendency predominates.

The extroverts are the persons who turn out to the world about them. They love to be with people and let others know their feelings and thoughts. Since they value things, activities with people, and a feeling of importance, they tend to be actively engaged with people, things, and activities.

The introverts are those who like to take a little of the world inside to think about. They like to be alone or with people whom they know well. Keeping feelings and thoughts much to themselves, they value ideas, imaginations, dreams, and feelings. Much of their activity takes place in thinking, dreaming, and imagining.

Jung did not think of one type or the other as being the more desirable. They are different, that is all. There is much that is of value about extroverts. Likewise, there is much that is of value about introverts. There are both well-adjusted and poorly adjusted people in each group.

Many psychologists do not believe that people can be labeled as either extroverts or introverts. But rather they believe people have some of the characteristics of both and perhaps should be called ambiverts (ambi meaning both).

We should also make clear that these same terms, introvert and extrovert, are sometimes used in another way. That is, they are used to describe the person's adjustment to his or her environment. In this second meaning, it is not so desirable to be called an introvert. For the term thus used means that you turn away from people because of feelings of inferiority. In this "adjustment" sense, it is desirable to be called an extrovert. The term thus used means that you can turn your attention away from yourself and enjoy wholesome activities with others.

However, as Jung used the terms, *introvert means that there is great interest in the world of the mind. Extrovert means that there is great interest in the external world.*

Alfred Adler (1870–1937), an Austrian psychiatrist, felt that *the source of determinism[2] for a person was his or her will to power.* This, he believed, was the primary motive of people. Adler saw the will to excel in social, economic, and sexual competition as the main consideration in people's lives. Failure to excel in these basic areas, Adler asserted, led to an inferiority complex which in turn was responsible for people's great efforts to compensate for their defeats. According to Adler, personality development progressed along a road paved with evidence of either personal superiority or inferiority.

Factors affecting personality development

There are three main factors that affect personality development. These are the home atmosphere, the person's discipline, and the adult models. A positive home atmosphere leads toward individual initiative and learning attitude. It leads away from anxiety, conflict,

2. Determinism as used here means that nothing in the individual's emotional or mental life results from chance but rather from specific causes or forces known or unknown.

defense, and escape. Family, friends, school, neighborhood, past experiences, and future plans affect what persons are and what they may become. Each person is different. Even in the same family, each child has a unique position in relation to other family members. Each person has his or her own experiences involving particular people, places, and things that are unlike anyone else's experiences. The total of his or her reactions to all of these unique experiences shapes his or her personality.

The home atmosphere is probably one of the most influential factors in personality development. Here are conditions which stimulate personality growth. A favorable developmental climate includes the following.

1. affection that gives security

2. discipline that is consistent and results in learning

3. parents or older persons who are models for a positive identification and sources of standards and understanding when difficulties arise

Your personality is a positive force in your development if it makes you happy, makes your associates happy, and is an asset to society. In other words, your personality is a good one if you are likeable, successful, honest, and responsible. You enjoy life, your emotions are pleasant for you and others, and you meet your troubles and disappointments courageously.

Developing and improving personality

The question of whether personality can be improved puzzles some people. They argue, "If personality is a reflection of my inner self, if it represents me, there is not much I can do about it. After all, if it is my nature to act in a certain way, I must accept it and let it go at that."

It is true that if you are tall or short or have big ears, you cannot change these physical characteristics. They are part of you. Being tall does not mean that you must stoop to appear shorter. Your big ears do not bother others as much as they bother you. It would be wise to concentrate on and develop other aspects of your personality. Emotional habits, such as a quick temper, irritability, and shyness are parts of your personality which can be changed. Since you were not born with these traits, you must have acquired them. Habit patterns can be altered.

Everything wants to exist as it is. A cat wants to act like a cat, and you want to be you. If anything or anyone prevents you from acting as you are, you try to overcome the obstacle. You also try to prevent change, even though it may be good for you, because of certain patterns of behavior. It has been said that if anything affects your eye, have it removed. If anything affects your mind, just put up with it. This may not be entirely true. You may have become accustomed to your likes, dislikes, and idiosyncrasies. Do not feel too badly if you want to remain as you are. There is some rigidity in every one of us.

There are four steps in the process of personality improvement and correction.

1. realization of the need for improvement

2. strong desire for improvement

3. analysis or stocktaking of one's strong and weak points

4. a systematic plan for improvement

Personality improvement cannot be neatly rounded out in six weeks or a semester. It is something that should continue indefinitely. None of us will ever be perfect. There will always be room for improvement. It is true that you may be able to remake yourself in three months of concentrated effort. You may be so changed and improved that friends who have not seen you for a time will hardly recognize you. However, without the strictest self-discipline and continued effort you may slip back into your old ways. This will be the case especially if these old ways represent habits of many years' standing.

Classification and improvement of personality traits

The personality traits which describe each person fall into a number of broad classifications:

Physical appearance	posture
	body build and size
	complexion
	hair and eyes
	facial expression
	appropriateness of clothes
	condition of clothes

Intellectual accomplishments	range of ideas
	manner of speaking
	topics chosen for conversation
	quickness of mind
	ability to judge values

Emotional adjustment	likes and dislikes
	degree of aggressiveness
	response when things get difficult
	calmness and self-reliance
	ability to control anger
	sense of humor

Social qualities	conduct in the presence of other people
	knowledge and practice of rules of etiquette that govern society
	obedience to the prevailing customs and conventions

From these classifications of personality, however, you should not assume that behavior can be divided into exact pieces. Behavior is mainly social in character. When judging a person's emotional make-up, the evaluation of traits is made in terms of some kind of social setting. One who has spent most of life in solitary confinement would have had little social experience. The evaluation of his or her personality by the usual standards would be impossible.

Personality has been divided into the convenient classifications above so that it will be easier for you to analyze and study yourself. You can find out what makes a well-developed personality and improve your own personality so that you will be more effective in human relations. Remember only you can change you. You can change no one else.

Questions

1. Demonstrate your knowledge of each of the following terms by giving a definition, by using it in a sentence, or by giving an example.

personality	ideal self	superego
introjection	personal self	introvert
sublimation	ego	extrovert
social self	id	mesomorphic

2. Make a personality inventory and indicate ways of self-improvement.

3. What factors are prominent in personality development and personality change?

4. What kind of behavior might be exhibited by a very short man? Whose theory would explain this?

5. What are the important factors in the child's environment that shape his or her personality?

6. Give an example of how the self concept might function as a determiner of action.

7. Why is it necessary for a person to play an appropriate role to fit each situation?

Further reading

Arndt, William B. *Theories of Personality.* New York: Macmillan, Inc., 1974.

Baltes, Paul B., and Schaie, K. Warner, eds. *Life Span Developmental Psychology: Personality and Socialization.* New York: Academic Press, Inc., 1973.

Bernard, Harold W. *Personality: Applying Theory.* Rockleigh, NJ: Holbrook Press, 1974.

Hall, Calvin S., and Lindzey, Gardner. *Theories of Personality.* 3rd ed. New York: John Wiley & Sons, Inc., 1978.

Hurlock, Elizabeth B. *Personality Development.* New York: McGraw-Hill, 1973.

Kagan, Jerome. *Personality Development.* New York: Harcourt Brace Jovanovich, Inc., 1971.

Lazarus, Richard S. *Personality.* 2nd ed. Englewood Cliffs, NJ: Prentice-Hall, Inc., 1971.

Chapter 4

Our maturity

Graduation is seen as the completion of formalized school and the commencement of the work toward life goals. What will be my life goals? What should I decide to do with my life? Whom should I choose to work with? How should I begin my career?

Reprinted by permission of Rick Detorie.
From *Saturday Review,* © 1977 by Saturday Review Magazine Corp.

"Read it again, only this time with more emphasis on character development and less on plot mechanics."

When should I marry? Where shall I live? What am I most capable of doing? How do I define success? What is happiness? These are some of the questions that you may ask as you mature.

One is never fully mature. When one accomplishes one stage of maturity other stages are waiting. For example, when you have finally figured out how to be a highschooler, you are graduated and you have to figure out how to be a college student, or an employee, or a member of the armed services, or whatever you choose. The life cycle has tasks to be done at each stage. When these are done you progress to the next stage with its list of tasks. One is never fully mature because there are always new challenges to face. There is always the question, "Now what?"

In circa 42 B.C., Publilius Syrys said, "It takes a long time to bring excellence to maturity."[1] Wordsworth stated that the child is the father to the man.[2] Milton said, "The childhood shows the man as morning shows the day."[3]

1. The translation (Maxim 780) is by Darius Lyman.
2. Wordsworth in "My Heart Leaps Up When I Behold."
3. Milton in *Paradise Regained,* Book III, Line 220.

Definition of maturity

Maturity is the ability to face your assets and your liabilities and handle them intelligently. When you are judging your degree of maturity, you think not only of your ideas, ideals, or specific goals. You also think of those levels of achievement that indicate whether or not you are ready for adult experiences, privileges, and responsibilities. This becomes apparent as one grows and develops. Have you ever laughed about a past action of yours in light of your present maturity?

There is no need to be too critical for there are stages of maturity. Mature behavior at one age and stage of development is immature behavior at another age and stage. There is no time in life at which one can say, "Now I am completely mature; I have experienced all possible things. I know that I will act with intelligent judgment." Maturity is a growing process that is lifelong. Each age brings new situations with which one must cope.

By definition, maturity is revealed whenever a person uses all the resources he or she has to move in the direction of his or her full potential. In other words, the one who is best adjusted has reached the highest level of maturity within his or her capacity.

The following examples are not meant to indicate a norm, but to further explain the discussion above:

Dawn is a six-month-old baby girl. She responds to her name with a smile. She manipulates her toys with her hands and plays alone for 30 to 45 minutes at a time. When she sees her food being prepared, she is patient for a short time. She recognizes her parents' voices and their images. When she is tired of a position, hungry, or lonesome, she cries. Although she likes to try to sit alone she frequently falls over. This frightens her and she cries to be consoled and reassured. For her age and stage of development and for her available resources, she is mature. However, if she still performed in the same way at eighteen months, she would be immature.

Ronald Gum is seventeen years old. The Gum family lives on a farm. Mr. Gum is a firm but gentle man, warmly human, and respectful of the rights of his wife and children as human beings. He has, at the same time, considerable self-assurance and is the head of the family. The mother says, "The kids know that when Dad says something he really means it. He doesn't scold them or give them a lot of direction, but whenever he does talk they listen."

In the course of Ronald's life he and his father have spent a great deal of time working together. Mr. Gum says, "Ronald's an A-1 worker. He can do just about anything, and anything he does, he does well. We all think a lot of him. He knows what is right. We have always been proud of the way he's done in school and the way he gets along. We're proud of him." Ronald says, "Oh, sure, lots of times I have to work when I don't want to but Dad always tries to fit the work into my schedule so I have plenty of time to do other things too. We usually talk it over and plan ahead. It's pretty interesting working with Dad. He's like a magician with plants."

Ronald once said of his mother, "If Santa Claus were a woman, Mom would be a good Santa Claus." It is difficult to improve on this description of Mrs. Gum. She is a jolly person. She is also generous and thoughtful of others.

In spite of the essentially accepting attitude that characterizes Mrs. Gum, she puts considerable emphasis on her values. She says, "I'm a stickler for keeping promises you make. I think it's not fair to yourself or others to go back on promises." Like her husband, she has genuine respect for other people as individuals and has a sincere interest in them. She, too, has fundamental self-assurance.

Mrs. Gum respects Ronald's judgment. For example, Ronald had been going out often and staying up late several nights during the week. She had been somewhat concerned and asked Ronald if he did not think his school work might suffer. When Ronald said, "No, Mom, I won't drop behind," she didn't say any more because she felt that Ronald knew what he was doing. Mrs. Gum tries not to tie Ronald down or censure him for his activities. Rather she has encouraged his participation in activities outside the family. Ronald reports, "My folks very seldom tell me when I should be in. I can usually judge for myself."

From the beginning, Ronald Gum has known what his parents expect of him. Broad limits have been established and are consistently maintained. Ronald has learned that meeting his parents' expectations brings him rewards, abundant approval, and considerable freedom to express himself.

Now let's look at the case of Diane K. who has not used all her resources to move in the direction of her full potential. Diane K. is 18 years old. She looks and acts more like 14. She has superior intelligence and vocabulary, good work habits, and above average grades. Yet her attitude is submissive. As soon as she begins to talk, she gives the impression of being younger than she is. She finds it very difficult to differ with anyone of authority.

Her present behavior follows an orderly development. She comes from a family of lower-middle economic class. Her mother died before she started school. Diane was shifted from relative to relative as she developed. The relatives would keep her until another child was born in their family. As she grew older, she was asked to come to the homes of those who needed extra help. Her father was a laborer. He attributed all events in his life to luck. It was either a time of good luck or poor luck. The whole attitude of the family has been one of submission to authority. Diane has the ability to do college work but has never considered college a possibility. She was greatly surprised to learn from her counselor that many students of her economic class had of their own initiative gone to college and earned their way.

When Diane thinks of the future she can't sleep, becomes tense, has a fear of mistakes, and a general lack of confidence in herself. She wants to assume responsibility. Yet her background causes her to fear every new venture that is not supported by authority.

Dr. Strecker defines maturity as "the ability to stick to a job, the capacity to give more on any job than is asked for, reliability, persistence to carry out a plan regardless of the difficulties, the ability to work with other people under organization and authority, the ability to make decisions, a will to life, flexibility, independence, and tolerance."[4] It is quite clear that Strecker here describes the maturity of adult development—an adult who has used all the resources he or she has to move in the direction of his or her full potential.

Types of maturity

We do not grow up evenly and consistently all at once. We have many ages and stages. There are many maturities to consider in any growing person.

The most common types of maturity are shown in the following list:[5]

1. chronological (how many birthdays you have had)

2. physical (how mature your body is)

3. intellectual (how grown-up your thinking is)

4. emotional (how mature your feelings and the ways in which you express your feelings are)

5. social (how mature your relationships with other people are)

6. philosophical (how grown-up your beliefs, ideals, purposes, morals and values are)

4. E. A. Strecker, *Their Mothers' Sons* (Philadelphia: J. B. Lippincott Co., 1946), p. 211.
5. Reprinted with permission of Macmillan Publishing Co., Inc. from *Family Living* by Evelyn Millis Duvall. Copyright 1950 by Macmillan Publishing Co., Inc., renewed 1978 by Evelyn Millis Duvall.

Chronological maturity. This maturity refers to age. It is definite. This maturity is used to judge the legal age for a driver's license, a marriage license, a permit to work or a permit to enter school, and the right to vote. Chronological age is only accurate for legal purposes. It is not an accurate indication of individual readiness for these privileges. But it is a definite measure. Chronological growth is unalterable. There is nothing you can do to change your chronological age.

Physical maturity. Physical maturity takes place over many years. It can be measured to some degree by looking into a mirror, or by measuring height and weight. Physical growth is orderly and sequential. However, it is irregular in pace. During the first year of life, one grows very rapidly. Then there is a slower pace until the big spurt toward physical maturity which comes between childhood and adulthood. This time of change is called puberty. Puberty is the period at which sexual maturity is reached. Pubic hair appears above the genitals and under the arms of boys as well as girls. It is at this time of puberty that the first ejaculation for boys and the first menstruation and breast development for girls take place.

There are great differences in the rate of growth toward physical maturity among individuals. Puberty is usually reached between the ages of nine and twenty. Girls tend to mature at an earlier age than boys do. It is difficult for a boy or girl to be the first in the group to reach puberty or to be the last. One should remember that there are great differences in the rates at which individuals mature physically. Physical growth depends upon individual and inherited growth patterns unless altered by malnutrition or medicine.

Intellectual maturity. Intellectual maturity is highly alterable and intellectual growth can continue as long as you live. Intellectual growth is dependent upon mental ambition and native intellectual ability.

A person is intellectually mature[6]

1. to the extent to which he (she) can understand meanings.

2. to the extent to which he (she) can make up his (her) own mind.

3. to the extent to which he (she) can look at self and problems from outside of self.

6. Reprinted with permission of Macmillan Publishing Co., Inc. from *Family Living* by Evelyn Millis Duvall. Copyright 1950 by Macmillan Publishing Co., Inc., renewed 1978 by Evelyn Millis Duvall.

4. to the extent to which he (she) can take responsibility for his (her) own behavior and its consequences.

5. to the extent to which he (she) is able to postpone judgments.

6. to the extent to which he (she) can take a problem-solving approach to life.

Our intellectual growth is irregular because it is so dependent upon our environment. When we are in an environment that stimulates us to think and to tackle real problems, we grow intellectually. When our environment is not stimulating, we mark time. We also frequently mark time when the environment demands too much of us. When we are asked to perform much above our intellectual growth, we tend to become discouraged. We stop trying to learn and grow. Intellectual growth is most rapid when we are challenged and gain some degree of success from that challenge.

Emotional maturity. Emotionally mature persons have a proper regard for themselves. But their interests also move out to include the activities and well-being of others. Emotional maturity helps one make and keep friends. It contributes more than anything else to happiness in marriage. It is essential to our social well-being. Most of our social problems are caused by emotionally ill and infantile people. As more of us develop emotionally mature personalities, our communities, our country, and our world will benefit. The following diagram shows the characteristics of the emotionally immature and the characteristics of the emotionally mature person.

Social maturity. Social maturity, which is largely learned, involves so many skills and attitudes that it is difficult to measure it accurately. Your social age is measured by your ability to get along with people. Here are some of the characteristics of socially mature persons.

1. They accept other people for what they are.

2. They avoid labeling other people. To call people names is very childlike and gives a false impression. If you label a group of people or a person, you blind yourself because you tend to stop thinking about them as persons. If you avoid labels, you leave the way open to meet, to know, and to enjoy a host of people. It is easy to put a false label on a group and to stop thinking about them. It is easy, but it retards social growth.

THE EMOTIONALLY IMMATURE   THE EMOTIONALLY MATURE

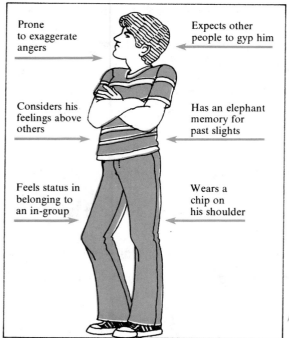

Prone
to exaggerate
angers

Expects other
people to gyp him

Considers his
feelings above
others

Has an elephant
memory for
past slights

Feels status in
belonging to
an in-group

Wears a
chip on
his shoulder

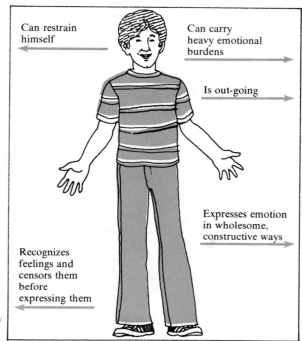

Can restrain
himself

Can carry
heavy emotional
burdens

Is out-going

Expresses emotion
in wholesome,
constructive ways

Recognizes
feelings and
censors them
before
expressing them

3. They have freed themselves from childhood dependencies upon parents. They make their own decisions. They take the responsibility for the consequences of their decisions. They ask advice of their parents, but realize that the final decision must be theirs. They establish an interdependency on a mature level with their parents. They do not blame parents for their own mistakes nor expect to be rescued financially.

4. They can meet strangers easily. They have mastered their social graces so that they enjoy meeting new people. They are at home with both sexes of all ages in any number of situations.

5. They enjoy planning with others.

6. They can accept and adjust to the rules and laws of the group of which they are a part. If the rules make sense, they obey them. If the rules need changing, they set about changing them. But they do so in orderly ways, according to the rules for changing rules.

Philosophical maturity. This maturity is the most difficult to achieve. It takes time, thought, and a love of wisdom. To be philosophically mature, you must understand yourself, your values, and your goals. Your philosophy embodies your practical and moral wisdom. It is also an indication of your ethics.

A group of young people were asked to characterize a person who has a good philosophy of life. These young people mentioned the items listed here.

1. He or she has few inner conflicts.

2. He or she has a sense of knowing where he or she is going. He or she strives toward conscious goals.

3. He or she lives primarily for long-term values rather than taking what is wanted at the moment.

4. He or she does not show fear or worry regarding non-essentials.

5. He or she has a grown-up conscience instead of a childhood conscience.

6. He or she shows social-mindedness and concern for the welfare of others.

7. He or she cannot be perfect in any one of these things, but shows growth in all of them from year to year.

An example of the ages of maturity

One might say that each person has six ages. We might have a boy, Jack, who is nineteen years old chronologically. His physical age may be fifteen as evidenced by his unreliable voice and whiskerless chin. On an emotional maturity test he may be twenty-one. His social maturity age may be twenty-five. He may be capable of doing college math and understanding meanings in the superior range of intelligence. He may be just beginning to formulate a philosophy of life. Thus, Jack's age is a composite of the six ages. The chronological age has been arbitrarily chosen for legal purposes because it is the one most easily measured. However, this is the age, or score, that contributes the least to Jack's behavior. When we think about our own maturity or the maturity of others, we will better understand behavior if we recognize that each person reacts differently to environmental and internal influences. This is because of our different stages and ages of development.

Characteristics of the mature individual

Maturity has many sides. Although one's growth toward maturity is never completed, we can measure maturity by looking at the characteristics of the mature person. This will be explored in terms of how a person meets basic needs as described in Chapter 1.

Persons are mature if they can support their own households. Mature persons make contributions to the vocational world. They can arrive at their own decisions and conclusions concerning the importance of those contributions.

Mature people value life. They value people. They value self. In this attitude of caring, they see themselves and their associates as persons of worth. They feel that each person has a reason for living and a life goal to achieve.

Mature persons strive to understand self and others. In this way they promote satisfying relationships.

Inner controls direct the behavior of mature persons. These persons do not behave in a certain way because they fear authority or punishment, but because they believe their way of life is right. Their moral codes are ones in which they accept responsibility for behavior.

Mature persons show controlled and directed emotionality. They are calm, deliberate, reflective, and capable of delaying responses when necessary.

Mature persons have an understanding of sexual anatomy, physiology, and reproduction. They use this knowledge in such a way that they feel experiences related to sex and reproduction are meaningful life experiences.

Maturity is never ending. All of the above is not enough to describe the mature person. As psychologist Fred McKinney states:

Not all persons who are heterosexual, sociable, and independent represent a high level of maturity in our complex civilization. This independence should go further. The best example of the mature person is one who not only supports himself but also controls to some extent his environment. Instead of being completely subjected to the forces of the outside world, he takes part in molding these forces. He recognizes talents, and he sees his place in the world; he sees future goals and moves toward them.

Maturity brings with it a point of view of life. If this is adequately verbalized, it deserves the title of a philosophy of life. It includes the individual's conviction of matters such as ethics, morals, politics, and the nature of the world and man.[7]

7. From page 468 of *Psychology of Personal Adjustment* by Fred McKinney. Published by John Wiley and Sons, Inc., 1961. Used by permission of the author.

Questions

1. Draw up a list of both mature and immature acts or attitudes that you have noticed in others or in yourself recently.

2. Write a sketch about the most mature person you know.

3. Our growth develops from dependence through independence and on to interdependence. Describe briefly two or three experiences to illustrate these three stages in your own growth toward maturity.

4. How do the following help or hinder your progress toward maturity?

   a. The ask-as-you-go or dole systems for getting money for your needs from your family.

   b. The appeal to "do this for mother's sake."

   c. Required courses and electives in your school program.

   d. The lowering of the legal minimum voting age to eighteen.

5. How do you rate your growth toward maturity? Write a sketch describing your stage and ages of maturity.

6. Is Ronald mature for his age and stage of development? Why?

7. Do Ronald's parents contribute to his maturity? If so, how? If not, how do they hinder him?

8. Is Ronald using all of his resources to move in the direction of his full potential? Explain your answer.

Further reading

Deutsh, Albert, ed. *Encyclopedia of Mental Health.* Volumes 1, 2, 3. New York: Franklin Watts, Inc., 1970.

Duvall, Evelyn M. *Family Living.* New York: Macmillan, Inc., 1971.

Fromm, Erich. *The Sane Society.* New York: Fawcett, 1977.

Lowe, Gordon K. *Growth of Personality: From Infancy to Old Age.* New York: Penguin Books, 1972.

Mussen, Paul H. *The Psychological Development of the Child.* Englewood Cliffs, NJ: Prentice-Hall, Inc., 1973.

Strecker, Edward. *Growth of Personal Awareness: A Reader in Psychology.* New York: Harrow Books, Imprint of Harper & Row, Publishers, Inc., 1973.

Chapter 5

Our adjustments to frustrations

Some people let others choose for them so they do
not have to make choices. Some people avoid
choosing by flipping a coin. These methods may
avoid frustration, but they rely on chance.

Reprinted by permission of Jeff Kaufman.
From *Saturday Review*, © 1977 by Saturday Review Magazine Corp.

"Some food on a plate, please."

People are frustrated when they are trying to go some place, get or do something and their efforts are hindered or stopped.

Our goal-directed activities are developed from our basic needs. A need, once aroused, causes activity until it is satisfied. The resulting tension makes us anxious, keeps us busy seeking ways to satisfy the need, and forces us to learn and to adjust. If we achieve adequate patterns of behavior for satisfying our needs, we lessen our adjustment problems. But if we are frustrated, conflicts arise.

Frustration factors

Obstacles in the physical environment. We may be flying to keep an appointment and fog prevents our plane from landing on time. The child in his or her high chair wants to get down. The man in jail wants to be free. All of these people find the physical environment restrictive and frustrating.

Biological limitations.   A promising pianist may suffer a crippling injury to her or his hand that forces her or him to stop playing.   An individual may not meet the physical requirements to be a flight attendant.

Complexities of psychological make-up.   Frustration may occur because we have to choose between two goals.   Both of them are attractive.   But one is near at hand, the other far away.   Choosing the near one does not necessarily mean giving up the remote one. But there may be considerable delay in reaching it.   For example, Don and Helen are dating each other.   They know that some day they want to marry.   They also want to obtain college degrees.   They know that they will have to pay their own educational expenses. They could marry immediately, give up scholarships, and work part-time and go to school part-time.   Thus, they could reach the one goal, marriage, immediately while slowly working on the remote educational goal.   They could also concentrate on the educational goal and achieve it before marriage.   Don and Helen choose to take full scholarships, work to support themselves and attain their educational goal before marriage.   Another couple might decide to make very different kinds of choices.

Frustration may occur because we are faced with two demands, both negative.   The small child who doesn't want to go to bed but who will be spanked if he or she doesn't go is one example.   He or she can choose either going to bed or being spanked.   Neither goal is a positive choice to the child.   As adults, we often are faced with a choice between two goals that have negative aspects.   We have to choose between two unpleasant situations.

Frustration may also occur if to reach a desired goal we have to accomplish negative tasks, that is, tasks that are of no interest to us.

Social environment.   Although social factors are present in the other three sources, we refer here to the conflicting mores and taboos. These are the opposing laws of society that sometimes thwart us.   We Americans stress getting ahead, beating the other fellow, advancing relentlessly.   But we also stress love and cooperation with others.   A conflict emerges between competition and cooperation.

Social regulations and conditions add to frustration in many ways.   You would like to be active in your city, state, or national government.   But the law says you are not old enough to vote.   You would like to travel and have new experiences.   Parents, schools, and financial problems keep you at home.

The frustration conflict

Frustration may result from having to choose between alternatives rather than from being prevented from doing something. Conflicts can be a frequent cause of frustration.

Young persons of late high school and early college age are often faced with conflicts. Some of these conflicts may be to go on with schooling or not to go on; to leave home and get a job or to stay at home; to go along with the crowd using alcoholic drinks or not to go along; to smoke or not to smoke; to marry or not to marry. The list continues on and on.

Kinds of conflicting situations[1]

Psychologists often speak of three kinds of conflicting situations: *approach-approach, avoidance-avoidance,* and *approach-avoidance.*

Approach-approach conflicts. When you are faced with two attractive choices that are mutually exclusive, you are torn between them. Both are positively attractive. You would like to do both, but you can't. This is called an approach-approach conflict.

A boy knows two very attractive girls. He would like to take both of them to the dance next Saturday, but two girls with one boy is just not accepted behavior for such an event. Since he can't decide which one to approach, he stays home alone the night of the dance. A girl wishes to buy a new dress for a party and finds two that are equally attractive in design, quality, and price. Since she can't decide which one to buy, she doesn't buy either.

Actually, in everyday life, circumstances intervene that often cause us to make a decision. The boy might just have happened to meet one of the two girls in the hall, stopped to talk a minute, mentioned the dance, and his whole problem would have been solved. If she said, "Yes," the conflict was over. If she said, "No," the conflict was likewise over, because now he could approach the other girl for a date. The girl trying to buy a new dress might have been influenced by the salesperson who merely

1. Slightly abridged and adapted from pp. 271–273 of PSYCHOLOGY: ITS PRINCIPLES AND APPLICATIONS, Sixth Edition, by T. L. Engle and Louis Snellgrove, copyright © 1974 by Harcourt Brace Jovanovich, Inc. Reprinted by permission of the publishers.

said, "You look very nice in that one." In many approach-approach conflicts we waver back and forth for a short time and then make a decision.

Avoidance-avoidance conflicts. When you are presented with two alternatives that are equally unattractive, you are facing an avoidance-avoidance conflict. To use the popular expression, you find yourself "between the devil and the deep blue sea."

As a student you may be faced with the unpleasant thought of having to study for an examination on an evening when there is a special program on television. An equally unpleasant thought is that if you don't study you may fail the exam, fail the course, and fail to graduate. You would like to avoid both situations—studying and failing the exam. Maybe you go to your room and sit down to study but cannot keep from thinking about what you are missing, so you go to the living room and watch the television program. However, you cannot enjoy the program because you keep thinking about the possibility of failing. Back you go to your room and open the book—then back to the living room. Such wavering is very unpleasant. You would like to 'leave the

"What do you mean you forgot?"

field'—to use a psychological expression. You decide to take a walk, you drift off into a daydream, you remember a task around the house that needs your attention. You try to avoid both the thought of study and the thought of failing.

Approach-avoidance conflicts. Sometimes you are attracted by certain aspects of a situation, and at the same time you are repelled by other aspects. This is approach-avoidance conflict.

You would like to approach a particular goal, but at the same time you would like to avoid it. It has both positive and negative value for you. You are pulled in opposite directions, liking and disliking at the same time. For example, you are at the beach, and a swim with your friends seems most attractive. You run down to the water's edge and a small wave covers your feet. The water is terribly cold. A swim suddenly seems like something to avoid rather than something to approach. You run back up the beach. Your friends call. You approach the water again, but it hasn't warmed up. You run back up the beach, and so on. You are faced with an approach-avoidance conflict.

Perhaps you are trying to decide whether or not to apply for admission to college. You have heard a great deal about the pleasures and advantages of college life, and you would like to approach it. However, you have heard of the long hours of study, of difficult examinations, and of the high expense involved. You would like to avoid these unpleasant features.

Conflict patterns

1. approach-approach	EXAMPLE: I asked my friend out to dinner. Another friend invited me to the theater both on the same date.
2. avoidance-avoidance	Teenager is told . . . be home at 11:30 P.M. or stay in all week after the party.
3. approach-avoidance	You want to get good grades but you want to avoid late and long hours of study.

Dealing with conflict

Reactions to conflicts are varied. The situation that creates a conflict for one person does not create conflict for another person. You may have had this thought as you read the examples which explained the kinds of conflict situations.

Communication can resolve conflict.

The major focus in a study of conflict must be on the factors that determine how a person views his or her situation. Each of the three types of conflict have been described in terms of situations.

Conflict situations which cause some uneasiness and which present the person involved with recognizable alternatives are met by everyone. They are helpful because they force us to make decisions and to move in some direction. First, however, we must learn how to handle them.

In some instances the resolution of the conflict may be made easier by taking the following steps.

1. Carefully define the goals and alternatives.

2. Obtain all available essential information about the goals and alternatives.

3. List the advantages and disadvantages under each goal.

4. Eliminate the advantages or disadvantages that seem insignificant.

5. Clarify the situation by discussion with a respected advisor.

6. Hold to a time limit for reaching a decision.

7. Accept the decision as the best one in light of the situation and the information available.

Frustration tolerance

Frustration tolerance is a term used by psychologists. It indicates the ability of a person to deal with frustration without becoming maladjusted or emotionally upset. When a turtle meets a situation with which it cannot cope, it withdraws into its shell. When some people meet frustrating situations, they may withdraw into their 'shells.' That is, they may not be able to tolerate the frustration. On the other hand, people who are in good mental health accept frustration as one of the realities of life. They may have to readjust goals and the plans for achieving these goals. But they do not feel that everything is hopeless. They may find it helpful to begin by tolerating little frustrations without becoming upset. For example, learning to accept an accident such as spilling a quart of milk over the kitchen floor. Frustrating situations do not seem so frustrating when one realizes that they are quite normal and that everyone experiences them.[2]

Considerable learning must occur in the development of frustration tolerance. For example, a person learns that immediate gratifications can be delayed. Further, he or she learns that long-term goals are sometimes best served by delaying immediate satisfaction or by avoiding an outward expression of frustration. Personal limitations and external obstacles cause all of us to give up some goals and objectives. The ability to tolerate frustration is necessary in order to gain personal and social effectiveness. The ability to tolerate frustration does not mean that one ignores all thoughts associated with unconscious impulses. It involves, instead, the conscious recognition of the objectives and the reasons for their being desired. It also involves an evaluation of how these objectives might be achieved, replaced by others, kept for another time, or abandoned.

Positive value of conflict and frustration

Frustrating experiences may disturb us. But they also may have value. In many cases frustration is necessary for learning and for growth. It has a role to help invigorate, enforce, and increase actions which uphold the values and goals of our Judeo-Christian culture. The struggles of the characters in John F. Kennedy's *Profiles in*

2. From page 270 of PSYCHOLOGY: ITS PRINCIPLES AND APPLICATIONS, Sixth Edition, by T. L. Engle and Louis Snellgrove, copyright © 1974 by Harcourt Brace Jovanovich, Inc. Reprinted by permission of the publishers.

Courage depict the positive value of conflict and frustration. Each story is an illustration of personal heroism, where each person faced conflicting alternatives with their resulting frustration. In one case a senator voted for a bill that was spiritually and morally right, but his vote meant that his constituents would not reelect him. In other instances it meant sacrificing a more prominent office or loss of face in the eyes of one's peers.

In meeting and overcoming frustrations, we learn, our personalities develop, and we adjust. The important point to consider is whether we have enough resources to handle frustration without becoming too upset. If a person becomes too upset, he or she may begin to rationalize his or her shortcomings or may withdraw completely instead of trying to find ways to handle the problems.

Questions

1. Define the following terms:
   frustration tolerance   conflict   frustration

2. Give examples of experiences of conflict and label them as to whether they are approach-approach, avoidance-avoidance, or approach-avoidance.

3. Which type of experience is the most difficult for you to solve? Why?

4. Below are some statements that indicate frustration. Indicate the correct frustration factor in each.

Frustration factors
a. Physical Environment
b. Biological Limitation
c. Psychological Limitation
d. Social Limitation

Statements that indicate frustration
1. "The women of the Smith family do not study to be dentists," said Jean Smith's father.

2. "Of course he won't play professional basketball; he won't inherit the build for it."

3. Because John Brown was reared in a small town without a swimming pool, he did not learn to swim.

4. It is bad luck for the groom to see the bride on the wedding day before the ceremony.

5. To do graduate work at Harvard successfully, a research study found that students needed to have an I.Q. score of 120 or over.

Further reading

Bailes, Frederick. *Is There a Cure for Frustration?* Marina Del Rey, CA: D. Vorss & Co., 1972.

Conaway, Judith. *I'll Get Even.* Milwaukee, WI: Raintree Publishers, Inc., 1977.

Deutsch, Morton. *The Resolution of Conflict: Constructive and Destructive Processes.* New Haven, CT: Yale University Press, 1977.

Engle, T. L., and Snellgrove, Louis. *Psychology: Its Principles and Applications.* New York: Harcourt Brace Jovanovich, Inc., 1974.

Frost, Joyce H., and Wilmot, William. *Interpersonal Conflict.* Dubuque, IA: Wm. C. Brown Company, Publishers, 1978.

Janis, Irving. *Stress and Frustration.* New York: Harcourt Brace Jovanovich, Inc., 1971.

Luria, A. R. *The Nature of Human Conflicts.* New York: Liveright, Subsidiary of W. W. Norton & Co., Inc., 1976.

Margolis, Joseph. *Values and Conduct.* New York: Oxford University Press, Inc., 1971.

Pincus, Lily, ed. *Marriage: Studies in Emotional Conflict and Growth.* Washington, DC: National Association of Social Workers, 1974.

Chapter 6

Our mechanisms for self-defense

There is a constant conflict between personality and environment. Sometimes the conflict is slight and sometimes severe. Conflicts occur because of inadequately satisfied needs. Inadequately satisfied needs call for face-saving mechanisms.

The person who has failed to satisfy a need, or feels that a failure is going to happen, finds it necessary to give some explanation for, or defense against, that failure. He or she feels a need to justify failure in his or her own eyes as well as in the eyes of others. This chapter is about defense mechanisms we use. They are helpful if used sparingly. They are hampering if abused or overused.

Approaches to defense mechanisms

Defense mechanisms are the face-saving means that we all use to satisfy conflicts between our personality and our environment. They are attempts to satisfy the need which was abandoned in favor of attempts to avoid the discomforts of failure.

There are three ways that one can approach this struggle between personality and environment. One can attack or fight, reinterpret or compromise, or take flight. The attack or fight approach is direct. The flight approach is indirect. While the compromise approach involves adjustment on the part of everyone concerned. The beachcomber and her dog may be in flight, or may be gaining the strength to return home to accept compromise.

Attack or fight approach.   One of the most primitive reactions to thwarted behavior is aggression or hostility. The attack or fight approach is direct and natural. This approach often changes the situation in a negative manner. It very often damages the relationship. Sometimes even ruins it. For example, Eric is very fond of Maria. Maria has dated Eric, but recently accepted a date from Mike. Eric was hurt and embarrassed because he considered Maria to be his girl. He waited for Maria and Mike in a local hangout where dating couples usually stop to eat. When he saw them, he challenged Mike to a fight. Mike was reluctant to fight and so Eric attacked him. He called Mike names and blacked his eye. Maria thought she liked Eric. But after this unprovoked attack on Mike, as she saw it, she never spoke to Eric again.

A milder form of the fight approach is argument. Refusal to cooperate and determined stubbornness are others. When one is angry he or she can fight by constant nagging and annoying. He or she can defy and refuse to do what is asked.

The fight reaction becomes serious if a person uses it too often or at the wrong times. The social non-conformists who are constantly fighting society use the fight reaction consistently by refusing to live the way the world does. This reaction is an unhealthy approach when, after a reform has been won, they still go on fighting.

Reprinted by permission of Jack Tippit.
From *Ladies' Home Journal,* © 1974 LHJ Publishing, Inc.

"I keep him around just in case anyone tries to skip out without paying."

Compromise approach.   The compromise approach involves the adjustment to both the demands in self and in the environment.   In constructive compromise your personality weighs the results of doing just as you wish against what you probably should do.   Then you make a decision which seems best for all concerned.   However, it does take mature people to adjust and settle differences by compromise.   For example, your wish may be expressed by an X; the other person's wish, by a Y.   The outcome may be xY, or Xy, or xy, or after much discussion and reinterpretation the final decision may be Z.   The small x would mean a small part of your wish attached to his or her wish was unchanged.   Xy would indicate the situation in reverse.   The small xy indicates a changing of both wishes, but keeping the original intent.   The Z decision indicates a new approach that pleases both people.

Successful living depends on how intelligently one can make compromises with self and others.   To give up now for future gains, to assume responsibilities for unpleasant tasks, to change wishes and actions after consideration are compromises that pay big dividends.

Flight approach.   Have you ever suddenly had a very bad headache when you were to speak before the Student Council? Did you even succeed in convincing a friend that he or she ought to speak in your place? As you look back, it was probably just the thought of speaking before your peers that made your head ache. You were taking flight.

Other kinds of flight reactions are expressed by tiredness, boredom, and lack of attention. Sometimes when a course is especially difficult for students either in subject matter or in a sense of security, they will use a flight reaction by daydreaming, sleeping, or making believe the situation is different.

Make-believe can be a worthwhile form of flight for small children. This approach helps them to cope with the lack of power over their environment. In make-believe, children can scold their toys and release their frustration. They can become brave firefighters or famous doctors. In fact, through play and stories, children learn to fit make-believe and reality together.

Only when this type of make-believe becomes a main adult activity is it unhealthy. Adults who cannot accept their environment as it is, often spend as much effort in trying to escape it in some way as it would take to change the situation constructively. The constant dodging of responsibilities or duties that are unpleasant is called "gold-bricking."

The flight reaction can be used too often and in too extreme form. Some people turn to alcohol to get drunk when they are worried or upset. Others run away from the situation by losing their memory. A few commit suicide.

Types of defense mechanisms

The three approaches to defense mechanisms, fight, compromise, and flight, have been discussed. The approaches are obvious behaviors. But the defense mechanisms are not obvious. There are thirteen defense mechanisms. Let's look at each one.

Reaction formation. *Reaction formation is a way you offset a very strong, unconscious urge by doing the opposite of this urge in your conscious behavior.* A person defends the self against unwanted, threatening thoughts, feelings, and wishes. First he or she may repress them and then compulsively think and try to feel the opposite. There are the parents whose unwed daughter gives birth to a baby and decides to keep that baby in the family home. They are unhappy about this event. They are upset by this interruption in their lives and their daughter's life. Outwardly they talk about the joys of having a baby in the house. They ask what they did with their time before the baby was born. There is the overprotective parent who represses hostility toward a child and becomes obsessed by thoughts that the child's health and life are in danger. There is the solicitous wife who represses hostility toward her traveling husband. She may say on his return, "I couldn't sleep or eat while you were gone. I kept thinking that you were in an accident."

Conversion. *Conversion is the mechanism by which you transfer the energy of a desire you can't express into a physical symptom or complaint.* A lot of ideas or wishes that come from the unconscious can't be expressed because the conscious part of your personality won't let them out. For example, have you ever felt anxious and upset about something for a long time but you don't want to complain? You may develop a headache that you just can't explain. Sometimes children develop upset stomachs the first time they go to visit relatives and spend the night away from their parents. They don't want to admit to homesickness so they transfer their lonesomeness into a physical complaint.

Conversion symptoms can become very serious. There are the persons who strive so hard to achieve but don't have the ability. If their personality won't let them admit the lack of ability, they may transfer that into a physical symptom such as a migraine headache or a crippled limb. Then they can blame their lack of success on the physical complaint and not have to face the lack of intellectual ability.

Compensation. *This is the mechanism that lets you make up for some real or imaginary inadequacy by doing well in another activity.* Toulouse-Lautrec was a crippled and unsightly person. But he compensated for his real physical inadequacy when he was able to become a great artist whose friendship was valued by many.

The process of turning a handicap into an asset is called *overcompensation.* As a child, Wilma Rudolph was not strong. Yet with practice and determination she became a fine runner and an Olympics winner. She had refused to compensate until she fought the inadequacy directly. She won. Actors often overcompensate by using physical defects such as a large nose or big mouth, skinny or fat physique, or prominent eyes as marks of distinction.

A deficiency may lead to *direct or indirect compensation.* A person may achieve success in some realm other than the one in which he or she is handicapped. There is the student who does not excel in school but becomes an outstanding community leader, an athlete, or successful shop owner. Arrogance, loud talk or clothes, strange gadgets on cars, as well as superior accomplishments in music, art, or scholarship may be compensation for an earlier feeling of inferiority.

Parents who wish to satisfy their own ambitions through their children are seeking indirect compensation. Parents whose youthful dreams of a medical career were frustrated by lack of money may try to satisfy their ambition by urging their children to become doctors. A parent whose marriage was unhappy may try to compensate by arranging a brilliant marriage for his or her child. Although such compensation sometimes brings satisfaction to the parents, it may seriously frustrate the children.

Compensation helps to solve problems when the path seems blocked in the direction that one wants to go. It makes many people strive and achieve much more than they would otherwise. It is a helpful or a harmful mechanism depending entirely on how it is used.

Rationalization. *Rationalization is a method of unconsciously justifying ideas and behavior in a way that seems reasonable to the individual.* The person who rationalizes gives plausible, socially acceptable, or "good" reasons for his or her actions or beliefs. In this way he or she avoids admitting the real reasons which are regarded as unworthy or improper, or which may not even be apparent.

There are many forms of rationalization. Perhaps the best known is the *"sour grapes" reaction.* This comes from Aesop's fable about the fox who wanted the grapes but couldn't reach them. After several tries, the fox declared, "I don't really want them because they are probably sour." This same attitude was shown by Barbara when she didn't get a part in the play that she had tried very hard to get. Instead of admitting her failure, she belittled the play. She said that she really didn't want a part. The director wasn't well trained. The play required too much work and too much time.

The "sweet lemon" form of rationalization is rationalizing in reverse. Instead of trying to convince ourselves and others that we did not actually want the thing we were after, we talk ourselves into believing that our present situation really is best. We say we are completely satisfied, and want nothing more. The status quo, or the existing state, assumes new value when changing it involves more talent or courage than we have or means that we lose status by the change. This is illustrated by the boy who says, "I'm not going to the dance. It is just as well. Now my family can save the money that it would have cost for my new tux." Or by the girl who says, "I wasn't chosen to be a member of the team. This will give me more time to spend on my physics course."

Rationalization is important psychologically because it helps us to maintain our self-respect and self-confidence. In everyday affairs we have neither the time nor the wish to track down and explain all our motives. Rationalizations provide protection against anxiety and failure.

But rationalizations may be harmful if carried to extremes. First, if we refuse to accept responsibility for our failures we shall never be able to overcome them. Second, rationalizations may in time shade into delusions. If we consistently blame others for whatever goes wrong in our lives, we may become completely dissociated from reality. We may develop delusions of persecution or of grandeur.

Identification. *Identification is a device whereby you automatically imitate the behavior and mannerisms of someone else.* You put yourself in his or her shoes.

R. R. Sears, who represents one point of view, claims that identification by a child comes from learning without anyone deliberately trying to teach him or her and without a conscious effort to learn. In this type of learning, called role practice, the child acts or pretends to act as if he or she is filling another person's role. Role practice occurs in fantasy, daydreams, or in play behavior. It can begin with a desire to reproduce pleasant experiences. Sears notes also that the role-practice behavior can represent an attempt by children to reassure themselves that they have their parents' affection and love. By assuming the parental role in fantasy or daydream, they can give themselves indirectly the affection they want.

Identification is often used by those who have been unable to reach their own goals. They gain satisfaction and enhance their self-esteem by identifying themselves with the achievements of others. This form of identification is called hero-worship. For example, there is the adolescent who follows the exploits of his or her football idol. He or she basks in the reflected glory of the hero's accomplishments on the gridiron. The hero may live next door, or may be somebody he or she has never met personally. Or the hero may even be a fictional character.

Not only adolescents but also adults often identify themselves with recognized prestige groups, especially when approaching a new situation. The boy who transfers to another college mentions his membership in a well-known fraternity. A woman making new business contacts points out casually but intentionally that she is an active member in a prestigious club.

People identify not only with specific persons, but also with certain groups. They join a club and it becomes their club. They speak of their school, their state, and their country. The achievements of their group become their achievements. They become upset when any slurring remark or attack is made against their group.

Whether or not identification plays a constructive role in the development of a person depends on three factors.

1. In the adjustment to society it makes a great difference whether one models oneself after a gangster, a saint, a doctor, or a mechanic.

2. The example set by one's hero or model may give direction and impetus to one's own activities.

3. In extreme cases of identification, one loses all sense of distinction between self and the person with whom one identifies. He or she actually believes himself or herself to be president, actor, or great inventor. Paranoia is the chronic mental disorder characterized by delusions of persecution and of one's own greatness.

Projection. *Projection is a device for assigning to others wishes or faults that you will not claim as your own.* This "misery loves company" process takes many forms. Pointing to guilt in others is so satisfying when one is troubled with impulses that lead to feelings of guilt in oneself. The many excuses for being late and for making errors fall into this category. "Most of the class is flunking the course," the socially busy sophomore tells his or her parents. "She had a bad reputation before I ever saw her, so she better not talk about me," argues the fellow who feels guilt for his behavior toward a girl whom he dated. He tries in this way to blame the beginning of the undesirable behavior on the girl.

The same process operates with respect to prejudice against other groups. The often contradictory nature of accusations against others becomes understandable when we realize that in the process of projection many different qualities that one finds disturbing to oneself can be attributed to others.

Consider a further consequence of the process of projection. After people have transferred their unacceptable or undesirable emotions or attitudes to other persons or groups, they are free to attack. Or they are free to direct suspicion toward others through insinuation, gossip, or slander. They feel justified in withholding certain privileges from others. Thus they deny others equal opportunity. They segregate or ostracize others because of their alleged characteristics.

So the projective mechanism gives people the satisfaction of defending virtue by attacking evil or weakness in others. They place themselves in a position of righteousness and moral vigilance. This helps to allay any additional doubts they may have about themselves.

Projection characterizes some extreme forms of personality disorganization. Delusions of persecution, for example, stem from one's tendency to project onto another one's own dangerous tendencies.

Regression. *Regression occurs when a person returns to previous levels of behavior.* A flight mechanism is often evident when a new baby is born into a family which already has a toddler. The older child often reverts to bed wetting or thumb sucking or drinking from a bottle. This may happen even though the child has long since learned to use the toilet and to drink from a glass.

Homesickness and other forms of regressive behavior are likely to occur especially in overprotected and overindulged persons. Another factor which contributes to regressive behavior is that we usually recall pleasant experiences and make the past appear more attractive than it actually was.

A general meaning of the term regression is using primitive or earlier behavior in response to frustration. "Primitive behavior" refers to early, learned actions that are less refined, less differentiated, and less effective than those learned later. In such instances, relative to their general capabilities, people display behavior that is unorganized, gross, and ineffective. Regression in this sense does not imply the return to a specific behavior characteristic of an earlier period. But rather implies a return to earlier and often less complex stages of behavioral organization. Regressive behaviors of this type are not lasting. Some people may be petulant, childish, tearful, or ineffectual for a time. But upon reaching their objectives, or their substitutes, or a decrease in the need for the objective, or diversion of attention, these persons again show the purposeful, organized activities of which they are capable.

Repression. *In repression, wishes, thoughts, and feelings associated with pain and unpleasantness are shut out subconsciously from awareness.* Consider all the unpleasant aspects of life that you do not think about. There are the embarrassing moments, the times when you have felt that you acted foolishly or showed unusual ignorance. There were the times you took advantage of another. There were the terrible sights of cruelty or an accident.

This flight reaction greatly complicates our adjustment to our problems. On the other hand, it would be a doubtful advantage if we remembered everything that happened to us, the relevant and the irrelevant, the wrong solutions or answers along with the right ones. Forgetting is a dynamic process. That is, we forget or remember experiences in accordance with our needs. Dismissing unpleasant memories from consciousness protects us against experiences that threaten or disturb our self-concept.

Suppression. Suppression is a conscious and deliberate act. *Suppression is a willful tendency to dismiss a thought or an unpleasant experience that is socially taboo.*

The art of being tactful is largely a matter of suppression. The person who ignores mature tact for the sake of cruel "truth" is being unkind toward others. He or she is not likely to have many friends. It is certainly not advisable for married persons to dwell upon the negative aspects of each other's personalities. Of course, frankness also has a place in society.

Fantasy and daydreaming. These are imaginative and pleasant ways to escape. One finds relief from frustrations by living in a world of one's own.

Whether a daydream is psychologically desirable or undesirable can be determined only by a study of the daydream and the conditions under which it occurs. If the fantasy or daydream becomes an end in itself so that a person stops trying to succeed in the world of reality, the desirability of the thinking is questionable. On the other hand, the daydream may be little more than an inexpensive form of entertainment. It may be no more undesirable than temporarily losing oneself in a movie or television program. Daydreaming that leads to positive action can be highly desirable.

Daydreams and fantasies, then, depending on how often we use them and how important they are to us, may operate in many different ways and affect our adjustment. All of us have spent time daydreaming. Perhaps the success of such plays as *Harvey,* with its imaginary rabbit which made life more interesting for Ellwood P. Dowd, is due to the fact that many of us have felt the world of daydreams and fantasy more satisfying than everyday existence.

Many inventions, social reforms, and plays have been born out of daydreams. Daydreams, in fact, are often first steps in the minds of people who create new things and develop new insights in old institutions or ideas. The daydream that materializes into reality has touched all our lives. Edison's idea of the incandescent light was certainly thought of as fantasy. Air flight was a huge daydream before the Wright brothers transformed it into reality.

Withdrawal. *Withdrawal is a retreat from the situations in which people feel frustrated and unable to adjust.* It may take various forms. People who are reserved and formal in their dealings with others may be showing symptoms of withdrawing. Their aloofness may be a screen to hide deep-seated feelings of inferiority. These persons may keep others at a distance for fear that they may come to share their low opinion of themselves. Their acquaintances, therefore, can never feel that they really know them. Such persons have no confidence in themselves or in others.

Some people avoid the problems and conflicts of everyday life by withdrawing into illness. They may not deliberately make themselves ill. But they do become especially sensitized to certain physical disturbances that other people might not notice.

Apathy and lack of interest also may be symptoms of withdrawal. Some people, in order to justify their withdrawal, profess a lack of interest in others.

What we popularly describe as narrow-mindedness is also a form of withdrawal. Narrow-minded people are unwilling to expose themselves to ideas contrary to their own. They dismiss as "propaganda" anything that opposes their own prejudices. They avoid opinions that threaten theirs. They withdraw from contacts with those who disagree with them. To some extent this is true of all of us. We are all selective in what we listen to and read. But when this selectivity becomes so pronounced as to blur our view of reality, then it is maladjustive.

Displacement. *In displacement, one transfers the emotion connected with one person or thing to an unrelated person or object.* The displacement process has been illustrated by Norman Rockwell in a cartoon where the boss bawls out the husband, the husband yells at his wife, the wife spanks the child, the child pulls the cat's tail, and the cat eats a mouse. Thus ends the displacement sequence. (Of course, one can imagine that the mouse caused the cat to experience indigestion.) The implication of the sequence is that since each is unable to express hostility toward the source, he or she redirects pent-up feelings toward his or her subordinate. Since a clerk can't get angry at the difficult customer, displacement may be the answer for him or her.

Hate, annoyance, and irritation are not the only things you displace. You can displace love. It is a healthy kind of displacement when you feel secure because you believe that people love you. You then can pass on some of that love to people who you know don't love you. Some displacement of love is unhealthy. For instance, there are people who give all of their love to a dog when there are people around them who need love more. Although some people overuse displacement, others use it only occasionally.

Idealization. *Idealization is the over-evaluation of someone or something.* The idealized person is seen as more capable then he or she really is. The idealized thing or object is prized more than it is worth. For example, Rachel describes her friend, Hector, as the best looking, smartest young man at Community High. When Rachel's friend, Sandy, sees Hector, she sees that he is not good-looking and has a bad case of acne.

General principles

In summary, these five general principles about the nature and function of defense mechanisms should be reviewed. First of all, the escape mechanisms are learned forms of behavior. This learning may be formal or informal, conscious or unconscious. However, people learn to establish an emotional equilibrium. The defense mechanisms help them establish a state of balance, or adjustment, among opposing influences, interests and needs. These mechanisms protect a person from threats to his or her security. They are adjustive or maladjustive, depending upon the extent to which they are used. They are adjustive if they provide flexibility in problem solving. They are also adjustive to the extent that they help a person to face reality and to cope satisfactorily. They are maladjustive when they prevent one from making an objective analysis of self in relation to the problem. They are also maladjustive when a person is blinded to the possibility of alternative courses of action.

Questions

1. Define the following terms:

   compensation   repression   withdrawal
   rationalization   regression   displacement
   identification   fantasy   maladjustive
   projection   conversion   reaction formation
   idealization   suppression

2. Give contrasting examples to show when the adjustment approaches of fight, flight, and constructive compromise would be helpful and when they would be harmful.

3. Joan Brown is a girl who is withdrawn. Give some examples of how she might act in a club meeting.

4. What are the advantages of daydreaming?

5. When Jerry, who is four years old, found he had a new baby sister, he began to suck his thumb. What is the flight mechanism that Jerry is experiencing?

6. At age ten Betty was bitten by a dog. This experience frightened her and left her scarred physically and emotionally. When Betty is asked about the scar on her hand, she says that she doesn't remember how she got it. What mechanism is Betty using?

7. Below are listed the mechanisms people use. Also there are some examples of these mechanisms. Try to match a mechanism which fits each of the examples.

   Mechanisms

   a. rationalization   e. displacement
      (sweet lemon)   f. rationalization
   b. compensation   (sour grapes)
   c. identification   g. conversion
   d. projection   h. reaction formation

EXAMPLES:

1. "We haven't a very warm home. We have no running water. But it is good for the children to learn to do without these things. They'll appreciate them more later on."

2. "My wife wanted me to have this fishing equipment to even up the cost of the garbage disposal that she added to our kitchen."

3. "Every time Mickey embarrasses himself by talking too loud at a party, he feels that he must buy his wife a gift."

4. "Don loves to joke about his big nose."

5. Cecilia has recently had a back operation. When her sister realized her discomfort, she had such a sympathetic backache that the nurse had to get a straight chair for her to sit on.

6. Lucy's mother works every day. While Lucy stays with her sitter, she likes to walk around the house in her mother's high heeled slippers.

7. "Her son was picked up by the police for speeding long before my son ever rode with him."

8. "I would have been on time this morning if my mother had made me get up."

9. When asked why she was crying, four-year-old Jackie said that it was because her bike wouldn't stand up.

Further reading

Dollard, John, and Miller, N. E. *Personality and Psychotherapy.* New York: McGraw-Hill, 1950.

Engle, T. L. *Psychology.* New York: Harcourt Brace Jovanovich, Inc., 1975.

Hall, C. S., and Lindzey. G. *Theories of Personality.* 3rd ed. New York: John Wiley & Sons, Inc., 1970.

Hilgard, E. *Introduction to Psychology.* 6th ed. New York: Harcourt Brace Jovanovich, Inc., 1975.

Kagan, Jerome. *Personality Development.* New York: Harcourt Brace Jovanovich, Inc., 1971.

Moustakes, C. *Personal Growth: The Struggle for Identity and Human Values.* East Dennis, MA: Howard A. Doyle, 1969.

Porter, Burton F. *Personal Philosophy: Perspectives on Living.* New York: Harcourt Brace Jovanovich, Inc., 1976.

Sears, R. R.; Maccoby, E. E.; and Levin, H. *Patterns of Child Rearing.* New York: Harper & Row, Publishers, Inc., 1957.

Chapter 7

Our attitudes

The influence which attitudes have upon behavior is found in both scriptural and classical literature. "As he thinketh in his heart, so is he." Disraeli wrote, "We make our fortunes and we call them fate."

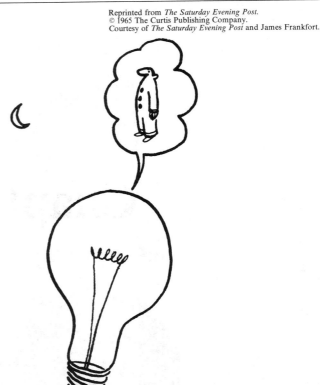

Composition of attitudes

Attitudes are made up of three parts. The *affective or emotional part* refers to the feelings of good or bad, like or dislike, for the object of the attitude. The *cognitive part* is viewed as the information, knowledge, and beliefs which the individual has about the object of the attitude. *The behaviorial or action part* of the attitude describes the response associated with or to the object of the attitude.

The parts of an attitude are related to each other in that each part reacts with the other parts and the intersection completes the whole attitude. For example, a high school student might say, "I have this teacher who's a real square in the way he thinks, and practically every time we talk, we get into an argument. But I notice that even when we see something exactly opposite and we are not going to compromise—no way!—he listens to me. Maybe that's why I still like him."

Probably so! Having someone listen makes the high school boy feel worthwhile. When we listen to each other, we convey respect. The boy knows that he and his teacher view the knowledge from opposite sides, but his action is *like* because the teacher gives him self-respect, a chance to disagree. His reaction to the teacher is to like the teacher even when they disagree.

Another high school student discussed a situation in his community. "What gets me are the things you can't really lay your hands on. I guess attitude would be the closest word for it—the attitude that we can't really think yet, that what we have to say rates a kindly pat on the head. Here's the situation. People started a block association in my area of town. Nobody invited the youth . . . but called us the 'youth resources' of the neighborhood. We thought it was our neighborhood too, so a few of us went. The Chairman, a man about 50 years old, talked about a community track meet. Another fellow about 40 offered to coach us. The women thought food and craft booths would make it festive. Not a person there asked us, the youth, what we thought. Or if we'd help. Or even if we liked the idea . . . *but* we were supposed to do the running." In this example all three parts of attitude formation are violated. Thus, there is no rapport between this group of adults and the adolescents.

A balanced attitude is one in which each of the three components or parts are about equally developed.

Function of attitudes

The *functional approach* to attitudes shows people as working or striving toward certain goals. The attitudes are analyzed in terms of the degree or extent that they enable the individual to obtain the these goals. Attitudes can be divided into four functions. The four functions are adjustment, defense, knowledge, and the expression of the values which the individual holds.

The *adjustment function* of attitudes recognizes that people try very hard to gain the most rewards or positive responses from the environment around them. People also try to minimize the negative responses or the penalties. People develop favorable attitudes toward those experiences, things, or people which are associated with the satisfaction of their needs. The people, experiences, or things that thwart, frighten, or punish develop favorable attitudes.

The *defense function* of attitudes revolves around the idea that people protect themselves from anxiety by blocking out threatening external and internal situations. Attitudes can function like defense mechanisms to protect people from acknowledging their conflicts and deficiencies. For example, prejudiced attitudes help to maintain the self-concept by enabling one group of people to have a sense of superiority over another group of people.

The *knowledge function* refers to the fact that people seek knowledge to give meaning to what otherwise would be an unorganized world. The attitudes in this frame of reference give people a basis for understanding their world. The knowledge gives predictability, consistency, and stability to their idea of the world.

The *expression of values function* of attitudes involves the notion that attitudes give positive expression to an individual's central values which make up self-concept. Satisfaction is achieved from the expression of attitudes which reflect one's cherished beliefs and one's self-image.

Social influence on attitudes

1. The attitudes of people are strongly influenced by the groups to which people belong and those to which they want to belong.

2. Attitudes which people make known publicly are harder to change than private attitudes.

3. Any successful attempt to develop or change attitudes must provide continuing social support for people to hold the attitudes.

4. There is considerable evidence that as one's reference group changes, so do one's attitudes.

5. There is also considerable evidence that if a group decides to adopt new attitudes its members will also adopt the new attitudes.

6. Audience participation in group discussions and group decision making help to overcome resistence to developing the new attitudes the communicator is presenting.

Experience and attitude

The following editorial from *Psychology Today*[1] tells how Abraham Maslow's attitude toward life and work changed as he experienced a massive heart attack and recovered. "I've been doing the preface for months when it should have taken only a couple of days. In fact, I permitted myself to hold up everybody and to write and rewrite and fiddle with it."

Abe did not let Harper & Row send the revision to press until he could say, "this is complete, this is the way I want it to be." The first copy reached his desk in Menlo Park, California on the day before a massive blockage stopped his heart.

There was just time for him to rejoice in what he had fiddled with: he had transformed M & P [*Motivation and Personality*] into a tough case for the validity of human motives of higher order than psychology generally assigns to man. So the book, once a tentative statement of theory, had become a triumphant summary of Maslow's lifelong struggle to prove that "wonderful people can and do exist—even though in very short supply and even though having feet of clay."

1. Reprinted from PSYCHOLOGY TODAY MAGAZINE. Copyright © 1970 Ziff-Davis Publishing Company. Used by permission of the publisher.

A Jew born in Brooklyn, Maslow took his Ph.D at the University of Wisconsin and developed a gift for well-controlled experiment and precise technical thought. Later, as chairman of the Department of Psychology at Brandeis and as 1968 president of the American Psychological Association, he angered the strict behaviorists of APA by grasping their research and theory and then insisting that it did not account for the whole personality.

He carefully defined what he called the "B-values"—the needs beyond self-interest—and he searched for them in "self-actualized" persons. Out of the exciting hope offered by his brilliance, young behavioral scientists founded the humanistic school of psychology, now a bold movement that is spreading like a religion across the U.S. and colonizing Europe.

In one draft of the M & P preface that he brought to us on a visit, Maslow wrote of the anguish of his early years, "doggedly pursuing an intuitive conviction and, in the process, defying some of the most basic canons of scientific method and of philosophical criticism . . . These were, after all, rules which I myself had believed and accepted, and I was very much aware that I was skating on very thin ice. Accordingly, my explorations proceeded against a background of anxiety, conflict and self-doubt."

Abe had a capacity for monumental rage at the purveyors of cynical views of man. Because of it he barely held himself back, in his last months, from savage attack upon certain heroes of the New York literary Establishment.

But he had an even bigger courage, a joyful affirmation of life that surged through the long tapes he often dictated for us, encouraging *Psychology Today* to explore questions that have no easy answers. Much as we loved this beautiful man, we did not understand the source of his courage—until the last cassette came in. It was a tape about the subject of the current issue—death.

Maslow talked with intense introspection about an earlier heart attack that had come right after he completed an important piece of work. "I had really spent myself. This was the best I could do, and here was not only a good time to die but I was even willing to die . . . It was what David M. Levy called the 'completion of the act.' It was like a good ending, a good close. I think actors and dramatists have that sense of the right moment for a good ending, with a phenomenological sense of good completion—that there was nothing more you could add . . . Partly this was entirely personal and internal and just a matter of feeling good about myself, feeling proud of myself, feeling pleased with myself, self-respecting, self-loving, self-admiring . . .”

“My attitude toward life changed. The word I used for it now is the post-mortem life. I could just as easily have died so that my living constitutes a kind of an extra, a bonus. It’s all gravy. Therefore I might just as well live as if I had already died.

“One very important aspect of the post-mortem life is that everything gets doubly precious, gets piercingly important. You get stabbed by things, by flowers and by babies and by beautiful things—just the very act of living, of walking and breathing and eating and having friends and chatting. Everything seems to look more beautiful rather than less, and one gets the much-intensified sense of miracles.

“I guess you could say that post-mortem life permits a kind of spontaneity that’s greater than anything else could make possible.

“If you’re reconciled with death or even if you are pretty well assured that you will have a good death, a dignified one, then every single moment of every single day is transformed because the pervasive undercurrent—the fear of death—is removed . . . I am living an end-life where everything ought to be an end in itself, where I shouldn’t waste any time preparing for the future, or occupying myself with means to later ends . . .

“Sometimes I get the feeling of my writing being a communication to my great-great grandchildren who, of course, are not yet born. It’s a kind of an expression of love for them, leaving them not money but in effect affectionate notes, bits of counsel, lessons I have learned that might help them . . .”

Attitudes and your way of life

Your philosophy of life is your deliberate effort to make your beliefs, morals, and behavior patterns sensible. It is an effort to put them all together so that you have a basis for action. Your personal philosophy can be defined in this way. It is the conscious statement of your credo or set of opinions and attitudes that are formed and reformed as you unify your thinking.

However, your way of life is formed by the attitudes that you have gained from the mechanisms previously discussed in Chapter 3. Many people reach maturity without questioning their behavior. Yet they consistently act in definite directions. Attitudes and habits guide their actions. Their behavior toward others, their sincerity, and their dependability suggest certain attitudes. These attitudes and traits may or may not be socially-oriented. For example, criminals may justify and rationalize their behavior as they relate to others in their antisocial environment.

Attitudes can be developed by education, society, propaganda, prejudice, and superstition; moods or emotions; and by generalizing from facts. Differences in attitudes are not only important because they determine social behavior but also because they affect one's emotional adjustment. Persons who always think they are getting "a raw deal" are usually being treated as everyone else is being treated. It is attitude which creates the "raw deals." Our attitudes color the world in ways that greatly affect our general outlook and happiness.

Attitude analysis

There are opinion polls and standardized tests which measure attitudes. These are worthwhile when one is trying to measure other people's attitudes. Also, they are important when the attitudes of groups of people need to be measured. However, we are going to ask you to measure your own attitudes without your having the aid of a standardized test. We want you to explore your attitudes and then write them down.

The objective in writing this attitude analysis is to further your understanding of yourself. It is not to be written for someone else to read. It is for you. It should represent a critical analysis of the factors and experiences which have formed the attitudes and feelings you have about the topic you have chosen. You may choose any area for an analysis. For example, consider attitudes about education, children, parenthood, love, friendship, pets, honesty, religion, and so forth. There is no limit to the topics which can be analyzed. Choose an area that has special appeal to you as well as possible answers. It is assumed that if you are able to analyze adequately your feelings and attitudes in one area, you can apply your analytical skill to other areas. Then you should be more able to understand your own behavior.

Before you start to write your analysis, make an important decision. Decide to be as objective and as honest as possible. Otherwise the value of the analysis is lost. Your goal is to examine what your attitudes and feelings about a topic really are. Try to discover how and why you came to feel as you do. Therefore, do not approach this task with an attempt to write what you think your attitudes should be, or what you think others think they should be. Look at your attitudes as they really are.

An adequate and thorough analysis will call for a lot of thinking—deep thinking. First of all, try to record and examine what your attitudes and feelings are. Then trace your past experiences which relate to these feelings and attitudes as far back as you can remember. Since it is highly unlikely that you can recall every detail in chronological order, it is better not to start with the hope of writing your analysis from beginning to end. As you try to recall your earlier experiences, one thing will lead to another. Therefore, use small sheets of paper or file cards. As you recall various thoughts, record each one. Identify the approximate date, age, or whatever is needed to classify the thought. When you are certain that you have recalled all that you can, sort the notes. Then on the basis of these thoughts, write your complete analysis.

Undoubtedly, some things will be remembered more easily than others. But from what we know of how the mind works we are relatively sure that many experiences, which may not be recalled immediately, may be remembered later. If you seem to have no recollection of some particular time of your life, or if there are some things that do not seem quite clear, don't give up. Try hard to recall the experiences or circumstances.

Work on your attitude analysis with dedication to self-understanding. As you work, your attitudes may be strengthened by considering this statement attributed to Socrates, "The unexamined life is not worth living."

Questions

1. Write an example that reinforces or discredits the quote from Disraeli, "We make our fortunes and we call them fate."

2. If John Jones has never analyzed his attitudes, how is it possible for his attitudes to cause him to act in definite directions?

3. How can an attitude be changed?

4. Marie Barry says that she has no attitude toward snakes because she never thinks about them. Is she correct? Why?

5. What is the difference between an attitude and a personal philosophy?

6. Let's look at two college roommates and their attitudes toward study. Libby and Helen are enrolled in the same English class. An announcement is made that a written paper is due the next day. The girls have no other required assignments.

Helen realizes that she can best enjoy the remainder of her day if she goes to her room at once. There she makes an outline of the theme, determines references to be cited, plans her writing, and decides how much time will be required. Then she writes the paper. She finds it exciting to write. At supper time her work is completed. She goes to supper with the satisfaction of having completed her task and now has time to relax in any way she wishes. She may turn to a new job, using the zest that results from a completed one, or she may go to a show, engage in a game, or read.

Libby says, "I have all night to do this. I'm tired after a day's work. I ought to go get a soda." She meets some friends and spends the time until supper talking. She eats a hearty meal, lounges on her bed while reading a magazine, and then decides to take a nap. She sleeps an hour, wakes up too befuddled to work. She decides to set the alarm clock so she can awake for an early morning session. She awakens at four, goes to her desk, and spends a half hour trying to recall the specific requirements of the paper. She becomes panicky as daylight comes. She writes as well as she can under the strain. Finally, she finishes the theme and dashes to class without breakfast.

What attitudes toward work or study are depicted by the two cases? How could Libby's efficiency be improved? Which girl do you think is getting the most out of college? Explain your answers.

Further reading

Allport, Gordon W. *Personality and Social Encounter.* Boston: Beacon Press, 1964.

Bettelheim, Bruno, and Janowitz, Morris. *Social Change and Prejudice.* New York: The Free Press, Division of Macmillan, Inc., 1964.

Heidenreich, Charles A. *Personal and Social Adjustment.* Fair Oaks, CA: Heidenreich House, 1970.

McKinney, Fred. *Psychology in Action: Basic Readings.* New York: Macmillan, Inc., 1973.

Miller S.; Nunnally, E.; and Wadsman, D. *Alive and Aware.* Minneapolis, MN: Interpersonal Communication Programs, 1975.

Stinnett, Nick, and Walters, James. *Relationships in Marriage and Family.* New York: Macmillan, Inc., 1977.

Wolman, Benjamin, ed. *Handbook of General Psychology.* Englewood Cliffs, NJ: Prentice-Hall, Inc., 1973.

Chapter 8

Our mental health

The serious problem of mental illness is not humorous. We may use it as a source of humor because it is too painful to think about. Perhaps James Thurber had this in mind when he wrote, "Humor is emotional chaos remembered in tranquility."

Reprinted by permission of Robert Schochet.
From *Saturady Review/World,* © 1974.

"Up a lazy river . . . by the ol' mill run. . . ."

The healthy self

The previous chapters in this unit should help develop an understanding of the healthy self. To the question, "What is a healthy self?" three major ideas are proposed.

First, *people are called mentally healthy when they understand themselves, their motivations, drives, wishes, and desires.* This self-knowledge is regarded as healthy when it leads a person to accept oneself while recognizing faults and assets in past as well as in present behavior. Although people think they know themselves, many actually do not. This is why it has been pointed out that a healthy self-image is a correct one. It is not easy to decide whether a self-image is correct or incorrect. It may be idealized or under-rated. It may also be in conflict with what close friends think about a person. Many psychological conflicts arise because people see themselves as being different from the way others see them.

Second, *a healthy self views the person not at any one moment,* but sees the person from a perspective that covers his or her life span to the date of measurement. This kind of analysis examines the person's previous growth and the result of this progress. It is often described as self-realization, self-actualization, growth, or becoming. The idea appeals to many people because it recognizes that psychological development is a growth toward one's highest potential. That is to say, the person has made positive growth toward development in each age and stage of life. The person has developed a distinct and special character.

Third, *the healthy self is concerned with integration of a personality.* Integration indicates whether a person's conscious outlook on life is unified or is contradictory in its elements. The balance between the various parts of personality is regarded as flexible. A flexible balance is, perhaps, best illustrated by thinking of a person under some considerable stress. Where the balance is rigid (that is, unhealthy), such a person will appear not to respond at all to the stress. However, after a certain degree of stress, he or she may go to pieces completely. Where the balance is flexible (that is, healthy), response to stress will appear sooner. This will be, perhaps, at a point where readjustments are still possible. The most frequent response to stress is some degree of anxiety. In contrast to popular belief, anxiety is a sign of health not one of ill health. For example, Ms. Romero is a young attractive librarian in a large suburban school. To keep order in the library so that students can study, she often has to ask other students, who come to the library to disturb others, to leave. Some of these students have threatened her when they have been asked to leave for disciplinary action. Ms. Romero's apartment is six blocks from the school. She must walk because she doesn't own a car. There is a vacant lot by the newsstand, where these students usually gather. Ms. Romero must walk by this vacant lot on her way home. She is always somewhat frightened as she walks in this area at night. Sometimes when there is a gang gathered, she stops at the newsstand and calls a cab. Ms. Romero's anxiety and precautions are a sign of good sense, not a sign of ill health. However, it is true that many forms of mental disease are characterized by states of intense anxiety with which a person cannot cope.

The mentally healthy person

The following characteristics of the mentally healthy person are similar to those of the mature individual, the well-integrated personality, and the developing character. This similarity is natural because mental health is achieved by the factors that contribute to self-understanding. The mentally healthy person is one who has these qualities.

1. enjoys life

2. realizes that any unhappiness he or she experiences has understandable causes

3. is generally self-confident

4. is able to maintain close and satisfying relationships with a few people

5. is able to meet problems without becoming more disturbed by them than their degree of seriousness would warrant

6. is sensibly concerned about health and is neither overly interested in body functions nor repelled by them

7. is able to express justifiable anger in a socially acceptable way

8. is not afraid of people, things, or situations except where there is reasonable cause to be afraid

9. has a conscience that helps him or her keep behavior acceptable for self and others

Mental health and humor

A sense of humor implies certain desirable abilities and attitudes. It is an index of good mental health. A sense of humor suggests that one is able to have a light, playful attitude toward the world at certain times. One can detach self from the seriousness and the cares of reality. One can deal with life in a lighthearted way. This attitude means that a person is not frightened by the situation, but is in control. It means that the person can relax his or her defenses against threat. He or she has an inner strength. He or she can stand anxiety and frustration for the moment.

A sense of humor shows that one can laugh and not take himself or herself too seriously. He or she has a good attitude toward impulses, wishes, illnesses, and physical handicaps. The extreme moralist, or prude, on the other hand, cannot take a friendly look at self. This kind of person judges self by a stern rule.

A person with a good sense of humor can enjoy the pleasure of self-indulgence. He or she can share feelings with others. This is what it means to be free to laugh. Laughter itself is a universal expression of emotion. All people of all ages know laughter. Marcel Marceau, the famous French mime, for example, is able to make people laugh by his comic antics without saying a word. Laughter is above culture, era, and civilization.

People laugh for many reasons. Besides the laughter at the comic, there is laughter that is expressed to hide other feelings. People laugh to hide unhappiness or distress. They laugh to cover up social discomfort. They laugh when they want to deny the seriousness of a situation. They laugh when they want to hide the fact that they are angry. People laugh when they are suddenly relieved from fear. They laugh when they are pleasantly surprised. Children laugh in play just from happy spirits. Even infants smile and laugh. These expressions become social responses and ways to communicate emotionally with another person.

According to Freud, humor provides two different sources of pleasure. There is play pleasure. That is, the pleasure of playing, thinking, and acting like a child. There is release of inhibition of unacceptable wishes, particularly the wish to injure or to hurt.

Reprinted by permission of Malcolm Hancock.
From *Saturday Review/World*, © 1974.

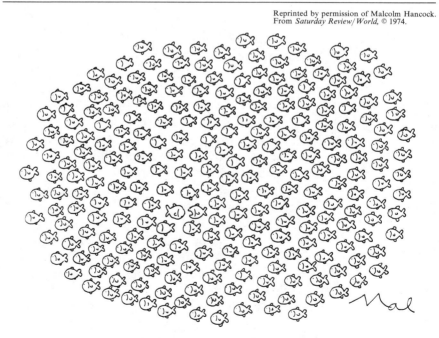

"Mortimer, can't you do anything right?"

With the first source of pleasure, humor lets one go back to a childish level as a relief from the seriousness of living in a real world. Humor allows us to return to the time when thinking and acting involved little trouble or conflict. By means of techniques like a play on words or punning, humor causes laughter as an expression of this sudden pleasure. In a sense, humor means being foolish, or being able to think in a nonsensical way. Everybody recognizes how much humor depends upon childish ways of thinking and upon feelings. One can, in humor, suspend the rules of logic, reality, and reasonableness. Rules of language can be violated in the name of humor.

Humor also serves as an expression of a variety of feelings that are inhibited. By means of satire and wit, people often can express their hostile feelings without appearing angry or being punished. The laughter that this humor brings is the reassurance that the true feelings expressed in the humor are recognized but accepted playfully. When one is angry with another person it is easier and sometimes more effective to make a witty remark than to attack the person directly. For example, a teacher was taking a class of fifth graders on a field trip. One pupil began to yawn . . . then another followed and still another. Rather than scold them, the teacher asked, "Do you have a yawning permit?" The pupils laughed. The yawning stopped. For the rest of the trip, the pupils listened and saw what they had come to see.

Off-color humor serves several purposes. First, it serves as an outlet for interest in sexual matters. By sharing the laughter at off-color jokes, some persons enjoy vicariously the pleasures of sex. Off-color jokes provide some persons with the opportunity to laugh at the sexual inadequacies of others. Thereby they reassure themselves of their own sexual potency.

Off-color jokes also provide people with the opportunity to belittle the actions and feelings of those who violate the sexual taboos. Very often people fear these feelings within themselves. By ridiculing sex offenders, people are able to feel superior and unafraid. Again, the sharing of laughter becomes a form of self-assurance.

However, when people become preoccupied with off-color jokes, they are obviously showing some symptoms of disturbance. Sex is likely to be a problem. By seeking this outlet, it is possible that they are not able to resolve their sexual problems in more direct and appropriate ways. For example, men, who are particularly frightened by women or who are hostile toward them without being able to express it directly, may tell off-color jokes at the expense of women.

In this way they try to reassure themselves of their adequacy. People who are unable to fulfill sexual desires may substitute talking about sex or joking about it.

Generally, sick humor refers to the kind of humor that not only pokes fun at sacred institutions and revered persons, but does so with violence. For example, many sick jokes are addressed to the murder and dismemberment of people in authority, members of opposing groups or to opposing ideas. The reaction to this form of humor may be one of shock, and the laughter that it may produce includes discomfort and embarrassment. Sick humor often demonstrates the so-called double-edged sword of humor. In other words, there is a very fine line between its pleasure-giving qualities and its ability to arouse discomfort.

Sick humor seems to be most appreciated by adolescents who often rebel against tradition. For adolescents, the sick joke is another way of attacking authority and breaking with parental control. Many adolescents belittle family relationships and affection. The institution of the home is often attacked as sentimental, old-fashioned, and useless. In a sense, sick humor is a sign of the times. Each era has its own forms of sick humor.

Maintaining mental health

People can be helped to maintain mental health if they

1. develop patterns of living that reinforce their basic psychological needs; love, a sense of security, respect for others, a philosophy of life, and satisfying relationships with others. As they make a conscious effort to move from self to others, they satisfy these needs. Thus, they move from discomfort toward comfort, from being ignored to being admired, from being disliked toward being loved. They move from failing toward succeeding, from monotony toward new experiences, from danger toward tranquility. Satisfaction may be obtained by conscious effort to bring about such movement.

2. live to meet their own goals, values, and standards without trying to compete or compare themselves with others.

3. usually think kindly of others.

4. try to make others happy when they are around.

5. achieve within their own range of abilities. This requires them to carefully evaluate themselves and to know where they may be expected to find successful experiences.

6. believe that their problems and peculiarities are similar to those of others.

7. recognize reality as the state of affairs with which one must deal. Reality may be altered but not ignored.

8. develop the ability to face the world alone with confidence. A desire to make the best of whatever happens is basic. Self-reliance is built by being independent of any particular person or type of person. It is gained by handling specific situations over a period of time.

9. ignore the common compulsion to save face, to prove that they have always been right, or to try to make another person admit fault or error first.

"Some people perceive their power or influence being many times as great as it actually is. When this happens, reality could come as a shock. On the other hand, with a good sense of humor, one can recognize one's own folly, and accept gracefully those normal human powers that provide functional adequacy."

D. G. Westlake

Depression

Depression ranges from a case of the blues to the depths of despair with its accompanying loss of hope. In their least intense forms stress and strain are experienced by everyone. Relief can come for the mild cases called the blues, by reassurance from our friends, a sunny day or a pleasant change. However, for approximately eight million Americans depression is severe enough to cause them to require treatment by their doctor. Another 250,000 people require hospitalization, often because of suicidal intentions. Suicide is the eleventh most common cause of death in this country, and the fifth most common among children and adolescents.

The causes of depression are virtually unknown. The ancient explanation of an imbalance among the bodily juices does not seem too far removed from the truth. There is certainly a connection between diet imbalances and depression; use of stimulants and depression; use of depressants such as alcohol and depression; fatigue and depression. The common person and the great leader have been victims of depression. Winston Churchill spoke of the "black dog" of depression that often overwhelmed him with a sense of hopelessness.

Depression is thought of as involving loss, whether real or imagined, of a particular person, object, belief, or value to which one is attached. Depression can be caused by the loss of something that one expects another person to value such as the loss of a loved one or the loss of something with no apparent value. But it has value for the person who lost it. This attachment and loss behavior can be seen in many different forms of depression.

For example, after a forest fire many people whose homes are destroyed show depressive symptoms. They lose interest in the outside world, are unable to perform useful tasks, and lack motivation. But at the same time, they do not have the characteristic self-reproach and self-abasement found in other, more serious forms of depression. This occurs because they did not initially cause the forest fire. It was beyond their immediate control. When deep depression occurs the person often feels that he or she should have been able to change the situation. Or he or she feels his or her particular behavior was the cause of the tragedy. A person may feel more depressed by the loss of an automobile that caught fire from a neglected cigarette than by the loss of a house in a forest fire spread by high winds. The cigarette that caused the automobile to catch fire was due to the person's carelessness. The house was out of the person's control. It was an act of nature.

The degree of attachment one has to things, not their material wealth, is what determines the extent of the depression response to a loss. If the attachment is small or the setback temporary, then the reaction may be normal feelings of "the blues" that disappear in a short time. At the other extreme are the abnormal feelings of intense despair, a sense of losing all that makes life worth living. This is the common theme of romantic novels when the young lover loses his love and takes drastic measures. Another example of the degree of attachment is illustrated in the case of Helen. Helen's mother gave her an inexpensive ruby ring that her stepfather had given her years before for her sixteenth birthday. Helen later bought herself a valuable diamond dinner ring. She would feel more depressed if she lost the ruby ring than if she lost the diamond cocktail ring. The ruby ring has sentimental and family value while the diamond ring has only money value.

Depression may also occur from the excessive attachment to a career or public image. For many high achieving people, love and acceptance come to be associated with achievement and compliments from peers and superiors. If a person fails or does not achieve some important goal, then depression may occur. If the image or the career is damaged the person may withdraw, develop illness, or feel the need to move away from familiar surroundings.

Depression related to success happens to some high achievers. A person receives a promotion or reaches a long-term goal such as getting the house of his or her dreams. Then he or she experiences depression that has no explanation either to the person or to family or friends. Most psychiatrists believe that the depression is caused by two factors.

1. The intense pressure necessary for attaining the goal becomes a needed impetus to activity.

2. The person's fear that somehow he or she will ruin his or her accomplishment or that it really is not deserved.

Depression basically has three degrees of severity with incomplete unresponsive withdrawal on one end and "the blues" on the other.

[1] *"The blues" or mild depression involves low mood and pessimism about the future.* At this level of depression the individual is lethargic and feels unable to deal with simple, everyday affairs.

Moderate depression is characterized by markedly slowed thinking and action. It is during this stage that the individual blames himself or herself for everything. Minor setbacks become catastrophes in his or her mind. This is perhaps the most dangerous of depressions because it generates suicide.

Severe depression is characterized by complete withdrawal and unresponsiveness. The person often curls up on the bed in the position of the fetal state, or sometimes rocks back and forth, completely unaware of others or their needs.

Questions

1. What is basic to good mental health?

2. How does the humor one uses define personality?

3. Why do some adolescents like sick humor?

4. What needs are expressed by one who constantly employs off-color humor?

5. Is humor universal? Explain.

6. What are the common threads that tie together the mature person and the mentally healthy person?

7. Write a description of a mentally healthy person.

8. What are the three major categories of depression?

9. What is the relation between loss and depression?

10. What might you do to help a friend maintain good mental health?

Further reading

Barrett, Roger K. *Depression—What It Is and What To Do About It.* Elgin, IL: David C. Cook Publishing Company, 1977.

Beck, Aaron T. *Depression Causes and Treatment.* Philadelphia: University of Pennsylvania Press, 1972.

Cammer, Leonard. *Up from Depression.* New York: Simon & Schuster, Inc., 1969.

1. From "The Anatomy of Melancholy" by David Elkind and J. Herbert Hamsher in *Saturday Review*, September 30, 1972. © Saturday Review, 1972. All rights reserved. Used by permission.

Deffner, Donald. *You Say You're Depressed.* Nashville, TN: Abindgon Press, 1976.

De Rosis, Helen, and Pellegrino, Victoria. *The Book of Hope: How Women Can Overcome Depression.* New York: Macmillan, Inc., 1976.

Deutsh, Albert, ed. *Encyclopedia of Mental Health.* Volumes 2, 3, 4. New York: Franklin Watts, Inc., 1970.

Elkind, David, and Hamsher, J. Herbert. "The Anatomy of Melancholy." *Saturday Review,* September 30, 1972, pp. 54–59.

Tussing, Lyle. *Psychology for Better Living.* New York: John Wiley & Sons, Inc., 1959.

Chapter 9

Our view of religion

In order to understand ourselves, we need to understand our religious beliefs and our religious commitments or our lack of them. The part of religious doctrine to which you are committed is very important to your development.

Reprinted by permission of Robert Censoni.
From *Saturday Review,* © 1971.

"I know this wart bit is a myth, but we still have the stigma."

However, the part that you don't buy is equally important. As we mature and gain insight about ourselves and others, we learn that trust must be earned. It is not given blindly out of respect for one's position or for a particular institution because respect and trust should be deserved. With maturity, we begin to recognize that living up to high ideals is easier in thought than deed.

Is religion basic?

When basic needs were discussed in Chapter 1, we saw that one need was to have a religion and/or a philosophy of life. For some of us, our religion is our philosophy of life. We live our religious convictions. They form our life pattern. For others of us, our philosophy of life reinforces our life choices. Others of us have combined religion and philosophy and have a basis upon which to act. Which is best—a religion, a philosophy, or a philosophy and a religion? This question can only be answered by each of us.

Definition of religion

Those who value religion say it is the outward quest for truth and the inward struggle for integrity. Religious beliefs are seen as enriching one's search for the meaning and the purpose of life. Religion may also be defined as the way by which some people try to find their place in the universe. They develop valid goals within the framework of the forces which control their destiny. This definition suggests that religion is one's attempt to give meaning to life, especially one's own life and death. People who value religion consider it a way to give meaning to life in the face of the more immediate frustration of cherished goals. They also believe it is necessary to

"I'll buy that."

help one face the death of one's only body. In brief, religion may be betting one's life that God exists and is good.

The people who do not value religion describe it as the opiate of the people. They feel that religion leads to dependency on a set of meaningless rituals and beliefs. They consider religion a way to rule people by exploiting their fears, especially their fear of the unknown. To the opponents of religion, religion is a malady which makes people hate and suppress their natural tendencies.

Social change and religion

Our society is questioning some of the traditions, rituals and religious practices. Some people feel that society needs to return to the fundamental religious beliefs. On the other hand, discoveries appear to contradict fundamental beliefs. What does all of this mean?

The individual and change

The changes in religion and our acceptance or non-acceptance of them is influenced by our stage of development. Children, because of their position in the life cycle, are very religious. At first they hold to child-like beliefs. Later they accept the standard ideas of their family and peers. Intellectual doubts start at a mental age of 12, followed by emotional stress. These conflicts are often resolved at about the age of 16, either by conversion to religion or by a decision to abandon the religion of childhood. During the years from 18 to 35, there is a sharp decline in all aspects of religious activity except for those who felt a religious calling earlier. Then there is a steady increase from about 35 until old age, which is marked by a widespread belief in God and the afterlife.

Some individual thoughts

The basic psychological need for a religion and/or philosophy of life is met differently by each person. The following sketches may help you recognize and appreciate the many ways in which people try to meet this need.

MRS. WILSON: I believe that one should go to church every Sunday. It is important to be a part of the church organization, to work for the church causes, and to support the church with time, energy, and money. I believe in life after death and believe that I will meet my loved ones who have gone beyond for an eternity together in

"What gets me is that having to love everybody
whether you like them or not."

heaven. In order to accomplish this, I must follow the doctrines of
my church in my actions, thoughts, and deeds. I worry about members of my family and my friends who do not closely follow church
doctrine. I feel that people who do not regularly attend church are
not really preparing themselves for life after death or giving their best
to their family and their community. I am 63 years old, have been in
the choir for forty years, and have held most of the church offices. I
am a deaconness and am on the ministerial board.

MRS. WEBER: I am a widow, twenty-eight years old, with three
sons. I believe that God is love. I attend church every Sunday and
see to it that my sons also attend. I don't believe that church atten-
dance makes me any better, but it gives me support. When you lose
your husband suddenly and have the added responsibility of being

both mother and father, it is helpful to feel that there are people and an organization for support. I really don't believe in a hereafter or that going to church makes me any better than anyone else. I do, however, think that it may give my sons a focus upon which to make decisions and a stronger foundation by which to judge experiences.

TOM (*college sophomore*): I really don't have any guidelines. I feel that what I do is really up to me, not anyone else. For the first twelve or thirteen years of my life I more or less just accepted what I had learned as being the right and truthful way of thinking. Anyone who didn't agree with what I had learned was just wrong. Then, suddenly, I began to question what parents and authorities said. I began to want to know whether a thing or a situation was this way or that way. The questions weren't answered for me and it really disturbs me a lot. I'm searching now, so I can't say what guidelines I'll use or what ethics or morals I'll follow. I'm just confused.

DOUG (*high school senior*): I try to be kind, honest, and considerate of people at all times and hope to do something useful in my lifetime. When I am faced with a hard decision or get myself into a tight spot, I think about my beliefs about people and my belief that God is with me. Then I feel that if I try to do what's right, everything will come out right in the end. When I question my beliefs I feel strengthened and convinced that I should follow them more closely. I think over bad decisions and troubles that I have experienced. Each time I find that if I had been completely honest with someone or done as I thought God would have wanted me to do, these bad decisions would have righted themselves more quickly or been avoided entirely. As I get older, these beliefs seem to triumph more often. I believe that with these beliefs I will make a worthwhile contribution to our society.

NANCY (*high school junior*): As far as I'm concerned, my main judgment of right and wrong comes from the Ten Commandments. I believe in following their teachings as closely as possible. Even though the Bible has many debatable points, I believe that the Ten Commandments are very valuable. I cannot accept many of the stories in the Bible, but I do not think that this weakens me in any way as I think its authors meant well in trying to get a general point across—the goodness of God. In making my personal decisions on debatable moral or ethical questions, I rely on rather impulsive actions, stemming from parental or family influence, peer group influence, and what I think is acceptable to me at the particular time. My religion only enters into my decisions which have to do with strong questions, such as stealing.

KENT *(high school sophomore)*: I don't believe in a strong religious belief. I don't believe that man was made all of a sudden. I believe in evolution. I believe that all religions are right; men can believe as they wish. As for me, I follow all laws and rules (but try to change them when I believe they are wrong) and try to do right to all people regardless of race, creed, age, religion, or position. I like people, all people, and enjoy making them happy. I try to be extra kind to little children because they particularly need love. My decisions are based on what is right for others and on how I want others to treat me. Of course, I haven't met a strong challenge, so perhaps my beliefs aren't any good.

The church and change

Although it is commonly agreed that the church will change because of the unique and pressing problems of this century which require a commitment in one direction or another, there are many people who are not sure of the best direction for the church. Even members of the same congregation may differ as to degree of change and direction. Even so, two main directional changes seem possible.

Some people think that religious institutions might change in the position they take in the community. Thus, religious groups would live their teachings by actively denouncing war and working for peace. They would act as leaders and supporters of poverty programs, urban renewal, and slum clearance. The main concern of churches would become the conscience of movements for social improvement. The clergy would step out of the limits of the church and mingle with the laypersons wherever they are. Thus, the church would see God as the basis of being, the force of life, the principle of love, ultimate reality. God, then, would be the love we encounter when we turn to help others. Prayer would be essentially a dialogue of love. Salvation would be being loved in a community characterized by love. Thus, the change would involve love, community, and social action.

Other people believe that religious institutions should be more concerned with spirituality and mission. Thus, the churches could take the direction of inwardness, of personal experience, and of a new search for identity. The church and its leaders would advocate more of a withdrawal from society as a whole and more of an introspective awakening of the purely spiritual mind. In this way, a new and more ultimate relationship with God might be achieved.

Need for faith and knowledge

Margaret Mead, the late anthropologist, has aptly described this country's religious confusion and need for a new religious commitment in these words:[1]

It is the way of those who follow the Judaeo-Christian path to be troubled, to search the sky and their own hearts for signs and portents that all is not well. Such exercises of furious and exacting imagination often are followed by long periods of what some call stagnation and apathy and others call betrayal—times when the flame of religious witness burns very low, the young men who should be seeing visions turn elsewhere and the life of the church gives little light to the world.

We are just emerging from a period in which it seemed that the churches were powerless to wrestle with new forces of world-wide revolution, with new forms of warfare that threaten all mankind, and with new powers derived from science that give man incalculable capacities either to destroy the world or make it anew. With these earth-shaking changes, a new sense of helplessness, of being strangers in a world too large to love, has fallen upon many churches. . . .

Today churches have a threefold task: to understand what is happening, to use with wisdom and dedication all that is known, and to demand that the search for new knowledge continue unabated.

In particular, we need the support of the churches for the application of all existing knowledge to the cause of world order, international law and world-wide institutions; the establishment of food banks around the world to guard against famine; application of known methods and continued research on new methods of conception control to bring the population of the earth into balance; interim measures to bridge the gap between the richest and the poorest countries; the equalization of opportunity for racially and socially deprived peoples in all nations; the purposeful, controlled planning of our growing cities; opportunities for youth to participate responsibly in the modern world.

Only with such support from the churches can we hope to build a world in which the people of each nation are the keepers of the people of each other nation. With knowledge and no

1. Excerpts from pp. 17, 23–24 in A WAY OF SEEING (1974) by Margaret Mead and Rhoda Metraux. Copyright © 1967 by Margaret Mead and Rhoda Metraux. By permission of William Morrow & Company.

faith, we may well see a world destroyed. With faith and no knowledge, we may still see a world destroyed. With faith and knowledge bound together, we can hope to cherish and protect the lives of men and the life of the world.

Questions

1. What part does religion play in your life today?

2. Should your church change? If so, why? If not, why not?

3. Should other churches change? Why? Why not?

4. Why is religion considered a part of human relations?

5. Is religion basic? If so, why? If not, why not?

Further reading

Aubert, Roger. *Church History in Future Perspective*. New York: The Seabury Press, Inc., 1970.

Blake, Eugene. *Church in the Next Decade*. New York: Macmillan, Inc., 1966.

Bostrom, Christopher. *Philosophy of Religion*. New Haven, CT: Yale University Press, 1962.

Brantl, George. *Catholicism*. New York: George Braziller, Inc., 1961.

Cohn, Steven M. *Philosophy of Religion*. New York: Harper & Row, Publishers, Inc., 1970.

Collins, James D. *Emergence of a Philosophy of Religion*. New Haven, CT: Yale University Press, 1967.

Dunstan, J. Leslie. *Protestantism*. New York: George Braziller, Inc., 1961.

Gard, Richard A. *Buddhism*. New York: George Braziller, Inc., 1962.

Hertzberg, Arthur. *Judaism*. New York: George Braziller, Inc., 1962.

Hick, John. *Philosophy of Religion*. Englewood Cliffs, NJ: Prentice-Hall, Inc., 1973.

Lewis, M. D. *Philosophy of Religion*. New York: David McKay Co., Inc., 1975.

Luckmann, Thomas. *The Invisible Religion*. New York: Macmillan, Inc., 1970.

Chapter 10

Our insight into philosophy

One's philosophy may be like the symbol of a dream . . . a collection of shapes, concepts, and designs that is difficult to define or understand. It takes years of reflective thinking, study, and living to untangle what we really think.

One may be at different levels in philosophical development. A person may have a philosophy which deals with some one area of experience and not with another. You may have developed a philosophy toward education but not toward knowledge. You may have a philosophy about honesty but not integrity. In other words, philosophies are often fragments.

However, all people, unless spoiled by a faulty education or by some intellectual vice, have a natural understanding of some of the great truths. Those whose understanding has never been cultivated are not able to give any account, or at least not a satisfactory one of their convictions. That is to say, they cannot explain why they have certain beliefs. They may feel a certain way about a particular subject after much thought. Later, with study, they find that their thought is similar to that of someone who wrote centuries ago.

One's philosophical thoughts direct one's life. They determine actions, activities, and behavior. It is important to consider some of the philosophical questions, recognizing that only time, effort, and the insight of maturity will give satisfactory answers.

Reprinted by permission of Peter Paul Porges.
From *Saturday Review,* © 1967.

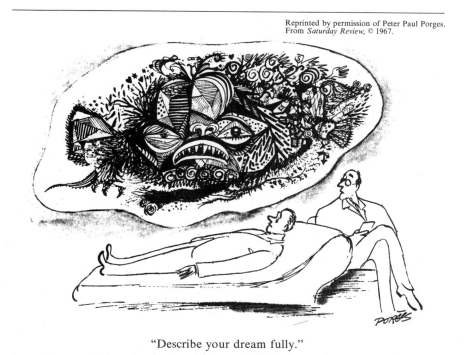

"Describe your dream fully."

Philosophy and the person

Ordinary knowledge consists for the most part of opinions or beliefs, more or less well founded. But it also implies a solid kernel of genuine certainties in which the philosopher recognizes the following.

1. data of the senses (for example, bodies have length, breadth, and height)

2. self-evident truths (for example, the whole is greater than the part; every event has a cause)

3. consequences (for example, the outcomes of behavior)

These certainties arise spontaneously in the mind. They may be called an endowment of nature proceeding from the natural perception, consent, instinct, or natural sense of the intellect. Since the source of these certainties is human nature itself, they will be found alike in all people. They may, therefore, be said to belong to the common perception, consent, instinct, or that which is called the "common sense" of all people. The great truths without which one's moral life is impossible belong in this area of common sense.

Listing some of the things philosophy may do for us may show why a person needs a philosophy for living.

1. Life forces us to decide questions of right and wrong, truth and falsity, ugliness and beauty. Each person must make decisions and act. In order to decide well and to act consistently, we need a philosophy of life. Our decisions must be made in light of our goals, beliefs, and understanding of the world around us. Philosophy may furnish a basis for social action as well as for personal conduct.

2. Our conduct is our own. We are really free only when we rely upon inner controls or self-chosen ends. If a person does what he or she does merely because of tradition, culture, or law, he or she is not really free. When Aristotle was asked the value of philosophy, he answered that it allowed him to do willingly what others did because of fear of the law.

3. Philosophy may help us cultivate a wide range of appreciations and sympathies. Such a broad range of interests and appreciations is a condition for ultimate intellectual and emotional living. We need to reach out to the great masters who have lived and thought deeply. They can open up new vistas of thought for

us. We also need to reach out to people who are less fortunate and who need understanding. We should develop a sufficient depth of inner life and a range of appreciations in art, literature, nature, and great ideas to have life bring us zest and happiness.

4. We live in an age of uncertainty and change. Under such conditions, we need a scale of values and a sense of direction. Just as we feel a physical discomfort when we see cruelty and injustice, we feel mental discomfort when we are in the presence of confused ideas. To achieve unity, we must gain an inner integration to know what to approve or to disapprove.

What is philosophy?

Philosophy is approached and defined from different points of view.

1. *Philosophy is an attitude toward life and the universe.* The mature philosophical attitude is a searching and critical attitude. It is also open-mindedness. It is the willingness to look at all sides of an issue.

2. *Philosophy is the method of reflective thinking and reasoned inquiry.*

3. *Philosophy is a group of problems.* There are certain problems which perplex people and for which philosophers seek answers. A philosopher's question is not, "Did John tell Mary a lie in the student council meeting?" But rather, "What is truth or the distinction between right and wrong?"

4. *Philosophy is a group of theories or systems of thought.* Some people think of philosophy as certain world views. They think of certain terms like idealism, realism, pragmatism, humanism, pessimism, optimism, and materialism. To others, philosophy means the various theories or systems of thought found in the history of philosophy. These theories are attached to the names of the great philosophers. These philosophers are men like Plato, Socrates, Aristotle, Augustine, Thomas Aquinas, Descartes, Spinoza, Kant, and James, to name a few.

Definitions of philosophy

There are many different definitions of philosophy. Will Durant has defined philosophy as total perspective, as mind overspreading life and forging chaos into unity. He also says that philosophy is harmonized knowledge making a harmonious life. It is the self-discipline which lifts a person to serenity and freedom.[1]

Another writer, Jacques Maritain, calls philosophy human wisdom. He says that philosophy alone among the branches of human knowledge has for its object everything which is. Philosophy is the science which by the natural light of reason studies the first causes or highest principles of all things. In other words, it is the science of things in their first causes, in so far as these belong to the natural order.[2]

Most definitions seem to describe philosophy as embracing a life view. A life view is a doctrine of values and purposes for living. Thus, philosophy is the attempt to give a reasoned conception of the universe and one's place in it.

Most of the definitions of philosophy emphasize the use of reflective thinking. They state or imply that the aim of philosophy is to gain unity and to see life in its totality. Consequently, we may say that philosophy is a study of nature, in both its inorganic and organic aspects, and in its social and spiritual aspects. Philosophy seeks to bring together the results of the sciences with the principles of morality and religion.

Philosophy and change

Philosophy, unlike religion, is not directly affected by change. There is such a variety in philosophies that truth, rather than being altered by change, merely moves in and out of vogue. The philosophies that are in favor during a certain period of time tend to describe that particular time. For example, Stoicism and Epicureanism flourished when the Greek city-states were disintegrating, about the 4th century B.C. The Stoics believed that people should accept their fate without complaint. Indeed, they should suppress any and all emotions and live the unbending life of duty and reason. The Stoics believed it was essential to be indifferent to pleasure or pain, joy, or grief. The Epicureans, on the other hand, believed that pleasure was the only good in life. However, the basis of this belief was that genuine pleasure comes from a life of prudence, honor, and justice. As scientists, the Epicureans believed that reality is a grouping of material atoms in random movement. They held that the world is governed entirely by chance, not design.

1. Will Durant, *The Pleasures of Philosophy* (New York: Simon & Schuster, 1953), pp. xi, xii.
2. Jacques Maritain, *An Introduction to Philosophy* (Mission, Kans.: Sheed Andrews & McMeel, 1962), pp. 64, 67, 69.

The rise of nationalism in the nineteenth century in Europe brought a renewed interest in national language, background, poetry, traditions, and culture. This century was marked by a cultural nationalism, romanticism in literature and the arts, and an interest in history. During this time, however, there was also a recognition of value in the person.

The philosophies of the present reflect conflicting interests. Nationalism advocates a national unity, independence, uniqueness, and

Reprinted by permission of Anthony Taber.
From *Saturday Review,* © 1977 by Saturday Review Magazine Corp.

"Some days I can't help wondering if they're
laughing with us or at us."

subjection of each person's interests to those of the nation. Individualism assumes the individual, not society or the nation, is the first consideration.

The present time has been described as a time for philosophical pragmatism. This American philosophical movement, founded by C. S. Pierce and William James, has these characteristic doctrines.

1. that the meanings of conceptions are to be sought in their practical bearings

2. that the function of thought is as a guide to action

3. that truth is to be tested by the practical consequences of belief

The twentieth century has also been described as a time for materialism. This ethical doctrine holds that consideration of material well-being, especially of oneself, should rule in the determination of conduct.

Hedonism can be described as the doctrine that pleasure is the sole or chief good in life. Further, that moral duty is fulfilled in the gratification of pleasure-seeking instincts and dispositions. Today's change in moral codes, dress, and leisure-time activities is seen by some to be the beginning of a world of hedonists. As such, our time is likened to the Roman Empire with predictions of a repetition of history.

Idealism is a theory which states that all that exists is a form or object of experience. Idealism regards reality as essentially spiritual, the embodiment of mind or reason. Idealists identify reality with perceptibility. They deny the possibility of knowing anything except the mental life—the life of thought, ideas, and ideals. On the other hand, materialism denotes an absorption in material ends. Materialists identify reality with what they can feel, taste, touch, and smell. They tend to give greatest importance to material interests and possessions. In popular usage, the terms "idealism" and "materialism" often imply moral attitudes. In this context, idealism suggests a devotion to high ideals or an optimism about the ultimate goodness of people. Materialism suggests a devotion to more material ends. The terms as used in philosophy, however, denote opposing views of the nature of reality.

Philosophical trends

Philosophical trends in the future are seen as hedonistic or idealistic, depending upon the pessimism or optimism of the viewer. In hedonism and idealism we have primary philosophical convictions.

Pessimism and its opposite, optimism, are only secondary philosophical theories or convictions.

This brief section on philosophy and change is intended to help you understand some of the dynamics of change. From this discussion, you can see that contradictory philosophies can and do exist at the same time. Although certain philosophies may be in the foreground during certain times, other philosophies are also present. The dominant philosophies may give historical focus to a particular century. In our own time, we may be described as a civilization given over to hedonism, idealism, materialism, and/or pragmatism. As you think of yourself and what means most to you, however, you may find that you are a stoic, an epicurean, or an interesting, new philosophical mixture.

Questions

1. Define philosophy from your point of view.

2. Re-read the statements that describe some of the things that philosophy does to aid people. List some examples from your own life that reinforce these aids.

3. What directions would you like to see the philosophy of the twenty-first century take? Why?

4. Write a paper on a philosopher or philosophy of your choice.

5. Santayana said, "It is a great advantage for a system of philosophy to be substantially true." What ideas does this statement bring to your mind?

6. Discuss Montaigne's statement, "Admiration is the foundation of all philosophy, investigation the process, and ignorance the end."

Further reading

Durant, Will. *The Pleasures of Philosophy.* New York: Simon & Schuster, Inc., 1953.

Maritain, Jacques. *An Introduction to Philosophy.* Mission, KS: Sheed Andrews & McMeel, Inc., 1962.

Chapter 11

Our personal philosophy of life

Our own personal goals and values are the threads
that weave the fabric of our philosophy. Chapters 9
and 10 gave us a bird's-eye view of some philosophical
concepts and reasons for religion. In this chapter,
we'll consider our own personal values and goals.

Values

Values are many things.   They are our objectives and our goals. In this sense they are real, tangible, and attainable.   Yet values are more.   Values are the ideals toward which we live and those things which we hold most dear.   Our ideals are motivational forces toward the goodness in our lives and the humanity in the human spirit. Values are the importance we give to ideas, goals, and attitudes. This makes it possible to put ideas, goals, and attitudes in an order which encourages decision making and consistent behavior.   For the group, *values are the accepted rules which direct behavior toward the very best we know from the experiences of others.*   For the person, *values are the rules, the goals, the ideals, and the judgments which integrate the personality.*   They make one's personality predictable, consistent, and whole.

Our values are our yardsticks by which we measure our own behavior.   They are the controls, the direction of our actions.   By them

From *Saturday Review,* © 1972.
Reprinted by permission of *Saturday Review* and Henry Martin.

"Harvey Donaldson, how come you preach liberalism
but practice conservatism?"

we judge our everyday actions as they relate to us and others. Even more, we use our values to judge our behavior as it relates to our future. Values serve as brakes on desire for immediate gratification and satisfaction. They are holding qualities which keep us steadily moving toward that which we believe. They also indicate the worth of that for which we must wait. By our faith in these values, we move closer to them as ideals. William James, an American philospher (1842–1910), showed his values in the following excerpt.

> We have little to fear, declares James, so long as we sustain our affections, so long as we have a home to play in, and a family to play with. This is the meaning of Pragmatism—the philosophy of the practical life—as applied to our family relationships. The family satisfies our universal hunger for "the dear togetherness." In mutual service, every member of the ideal family arrives at its fullest spiritual growth. He finds that it pays to make our home cheerful with the brightness of love.
>
> In the development of his pragmatic idea about family relationships, James widened the boundaries of the home to those of the world—here again we have the philosophy of a united mankind. The world, he observed, is our common home, and all its inhabitants are the members of our single family. The most profitable business of life, therefore, is the friendly exchange of affection and good will among all men.[1]

Our moral values are our group experiences at their very best. They are our group aspirations which protect our institutions of freedom and democracy. They protect our homes and the love between generations. They protect our schools. They protect our free economy which is built around the profit motive. We respond to our moral and religious values with respect. They are obligations and objects of reverence from people, and for people. *Because of our moral, spiritual, and religious values, we become persons of dignity, worth, and integrity.*

Values for society are the general principles which guide our group behavior. When a nation or a society loses its values, its understanding of them and their reality, then the nation or society deteriorates. If a nation lets its values degenerate, proclaims them but does not live by them, then disintegration of the culture is inevitable.

Values and the personality have important interrelationships. Personality has been defined as our usual ways of behaving with

1. Henry Thomas, *Understanding the Great Philosophers* (New York: Doubleday & Co., Inc., 1962), pp. 330–331. Reprinted by permission of the publisher.

other people. If you would know your own values, consider how you behave with others. Behavior always has within it conformity to the larger moral, spiritual, religious, and social values of the group. Without healthy, creative conformity in light of the best we know, there would be no order in personal or group life. Chaos and anarchy would result. Individuality and creativity can never arise from chaos or rigidity. The inner self, the core of personality, is composed of those values that people regard as the most important, drawn from their experiences. These are the values which carry people toward their goals and gain for them basic satisfaction in life with themselves and with others.

Each is a person in his or her own right, but he or she is a person among other persons. William Menninger has said that our personalities are all that we have been, all that we are, and all that we

"I'm afraid I have no opinion at the moment.
All my journals of opinion have been late this week."

will be.   They are not static because our ways of behavior change to meet new situations.   Our values which we use as guide posts change.   The integrating principles of personalities are values from past experiences which we build into the future.   These values continue through growth toward our ultimate objectives.   They give consistency to our outlook and predictability to our behavior.

Developing a personal philosophy

Values and their organization into a personal philosophy grow in a random way.   They grow through trial and error as we try to solve our problems.   If the solution of a problem is a physical one, without our thinking in terms of ideas, it probably does not become a part of our philosophy of life. *Values develop as the result of the consistent example of those whom we respect, the teaching of dedicated teachers, and of our own personal study.* Much of a personal philosophy may be taken from a writer, from the Bible, the Torah, the Talmud, or from proverbs of an unknown source. If these ideas are to become a part of our personal philosophy, we must experience real satisfaction as we see their roles in our behavior. They must have the vividness of insights or discoveries. The words, "Do unto others as you would that they would do unto you," mean little until one has found through experience the meaning and value of them. Rarely does a personal philosophy come from a single experience. Single books, courses, or essays may sum up one's attitude and the reactions that have grown from numerous personal experiences. One does not build a philosophy of life during one weekend when writing a term paper. But one can bring to consciousness attitudes that have had a long previous existence.

One's personal philosophy, like all such complex patterns of experience, is influenced by the many other aspects of one's personality. Intelligence, temperament, physique, physical urges, and emotional experiences play a part. Contacts with other people, books, plays, sermons, and lectures, play a part. The compatibility of one's philosophy and behavior depend upon the extent to which philosophy has taken into account one's basic constitution and past experiences.

Value of personal philosophy

A philosophy of life should guide behavior. It should allow a person to act on the basis of rational principles rather than through fear, selfishness, or social pressure. It, however, cannot ignore inner feelings such as anxiety or outer forces such as social standards. Awareness of these standards helps in the development of one's philosophy. If the philosophy helps self-understanding and involves acceptance of oneself, it can be a real source of direction. A personal philosophy brings relative peace to most people. It provides perspective. It allows one to see oneself in retrospect and to project ambitions realistically. Philosophy enables one to organize values so that they will form a "united front" and strength of conviction when there is conflict or need for decision making. History shows that those people who have received the gratitude of society became immersed in worthy causes, so that their personalities and the causes were indistinguishable.

Formation of values

Values are the end product of human experiences. They are recognized generally as supporting the human personality. Values are convictions of the richness of living and the knowledge of what it takes to make life good and worthwhile.

Every person can take part in the formation of his or her own values. This participation is not a matter of age or maturity. Every age can take part in the creation of values by living, exploring, and experiencing them. *One can discard the values that are unworthy. One can strengthen those which are worthy. One should share this creation with those who are older and wiser in experience.* Value formation is as dynamic as life itself. Out of living, out of creativity, out of change, and out of progress, grow values which people have to meet their ever-changing needs.

Value stability

Values that change and grow in strength are those which are created out of new and different situations. Values that are steady are those which hold us steady. They are time-proven. They are our religious, spiritual, and moral values. Our religious and our spiritual values are our eternities. They are the ideals toward which we grow. For us in the United States, our Judeo-Christian faiths bring forth two major values. We believe in the dignity and worth of each person, regardless of race, creed, color, or abilities. We believe that we were created in the image of God. We believe as well in the brotherhood of all men under God. These are eternal values toward which we strive, work, and live.

A personal philosophy can give perspective to one's self, foster personal growth and adjustment, and increase creativity.

Some thoughts from philosophers

Philosophers have written about various values. Each philosopher writes about those values that seem to be of greatest worth to him or her. The following quotes are included.

"In the long run," declared Gandhi, "all men have an equal destiny. All are born in order that they may study how to serve God's plan. Every one of our lives is a special task assigned for our education in cooperative living. And our greatest duty is to teach and to befriend our less fortunate brothers... The purpose of man's life is to lighten the sufferings of his fellow man."[2]

Santayana declared, "It is war that wastes a nation's wealth, kills its flower, narrows its sympathies, condemns it to be governed by adventurers, and leaves the puny, deformed, and unmanly to breed the next generation... (Therefore) instead of being descended from heroes, modern nations are descended from slaves."[3]

Friendship, to Emerson, is the most sublime thing in the world. "The essence of friendship," writes Emerson, "is 'entireness,' the fusion of different personalities into one essence. This fusion enables men to rejoice in one another's triumphs. I feel pride in my friend's accomplishments as if they were mine."[4]
Emerson believed that cultivating the art of friendship enabled one to come close to the heart of reality; that true friendship brought one in touch with the divine meaning of life.

Kant stated that morality, like mathematics, prompts us to live in accordance with the harmonious process of life. "Act as if the maxim of your conduct were to become by your will the maxim of all the world's activity."[5]

Croce said that Christianity, like Judaism, Buddhism, and Mohammedanism, "lives on in spite of its defects because it has a vital function and satisfies a universal need."[6] The important thing in life, Croce maintains, is not only to conceive the right image, but to perform the right act.

Formulating a philosophy

Your philosophy of life is your deliberate effort to make your beliefs, morals, and behaviors sensible and unified. By such effort you have a basis for action when confronted with problems.

2. Ibid., p. 357.
3. Ibid., p. 343.
4. Ibid., p. 322.
5. Ibid., p. 257.
6. Ibid., pp. 308–309.

Your philosophy of life is not necessarily your way of life. Your way of life is composed of attitudes, traits, habits, and directive motives that you use but that you have not defined. They may become a part of your philosophy at a later date. Your personal philosophy is the term reserved for your conscious statement of your credo. Your personal philosophy of life is composed of your real beliefs after you have thought through your attitudes, values, goals, and experiences. As an example, the following reflections are those of a forty-year-old scientist.

At each stage of my adult life, my decisions with respect to my profession have been influenced by what seems to be an inherent desire to make a contribution to mankind as meaningful as possible with the limited capability and time alloted to me. I feel little ambition for public acclaim, but sense gratification in successful completion of a task which represents my best efforts.

Moderation governs most of my actions—eating, drinking, exercising, emoting, spending, and so on. My wardrobe is small. We live in a house more modest than my income allows. While we have traveled to Europe, Canada, Mexico, the Caribbean, and all of the United States except Alaska, each trip has been planned with economy in mind. The friendships, experiences, knowledge, photographs, and memories acquired in our travels are among my most valued possessions.

My interests are varied enough so that I have never become totally involved in any one pursuit, hobby, or even in my work. I consider diversion extremely important to one's health, and lively fun as essential to happiness. We are regulars at the theatre, concerts, and movies. I thoroughly enjoy all sports both as a spectator and participant. I play guitar, banjo, ukelele, and sing folk songs. I am even known among my friends as a joke teller.

I do not participate in an organized religion, but could never be described as an atheist. I am constantly awed by the order of our universe which I cannot disassociate from a concept of God. I firmly believe that man could live happily and peacefully if he could learn and practice Judeo-Christian moral teachings.

Questions

1. Define the following terms:

values	interaction	realism
eternities	creativeness	

2. Write your personal philosophy of life. There is no experience that can give you more personal insight. You may use whatever method you wish to write your philosophy. But if you want a suggestion you might work through these steps:

   a. List ten values that you hold most dear.

   b. Rank the ten values in the order of most important to least important. This is very difficult. As you do this take note of your thoughts. These thoughts will help you formulate your philosophy.

   c. Now list the goals that you hope to accomplish this year, in the next five years, next ten.

   d. Now compare your goals with your values. Are they compatible?

   e. Think of the people in your life whom you respect. What do you respect about them?

   f. Think of the maxims and creeds which you hold dear. Do you believe them in your heart or do you think that you should believe them?

3. Now with this evidence about your own thoughts, write the philosophy that seems to represent YOU.

4. Here is an autobiography written by a young man after college graduation. What are his values? What philosophy does he portray from this autobiographical sketch?

At the age of six I started school and quite fortunately I found the teacher, the kids, and the school work very much to my liking. From the first day, I knew that some day I would go to college.

I was always a runt. I can remember one of our neighbors saying. "It's no wonder you stay thin, you run everywhere you go." I was very headstrong and liked to see things done my way. Therefore, from the ages of eight to twelve I found myself in a fight on the average of about four times a week. I never lost a fight. Eventually, I learned, however, that I could solve my problems much more satisfactorily in a peaceful manner. Since that time I cannot remember having a serious argument with anyone.

I have always been extremely interested in athletics. Despite my small size I played on the grade school varsity basketball team every year after third grade. My favorite sport was basketball although I played them all.

I graduated at the head of my class and went into high school standing an even five feet tall and weighing an even one hundred pounds. Again, despite my stature, I was fortunate enough to play some varsity basketball in my freshman year.

During my sophomore year, I started to grow up. I also started to look for the "right" girl. And I didn't have to look very long, for during my junior year I began going with a very cute blonde who turned out to be the one.

During my high school years I was president of the freshman class, student council representative four years, president of the student council two years, and captain of the basketball team two years. I was first place winner in oratory in the conference speech contest. During my senior year, I set a high jump record in the conference track meet. I played the lead role in the class play. I graduated valedictorian of the class.

I entered state college where I put myself through school without financial assistance by working in the school cafeteria during the school term and doing carpentry each summer. I majored in chemistry and minored in mathematics. My campus activities included the following: President of Alpha Phi Omega fraternity; President of Sigma Zeta honorary science society; secretary of Men's Union; vice-president of the senior class; vice-president of Cavaliers, honorary organization of twelve senior men; an active member of Tau Beta Rho, Math Club, Varsity Club, and the President's Council. I played varsity basketball three years and was graduated from college with high scholastic honors.

The aforementioned blonde and I went to college together and found each other's company very pleasing. We took the vows of marriage in October a year after college graduation and now find happiness in living in an apartment in the town where we both teach.

I value my relationships within my own family above all. While my wife and I were happy before we had children, our family provides an even richer fulfillment. I feel our greatest challenge is to provide a home so that our children will arrive at adulthood healthy in mind, body, and spirit. I have no specific goals for our children, but I would hope to instill in them a desire to do well in whatever their capabilities allow them to undertake.

Further reading

Beck, Robert N. *Perspectives in Philosophy: A Book of Readings.* New York: Holt, Rinehart & Winston CBS, Inc., 1975.

Bellanca, James A. *Values and the Search for Self.* West Haven, CT: National Education Association, 1975.

Hartshorne, Hugh, and May, Mark. *Studies in the Nature of Character: Studies in Deceit.* New York: Macmillan, Inc., 1975.

Strom, Robert D. *Values and Human Development.* Columbus, OH: Charles E. Merrill Publishing Company, 1973.

UNIT
2

Understanding
Others

Chapter 12

Relationships with parents

Adolescents are torn between the indulgences of childhood and the privileges and responsibilities of adulthood. Parents want children to become independent and responsible adults but the process of letting go requires conscious efforts.

"When I clap my hands three times you will double my allowance.
Are you listening?"

Definition of adolescence

The term adolescence comes from a Latin verb meaning "to grow up." It is defined as the period of life from puberty to maturity. For the biologist, adolescence is the period of rapid growth. It begins with a speeded-up phase that continues until the attainment of sexual maturity. It merges into a slowing-down phase, and stops when skeletal growth has ended. But adolescence is also a social phenomenon. How long it lasts is determined not only by biological factors but also by the way the particular society defines childhood and adulthood. The sociologist may describe adolescence as a period when society no longer regards young persons as children but has not yet given them full adult status.

Two conflicting ideas can be found in these definitions. In one, adolescence is a period of positive attainment, of growth, and of maturation. In the other, it is a period of transition.

"... Son, did I ever tell you what a thrill it was
the first time I shaved?"

Developmental goals of adolescents

In order for adolescents to move from the dependence of childhood to the independence and interdependence of adulthood, they must reach certain goals. Adolescents may be working on a number of goals at the same time. Success in one makes progress easier in another. Failure in one may interfere with accomplishments in other areas of life. In reaching these goals, adolescents are trying to define the place they will occupy in adult society. The older the adolescents the more they face the problem of position in the adult world. This world includes independence, marriage, jobs, and politics. Adolescents must find their identities as themselves rather than as members of either their families or their gangs. In reaching these developmental goals, young adolescents are concerned with who they are and what they are. Older adolescents are concerned with what to do about it.

There are many ways to list the goals of the adolescent period. The ten goals listed below range from goals for early adolescence to those for later adolescence.

1. achieving physical competency—accepting and making the most of one's physical capacities

2. getting along with one's family—gaining emotional independence from parents and other adults without hurting their feelings too much

3. getting along with age-mates of both sexes—making friends, learning to work with others for a common purpose

4. achieving scholastic success—including choice of courses, relationships with teachers, and development of communication skills—speaking, reading, writing, listening

5. making sound educational plans—choosing, preparing for, and entering a vocation for which one has the necessary ability and interest

6. developing a workable set of values, moral standards, and religious beliefs—evolving a functional philosophy of life which takes into account one's place in the world

7. developing socially responsible behavior

8. achieving identity—discovering and developing one's most acceptable self

9. preparing for marriage and family life

10. being economically independent—including not only the ability eventually to make a living, but also the ability to earn enough money, while going to school, to satisfy one's needs and desires

These developmental goals are accomplished over a number of years. All of us must work on them in one way or another. By accomplishing them, adolescents are able to bridge the gap between what they were as children and what they are to become as adults. If a person has done well with these goals up to a certain age, he or she is likely to complete them successfully.

Tasks of parents of adolescents

Parents of adolescents have many tasks to do. The purpose of this section is to help adolescents appreciate the role of their parents during this time. Just as children grow and develop from one stage to another, parents must grow and develop in relation to them. Some parents can meet dependent needs easily but are unable to give up being the central figures in their children's lives. This is particularly true when they have devoted all their time, energy, and money to their children. Parents whose children have been the main focus of their existence, see puberty as the beginning of a change that will lead their children out of the home and into their own lives. They fear loneliness and being left alone because they are unable to develop a more mature relationship with their children. They feel unable to cope as equals with their children.

The emergence of sexual characteristics in adolescents may be threatening to parents. There are several reasons for this sexual threat between child and parent. The parent may envy the physical beauty or physical prowess of the child of the same sex or of the opposite sex. For example, an insecure mother may see her beautiful young daughter as a threat to her relationship with her husband. The daughter may challenge the mother through comparisons made by friends and family. The father, who may have always been physically undersized, insecure, or clumsy and whose head is becoming bald, may feel threatened by his tall, handsome athletic son. In addition, young girls try out their manners and "line" on their fathers. Young boys try out their manners and "line" on their mothers. The insecure parent may feel that he or she is being replaced in the affection of his or her spouse.

The parent who does not understand this stage of development may not recognize these sexually charged advances as tryouts of young adult wings. Without this kind of recognition, the parent may be either repulsed or attracted. Either reaction would damage the relationship. For, on the one hand, repulsion would create insecurity in the adolescent. On the other, attraction on the part of the parent would leave the parent feeling abandoned when the young adolescent moves on to a relationship with the opposite sex in his or her own peer group.

The emergence of sexuality in the child is frightening to parents who have never worked out a mature solution for their own sexual feelings. They may fear that the adolescent will display forbidden impulses and wishes which they themselves harbor. They may react by projecting their own inner concerns onto the child. Unjust accusations of sexual misbehavior are often the result. Sometimes this action on the part of the parent develops in the adolescent a sense of guilt or a sense of "I might as well do what I'm accused of."

Parents have to learn how to let go and how not to let go. Before late adolescence, however, children need the assurance that their parents are not letting go for good. Adolescence, by contrast, is an exercise in letting go for good. It is preparation for a new kind of relationship between parent and child. One that is based on mutual respect between older and younger adults. Parents must give up their children. Remembering the adolescent's own perplexity and ambivalence, parents must likewise help adolescents give them up.

Parents must be at least as committed to the adolescent's need for independence from them as he or she is. This, however, does not mean that they abruptly throw adolescents on their own resources. Adolescence is a preparation for independence, not a time when it is imposed all at once. Adolescents' demands for self-determination are, in part, a demand for reassurance that they are capable. They want their parents to stand by them while they try their wings. If parents literally give adolescents everything that they claim they want, they may frighten them. They need their parents as sounding boards for their ideas and their decisions. Adolescents, in their ambivalence, will often fight hardest for something they are afraid to have. But parents must be aware of their own ambivalence as well as that of the adolescents. They must be basically and firmly on the side of the adolescents' freedom. If they are, they can set forth consistent, clear, and sincere growing standards for adolescents to meet.

Parents must also resist taking literally the adolescents' defiance and belittlings of them. These statements spring less from a sweeping rejection of parents than from the adolescent's need to assert self as somebody different and independent. In the language of adolescent ambivalence, "I hate you" sometimes means, "I'm afraid I love you too much."

Adolescents who have no conflicts at all with their parents may have evolved elaborate techniques for lulling their parents' concern. Outside the home they may do exactly what suits them. Or, more usually, they may have been cowed or manipulated into inert acceptance. This inert acceptance can prevent growth toward maturity. These adolescents may remain their parents' good children who stay home, voice their ideas and attitudes, and fear to dissent. They become their parents' companions and nurses. They become lonely and alone when they themselves become old.

Adolescents who can think and act for themselves should try out and oppose the ideas with which they disagree. Usually, it is only when one doubts the worth of one's own convictions that one is unwilling to risk the survival of his or her ideas in the marketplace.

While some disagreements during the development of interdependency arise between adolescents and parents, this time should not be one of constant storm.   Stress and hostility carried to extreme may be signs that the parents are pressing too hard or that the adolescents have a false idea of their role.   More often, however, it means that earlier, unresolved developmental issues have been reactivated by the adolescent crises.   When this happens, a psychiatrist, a psychologist, a family counselor, or a neutral person may be needed to help both sides see the issues more clearly.   Adolescence is a time when stresses from earlier stages of development are laid bare.   It may also bring out hidden conflicts between parents.   When youngsters become overly suspicious of other people's attitudes and intentions, unduly guarded, or excessively violent, there is reason to suspect that their difficulties date back before adolescence.   Circumstances may have flawed their basic trust.   They may have failed to develop an adequate degree of autonomy.   They may have developed excessive guilt about their bodies and their bodily functions.   They may have met social rejection.   They may have become drawn into parental discord.   However, the experiences that a child had at two or five or ten are a part of him or her at fourteen, seventeen, or twenty.   It does not help to blame the past for present behavior.   One must instead deal with the person that he or she has become.

Parents, as you can see, have many tasks to perform during the adolescent period.   Adolescents need to recognize the impact of late adolescence on the status of parents in order to understand the interrelationships at this period of family development.   As an adolescent, you need to forgive and forget past mistakes made by your parents just as you wish them to forgive and forget yours.

Sexuality in adolescence

The sexual awakening that comes with biological maturation is one of the main concerns of parents and adolescents.   The concern of this age is to learn to deal with his or her own sexuality in the service of mature love and to transform surplus sexual energies into productive work.   Adolescent sexuality concerns the following points.

1. how sexuality appears to the adolescent

2. our society's often ambivalent ideas about sexuality

3. what the facts seem to be

4. the job that the adolescent has of reconciling his or her feelings with values, imposed restraints, and the evidence of widespread violation of these restraints

5. the secondary feelings of guilt, anxiety, and tension that are likely to be accompanying sex in our society

The sexual capacities that come with puberty are not the same for boys and girls. The sensation accompanying sexual desire, in boys, is centered in the genitals. It can be aroused by a variety of external stimuli—pictures, words, jokes, or by random thoughts, or it may be deliberately sought. Among girls, there are wide normal differences. Some girls experience desire in much the way that boys do. Others may not experience direct sexual urges until later in life. Most adolescent girls, however, experience sexual desires that are diffuse and not as clearly distinguished from other feelings. These feelings may be evidenced by romantic yearnings, maternal cravings, enthusiasm, pity, sensual pleasures, or even such emotions as anger and fear.

For boys, sexual cravings are not necessarily associated with notions of love. Such arousals are a natural part of his physiology and require no overt action. If a girl invites a boy's favors, even though she yields herself only within sharply defined limits, the boy may very well be easily aroused whether he feels an affection for the girl or not. Even if there is affection, it is certainly different from the emotion he feels in later years as a husband and father. The qualities that he sees in the girl might be projections of his own needs onto a convenient object. This may have little to do with her actual characteristics.

For girls, love usually takes priority over sexuality. Young girls strive to fall in love, partly because it is the thing to do and partly because it seems to answer some inner need. True sexuality and mature affection include respect, understanding, appreciation, and tenderness. They can come only after the girl or boy has found security in the presence of someone else. For the adolescent girl, relations with the opposite sex seem to be directed consciously toward finding love. Although boys are not always aware of it, girls are usually seeking a husband, or practicing finding one. Going out with boys may also have meaning in the competition with other females, as a kind of self-esteem or evidence of desirability. Some boys, too, are seeking a wife or practicing finding one. But, in surveys of a large number of boys, marriage ranks behind sexual stimulation and gratification, companionship, and love as the motive for dating.

Intellectual curiosity about sex is greatly intensified in adolescence. The curiosity goes beyond information about the physical being. One of the difficulties comes from the idea that there must be something more that one does not know about. Many adolescent discussions of sex have as their theme the search for the "something else." This craving for knowledge is not merely a desire to find out what sex does or should feel like, but what it is like to the opposite sex. In folklore, in literature, in scientific publications, there is an ignorance of female sexuality. Boys often project their own sexuality onto girls or see girls as indifferent or hostile to sex. Girls have a better idea of what boys are seeking, but are not particularly understanding or sympathetic with such different goals.

The sexual standards for boys and girls are confusing to adolescents and to their parents. While boys are expected to restrain their urgings, it is nevertheless often taken for granted that they will "sow some wild oats." As a result some boys are ashamed of their virginity, while others cling to it. For girls, the formal standards still remain, reinforced by fears of unmarried pregnancy, the desirability of being a virgin at marriage, and the lesser acuteness of sex drives. Ambivalence does enter, however, in two ways.

> According to Stone and Church: First, there is the matter of maintaining popularity with the peer group, and more particularly with the boys who are potential husbands, which may require promiscuity or near-promiscuity. Second, there is the effect of the moral revolution, which has produced a psychiatrically backed mythology attributing to girls a sexuality identical with that of boys. Particularly in the educated classes, this has had the result of making many girls feel that to be normal they must want sexual experience, that they should attain a sexual climax readily, that they should engage freely in sex. It is probable that this view has left a fair number of girls and young women feeling guilty and inadequate because their own feelings fail to correspond to what they have been told about them. It is also likely that some girls have become actively promiscuous in search of what they are told to believe is normal experience, and have ended up feeling cheated, blaming either their own "frigidity" or the inadequacies of their partners. In short, works such as Kinsey's have been treated not only as descriptions of what does go on but have also been taken as prescriptions for what should go on.[1]

We have talked about how sexual capacities differ between male and female. We have discussed some of the natural tendencies and

1. From p. 314 of *Childhood and Adolescence: A Psychology of the Growing Person*, by L. Joseph Stone and Joseph Church. © Copyright 1957, 1968, by Random House, Inc. Used by permission of the publisher.

cultural ideas about sex. Now it is important to consider some of the attitudes. We must develop understandings and feelings so that we can make positive progress in becoming a man or becoming a woman. We must realize that our own sexuality is an important part of our whole personality. Sex cannot be singled out just on its own. It is part of the whole life of a person. It has many purposes. It is not only a part of the marriage relationship, but it is also a power that gives life, color, creativity, and meaning to all human relationships. If we limit our concept of sex purely to the physical act, we limit our whole lives. For this single physical act is not enough to carry us throughout adulthood.

Knowing the differences in male and female sexual make-up should enable each sex to help the other in the understanding and appreciation of their own sexuality. In this way it becomes an integral part of a mature individual's personality that is ready for a mature and loving marriage. One must realize that sex is an important part of marriage, of course. But the real part of marriage, the strong part, is based on the trust and companionship that the woman and the man create in their relationship. This is what will help them as they face the changes in society and in their life together.

Our relationships are the most important structures of our lives. Whether it's parent to child, friend to friend, brother to sister, boy to girl, or man to wife—the moralities, the ethics are the same. *Sexual morality is no different from any other morality. It has to do with the honesty of our relationship to each other, the trust and confidence we have in ourselves, the trust and confidence we have in each other, the conviction we have that the other person's welfare is more important than our own.*

In matters of sexual morality as well as in any morality, one must look beyond the present moment and realize the future consequences. People use sex to prove certain things, their femininity or masculinity, or their independence from their parents. People also use sex to get something they want. They use it as a bribe or as punishment, revenge, or reward. When sex is used in any of these ways it becomes an object used for gain. This means that people themselves are using each other as objects. This is exploitation. It may work at the moment, but in the long run people will feel cheated.

Adolescent-adult

Adolescents can more easily enter the adult world if they are a part of it, not alienated from it. Some adults feel that the problems of the world come soon enough. Let youth enjoy their childhood. However, one of the worst aspects of any alienation of young people from the adult world is that they are cut off from discussions of adult problems. To live such problems vicariously is the necessary preparation to making responsible decisions when these problems are actually faced. *Adolescents should not be protected from money worries, business troubles, domestic issues, and the topics of sex, birth, marriage, and death, including the personal tragedies involved in illegitimacy, marriages based on expediency, and delinquency. To isolate them from adult concerns is to do them a great disservice.* Young people must not be protected from the troublesome aspects of civilized living. Adolescents are ready to respond to any overture which welcomes them into the adult community and which demonstrates a genuine desire to acknowledge their opinions. The adult community, in turn, needs the idealism of adolescents.

Questions

1. Define the following terms:

   adolescence   sexuality   ambivalence

2. How might the Peace Corps help an adolescent achieve his or her developmental goals?

3. List the characteristics of parents which would be most helpful to an adolescent as he or she strives for adulthood.

4. What factors complicate the struggle of many adolescents for emancipation from the family?

5. How might a group of adolescents be encouraged to raise their standards with respect to boy-girl relations?

Further reading

Hilgard, Ernest R. *Introduction to Psychology.* 6th ed. New York: Harcourt Brace Jovanovich, Inc., 1975.

Duvall, Evelyn Millis. *Parent and Teenager—Living and Loving.* Nashville, TN: Broadman Press, 1976.

Grinder, Robert E. *Adolescence.* New York: John Wiley & Sons, Inc., 1978.

Manaster, Guy J. *Adolescent Development and the Life Tasks.* Boston: Allyn & Bacon, Inc., 1977.

Sebald, Hans. *Adolescence: A Social-Psychological Analysis.* Englewood Cliffs, NJ: Prentice-Hall, Inc., 1977.

Wattenberg, William W. *Adolescent Years.* New York: Harcourt Brace Jovanovich, Inc., 1973.

Chapter 13

Relationships with brothers and sisters

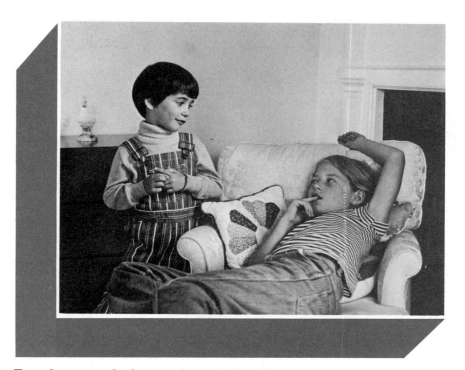

Brothers and sisters in the family often play the role
of confidant, listener, and sharer in the exploration of
the world around them.   Children share their
observations and insights with each other.

Drawing by V. Gene Myers. From *Saturday Review,*
© 1977 by Saturday Review Magazine Corp. Reprinted by permission.

"I'm not sure. I think it has something to do with
the eternal revenue service."

This chapter poses questions about brother/sister relationships. We will discuss the rivalry of brothers and sisters, their competition, their position in the family and personality, and the adolescent and brother/sister relationships outside the family. With these topics in mind, we shall try to understand ourselves and our relationships with brothers and sisters.

Brothers and sisters

No two children have the same family. This is true for all families. This statement is startling until one stops to consider it. The firstborn comes into a family of father and mother. He or she is the only child. The parents may be a little concerned about being able to handle this new family member. They may also be worried about money, their own relationships, and their status in the community and in their profession. The second child is born to a family composed of three, instead of two. The parents feel more competent in their ability to handle a baby. Perhaps by now, parents are more settled in their careers and are more aware of the demands of parenthood. The third child comes to a family of four, one that has established itself as a family. Perhaps a grandparent has been added. Whether the family changes are positive or negative is not important. The emphasis is on change. The family changes as it grows. Thus, no two children have the same family.

Rivalry

The child's first experience with competition usually occurs within the home. Rivalry between brothers and sisters is almost universal. This can be seen among American families, where children's expression of aggression is more tolerated than in other societies. Rivalry tends to be greatest when the children are more than eighteen months but less than thirty-six months apart in age. However, spacing to avoid this critical period is not likely to make any practical difference. The jealousy of the older child is focused on being pushed out of his or her privileged place in the parents' affections. It is the older child whose reaction is likely to be most intense. Baldwin's study showed that this reaction may be caused by the changes he observed in the behavior of mothers toward an older child before and during pregnancy. The changes were also noted after the birth of the baby. The changes were dramatic. Over a period of a few months, the mothers showed a marked drop in affection, approval, and attention. There was a corresponding rise in parental restriction and severity in discipline.

This finding points to a major principle for dealing with children's rivalry, or more realistically, for restricting it. It is important that the transition in the psychological status of the older child be neither too sudden nor too severe. At the same time, it is futile and foolhardy to try to eliminate such a change altogether. Rivalry is a natural part of growing up. Each child wants to be first in the eyes of his or her parents. Each child tries to achieve this status.

One of the ways in which children try to get over the pain of having younger rivals is to act as if they are no longer children by competing on the same basis as the baby, but as if they are a third parent. Usually the left-out feeling is more apt to be experienced by the first child when the second baby arrives. He or she has been used to the spotlight and has had no practice in sharing his or her parents' love with others. Middle children do not have to decide between being a parent and being a baby when a new infant arrives. They can see that they are still just one of the children.

When a condition of intense rivalry exists, it is sometimes openly displayed, sometimes not. It shows directly when a youngster tries to harm a baby brother or sister. It may appear indirectly when a child tries to mutilate a toy. Sometimes, however, children suppress feelings toward a rival and even convince themselves that no rivalry exists. There are adults who will say, for example, that they had no idea of their bitter feelings toward a brother or sister until they reached adulthood. Adults who have acknowledged only a mild rivalry in their childhood may, in discussing early experiences, burst into a rage and a flood of tears.

Parental attitudes toward children's rivalries will be influenced by their own experiences. Parents' childhood rivalries may persist in their lives as parents and cause them to treat their children as potential rivals. Adults who have not resolved their own feelings of rivalry may introject those feelings into the competitive struggles of their own children. This makes the competition among their children more dramatic than it would normally be without their interpretation.

If parents or other adults are obviously unfair or if they openly favor and admire one child more than another it is understandable that the unfavored child might feel hurt. However, rivalry shows that we cannot understand what will actually happen in a social situation simply by studying the characteristics of each person involved in the situation. Nor can rivalry be averted simply by manipulating the environment.

Rivalry becomes an acute problem if one or all the children in the family happen to be possessive, or if the children are demanding. Some youngsters seem more inclined than others to want to have everything for themselves. They want all of the attention, all of the care, all of the favors. Others, even at an early age, seem to find it easier to share.

Jealousy

Sometimes parents unwittingly discriminate against one child by showing greater admiration for another child. It is only human for adults to prefer some traits and characteristics to others. One child may get the notion that he or she does not rank as high in the parents' estimation as does his or her brother or sister. Where there are children differing in age, sex, interests, and abilities it is impossible for parents to treat the youngsters in a way that seems fair to all. It is, therefore, likely that all children near each other in age will show signs of jealousy at some time.

The link between jealousy in early childhood and a jealous disposition in later years has not been traced adequately in scientific studies. Children normally lose their obvious symptoms of jealousy as they grow older and become absorbed in interests outside their family. However, there are times when they may show even more jealousy toward their daily associates.

Among adults, the degree of jealousy a person shows frequently bears little relationship to his or her status or power as compared with others. The person who has achieved the appearance of success will sometimes begrudge the recognition bestowed upon an underling. This action is like that of a big hound that bristles when his master pets another dog. A person who was intensely jealous of a younger brother may, as far as he can see, have outgrown this jealousy. But traces of these early bitter experiences may remain, even though jealousy is no longer shown toward the brother. An attitude of jealousy persists in an adult, for example, if he or she feels hurt when another gets recognition or wins good fortune. His or her feelings may also express themselves in the way he or she takes sides against some people. These people represent objects of jealousy similar to those that were represented by a brother or sister at an earlier age.

Position and personality

A person's behavior is likely to be affected by the social position he or she holds in relation to the positions of other significant persons in his or her life. The relationship to others is an important variable in his or her development. Of all others, brothers and sisters are likely to exert the greatest influence on him or her.

The following results have emerged from a study of the personality patterns of five- and six-year-old children in relation to the order of birth (firstborn or secondborn position), sex, and age spacing. These results can be attributed to a brother's or sister's direct effect upon the behavior of the child. For brothers and sisters who are far apart in age, the effect is likely to be indirect, showing itself through differences in parental behavior.

The studies indicated that firstborns tend to be more self-confident and to have fewer nervous habits such as nail-biting and thumb-sucking than do the second children. Firstborns, close in age to their brothers and sisters, do not recover from upsets as readily as do the second children. Second children are less hesitant to express anger.

Particularly at the two-to-four-year age difference, the child whose brother or sister is of a different sex is more self-confident, cheerful, active, healthy, less changeable, and more inclined to recover poise easily. These differences have been interpreted as suggesting a greater degree of stimulation between members of pairs of different sex than between members of pairs of the same sex. In other words, in families of two children there is more stimulation if the family is composed of a boy and girl rather than being composed of two boys or two girls.

Differences in personality related to differences in age spacing are greater for boys than for girls. The two-to-four-year spacing, especially for firstborns, seems to be more stressful than shorter or longer age-spacing. Firstborn boys of the two-to-four-year age-spacing are confident, emotionally intense, excitable, moody, angry, and decisive. They are more given to alibiing, projecting the blame, and losing purpose than those boys whose brothers and sisters are closer or more distant in age.

The adolescent and brothers and sisters

The adolescent may respond to a new child by developing parental feelings that will lead to caring for the baby like a mother or a father. It is also possible that he or she may feel acutely jealous and see the baby as a rival for the parents' affection. If his or her understanding of the roles of sex in procreation is poor, the birth of a brother or sister may be distressing. The adolescent may displace his or her aversion to sex onto the parents and the new child whom he or she then shuns. It should be stressed that the birth of a brother or sister need not lead to conflict. If it does, it indicates that earlier issues have not been resolved in a healthy way.

With adolescence, some changes may occur in brother and sister relationships. Conflicts about dominance and submission are likely to become more acute in adolescents in relation to their brothers and sisters. They will demand more privileges and more recognition than the younger children. They will challenge the leadership of older brothers and sisters. As they become more aware of body changes and sensual feelings, they may become uncomfortable with brothers and sisters of the opposite sex.

The situation becomes more serious when parents prefer one child to another. Parental favoritism may decrease the adolescent's self-esteem and generate hostility. The presence of more brilliant and successful brothers and sisters may prevent the adolescent from perceiving self as a competent person.

Associations and role

Some recent research has shown that sex-role learning is in part a function of the sex of the child and the position in the family. For example, a boy with an older sister has more feminine traits than a boy with an older brother or a boy with a younger brother or sister.

The social learning in a family of two or three boys close together in age leads to high sex-role masculinity and high interest in conventional economic activities. The first-born boy is singled out from the second-born male by his interest in a strategic success style. The latter is singled out by his interest in a power success style.

A strategic success style is best described as a position of behavior that is directive and projective. The individual is capable of commanding and directing others in an indirect manner or through the use of strategy. For example, the first-born male in the family in our society must play the role of the older protective brother. He must not use his greater physical strength to make his little brother perform in the way he wishes. Thus, he learns to use psychological means or a strategic success style to manipulate the younger brother. The younger brother, however, can respond with his fists, since there is no stigma against hitting a bigger, older boy. Hence, for the second-born male, a power success style is fostered.

The family made up of girls has a high femininity role and an interest in routine occupations. However, the success styles are reversed from those of the all-male family. The first-born girl is distinguished by an interest in a power success style. The second-born girl is distinguished by an interest in a strategic success style.

The social learning in the boy-girl or girl-boy family contributes to an interest in expressive creativity. The older brother and the younger sister relationship often is the most creative combination.

Relationship outside the family

If brothers and sisters are fairly close in age, and are all within the age span of the school years, their contacts at home are likely to be marked by taunting, bickering, battling, and bedlam. These activities are interspersed with some joint activities. There will be some comparing of notes on people and school, and some sharing in whole-family enterprises and chores. However, outside the home, brothers and sisters close ranks in family unity. The terms "kid sister" and "big brother" may be used in disgust, but they also carry affection. In the case of brother-sister unity, the same children who criticize their parents freely will not tolerate any criticism of them outside the family.

In conclusion, studies point out that brothers and sisters do not want their parents to be pals. They have plenty of their own age group outside of the family to serve as pals. Children at all ages need parents as parents, which means as adults and not as pseudo-children. Children need parents as refuges when cut off from the gang, when sick, or at other threatening times. There are simply times when children want to be members of the family, trading news and jokes and confidences, asking for information, advice, and help.

Questions

1. Define the following terms:

   strategic success style   jealousy
   rivalry   power success style

2. What are the most important factors concerning sibling relationships and personality?

3. Lucy is two years older than her sister Kristen. They are the only children in the family. What characteristics might you expect them to manifest?

4. Give an example of family unity shown between brothers and sisters outside of the home.

5. What are the major causes of brother-sister rivalry?

6. How does rivalry cause jealousy?

7. Interview some of your friends who have younger brothers and sisters. What are their main concerns?

Further reading

Bohannon, E. W. "The Only Child in the Family." *Pedagogical Summary* 5 (1898):494.

Bossard, J. H. S. "Personality Roles in the Large Family." *Child Development* 26 (1955):71–78.

Goodenough, F., and Leaky, A. "The Effect of Certain Family Relationships Upon the Development of Personality." *Journal of Genetic Psychology* 4 (1927):45–71.

Koch, H. "The Relation of Certain Family Constellation Characteristics and Attitudes of Children Toward Adults." *Child Development* 26 (1955):37.

Lasko, J. K. "Parental Behavior Toward First and Second Children." *Genetic Psychology Monographs* 49 (1954):97–137.

McCandless, B. R. *Children: Behavior and Development.* 3rd ed. New York: Holt, Rinehart & Winston, CBS, Inc., 1977.

McClelland, D. C. *The Achieving Society.* Pap. text ed. New York: Halsted Press, Division of John Wiley & Sons, Inc., 1976.

Schacter, Stanley. *The Psychology of Affiliation.* Stanford, CA: Stanford University Press, 1959.

Sutton-Smith, Brian; Roberts, John M.; and Rosenbert, B. G. "Sibling Association and Role Involvement." *Merrill-Palmer Quarterly* no. 1 (1964), pp. 25–38.

Toman, Walter. *Family Constellation.* 3rd ed. Pap. text. New York: Springer Publishing Co., Inc., 1976.

Welsh, George. *Creativity and Intelligence: A Personality Approach.* Pap. text. UNC Institute of Research in the Social Sciences, 1975.

Chapter 14

Relationships with older people

Aging or growing old is made difficult in our culture because the views of older people are different from the views held by younger people. The real threat for older and aged people may be due to our preoccupation with younger people.

Reprinted by permission of Don Orehek.
From *Saturday Review,* © 1969.

"It's her last wish upon retiring after twenty-five years!"

It is important in our culture to look and act young. It is a compliment to be called young. The problems of older people are increased because people fail to recognize that aging is part of the process of growth.

Shakespeare, in *As You Like It,* wrote about the aging process in Jacques' famous soliloquy on the seven ages of man.

All the world's a stage,
And all the men and women merely players.
They have their exits and their entrances;
And one man in his time plays many parts,
His acts being seven ages. At first the infant,
Mewling and puking in the nurse's arms.
And then the whining school-boy, with his satchel

And shining morning face, creeping like a snail
Unwillingly to school. And then the lover,
Sighing like furnace, with a woeful ballad
Made to his mistress' eyebrow. Then a soldier,
Full of strange oaths, and bearded like the bard;
Jealous in honour, sudden and quick in quarrel,
Seeking the bubble reputation
Even in the cannon's mouth. And then the justice,
In fair round belly with good capon lined
With eyes severe and beard of formal cut,
Full of wise saws and modern instances;
And so he plays his part. The sixth age shifts
Into the lean and slipper'd pantaloon,
With spectacles on nose and pouch on side!
His youthful hose, well saved, a world too wide
For his shrunk shank; and his big manly voice,
Turning again toward childish treble, pipes
And whistles in his sound. Last scene of all,
That ends this strange eventful history,
Is second childishness, and mere oblivion,
Sans teeth, sans eyes, sans taste, sans everything.

Definition of aging

Aging is a process. It begins before birth and continues until death. As such, aging is a part of human development. However, the term aging usually means the later stage or stages of the process. The chronological age arbitrarily selected at which aging is legally said to begin is the age of seventy.

Family structure

History shows that there has been a transition from the extended family to the nuclear family. The extended family is a family unit that includes mother, father, and children, and is extended to include grandmother, grandfather, aunts, uncles, and cousins. The nuclear family consists of the immediate family unit of mother, father, and children. The independent nuclear family seems destined to be the family of the future. In the past the patriarchal extended family and the matriarchal extended family were most common.

Reprinted by permission of John Ruge.
From *Saturday Review,* © 1971.

"DAD! Oh, I'm sorry, Sir. I thought you were my father.
You all look alike, you know!"

The extended family

The large patriarchal family gave the authority and decision-making for the family to the oldest male member. This type of family exists today in some countries. The patriarchal extended family was an economic unit of production in farming and in trading. It has been threatened by industrialization, the growth of cities, and the rise of individualism. It still develops when the owner of a family business hires his sons and perhaps sons-in-law.

The matriarchal extended family is made up of the grandmother, her daughters, and granddaughters. Husbands and wives in this family structure enjoy much of their recreation and social life separately. There is a system of mutual help in time of need. This help is given by grandmother, daughters, sisters, and granddaughters.

In this system, the husband controls the money. He does not tell the wife what he earns. He gives her the housekeeping allowance customary in the neighborhood. Those participating in the matriarchal extended family believe that a good husband-wife relationship is

Reprinted by permission of Mischa Richter.
From *Saturday Review*, © 1971.

"OK, there ain't no Santa Claus! How does a senior citizen
who lives in the North Pole and is a philanthropist strike you?"

one with division of labor rather than with joint activities and shared interests.

The matriarchal extended family appears to be established in communities where the residents are employed by local industry. It is most stable where at least three or four generations have been born and reared in the same locality.

The independent nuclear family

The chief characteristics of the autonomous nuclear family are as follows.

1. equal authority is shared by husband and wife

2. division of labor between husband and wife is flexible and roles are easily reversed

3. compatibility of personality and complementary differences are regarded as desirable by the couple for a happy marriage

4. nearly all friends are joint friends of husband and wife

5. there is a minimum of social control by friends and neighbors

6. leisure-time activities are shared, with emphasis upon entertaining and being entertained by friends

The independent nuclear family has the characteristics which seem adapted to the urban way of life. Husband and wife no longer seek their chief companionship outside the home, the husband with friends and the wife with relatives, as in the matriarchal extended family. They find companionship with each other. They select friends on the basis of interests and similar backgrounds. These friends are likely to live in other neighborhoods. The couple is freed from the control and the responsibility of relatives and neighbors.

Changes in the relations of aging parents and their adult offspring

The independent nuclear family is a product of the effects of the economic and social trends of the times. The adult offspring probably have a higher educational level, different tastes, and more sophisticated interests than their aging parents. The aging parent threatens the status of his or her adult children both psychologically and economically. With our fetish for youth and its charms, the young adults are threatened by the mannerisms of their aging parents. They recognize that these symptoms may too soon be their characteristics. It is easier to ignore the advancing years when one isn't reminded by the presence of an aging relative. Also, the adult offspring with their changing status strive toward upward mobility economically and socially. Acquiring automobiles, better housing, and prominent club memberships places economic stress on them. The care of the aged parent is an additional strain.

A small number of aging parents still live with their adult children. It is, however, important to distinguish cases where the adult offspring live with their parents and those where the parents live with their adult offspring.

Where the children who are now adult live with their parents, the older generation takes the dominant role. The aging mother, if physically able, is in charge of the housekeeping. This arrangement proves more satisfactory to the older generation than to the married younger couple. In general, it works better if the daughter and her husband live with her parents than when the couple live with the husband's parents.

If the aging individual or couple live with a married son or married daughter, the arrangement is generally difficult on both sides. It is likely to be especially frustrating to the older people who frequently feel in the way and useless.

Aloneness and alienation

With tremendous advances in industrialization, urbanization, communication, technology, and science, the pace and complexity of social life have multiplied. The same forces that conquered disease and deprivation in earlier times have created a new stress in modern times.

For individuals or for societies, periods of rapid change tax older ways of life. For example, movement of population resulting from industrialization and urbanization strains the traditional family organization and roles. Grandparents are cut off from the emotional and economic support of their children. Meanwhile they are being kept alive longer by medical advances. The offspring lose the skills

No alienation here. "I'm Grandpa's sweetheart."

Companionship
continues to grow.

and knowledge of their parents, while having to deal with the problems of their own children. These children lack the emotional acceptance and guidance of the extended family and instead have to
seek status and achievement with their peers.

With these thoughts in mind, one could say that each group is
alone and distinct. However, there is aloneness that is privacy and
there is alienation. Many in the older generation and many in the
younger generation are growing up alienated, unable to attach to
other people. Such people are lonely and alone, but not because
they enjoy their own aloneness. Rather it is because they are incapable of enjoying relations with others or incapable of making relationships with others. When this incapability exists, old age is not
seen as a part of life, as death, birth, and puberty are seen as a part of
life.

It is often stated that older people "want to be needed." Here is
an interesting reflection upon the state of real affairs. If they were, in
fact, needed, they would not need to wish it to be so. Older people,
while wanting to receive recognition for having been useful, find that
it is present activity that is rewarding and not past activities.

The problems of aging are increased by the inability of our society
to create satisfying places and worthwhile roles for older persons.
The old family system had a place for older persons. But modern
society has little room for them. This, however, is not a matter of
aging alone. It is a reflection of the larger social changes which have
taken place. In a society such as ours, in which high values are

placed upon economic and social success, family unity is all too often incompatible with occupational and social mobility. One must often make a choice which can work against the older persons within the family.

Many of the stresses of modern social life are by-products of social change. It is useless to wonder if life would be better if the "good old days" could be restored. For society can no more retrace its history than an individual can regain the pleasures of childhood. More important is the question of whether new values and institutions can evolve that will permit not only greater freedom from stress but also greater opportunity for harmonious and creative living.

Interaction between individuals

Older people are part of our ongoing society. Their characteristics are developed in large part through social interaction. The interaction between people develops a series of stages in the process of socialization. There is a saying which states that what one is at fifteen is what he or she was given; what one is at sixty is what he or she has made of himself or herself. People who have a satisfying old age are people who are doing things that interest them. They are involved with life. They are involved with people. Such persons will be sought by people of different ages. They will not be put aside. They are people who are alive. They are alive because they grew that way. They are people who have resources and are engaged in life now. They grew up engaged in life. They did not protect themselves from work. They did not protect themselves from exertion. They were willing to go out and get involved with people. They are the old people that young people like to talk to, the people they like to visit.

Old age is a developmental stage in the continuing process of socialization which we call aging. The aged of today are yesterday's children. The aged of tomorrow are the youth of today. The problems of our youth predict the problems of our old age. The behavioral patterns followed by us today, and the adjustments that we make to the situations in which we find ourselves, all reflect the kinds of persons we shall be in the future. To illustrate this, let's think about two girls in senior high school. Jean and Polly are both seventeen. Both are reasonably attractive and intelligent. Jean babysits for extra money, tutors some children of the inner city in reading, reads stories to some of the older ladies in a rest home, has taught herself to play a guitar, and has a vast number of friends of all ages and stations. Polly is restless if she doesn't have a weekend party or date. She complains that her parents do not give her a large enough allowance and that she never has anything to wear. Polly is bored. She can't wait until graduation.

The actions, attitudes, and adjustments of these seniors at seventeen predict the kind of people they may be at seventy. Those who learn to interact, to become involved, who cultivate the art of social interaction, will not be alienated at any age.

Planned communities

For people of various ages and stages of development to learn to interact with each other, they must know each other. Our planned communities with their same-age groupings have developed alienation between different ages. These communities have grown up with populations of the same age. The people who live in one kind of planned community are people in their late 20's through the early 40's and their children. There are almost no older people and relatively few adolescents. This development of a society with a sameness in age structure creates problems for our youth. Older persons have always provided us with role models. They have given us understandings of what it means to grow old and how to change and adapt to the later years. If there are no older persons around, young people have no models after which to pattern themselves as they themselves grow older. There is also a reverse process in these communities. If the planned community is composed of older people, they do not have a chance to know and observe the young people. Their only knowledge of youth and their activities is that of the 8 to 10 percent who make newspaper headlines.

In the planned communities occupied by the young, people don't die. What happens then is that young people have no way of adapting to bereavement. They don't learn to accept death as a part of life. The people who can die gracefully are those who have lived a rich life. The people who are afraid to die are those whose lives are empty. They always hope somehow or other that they will catch up with something real in life. When our vital old people die, we are the ones who suffer. It is not a tragedy for them, it is part of the life process.

To further discuss the importance of the need for the different ages to know each other, Dr. Dorothy Lee, an anthropologist, tells this story.

"I recall that one of the teachers in a Hopi school reported that the Hopi children had been given a party in the school, but did not turn out. When they were asked why, they said, 'What would we do all alone? We would be just children. There weren't going to be any parents to watch us, no grandparents to tell us stories, and no babies to hold or watch, just children our age.' They did not enjoy themselves just being alone, because they felt that a rich party included even babies."

When we can have gatherings where all ages participate and mingle, we won't have the deep misunderstandings about the various stages of development.

Preparation for old age

As stated previously, one starts to prepare for old age at birth. However, it is not until people approach middle age that they really begin to concern themselves with questions of security, health, and death. The past experience of the person, at this mature stage of development, plays an important role in his or her growth toward maturity. All age groups are influenced by their early years and experiences.

The great challenge of middle age lies in the necessity to adjust downward from the previous period of activity and responsibility. Skill and self-understanding are required to change to a slower pace. There is a need to release control and to accept the shift in

Reprinted by permission of Robert Censoni.
From *Saturday Review*, © 1971.

"How can we break it to the Queen that we're changing
from a monarchy to a republic?"

attention from oneself to others. Above all, one must find satisfaction and stimulus in younger people, despite differences in values between generations. The world does not fall to pieces because familiar ways change and/or take on new forms. Life does not end when one is less needed in a family or in a job.

Acceptance, flexibility, and independence are the cues. A certain degree of vicarious living through one's children's lives is natural and even healthy. But a person should not depend upon his or her family to supply the energy and motivation for his or her own life at any age, perhaps least of all in middle age. Free from restricting and confining family ties, many people find in middle age their first opportunity to be truly independent. Adult offspring should be viewed as friends, peers, and colleagues. Not as indebted persons obligated to support parents or to accept parental authority and guidance.

Questions

1. Define the following terms:

   aging
   matriarchal extended family
   the nuclear family
   the patriarchal extended family
   the independent nuclear family

2. What social changes affect the relationship between aging parents and their adult offspring?

3. The Swedish people have a saying, "Heaven in this world is to be alone when I want it; Hell is to be alone when I don't want it." What is the relationship between this saying and the role of the grandparents in our society?

4. Which characteristics of the independent nuclear family meet basic psychological needs?

5. How might the characteristics of the independent nuclear family conflict with the role expectations of the older generation?

6. What causes adult offspring to feel threatened by their aging parents?

7. What is the difference between alienation and aloneness?

8. How does our society compound the problems of the aged?

9. If death is part of the life process, how can one best accept it?

10. What are the characteristics of an older person who has "grown old gracefully"?

11. Discuss this statement: "A community without its senior citizens is as artificial and wrong as a retirement community without any young people."

Further reading

Emerson, Geraldine M., ed. *Aging.* New York: Halsted Press, Division of John Wiley & Sons, Inc., 1977.

Hess, Beth B. *Growing Old in America.* Pap. text. Brunswick, NJ: Transaction Books, Division of Transaction, Inc. Rutgers—The State University, 1976.

Huyck, Margaret H. *Growing Older.* Pap. text. Englewood Cliffs, NJ: Prentice-Hall, Inc., 1974.

Jhabvala, R. Prawer. *The Nature of Passion.* Reading, MA: Allen Unwin, Inc., 1956.

Lee, Dorothy. *Freedom and Culture.* Englewood Cliffs, NJ: Prentice-Hall, Inc., 1961.

Maurus, J. *Growing Old Gracefully.* Pap. text. Canfield, OH: Alba Books, 1977.

Percy, Charles H., and Mangel, Charles. *Growing Old in the Country of the Young.* New York: McGraw-Hill, 1974.

Simmons, Leo W., ed. *Sun Chief: The Autobiography of a Hopi Indian.* rev. ed. New Haven, CT: Published for the Institute of Human Relations by the Yale University Press, 1963.

Zborowski, Mark, and Herzog, Elizabeth. *Life Is with People: The Jewish Little-Town of Eastern Europe.* New York: International Universities Press, Inc., 1962.

Chapter 15

Relationships outside the family

In Western industrialized society, a person's job is a means of earning a living and establishing oneself as an adult. In evolving a social role through work, a person can judge his or her own adequacy, worth, and contribution as an adult.

The idea of establishing oneself early in an occupational role is so important that we give great emphasis to vocational guidance in secondary schools. We ask many preschool children what they are going to do when they grow up.

Working

A person's job gives the person identity as an adult. Work is important simply because so much of one's life is devoted to it. People spend more than one-third of their waking hours at work in the course of a working lifetime. Work frequently precedes marriage and usually continues long after children have become adults. Within this time span, a person establishes relationships with other people. These relationships give status, prestige, affection, social membership, and support during personal emergencies. These relationships influence family life but are often apart from the family.

A job is a means of developing comfortable relationships with other people. Some people prefer to work closely with others. They

Reprinted by permission of Leo Garel.
From *Saturday Review/World,* © 1973.

"I'm warning you, Donald, if you don't behave yourself
I'll tell your parents you're a musical genius."

From *Saturday Review/World*, Copyright 1974.
Reprinted by permission of *Saturday Review* and Henry Martin.

"How would you like to start at the top?
We have an opening for a chairman of the board
of a beleaguered and bankrupt railroad."

seek jobs which provide this closeness. Others, to be comfortable, seek out more isolated jobs. When people are forced into situations in which the work environment is not comfortable, they are often unhappy in their work.

Balanced distance from other people has a counterpart in balanced distance from other aspects of life. In going to work, many people can separate themselves temporarily from personal and family concerns. When they return from work, having put these concerns aside for the day, they are refreshed and better able to cope. This is particularly true for many women who go to work primarily for relief from home and family pressures.

A person's relationship to the organization in which he or she works is an important consideration. A business organization and its social structure have increasingly come to take the place of the disappearing small community. When ours was primarily an agricultural society, people depended on their neighbors for help in emergencies. Their roles in their communities were the avenues for achieving adult identity. Now a business organization often meets these needs for many people. This is particularly true for those in large organizations in metropolitan centers. This is evident in fringe benefits, especially in interest in and help for the retired employee. It is also evident when the role or status of a person is referred to. The person is identified not alone as "Mercedes Brown," but usually as "Mercedes Brown, Vice-President of I.V.M." or "Jan Smith, Supervisor at Alpha Electric."

Employer-employee relationships

Achievement, recognition, position, responsibility, and advancement are the factors most closely related to increasing work satisfaction. Note the close relationship of these to our basic psychological needs. Leadership or non-leadership, company policy, administration, supervision, and working conditions are the major factors responsible for job satisfaction or dissatisfaction.

Despite many studies, there is no common agreement on the qualities of leadership. What makes a good leader seems to vary with the group to be led, its task, and the conditions under which it operates. This becomes very evident in Golding's *The Lord of the Flies,* when one compares the leadership qualities of Ralph and Jack.

However, from the cartoonist's point of view, employers might be more successful if they looked for a new employee who showed creativeness rather than one who represented the norm. Paramount to good employer-employee relationships is mutual respect. A good executive, whether in a work situation, social club, or educational organization, is a leader. A leader must be able to permit subordinates to depend on him or her. At the same time the leader must be able to depend on the subordinates. The leader must give them consistent support and respect if he or she is to foster their psychological growth and their assumption of responsibilities. The employer or leader must also keep a constant focus on the job to be done. He or she must create a work plan within which people can do the job.

How one dresses is not an indication of ability. However, for many people, personal appearance and dress speak first, before the

Reprinted by permission of Tom Stratton.
From *Saturday Review*, © 1976.

"Sorry, we have a dress code here".

real person is known. Employees should consider how they dress and present themselves in the most positive way according to current dress practices.

Perceptions and expectations

Relationships of employer and employee seem to have three problem areas which are the same for both small and large firms.

The first problem is the difference in perception between the expectations of the employee and those of the company. There is often considerable difference between what a person thinks he or she is to do on the job and what the supervisors expect him or her to do. These differences in perceptions and expectations result in built-in conflict and frustration.

The second problem is management's assumption, and usually the union leadership's as well, that people are motivated only by money. Despite considerable research most incentive programs and efforts to motivate people are based on monetary rewards. Furthermore, many businesses are organized in such a way as to ensure maximum control over people. This is on the assumption that they cannot be otherwise motivated or guided. From our earlier study of human needs, personality, and character development, one can see that these concepts of management are out-of-date. They result in irresponsibility, apathy, and hostility.

Here is an example that shows motivation precipitated for public good rather than for personal monetary gain. After an ice storm had disrupted its facilities, a public utility company made a survey. They found that there were no accidents while emergency work was being done to restore service. This was the case despite the fact that the work was done under great pressure and dangerous conditions. The workers were so motivated by the feeling that the community was depending upon them to restore service that they gave almost superhuman service.

A third problem, and one that is gaining in importance, is the feeling expressed in the phrase, "I don't know where I stand." This usually does not mean that the person is unaware of how the superiors judge his or her work. But rather it is the feeling that personal contact with superiors is so limited that nobody really cares. The fact that people are useful to their organization for limited skills does not make them feel useful as human beings. While no organization can use all of the skills and talents available to it, few people use more than a small fraction of their capacities in their work. Furthermore, many people live uncomfortably with the knowledge that they can be replaced.

In general, these dissatisfactions can be reduced if management recognizes the employee as a responsible adult. In our society, when people are eighteen years old they are credited with having sufficient intelligence to help elect the President and the Congress. In that way they contribute to the making of government policy. In business and industry, however, they may not be asked to share in a responsible way in decisions relating to their work. The use of suggestion boxes by some companies indicates how little face-to-face conversation goes on in such business organizations. Many company studies indicate that there are significant increases in productivity and decreases in the expression of various forms of hostility when people have a responsible share in planning the work they are going to do. Participation indicates also that management cares about employees and is willing to listen to them and to permit them to express their feelings about their work and work situation.

Work satisfaction and individual worth

An individual's feelings about his or her work can affect feelings about his or her home, family, and future. Years ago there was a *Saturday Evening Post* cover that showed a man being criticized by his boss, who in turn had an argument with his wife. She spanked the child, the child kicked the dog, the dog chased the cat, then the cat ate the mouse. This sequence was used to illustrate the escape mechanism of displacement in Chapter 6. That is, it explained the displacement of feelings from one situation in which they could not be expressed to another in which they could be expressed. A person's feelings about his or her work are frequently displaced onto the home situation. Anger and frustration on the job may well result in hostility and irritability at home.

On the other hand, people who take pride in their work, whose occupational identity is important, quite often extend that pride to include the appearance of their homes. Many home appliance and automobile companies reinforce this by making their products available to their employees at cost. For example, some will say that they must keep the lawn neat and the house painted because people identify them with their company. Their pride in the company enhances their pride in themselves, their families, and homes.

At the same time, the positive feelings about work are usually correlated with a positive, optimistic outlook on life. A person can be comfortable about the future when he or she trusts it.

When work experience holds no promise of further growth or achievement, people will invest the major part of their energies elsewhere. This often happens when some recognize they will stay essentially in the same positions for the rest of their working lives. If their salaries are adequate to meet their needs and if they can earn their salaries by meeting the minimum requirements of the job, they will do only that which is required of them. Some people in executive positions complain of the loss of initiative on the part of their subordinates. Sometimes when there is a greater investment in home and family the individual is provided with greater interest in life away from work.

The employee, young or old, who does not meet the employer's standards, is subject to a shock. Psychologically, hiring and firing on a job is comparable to the early childhood experience of being given or being denied love and affection. When a person is employed, he or she is told in effect that he or she is wanted and looked upon as worthy of working with others. When discharged, he or she is told that he or she is no longer wanted. The importance to a person of being wanted and needed, whether in or outside of the family, has long been recognized.

Conformity and the corporation

The recent Broadway play, *The Absence of a Cello,* by Ira Wallach, is a comedy based on the demands of large corporations and their effect on the life and the wife of a possible future executive. The college professor in Wallach's play resented his prospective company's interest in his personal life, which he regarded as an unwarranted intrusion into his privacy. The professor is asked to join the corporation as a consultant and also to do research on their business techniques. He is offered a salary of fifty thousand dollars, which is considerably more than a college professor earns. However, before the position is finalized, the professor and his wife are told that they must be visited in their home by the personnel executive of the company. The professor's hobby is playing the cello and his wife's hobby is writing. You can imagine the amount of music and unfinished manuscript that clutters their home. They also collect and study ancient ceramics, either whole or broken. The comedy begins when the doorbell rings to announce the company visitors. The cello is absent and the desk is transformed into a television table with the manuscript stored in the sound chamber. The visit goes well, but the professor decides that he and his family are not the people the executives in the company think they are accepting. He does not accept the position on the company's terms.

Corporate concern with the personal lives of executives is destructive if it is paternalistic, that is, if the corporation treats its executive and his or her family as if they were children. This generates resentment. In some cases, however, the corporation may not be concerned enough with the problems of personal life, and with the corporation's impact on personal life. This can result in the executive having to spend much time away from his or her family. The company often requires the executive to devote extended hours to the company's business. Community activity may also be expected. Many wives or husbands and children are angry, sometimes not consciously, at being deserted in this way.

People have always, in various ways, conformed to the demands of others in order to survive. To some extent we must all conform to remain in any community or work situation. The corporation does not create the conforming person. However, it may help to increase his or her numbers. Just as it is true that certain kinds of people are attracted to certain communities, so people are attracted to certain companies. For example, people who value job security above rapid promotion will tend to choose banks or public utilities. These institutions, in turn, because they deal in public service, will seek to hire people who can get along well with the public. Thus, in a general way, businesses tend to develop corporate personality types.

In most company structures, people move up because they gain the approval of their superiors. To that extent they conform to superiors' wishes and expectations. Many people are quite comfortable with such arrangements because the organization's controls enhance their personal control. The structure of the organization meets their psychological needs. In some cases, however, they risk losing their own purposes and goals and substitute those of their superiors. This results in subsequent discontent. Many people who wish to do so cannot leave large corporations because they would lose their vested rights in pensions and other benefits. These people often stay with the corporation but are frequently angry and apathetic.

Pecking order

In Chapter 8 of his book, *The Art and Skill of Getting Along with People*, Dr. Sylvanus M. Duvall discusses the importance of position in a group. He says that the "unofficial positions of status, rank, and power include not only those at the top and bottom, but everybody in between. Your relative position—your unofficial position—in any group is something referred to as your position in the 'pecking order.' This is a term that comes from a study of rank among flocks of chickens."[1]

In the study, it was observed that usually every chicken had a definite rank in the flock. Every other chicken knew what that rank was and scrupulously observed it. That is, each chicken knew which other chicken it could peck and which chickens could peck it.

When we think about it, we can see our place in such an order at school, at home, in a club, in church, and perhaps even at work. There are people who defer to you, and people to whom you defer.

In organizations to which you have belonged for a long while, you probably have come to sense who "rates" and who does not, and how much. Groups without formal organization also observe the pecking order. For example, at a class meeting about the annual dinner-dance, Mr. Talk-All-The-Time springs to his feet and gives his ideas

1. From the book *The Art and Skill of Getting Along with People* by Sylvanus Duvall. © 1961 by Prentice-Hall, Inc. Published by Prentice-Hall, Inc., Englewood Cliffs, New Jersey 07632. Used by permission.

on all facets of the party. The class lets him talk, but nobody listens. Miss Able Accomplishment then quietly makes a few proposals to which everyone listens. After discussion, Miss A. makes a final suggestion that is accepted. Of interest, however, is the fact that a person's place in the pecking order will vary in different groups. In the class meeting Miss Accomplishment may be topnotch and the one to whom everyone listens with deference and respect. However, in her church group or her work group, she may be only one of the persons whom everyone likes but whose words hold little significance for anyone.

It is difficult to decide why a person's rank is such-and-such in the pecking order. Here are some factors that Dr. Duvall identified:[2]

2. From the book *The Art and Skill of Getting Along with People* by Sylvanus Duvall. © 1961 by Prentice-Hall, Inc. Published by Prentice-Hall, Inc., Englewood Cliffs, New Jersey 07632. Used by permission.

Official position. (It always helps!) Although, under Mussolini, the King was powerless to affect national policy, he did enjoy status, and even a limited authority which he would not otherwise have had. The mayor who is a puppet of a political boss certainly has more power than he or she would have as an ordinary citizen.

The favor of those in power. Many people enjoy high prestige because they have the ear of the boss. Lysenko was a scientist who was able to talk scientific nonsense in the Soviet Union as long as he had the endorsement of Stalin. Being the fairhaired boy of someone in an important position can put you right up there. All of us try to help our friends. Those in positions of influence are no different. One interesting phase of this came out in a study of a thousand advertising executives who carried briefcases home with them at night. Investigation revealed that two thirds of them never opened their briefcases or did any extra work at home. Their bosses usually knew this. Yet they thought that taking the briefcase home showed the proper spirit. As a result those who brought their briefcases home had conspicuously better chances of promotion than those who did not; another instance of the importance of the favor of those in power.

The disfavor of those in power. Some people are deposed from higher positions, or fail to get promotions, because of antagonisms of those at the top. In this respect not only the higher-ups, but the subordinates may play a part. A group of children take a dislike to a teacher. They are so disorderly and cause so much trouble that officials believe the teacher to be incompetent. Or the group in an office wants to get back at the office manager. They sabotage him on every occasion, and the manager is dismissed. Sometimes such opposition is justified. Sometimes it results because the individual is too honest, too conscientious, and thereby arouses the antagonism of his subordinates.

Some people inherit it. Careful studies have shown that you don't buy your way into the top crust of American society. You must either be born there or marry into it. Business positions are more open. The son of the boss does not always succeed his father, yet there is no doubt that he has the first chance and the inside track. He is given the earliest and best opportunities for learning the business. He has the best contacts. If he has the ability it takes (and sometimes when he doesn't), he will get the top post if he wants it.

Some people are lucky. Luck is far less important than most failures believe, but it does sometimes play a real part—particularly in the matter of timing. A Hollywood scout drops in on a play to see a well-known star. The star is ill and her place is taken by an unknown understudy who does a superb job. Undoubtedly her talents would have come out sometime, but had the star been ill one day earlier or one day later, the movie career of the understudy would have been delayed, possibly for years. Some people have risen to the top because there happened to be a vacancy at the particular time when they were available and others, who might have done as well or better, were not.

A word of caution. Don't be too quick in labeling someone else's success as luck. Sometimes, though it appears to be, it isn't. . . . Sometimes the "lucky" person is one who has prepared himself or herself, watches for breaks, and grabs them when they come.

From the discussion of leadership, you can see that there is a hidden power structure in any group. This is particularly true in the world of work. As the pecking order points out, titled power is not always the effective power. The real leader may be someone with no title at all. Regardless of title, and sometimes in sharp variance with it, each person in any group has his or her place in the "pecking order."

Questions

1. Upon what does good leadership seem to depend?

2. As an executive of a large firm, you are concerned with maintaining good employer-employee relationships. What would be the theme of your instructions to your subordinates at a board meeting?

3. How would you help an employee develop the same perception of the expectations of the job that you, as his or her employer, have?

4. How does the importance of the job affect one of your associates, your parents, or yourself? Give some examples.

5. How do the work "satisfiers" reinforce our basic psychological needs?

6. How can a large business corporation cause one to conform?

7. Now that you are aware of a "pecking order," what are some of your observations about its function in your life?

8. What qualities seem to you to be the most important in a job?

Further reading

Adorno, Theodore W. et al. *The Authoritarian Personality.* New York: W. W. Norton & Co., Inc., 1969.

Allee, Warder C. *The Social Life of Animals.* New York: AMS Press, 1976. (Reprint of 1938 edition.)

Golding, William. *Lord of the Flies.* New York: G. P. Putnam's Sons, 1978.

Herzberg, Frederick et al. *The Motivation to Work.* New York: John Wiley & Sons, Inc., 1959.

Kozlowski, Lynn. *Motivation and Emotion.* New York: Harpers College Press, 1976.

Lasswell, Harold D. *Power and Personality.* Westport, CT: Greenwood Press, Inc., 1976.

Young, Paul T. *Motivation and Emotion.* New York: John Wiley & Sons, Inc., 1961.

Chapter 16

Relationships with love

Everyone has within them the urge to grow toward their fullest potential. The most lasting, worthwhile, and growth-producing love relationships are those that allow each member in the relationship to develop to his or her fullest capacity.

Love should grow. It should not start out full grown and then dwindle. Some of the saddest words are, "I used to love her, we thought we loved each other, or he said he loved me." The love relationship that grows and matures doesn't have these words. For example, Mr. and Mrs. Sanchez are celebrating their tenth wedding anniversary at a dinner for two in an elegant dining room. They begin to reminisce about their days together in college before their marriage, their first apartment . . . suddenly Mary Sanchez laughs and says, "How could I have thought that I loved you enough to marry you? Because in comparison to my love for you now, the love I felt then was small indeed. I wonder if on our twenty-fifth anniversary our love will have grown ever larger—if I'll consider our love now as small in comparison?"

"I hope so," said Mr. Sanchez. "I hope so!"

Definition of love

Today we examine love critically. Love is the ability to form meaningful and satisfying relationships with other human beings. It is essential to successful lives. Just as we play many roles, we have many loves in our lifetime. Past and present love relationships help us build toward future love relationships. Sometimes, if our past and present love experiences are not satisfying, it is difficult to build valuable future relationships.

One of Alice's strange experiences in Wonderland involves a Cheshire cat which sits smiling in a tree. While Alice is chatting with him, all at once the cat begins to disappear, tail first, until little by little the whole cat has vanished and only his smile remains. Alice

FRED BASSET

FRED BASSET by Alex Graham.
© Associated Newspapers Group Ltd., 1978.
Dist. Field Newspaper Syndicate. Reprinted by permission.

objects. She has seen cats without smiles but never a smile without a cat!

We, like Alice, can find a person without love, but not love without a person. Love becomes real through the thoughts and deeds of people in their relationships. We learn to love as we learn other abilities. Love can be given only if it has been received. The ability to love can be likened to a solar cell. The cell cannot work until it is charged. It needs to absorb energy before it can generate energy. Human beings are like the solar cell in their generation of love. They need to receive a great deal of love for a long period of time before they are able to return love to others.

The love ladder

The diagram below shows the stages of love as rungs on a ladder. In order to climb a ladder one cannot start with rung four or five because they are too high. One must start with rung one. The same is true for love. One doesn't start with love for the opposite sex or with marital love. One must start with love for self.

THE STAGES OF LOVE
(The Love Ladder)

10. Love of Another, The One

9. Love of The One

8. Love of Opposite Sex, All

7. Love of Opposite Sex, Older

6. Love of Same Sex, Older

5. Love of Same Sex

4. Love of Peers

3. Love of Entertainment

2. Love of Nurturer

1. Self Love

Stages of love

Self-Love. The first stage of love can only be attained when the basic needs are satisfied. Love is a learned response. One learns to love by being loved. When one's physical needs are cared for and one is comfortable then the world seems good and one can love oneself. The baby who is fed when hungry, given a drink when thirsty, diapered when wet, rocked and sung to when in need of a change of position, cuddled and made to feel secure when feeling alone and alienated is the lucky child who learns self-love. The child who misses all these positives in life is the person who is a seeker, a taker in the love relation. He or she spends much energy trying to gather responses to all of the basic physical and psychological needs discussed in Chapter 1. If this is not realized in childhood then one goes through life seeking this accomplishment. Unfortunately, many people never grow beyond this first rung of the love ladder. So they spend their lives being the takers, the seekers. They are the people who hope that love can fill their barren solar cells or "empty love buckets." The love bucket as referred to here is a metaphor. If one translated the need for love into a bucket one would find people with varying bucket sizes. However, before anyone can give love, that person's love bucket must be filled to overflowing. For example: if person X's love bucket is of one size, then person X can only show love when his or her bucket is brimful and overflowing. The extra love that is splashed out is the love that X can give to others. Thus, those persons whose love buckets are not full must be the takers or receivers of love until their needs are fulfilled. Unfortunately, many people are in this circumstance. However, there is always hope because, in time, if self-love needs are met then one can learn to love.

Love of Nurturer. The first person one learns to love is the nurturer. This is the mother, father, sister, brother or other person, the provider of food, drink, shelter, security, comfort. As the child's needs are met the child identifies with the provider of those needs. As the provider kisses, hugs, smiles, pats or comforts the child, the child returns the same responses as a copying mechanism or response. If the nurturer fulfills the child's needs the child learns to trust, to copy and to identify love and to learn to love.

Love of Entertainer. As the child grows in his or her love responses he or she soon learns that the person who changes the scene is also of importance. Thus, the child learns to respond to the laugh of the entertainer. He or she is the provider of games, the person who plays peek-a-boo, the person who reads stories, or sings songs. Or he or she is the person who visits or becomes a participant in the tea parties, the coloring books, the block building, the puzzle solving, the dances, and the playing with toys.

Love of Peers.   The next rung brings the child to the stage where the presence of another person of the same age is a delight. Playing beside an agemate in parallel play is gratifying. One can observe children playing with great delight in the vicinity of each other. During this stage of love development children enjoy agemates for play interaction. There seems to be no notice of sex or even of age, but just someone who will interact and love on their level. Sometimes during this stage, if a real friend doesn't emerge, the child has a make-believe friend or love object. This make-believe friend often needs to have a place at the table, a special chair. Sometimes this friend is responsible for broken china, eaten cookies, or rules that are not carried out. Often the child and his or her friends have beautiful imaginary adventures. It is great fun to watch children in this stage of love go from lovers, to tea party participants, to pretenders. They may pretend to be animals lapping up water from the same dish. In a matter of a few minutes all of these roles are played.

Love of Same Sex.   Boys with boys, girls with girls is characteristic of this love stage. The same-sex friend is the best friend. The boys have contests to determine who can spit farthest. The girls have contests to see who can ride a bicycle fastest. Often if people during this age are taken to the airport or on a trip, they will hold each other's hands, put their arms around each other, or indulge in other expressions of mutual love and respect. There may be friendly boxing, tumbling or wrestling, or kissing, pushing, and playing with hair or personal items. The same-sex best friend is often annoying to other family members but most important for the individual in his or her growth on the love ladder.

Love of Same Sex, Older.   The child during this stage has an older, same-sex idol. The youngster dresses, talks, walks, and imitates the manner and mannerisms of the older, same-sex idol. The idol may be a favored family member, a neighbor, a Hollywood star, or a famous personality. Often it is a combination of persons from which the youngster draws identity.

Love of Opposite Sex, Older.   During this stage, the person tries out flirtatious behaviors with a safe, older person of the opposite sex.   If there are good relationships in the family, the daughter may try her wiles on Dad while the son tries his line on Mom.   Perhaps you will remember being thrilled about attentions paid by the young, junior high teacher.   This is a natural, normal stage.   But it can meet with tragedy if the older person doesn't understand the advances of the younger person and actually acts on the offered behavior.

Love of the Opposite Sex, All.   This stage is often termed girl crazy or boy crazy.   The young person is interested in the opposite sex with no reservations.   For girls, if it's a boy, I'm interested.   For boys, girls are first in their thinking.   If the individual is alone, his or her thoughts are of the opposite sex.   Very often, boys at this stage draw sketches of girls.   The girls doodle love symbols while daydreaming about boys.

Love of the One.   Then one day, the marvelous creature of the opposite sex actually selects you to go some place.   It is so special and so exciting.   Who would believe that someone would actually prefer your company?   Thus the young person falls madly in love.   He or she is in love with love and only sees his or her partner through rose-colored glasses.   To him or her, the chosen person represents all of the positive characteristics of the opposite sex.   The fact that their romanticized version may be far from truth is of no importance.   This stage is sometimes called "puppy love" but nevertheless it is a very important rung on the love ladder.   When this attachment breaks up the individuals feel great hurt from a love lost.

Love of Another, the One.   Now, the individual is more willing to see his or her companion in his or her true light.   The love relationship is more realistic.   The loved one is seen as having some negative characteristics along with the positive ones.   In this stage there are several "the ones" with the individuals seeing themselves and their lovers more clearly each time.   After a period of successful dating one finally finds "the One" and the highest rung is reached with an ongoing, growing love relationship that endures.

Up and down the ladder.   Life and life circumstances push and pull us up and down on the love ladder.   For example, one finds the one, marries, and has an ongoing love relationship.   Then if the loved one dies, society expects the survivor to move back on the love ladder at

Reprinted by permission of Robert Censoni.
From *Saturday Review/World,* © 1974.

"I have a surprise for you, George.
Remember when I said we never do anything together?"

least to rung three or four, back with peers or back with same sex. The wife who loses her husband or the husband who loses his wife can now expect to do things with friends or with relatives. If she or he dates anyone of the opposite sex too soon, people may question the relationship.

Sometimes the venturing on the love ladder leads to too much too soon. In order to explain this concept, let's consider June D. June went away to college, lived in a co-ed dorm, and was overwhelmed by the attention she received from Chris R. She became pregnant. Chris wanted her to put the child up for adoption. After the adoption, June went back to school. By now Chris was interviewing for jobs and furthering his career. June felt alone and lonely so she returned to her parents. June returned to rung two of the love ladder. She now needs to work her way back up toward the goal of finding "the One."

Stages of love development

Love development starts with birth. It should be a step-by-step process that progresses through life to death.

Little babies are capable of loving no one at first. They have not had enough experience even to be aware that there are other persons to love. So they love their fingers and toes. They enjoy their bodies in a vigorous, lusty way as they kick, jabber, and laugh. This is called self-love.

It is quite possible that from time to time one still feels and acts as he or she did in that first stage. Haven't you seen yourself and others in front of a mirror admiring that new hair style, a new haircut, a dimple, or a clean shave?

This stage is so apt to recur all through life that we have a name for it, narcissism or self-love. This word comes from the old Greek story of Narcissus who fell in love with his own image in a quiet pool of water. He so adored his reflection that he pined away and died. Whereupon the flower that bears his name sprang up to mark his resting place. Today when persons love and admire themselves, we call them narcissistic.

Babies form their first attachment or love for the persons who satisfy their needs. In our society this is usually the mother. We have seen how the infant, taking food from his or her mother, becomes attached to the hand that feeds him or her, the arms that hold him or her. The child becomes attached to the mother figure or the person who is meeting his or her needs. As awareness of reality grows, the infant comes to realize how very little he or she can do for himself or herself. Mother, who does everything for him or her, represents solace, satisfaction, security. This type of love is called mother and/or father love.

The next significant period of love comes between the ages of six and twelve. The child has stepped out into a larger world. The world encourages him or her to form social attachments. These social attachments are usually with youngsters of the same sex.

These new relationships or loves are for the most part asexual. Boys play with boys, girls play with girls. A boy who shows an interest in girls is considered a sissy. A girl who wants to play with boys is called a tomboy. It is a period when children are encouraged to develop and accept their sexual roles in life by pursuing all the interests characteristic of their masculinity or femininity, with one exception: an interest in the opposite sex.

What kind of a woman will I be?

This is the age when a girl asks, "What is it like to be a woman? What kind of woman do I want to be?" To help her make this identification, she watches older women and has movie stars, outstanding women athletes, or some other famous women as her idols. She tries to be close to an older sister, to her mother, or to any favorite adult to see how they act in the hope of answering her questions.

Boys in this age group form attachments to male heroes. They too, are trying to answer the same questions. "What kind of man do I want to be? What is it like to be a man?"

It is important that boys and girls of this age are in close contact with adults with whom they can identify. This means adults who recognize the reasons behind these attachments and do not rebuff or ridicule young people for their efforts to please. The typical experience of the youngster falling in love with his or her coach, doctor, or college-age neighbor should be a happy one, guided and understood by the adults involved. It is a further step in the direction of the mature, heterosexual love which unites people in marriage.

"Love for love's sake" and "in love with love" are phrases that describe the stage of love development which encompasses love for all members of the opposite sex. Adolescents want to be where other adolescents are. Boys and girls at this stage of development need the hangout, ice cream shop, or youth center where they can come into contact with each other. They need the gang or crowd. Even though an individual has this great interest in the opposite sex, he or she isn't sure enough of himself or herself alone. He or she needs the security of the crowd and the noise of the records to cover up his or her own verbal inadequacies. He or she needs the chance to observe and to talk to many girls and boys. In this way he or she can begin to narrow his or her ideas about the kind of person he or she really likes.

When the individual passes this stage, the field has been narrowed. The young woman says she likes a boy who has certain characteristics that are important to her. She has developed standards for her dates. She knows the kind of boy from whom she will accept a date. She can say "no" to invitations from boys who do not meet her ideals. She has matured in her attachments. She is no longer in love with boys but interested in certain boys.

The young man also has developed a list of characteristics he is looking for in the girls he dates. He has an idea of the kind of woman he wants for his wife. He has given some thought to the type of home that he would like to have and to foster. The early rush for many dates and many types of dates has now been altered. He also dates with more definite ideas and ideals in mind.

Peer love.

Competitive fun.

Finally the love attachments settle on the one. The focus is on this person because he or she seems to be one's ideal and complements one's personality. One would rather be with this person than with anyone else.

Mature love for others

The person who has successfully come up the ladder of love development eventually reaches a kind of love that affects those with whom he or she is in closest contact. In addition it affects many people whom he or she has never met. He or she is concerned with the responsibility to all other people. Such an attitude is considered mature love for others. He or she does things to promote human welfare. The person feels warmly toward the men and women and children whom he or she meets. He or she has faith in the power of parental, fraternal, and romantic love. Mature love enables a person to promote brotherhood by helping to provide an opportunity for all to develop their best potentials and by giving the gift of loving support to enrich positive efforts. While it inevitably leads one into hard work and some difficult trials, this kind of love builds character. Its strength comes from an inner peace that enables one to bear the hardships of life. It can be attained only through the mastery of the other stages of love development that lead to it.

Love and infatuation

To love a person, one must know that person. What usually happens in "love at first sight" is that the two people are strongly attracted to each other, perhaps even infatuated, from the very beginning. Then this strong attraction develops into love without any break in the process. It only seems as if it were love at first sight.

Love at first sight may also be compulsive in nature. A person has a strong urge to love someone. This urge becomes focused on a particular person. What should be expressed as "This is the person I must love" is expressed by the persons concerned as "This is the person I do love."[1]

Such an urge to love is not uncommon during adolescence. This is the time when new emotions, with which the young person has not yet learned to live and which are largely the result of physical and psychological development rather than experience, begin to well up within the person. Such "love" may also be an outgrowth of a person's feeling of inferiority or the fear that he or she may never marry because of personal unattractiveness or the inability to meet members of the opposite sex.

Love grows out of an appraisal of all the known characteristics of the other person. Infatuation may arise from an acquaintance with only one of these characteristics.

When an individual is genuinely in love, he or she is in love with the other person as a total personality. His or her feelings grow primarily out of the relationship with that other person and his or her estimate of that person. An infatuated individual may be "in love with love."

Love is other-person centered. It is outgoing. It results in sharing. Infatuation is in contrast, self-centered. The other person is a means of self-satisfaction.

An individual in love works for the other person or for their mutual benefit. He or she may study to make the other person proud of him or her. Ambition thus spurred, he or she may plan and save for the future. This person may daydream, but the dreams are reasonably attainable. An infatuated person may lose ambition, appetite, and interest in everyday affairs. He or she often daydreams, but the dreams are not limited to the attainable but are given free rein.

---

1. Willard Waller, *The Family; A Dynamic Interpretation.* (New York: Dial Press, A Cordon Book, 1938), p. 284.

Love leads to idealization. But, because the ideal is partly an outgrowth of understanding and appreciation for another, it may be checked against reality without loss. In infatuation there tends to be idealization accompanied by a disregard of reality.

Two people in love face problems frankly and attempt to solve them. In infatuation, problems tend to be disregarded or glossed over.

Physical attraction is a relatively small part of a total relationship when a couple is in love. But it is a relatively greater part when the two are infatuated. Let us imagine, for example, that physical attraction is represented by a three-inch square. In infatuation, this square is part of a four-inch square; in love, however, it is part of a twelve-inch square because there are so many other considerations.

With mature people in love, an expression of affection tends to come relatively late in the couple's relationship. In infatuation it may come earlier, sometimes from the very beginning.

When a couple is in love, the physical contact that they have tends to have meaning as well as to be a pleasurable experience. But physical love is not usually considered an end in itself. It tends to express what the couple feels toward each other. In infatuation, physical contact tends to be an end in itself. For most infatuated people it represents only pleasurable experience, without meaning.

Love tends to endure. Infatuation may change suddenly, unexpectedly, and unpredictably. When love changes, the reasons tend to be more or less apparent. Infatuation may change for no apparent reason.

Two people in love are not indifferent to the effects of postponing their wedding. They do not prolong the period of postponement unduly, but they can usually wait a reasonable time. Most do not feel an almost irresistible urge toward haste. They tend to think of the period of postponement as one of further preparation. An infatuated couple tends to feel an urge toward immediate marriage. Postponement is intolerable to them. They interpret it as deprivation rather than preparation.

Complexities of love

The word love tends to be talked about without due consideration of its intended meaning. One may love to participate in certain activities or love to collect items and cherish the collection. One may love to eat certain foods or listen to a particular composer or a favorite musician. Thus one may say that he or she loves cats, loves oranges, or loves sports. Yet the word love as used in these examples is on a much lower plane than the word love which is told to a parent or husband or wife.

The facets of love that make this emotion generally sparkle are the relationships that produce a shared affection. To love and to be loved by a person is the brightest facet of all. The person who loves to hear of your experiences and whose touch and presence brighten your day is wonderful.

Marital love

A marriage based on a deep, shared love can be the very best kind of love. When two people love each other with romantic love, intellectual love, and physical or sexual love, they have the three ingredients for a mature and lasting love relationship. Romantic love is often described as the love of the courtship and honeymoon. Romantic love is the smile across the room, the kiss on the nape of the neck, the bouquet of roses, the thoughtful note, and the hand that pats a tired shoulder.

Intellectual love is the respect for the other person's intelligence, integrity, and opinion. It is the willingness to try to understand another's point of view. This love is probably the most important of all three. The respect for the intellect of another person is the foundation of conversation and communication. Without a sharing of ideas, ideals, opinions, and thoughts as well as humor, a couple cannot build companionship. Intellectual love is the basis of all relationships. It is an integral part of a lasting marriage relationship.

Sexual love is the joy of the other person's embrace, the warmth of physical closeness, and the desire to be the shared parent of a child that may be created from this love.

Love, however, is often identified and confused with sex. Sexual love is certainly a part of marriage, but only a part. For love to grow the other parts, romantic love and intellectual love, must be present. The amount of each of these loves will vary, because two people love each other as a result of mutual attraction.

For a lasting love relationship, each type of love—romantic, intellectual, and sexual—must be put into proper perspective and balance by the couple themselves.

Questions

1. What is the difference between love and infatuation?

2. We learn to love just as we learn to eat, walk, and read. Discuss the life experiences that are important in developing the ability to love.

3. How is love diffused to others?

4. What factors are involved when love dwindles?

5. What is narcissism?

6. Love involves empathy with the loved one.   Explain.

7. What are the three kinds of love that enhance a mature relationship?   Explain each.

Further reading

Bowman, Henry A., and Spanier, Graham B.   *Marriage for Moderns.* 8th ed.   New York: McGraw-Hill, 1978.

Duvall, Evelyn M.   *Marriage and Family Development.*   Philadelphia, PA: J. B. Lippincott Company, 1971.

Landis, Paul H.   *Your Marriage and Family Living.* 4th ed.   New York: McGraw-Hill, 1977.

May, Rollo.   *Love and Will.*   New York: Dell Publishing Co., Inc., 1974.

Chapter 17

Relationships in dating

Our relationships in dating occur in accordance with the kinds of persons we meet and the kinds of persons we are. Our social ability and our social competence determine the kinds of people who want to meet us.

Reprinted by permission of Jack Tippit.
From *Ladies' Home Journal*, © 1974 LHJ Publishing, Inc.

"You gotta watch out for *that* one . . . he'll give you a frog
and then forget all about you!"

Likes and dislikes

We have all at times wondered why we like some people at first
glance. We wonder why we have to know some people for a long
time before we begin to like them. We may wonder why we immediately dislike other people. Our likes and dislikes are not planned.
They have a basis in our individual make-up and in our past and
present experiences.

In dating, it is important to be aware of the principles of attraction. This is particularly true if we are attracted to the people who
are considered attractive by our friends and peers. Often when we
go with the crowd, we betray ourselves. We should remember that
we have individual needs. Conforming to the crowd's standards for
a date may not let us meet or date the person we can respect and love.

We should also consider our stage of maturity when we reject the
date that our parents recommend. We should ask ourselves if we
really reject the person or if we are just negative because we are
trying to establish our independence.

The persons who have grown up in homes where their needs were
met and who want to establish a home similar to their parental home
have an easier task in dating. They know the relationships that they

want to create and maintain. Whereas, they have a pattern to follow, those who reject their past home relationships look for something opposite. However, they are always confronted with the questions pertaining to the nature of being "opposite" or "different." They don't know what they are looking for because they have no pattern.

This lack of home pattern makes it necessary for one to be more cautious in the search for a mate. Coming from unhappy or broken homes, however, does not mean that persons cannot create happy homes. It just means that those persons need additional experiences in living before they can establish the kinds of homes that they seek.

When men or women are old enough to think of marriage, they may unconsciously seek out mates who resemble their parent of the opposite sex as they remember that parent from childhood days. They also may tend to see their role in the newly created home as played by the parent of the same sex. Thus, if one is unable to identify with his or her parents, he or she must make new identities which makes the task more difficult, but not impossible.

We tend to reproduce those relationships in which we found comfort as children. We are attracted to people who remind us of positive feelings and experiences in the past.

Principles of attraction

The principles of attraction are some of the unconscious tendencies that determine our preference for people.

1. We tend to like the people and the things that remind us of pleasant and comfortable experiences in our past, many of which go way back into our early childhood and are forgotten except for the powerful, unconscious role they continue to play in our choices. "I loved him the minute I set eyes upon him."

2. We tend to be repulsed by the people and the things that are associated with uncomfortable and unpleasant experiences in our past. The original, painful experience may no longer be remembered, but its influence continues to deflect us from anything and anybody that resembles some aspect of that unhappy situation. "Don't ask me why, I just don't like her."

3. We tend to be attracted to those people who reassure us, do not make us feel less worthy or less able or attractive than we like to think we are. "She's much too smart to suit me," or "I can't stand

him, he's always so superior," and "She makes me feel as though I am somebody."

4. We tend to seek the people who are considered attractive by those around us and to leave the unsought alone. "I want the kind of girl the other fellows will whistle at."

5. We tend to like those who satisfy some particularly hungry spot in our makeup. The boy who has not had as much mother love as he wanted may be strongly attracted to a mother type of girl.

6. We tend both to reproduce and to repudiate the relationships in which we grew up. A boy may be attracted to anyone who reminds him of his mother and who can reproduce the feeling of the old parent-child relationships. A girl may be unable to tolerate anyone who even remotely reminds her of her father, a repudiation of the former parent-child relationships. "I want a girl just like the girl who married dear old dad," or "I can't stand her. Who does she think she is, my mother?"[1]

The more attraction principles any one person has in his or her favor, the more attracted we are toward that person. For example: Helen, likes her father very much. She likes his mannerisms, the cool feel of his hands and his ability to fix things. Helen begins to date Don. She notices that Don likes to fix things, has hands that are cool to the touch. He reminds her of the positive mannerisms seen in her dad. Don is also popular with Helen's closest friends. Don also makes Helen feel witty, pretty, and capable. Don and Helen like to ride bicycles, read, and play accordion duets together. Don also likes to play the guitar while Helen sings. Thus, this relationship is strong because it reinforces four of the principles of attraction.

Opposites do not attract. Opposites may intrigue, fascinate, and interest us for a period of time, but a long-term relationship cannot exist between opposites. For example, if you are a person who always tells the truth, is responsible for your behavior, and respects property you cannot live with someone who lies, is irresponsible, wastes materials, and destroys property. The person who is extremely shy may enjoy the company of someone who is outgoing and able to meet friends. But the shy person is repelled by someone who expects or forces him or her to take the lead in social functions. Opposites repel. We are attracted to those who complement and enhance our attributes. We are not attracted to those who are totally opposite from us.

1. From p. 34 of *When You Marry* by Evelyn Duvall and Reuben Hill. © 1971. Used by permission of the publisher, D. C. Heath and Company.

Reasons for dating

Dating gives a person a chance to learn the ways of others without any permanent commitment or involvement. He or she is largely a product of his or her own experiences and family environment. Each person's ideas of people are conditioned by the characteristics of parents and close associates. Adequate evaluation of a possible mate means, most often, that persons outside the family need to be known and understood in the ways in which they think, act, and plan. Only as one has more acquaintances is a person free from the limitations of choice and action that are unconsciously imposed by the home environment.

Dating also affords a person an opportunity to improve communication and social maturity with members of the opposite sex. It takes time and experience to develop maturity in the heterosexual stage of psychosexual development. Dating gives a person a natural experience in which to develop these necessary social graces and competencies.

In addition, dating affords opportunities for young people to share with others the adjustments to the responsibilities of adulthood. For example, they become responsible for their conduct together without the watchful eye of parents or friends. They adjust to the possibilities for entertainment on a date. They adjust to the limitations imposed by money, transportation problems, and age requirements.

STAGES OF INVOLVEMENT

Completely
Unattached

Completely
Committed

Not dating

Casual dating only

Going steady,
for convenience only

Going steady,
with private understanding:
informal engagement

Formal engagement

They learn to respect differences in choices and decisions. They try to solve these differences in a mature manner. In short, they are learning to see to the welfare and well-being of the dating partner.

Current dating patterns

To discover what boys look for in girls and what girls look for in boys, the author talked with four classes of juniors and seniors who were studying marriage and the family. The students said that their expectations for dating partners were different from their expectations for possible marriage choices.

The boys said that for a date they were first impressed with appearance, personality, a sense of humor, an ability to participate in the activity of the date such as playing tennis, bowling, bicycling, and the popularity of the girl with their peers.

The girls said that for a date they were impressed with the boy's cleanliness or grooming, not necessarily his good looks, his cleanliness in speech and action, his popularity with the peer group, and what he liked to do on a date. The girls said that the boy's reputation was important. They also felt that the boy needed to provide some means of transportation. A car was important to a date. Both girls and boys felt that one dated for fun and excitement or a new experience so the date that was the most fun was the best date.

The boys said that their expectations changed if they were considering the girl seriously. Then her ability, her personality, and her character traits were more important than her looks. They preferred the girl whom they would consider marrying to be understanding, a good listener, and capable of managing a home and children.

The girls' expectations for mate selection were the boy's ability to earn a living, his loyalty to her and their marriage, his ideals, values, goals, his intelligence, and his desire for a normal family life and children.

Breaking-up

Breaking-up is hard to do. However, continuing a relationship when you are no longer really interested in the partner can be more difficult for both of you. When your dating has progressed to the point where it is not growing in a positive way, perhaps the relationship is over and it is time to date others. To continue a relationship when you are no longer interested in the other person is detrimental for each of you. So the best way to face a breaking-up is straightaway.

Many times damage is done if we break off a relationship by making up false excuses, by telling our story of disinterest to others who, in turn, are supposed to tell our date, or if we just get angry as an excuse to get out of the relationship. The truth may be painful but it is more reliable.

In breaking-up, find a time when both of you are free to talk out your feelings. Tell your partner those things about him or her that you like and have really appreciated. Tell the facts straight and as sincerely as possible as to why you want to end the relationship. Recognize that breaking-up is difficult. Appreciate the deep emotions that are felt. Listen to your partner. Try to see the partner's side of the breaking-up. Study each other's comments. Really use your communication skills. Recognize that the one you loved is neither a beast nor a heartless creature. Realize that the breaking-up has not destroyed everything you shared. It just leaves both of you free to recover and work at gaining the confidence to date and to love again.

Often consolation comes from recognizing that we can all grow from every relationship. It takes many dates and many different dating partners before we know what we want in a marriage partner. Some people return to a former partner after experience.

If you have been someone's steady date, then you are probably out of circulation. After the breaking-up you will be lonely, alienated from the group of daters, and free with time on your hands. Use that time to make yourself into a better partner—sharpen your skills. This is a good time to learn something new, to read, to learn a new sport or new game, to renew your friendships, to rejoin your family, to visit places of interest, or to revisit old haunts.

The dating process

The dating process is the chief method of mate selection in the United States. *Dating failure or courtship failure is the main cause of marriage failure.* Knowing how to meet and develop relationships with a number of potential marriage partners helps in self-understanding. Being able to date, so that one is free to become aware of personal values, emotional needs, interests, goals, and wishes enables one to choose wisely. When one dates, one is interested in developing the social skills of listening, conversing, and being considerate. Getting to know many different types of people with a variety of personality traits helps one to know oneself better. One can also gain insight into the kind of person with whom one would like to share his or her life. When young daters are afraid to break up or do not benefit from breakups, this is dating failure which causes marriage failure. In order to find the best mate one must be willing to look and to listen to the dictates of his or her heart, friends, values, and families. The best ally in the dating process is time. Time helps you to know yourself, to know your dating partner, and to grow into a couplehood. However, before one can become part of a couplehood, individualhood and/or adulthood should be accomplished. Partners need to mature enough to be aware of their strongest needs and the types of people with whom they are most comfortable, compatible, and companionable.

Questions

1. Give an example of experiences that you have had that explain the principles of attraction.

2. When is dating a person considered attractive by the peer group an advantage? a disadvantage?

3. How might your present home affect your choice of a dating partner?

4. Explain the statement: Opposites do not attract—opposites repel.

5. List five reasons for dating.

6. How have dating partners changed?

7. Why are breakups important to dating?

8. What is the value of time in the process of dating?

9. Why is it easier for one who has made a positive identification with home and parents to establish his or her own home than it is for one who rejects his or her home and parents?

Further reading

Duvall, Evelyn, and Hill, Reuben. *When You Marry.* Lexington, MA: D. C. Heath & Company, 1971.

Rogers, Carl R. *Becoming Partners.* New York: Delacorte Press, imprint of Dell Publishing Co., Inc., 1973.

Skolnick, Arlene. *The Intimate Environment: Exploring Marriage and the Family.* Boston: Little, Brown & Company, 1973.

Chapter 18

Relationships with questions of behavior

Questions of behavior have always been difficult.
How should I act?   What does this person expect of
me?   What kind of person do I want to spend my life
with?   What should my code of behavior be?

All of these questions plus many more are a part of and confused with our sexual attractions, sexual images, and sense of self. A person's inner dialogue can dramatically affect the outcome of a first meeting. People with self-confidence have a different inner dialogue than those without confidence. A person without self-confidence, for example, has an inner voice which says, "I wonder if I look right? I wonder what the other person is thinking about me now? I'm afraid that this person won't like me." On the other hand, the person with self-confidence has an inner voice which says, "I wonder what I can do to make this person feel more comfortable?" Thus the self-confident person tries to put others at ease. This sets off a chain reaction. He or she feels comfortable and likes the feeling. So others like the person for giving them the same comfortable feeling.

Moral codes in transition

On every side society is bombarded with examples of public and private immorality. It is as though expediency and opportunism are the base of ethics.

Moral choices are not easy. Society does not have standard, clear-cut, ready answers. Sex has come to play a role in every facet of life. Sex is used to sell everything from refrigerators to automobiles. Both sexes seek provocative appearances. Studies and surveys indicate a rise in sexual promiscuity.

The Judeo-Christian code is taught by adults as the most meaningful code to follow. However, the adult world does not provide enough models who live by this code. Adults often live by one standard but talk another. This is evident in the adult world's frustrated and

From *Saturday Review/World.* © 1974.
Reprinted by permission of *Saturday Review* and Nurit Karlin.

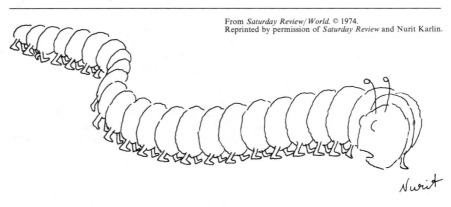

"Twenty-two's out of step. Pass it on."

juvenile obsession with sex. This obsession saturates the adolescent world with inescapable and distorted images. Yet the political speech-making and educational sermonizing stress such phrases as "moral and spiritual values" in a way that makes them appear to be a commodity to be bought and delivered, quite apart from the realities of life.

We must realize that there have always been people who deviated from society's moral codes with regard to sex. We have always had unwed mothers, illegitimate babies, venereal disease, and a variety of sexual practices that have led to serious consequences. Statistics show a continued increase in promiscuous behavior. Theories on promiscuity are numerous. Such behavior has become a subject of ever-increasing concern.

Premarital sex has various meanings for people. It can symbolize a struggle for independence, a desire to expedite maturity, or a need to keep up with the crowd and prove oneself. It can represent rejection of parents, teachers, or authority in general. It can be an expression of loneliness and a wish for affection. Or it can be used as a commodity. It may also occur as an aspect of the commitment of an engaged couple.

Recognizing the widespread confusion on the subject, one must either adopt traditional sex ethics and sex codes or develop a code which is personal but which also considers others. The widespread disregard of traditional codes of sex behavior and the increasing willingness to bring into the open relationships which have been considered wrong make it necessary for people to choose their own course of action. A person's choice will be most satisfactory if he or she understands the development of the person. Then in turn he or she understands self in relation to his or her own developmental stage. Some say that the break from the traditional codes gives a person freedom. Freedom, however, involves a willingness to take responsibility for one's own actions.

The responsibility for the adoption of an ethical code of sexual behavior is up to you. Its success or failure will depend upon your self-understanding, your ability to carry out the code in your life, and your capacity to make wise decisions and to assume responsibility for those decisions. You have the freedom of making choices. Once those choices are made, you are the one responsible for them.

Basis for decision

What value standards should one use in sex behavior? The decision will be easier if we think about the attitudes, decisions, and actions which seem to be most beneficial to the persons concerned.

If one acts to develop the following qualities, he or she has acted in the best interest of self and others.

1. increased capacity to trust people

2. greater integrity in relationships

3. cooperative attitudes

4. enhanced self-respect

5. general attitudes of faith and confidence in people

6. fulfillment of individual potentialities and a zest for living

If, instead, actions produce the qualities listed below, a person is being detrimental to self and to his or her relationships with others.

1. increased distrust of people

2. deceit and duplicity in relationships

3. barriers between persons and groups

4. resistant, uncooperative attitudes

5. diminished self-respect

6. exploitive behavior toward others

7. thwarted and dwarfed individual capacities and disillusionment

Perhaps another scale or balance that would help in making a decision would be for us to look at the requisites for maintaining love. As this author sees it, the requisites for the maintenance of love are these.

1. involvement in the welfare of the other

2. loyalty and trust

3. acceptance of the other with all his or her faults as well as his or her virtues

4. taking delight in the person, not for what he or she ought to be, but for what he or she is

5. willingness to put oneself in the other's place and, in addition, a desire to improve and make that place as happy as possible

If an individual acts in accordance with the ideas expressed above and in the illustration, the relationships with self and others will be more fulfilling and satisfying. If more people thought about their actions in these terms, perhaps it would then be possible to avoid unfair or hasty judgments concerning moral or immoral behavior.

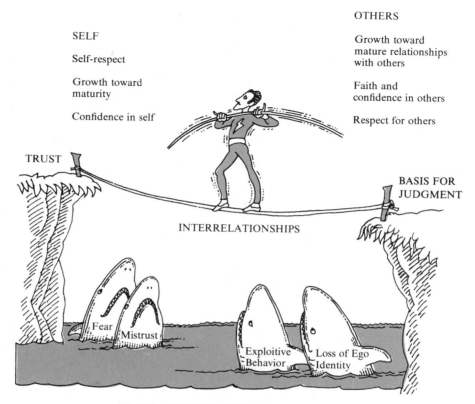

TO BALANCE OUR LIVES WE NEED
TRUST AND AN IDENTITY

Ethics and codes

Ethics is the discipline of moral values and duties, the study of the ideal human character. Moral codes are concerned with regulating human behavior so that a social order can be established and maintained. For example, it is important for children to know who their parents are. If there were no rules for behavior, a woman might not know which man was the father of her child. The man wouldn't know which child he fathered. In order for property to be passed down to children or inherited, the family needs to establish order. For the care, safety, and security of each person ethical standards need to be set. Such standards are developed to prevent injury or damage to others.

A case study

This incident in the lives of two young adults may bring about discussion that may help you make some personal decisions about your own ethical code.

This is the story of a girl we shall call Linda Ryder. She is 19, and when interviewed she was expecting a baby. She is a blonde girl with violet eyes and a habit of plucking at the long hair which keeps drifting over the right side of her face. She was wearing a simple skirt and white blouse. In spite of her pregnancy there was about her the coltish awkwardness of youth. She is a resident of the Florence Crittenden Home in Washington, D.C.

"They say it's the good girls who get caught," Linda said. "I was always a good girl, except with Joey. It isn't that I didn't know what we were doing. I guess it just never seems like it could happen to me."

Linda lived in a pleasant suburb of Philadelphia. Her father owns a small business in town; her mother is a partner in an interior decorating firm. Linda has a 14 year old brother.

Linda herself was always a pretty, popular girl. She brought friends home and never went with a wild crowd. At the end of her first college term she met Joey. "He was awfully goodlooking and a wonderful dancer, but that wasn't it. It sounds silly, but there was something in his eyes. He'd been hurt a lot, and his home hadn't been happy, and he didn't have any money at all. He was so sad and lonely.

"We just began going together. We read and studied together, and we talked about how much better this was than going out all the time with lots of different people. We used to talk about how this was the good kind of love, not like you get from your parents. I think they love you sometimes as if—well, almost the way a child loves a teddy bear. With us it wasn't like that. We were comfortable, and it really was good—then anyway.

"The rest just happened. We didn't use any—well take any precautions. It wasn't that we didn't know the facts of life. It just didn't seem right to be so businesslike about it."

Last April Linda and Joey made a mistake in timing. Linda had a feeling she was pregnant even before the biological signs. When the signs were unmistakable, her fear exploded into panic: "I cut a lot of classes. I began to go to the movies, why I don't know. I couldn't face telling Mother. And I couldn't bear what knowing about me would have done to Daddy."

Having to confide in someone, she told a more experienced girl friend. "I went to visit her for a weekend," said Linda, "and we tried everything from hot baths to hot gin. For three days I was the cleanest, drunkest pregnant girl in Eastern Pennsylvania. Nothing worked."

Linda lived alone with her knowledge for three weeks. "It seemed more like months," she recalled. "I didn't want to tell Joey, but finally I couldn't stand it anymore. I told him after class one day. He was drinking an orange soda. It's silly to remember that now, but he changed right from that minute. I know it took weeks, but slowly but surely he began to disintegrate right in front of my eyes. Right then all he said was, 'Oh, God, no,' and then we walked back to his apartment. We didn't say anything for a long time. I felt I couldn't reach him anymore. Finally I made him tell me what he was thinking, and he said, 'I'm sitting here being ashamed of you. God help me, I'm ashamed of you.' "

During the next awful week Linda and Joey drove to another town, where, under an assumed name, Linda got medical confirmation of her pregnancy. On the ride back they talked about an abortion, but neither of them had the money. "I never really wanted one anyway—not really," said Linda.

"I didn't mention marriage. I was waiting for him to. I didn't even mean it would have to be right then, but all he ever said was that it would be a disaster. Maybe he was scared. You know, it's awful when you know you aren't going to marry someone ever, ever, ever. You start questioning how much you really did love each other.

"From then things got worse. A couple of times he got really drunk, and once he even asked me how he could be sure the baby was his. I saw him only once after that.

"After we broke up I couldn't study any more at all. Then I had to tell Mother. When I finally got it out she just looked at me and then walked out of the room. When she came back the first thing she said was, 'We can't tell your father. He couldn't stand it.' "

Mrs. Ryder moved promptly on the practical arrangements. Through a family agency in Philadelphia she got maternity-home reservations. Through a friend she got Linda a job to keep her busy. Two months later Mrs. Ryder told Linda it was time to go away—before her father found out or the family's reputation was compromised. "It was sort of an ultimatum," Linda said. They told her father that Linda was going to visit a girl friend who had moved to Kansas. "We said it was because of the courses I'd flunked that I wasn't going back to school for a year," she said. And just about the time she would have been reentering college, Linda, alone again, got on the train for Washington and the Florence Crittenden Home. "There are people here I can talk to, and that helps," Linda said. "It's easier for some people to forgive than for others." Her mother has not been able to get down to see her.

So she waited. "The baby would be adopted," Linda said, "because I don't think any unmarried girl has the right to keep her baby, I don't think it's fair to the child.

"It's funny, though, a lot of the girls don't feel it, and I know I don't have the right. But I'm starting to feel like a mother and that this is also a child who will need a mother."

Linda hopes to be able to return to school, perhaps living with an aunt in Philadelphia and working part-time to help pay the bills. Beyond that, she doesn't know. "I want a home. I want to be married. I want children I can keep and love. Maybe that's why I'm here. Maybe I just need someone to love. I've been so lonely. . . ."[1]

Some other thoughts on sexual morality

Sexual Morality

Written by a high school girl—
Fall 1973

I don't believe in premarital sex. My reasons are personal.

I was raised with the idea that premarital sex wasn't good because there's such a big responsibility involved when you're playing with life. I was convinced that sex should wait for marriage, but then I met Dave. I grew to love him more strongly than I ever thought possible. Our relationship started growing strong physically and I was very confused because too much was happening too fast. I soon started thinking sex was all right because I loved him. He said we'd some day get married. I was virgin but there was peer pressure saying it's all right if you love him. I went along with it but all along I kept feeling such guilt. My friends told me sex would enforce our relationship but all it seemed to do was stagnate our relationship.

No longer did Dave just enjoy being with me doing the old things we thought were so much fun. He became preoccupied with sex. I wanted to get out of this jam. I began to realize Dave didn't love me anymore. I was just his possession. I told him I wanted to stop

1. From "Mothers Without Joy" by Jonathan Rinehart in *The Saturday Evening Post*, March 23, 1963. Reprinted by permission of the author.

behaving like this. But he said if I didn't give him what he wanted he'd leave me. I didn't want this to happen, so I gave him what he wanted. Such guilt overcame me that I was beginning to develop an ulcer. Then it happened; I was pregnant. I confronted Dave with it and he wouldn't believe me. He wouldn't pay for an abortion. I had to tell my parents. They were hurt but not as much as I was. Shame and guilt were all I felt. I realized how childish and foolish I was in believing it couldn't happen to me. I thought that Dave would marry me. I also fooled myself by going against my own moral standards and telling myself it was all right. This was the worst mistake I made. I should have trusted my own beliefs and none of this would have happened.

I don't think most of the girls who endorse premarital sex really know what they're committing. They've never been faced with a crisis such as unwanted pregnancy. They haven't realized how little the boy respects you if you give in.

My experience made me grow up so fast. I wish other girls would know what I know without having to do what I did to learn. I know I want sex but along with it I want love, respect, and responsibility. Only in marriage do I feel I can find this.

I wish girls would realize you don't find this in premarital relations. I've talked with a lot of guys. They all admit if a girl will give it to them, they'll take it, regardless if they love them or not. Sex does not always mean love. I wish others would learn this. It would save them from a lot of grief and harsh feelings.

I've made a mistake yet I've learned from it. I want so much more than sex out of a relationship. The pleasure of the mind is gratifying. It's wonderful just to enjoy being with each other and getting to really know each other. Sex can wait!

Sexual Morality

Written by a High School girl in
Fall of 1978

My morality code in regard to sex centers around the basic idea that sex is a very beautiful, tender act of love. It is for this reason that I believe in waiting until marriage before having sex.

When young unmarried people have sexual relations with each other, they are apt to encounter problems. They may have to face such situations as an unwanted pregnancy and venereal disease. Another serious problem involved in premarital sex is the emotional aspect.

Many young people become very disappointed and depressed when they fail to achieve the beauty of sex. By this, I am referring to the idea that sex will make them more of a man or woman. Their first disappointment often turns them off of sex completely.

These are just a few reasons why I believe in waiting until marriage. In my opinion sex is more than a physical action. It is an emotional act of love.

Though I myself do not believe in premarital sex, I do not condemn others. It has to be a personal choice. I do think, however, that each individual should consider all the possible consequences.

My sexual code is not limited to premarital sex. I have certain values in regard to petting and simple necking. I don't believe in petting because of the fact that once a couple has engaged in petting, it is often hard to stop at that point.

Necking, when it is used as a slang for kissing, is a very normal action. I have never considered it wrong or immoral. Kissing, holding hands, and other signs of affection are gestures of friendship and/or love.

I couldn't really say that I am definitely for or against premarital sex. I don't think that teenagers should have sexual relationships, in fact, I'm very much against it. I really don't see how teenagers can have sex thinking that they are in love. I'm nearly seventeen years old, and I still don't know what love is. At least the kind of love that I feel is an important part of a sexual relationship. I know a 16-year-old who has had several sexual encounters. Talking about it like it didn't matter who went to bed with whom. This really bothered me.

I don't see anything especially positive about having sex in the teen years. I would think that few relationships last a long time. All that I can see in it is trouble for the people involved. If teenagers feel that they have to have sex, I think they should give serious thought to what they're doing, and should take precautions. There is so much literature out about birth control that information about it is easily attainable.

I think that much of my own moral code concerning sex stems from discussions I've had with my mom, and also from the teaching of the Catholic church. I have formed my own ideas. I feel that sex is a beautiful and very intimate thing. I don't think that it should be taken lightly or given freely. This is the way I feel about premarital sex at my age.

I don't go for the image of the swinging single sleeping around with any one they happened to pick up at the bar that night. Whether this happens a lot in real life, I don't know, but I see it a lot in movies and on TV and I don't buy it.

Questions

1. Write a paper describing your personal ethics and moral codes. It is very helpful to put your thoughts down on paper so you can react to them. One gains personal insight and commitment.

2. What are the difficulties encountered in formulating sex ethics?

3. What is the main basis for decisions in our sexual behavior?

4. What advice would you give Joey?

5. Do you think that Mr. and Mrs. Ryder have a companionable relationship?

6. What advice would you give Linda?

7. What decisions do you think Linda should make for her future?

8. How do you account for Joey's attitude toward Linda? Linda's attitude toward Joey?

9. Would Linda have a problem if she had not become pregnant?

10. What problems will Linda face in a future marriage?

11. Will a future marriage produce any problems for Joey?

12. Does Joey need help in self-understanding? Why? Why not?

13. If no pregnancy had occurred, would Joey's opinion of Linda have been altered?

14. Does freedom carry responsibility? Explain.

Further reading

Genne, Elizabeth, and Genne, William. *First of All Persons: A New Look at Men-Women Relationships.* New York: Friend Press, 1973.

Jackins, Harvey. *The Human Side of Human Beings.* Seattle, WA: Rational Island Publishers, 1978.

Lemasters, E. E. *Parents in Modern America.* 3rd ed. Homewood, IL: Dorsey Press, Division of Richard D. Irwin, Inc., 1977.

Landers, Ann. *Talks to Teenagers about Sex.* New York: Fawcett Books, 1978.

Lorand, Rhoda L. *Love, Sex and the Teenager.* New York: Macmillan, Inc., 1965.

Smith, G. W., and Phillips, Alice. *Me and You and Us.* New York: David McKay Co., Inc., 1971.

Chapter 19

Relationships in alternative life-styles

The life-style a person chooses has a lot to do with all the information shared in Unit 1. The person's needs, personality, character, maturity, religion, and philosophy of life enter into the type of life-style.

Reprinted by permission of Norman Doherty.
From *Saturday Review*, © 1977 by Saturday Review Magazine Corp.

"Is this where I check in for the knight flight?"

Life-styles

Choice has been greatly expanded for both sexes. In the past, the life-styles for women and men were rigidly defined. There were certain games, behaviors, activities, emotions, and careers prescribed for men. Other choices were exclusively reserved for women. Men have been traditionally connected with the personal qualities of achievement, physical strength, aggressiveness, competitiveness, sexual prowess, and independence. Women, on the other hand, have been associated with tenderness, supportiveness, understanding, a low interest in sex, and a low interest in competition. They have been given a passive role.

Femininity and masculinity

People who showed traits of the opposite sex were regarded with some misgivings. Girls with well-developed masculine skills were generally accepted as tomboys. But after the age of twelve or thirteen, a girl who was a good ball-player or who played boys' games with boys was often regarded with some doubt. There were other more acceptable athletic skills such as swimming, water skiing, tennis, and golf.   But even in these sports, a girl who was more outstanding than boys was viewed with some skepticism.

Boys who had well-developed feminine skills and interests were regarded with amused tolerance as young children.   But if they grew up and acted like girls this was still generally seen as undesirable.[1]

Rigidly prescribed behaviors, activities, and career choices for each sex have cheated both men and women.   The society and the world have also lost out on the contributions that could have been made if people had been free to give to society according to their talents, skills, and intellects.   One can wonder what advances might have been made in medicine, science or law, if women had been admitted to the study of these professions in college.   What advances might have been made in the early lives of children if more fathers were free to be home to care for them.   Or if more men were teachers in the kindergarten and grade school buildings.   One wonders what might have happened in the League of Nations or in the United Nations assemblies if there had been an equal number of women negotiating or if the heads of states were women.   One also wonders what might be the state of the art of child care or housekeeping if there had been an equal number of men free to pursue these occupations.

Change affects life-style

Change is the one thing that is constant in our lives.   There is no society nor person that did not change in the past.   There is no society nor institution that is not changing in the present.   To avoid change is to avoid life.   What is new for these times is the rapidity of change.   Looking at change and its effect on our life-styles is tempered by our ability to remember and by our ability to forget.   We tend to remember the positive.   For example, we remember what we want to remember.   We say that in the past children were more respectful to their parents and teachers.   We remember that wives were dutifully enjoying the tasks of the household.   If we push back our illusion that surrounds the family life-style of the past and actually compare it with the family life-style of today we might better understand our relationship to the past and to the future.

1. From "Social Deviancy Among Youth: Types and Significance" by Robert J. Havighurst in *Social Deviancy Among Youth,* William Wattenburg, editor.   65th Yearbook of the National Society for the Study of Education, Chicago, 1966, pp. 61–62.   Used by permission of the Society.

Relationship to history

Population description

1880s. 80% rural. Urban middle class is 2%. 18% in cities are very poor. Children begin work at ages 9-12 in factories, in apprenticeships. Families do not move very often. Thus, they are known in their communities and have extended family support systems which nourish similar values and life-styles.

1980s. 80% urban. A new class, the urban middle class, makes up 50% of the population and lives in suburban homes. The rural poor have now become the city poor—the hearts of the big cities are where the poor reside. Families are very mobile. The mobility results in families living away from close extended family support systems.

Description of education

1880s. Most children are educated from the fifth to eighth grade level. An eighth grade education is enough for entry into the most popular occupations. Only 15% of the population goes to high school. The high school curriculum is organized for the development of "ladies and gentlemen."

1980s. Modern children from all walks and sectors of life are expected to attend high school. Students with great learning difficulties are expected to attend high school. Most careers demand high school, college, or vocational training for entry.

State of knowledge in child development—family life

1880s. The fields of child development, psychology, and family life were unexplored. Freud was the first to write about this area. His *Interpretation of Dreams* was not published until 1896. Children were regarded as inexperienced adults. The artists of the day drew children as miniature adults. Children were regarded as property, as owned by their parents for their parents to do with as they pleased.

1980s. Piaget's work on the child's cognitive structures comes into prominence. We realize that children think differently from adults.

The fields of child development and family life are being researched. Information about individuals and families is being gained not only in terms of life processes, but in terms of death education. Kohlberg's psychology of moral development gives new insight into conscience development.

State of medicine

1880s. Epidemics, nutritional and infectious diseases are common. These diseases kill one-half of the children born before their first birthday. One-half of the remaining children who survive the first year die before adulthood. Large families are common so more children will reach adulthood.

1980s. People expect that the children born to them will live. Mothers are expected to survive pregnancy and childbirth with no bad side effects. Parents expect the handicapped child to live and thrive.

State of vocations—nature of work

1880s. Work is connected with daily lives. The children experience the parent as a working person. Mothers work in the home in cottage industries. They make household items, preserve food, teach, and nurse in the home or near home. The children share the work experience.

1980s. Over 50% of the mothers with children are working outside the home. Children cannot experience their parents as working persons. Children are unable to share the work experience. They are years away from their vocational choice.

In the last one hundred years, society has changed and created a new developmental stage, adolescence. Persons at ages thirteen, fourteen, and fifteen have maturing adult bodies. But they are years away from entering any vocations. The adolescent society is often living in isolation from the adult society. Adolescents are cut off from experiencing their parents as working persons. They are cut off from the values of the adult world. Often they are cut off from the life processes of birth and of death. Adolescents are isolated from the older adults. The older adults are the carriers of the culture of the society. Therefore, if the children growing up in a society are isolated from other generations, changes in the society will occur more rapidly. The impact of the knowledge explosion and the new insights into the nature of behavior make it necessary to teach adolescents about these new things in relation to the old ones. The new body of knowledge only becomes understandable when it is put in the context of history.

Relationship to life-style

There are many life-styles from which choices can be made. The traditional life-style deemed to be most acceptable is that labeled "married with children," and with no premarital sex nor extramarital sex. This is the life-style that is given the most prominence in all major religions. It has been the one to try to achieve. Society has applauded those who followed this life-style. When society makes a life-style the most acceptable one, then those persons who have a different life-style are subject to suspicion. This is unfortunate because not all people should be married. Nor do all people want to marry. It is equally true that not all people should feel the need to be parents. Nor do all people want to be placed in the parenting role. However, when society makes one life-style as the most acceptable one then those who are outside that life-style are made to feel different. The married couple who is childless feels the pressure from family and friends to reproduce. If the couple remains childless, they are considered either selfish, infertile, insincere, or incompatible. This pressure from society causes many people to marry and have children. The sad result is that if the person really doesn't want to be married, the spouse may spend his or her life looking for another partner. Their children may spend their lives trying to find a parent.

There has always been a variety of life-styles. There are really no new ones. The only difference today is that some life-styles are more openly discussed than in the past. One has only to read history or other literature to realize that many different life-styles have always existed. Among the life-styles are: married—single, sex—no sex, children—no children, opposite sex—same sex, group—couple, commune—couple. The number of life-styles is almost limitless.

It is obviously not possible for all life-styles to become universal or the practice of the majority. All but one must remain minority practices for the simple reason that there can be any number of minorities but only one majority. The life-style of the majority is conventional, monogamous marriage. Unit 3 will discuss this life-style in detail because it is the life-style most commonly sought.

The variations in life-styles fall into two groups: the absence of marriage and modifications of marriage.

The absence of marriage

The absence of marriage can be due to factors beyond conscious control. The fact that in some parts of the society there are more males than females or more females than males could account for those who do not marry. The type of community in which one lives, responsibilities that prevent one from meeting eligible persons, occupational isolation or ignorance of ways of approaching the opposite sex can cause singlehood. Some people remain single because they have chosen a life's work which takes the place of a marriage. The deliberate choice of celibacy is such a factor. Other people remain single because they don't want the responsibilities of marriage, are disappointed in love or have lost a loved one through death and just never find anyone else who can measure up to their lost fiance. Others remain single because they fall in love with a married person. Some people are so busy accomplishing vocational or life goals that the time for marriage and a family passes them by. It is also common, especially for women, to have the responsibility for parents or dependent brothers and sisters and thus they are unable to be either emotionally or economically free to marry.

Modifications of marriage

The commune or community is an age-old life-style that is a modification of the majority style. There have been some very long-lived communes in history. However, most of them have been short-lived. There is a variety of combinations of life-styles represented. Some communes welcome everybody. Others only welcome those of a particular religion, value system, or educational level. A commune may be organized or may lack organization. The members may feel not only that organization is unnecessary but that its lack is a source of pride. In some communes there is a plan of work and in others there is not. Some communes are producing and self-sustaining. In some communes the children are cared for by their natural parents. In others, their care is scheduled by various group members. The communes which have lasted the longest were those that developed set patterns of behavior for members, where members had similar value systems, where the commune had observable goals, and where all ages were provided a place to live and given responsibility.

As we grow, so our life-style changes. Most of us will have several life-styles in our lifetime. For example, most of us spend our early years in the single, no-sex life-style. We may move out of our parental home into an apartment with a same-sex friend and thus have the single, same-sex, no-sex life-style. From there we may marry, living the marriage-no-children life-style; this may change to marriage-children life-style and so on. One's life-style changes with time as the stage of development changes with time.

Questions

1. How do rigid sex stereotypes cheat society?

2. Discuss how changes in history lead to changes in life-styles?

3. Are alternative life-styles a new idea in society?

4. What is the life-style of the majority?

5. Write a paper titled "Life-styles." Indicate which life-style you would choose and give the reasons why it would be acceptable to you. In your discussion indicate how this life-style reinforces your ideas, ideals, values, goals, and personal philosophy.

Further reading

Bernard, Jessie. *The Future of Marriage.* New York: Bantam Books, Inc., 1973.

Cox, Frank D. *American Marriage: A Changing Scene?* 2nd ed. Dubuque, IA: Wm. C. Brown Company, Publishers, 1976.

Otto, Herbert. *The Family in Search of a Future: Alternate Models for Moderns.* Englewood Cliffs, NJ: Prentice-Hall, Inc., 1970.

UNIT

3
Understanding Marriage

Chapter 20

Marriage and family forms

The forms of the family, the functions of marriage partners, and the identity of the kinds of families are not easily recognized in today's world. The family pattern becomes evident only after much study, thought, and observation.

Reprinted by permission of Robert Censoni.
From *Saturday Review,* © 1971.

"You've been walked and you've been fed.
Now I suppose you want love and affection."

Age for marriage

Every state has a certain minimum age at which individuals may marry. In the past, forty-four states required that the young man be twenty-one years of age before he could marry without parental consent. However, presently only seven states, Idaho, Kansas, Minnesota, Mississippi, New York, Oregon, and Utah require a minimum age of twenty-one for marriage without parental consent for the male. There is only one state, Mississippi, that requires the young woman to be twenty-one years old. The twenty-sixth amendment to the Constitution of the United States was proposed on March 23, 1971 and ratified on July 1, 1971. It gives the right to vote to citizens of the United States who are 18 years of age or older. The change in the legal minimum age for marriage has, no doubt, been due to the law that sets the minimum voting age from twenty-one to eighteen.

If parental consent can be secured the minimum age for both males and females is lower. See Table 1 on pages 222–223.

Changing population patterns

The United States began 1977 with an estimated population of 216 million, an increase of 1.6 million or 0.7 percent, over the January 1, 1976 figure. The Census Bureau estimates that the net gain resulted from about 3.2 million births, 1.9 million deaths, and net immigration of about 300,000.

Table 1[1]

Marriage Information, by State

Sources: Legal information, *Information Please Almanac* questionnaires to states; Marriage statistics, National Center for Health statistics, Department of Health, Education, and Welfare.

State	Legal minimum marriage age				Blood test required	Waiting period[1]		Marriages[2]	
	With parental consent[3]		Without parental consent			Before license	After license	1976[4]	1975
	M	F	M	F					
Alabama	17	14	19	18	yes	none	none	47,590	45,349
Alaska	16	16	18	18	yes	3 da.	none	4,878	4,734
Arizona	18	18	18	18	yes	none	none	28,312	26,558
Arkansas	18	16	18	18	yes	3 da.	none	22,630	24,337
California	18	16	18	18	yes	none	none	150,654	154,812
Colorado	16[21]	16[21]	18	18	yes[18]	none	none	27,144	27,565
Connecticut	16	16	18	18	yes	4 da.	none	22,648	23,389
Delaware	18	16	18	18	yes[11]	none	24 hr.[5]	3,943	3,947
D.C.	—	18	18	18	yes[7]	5 da.[5]	none	4,681	4,911
Florida	18	16	18	18	yes	3 da.	none	86,170	85,427
Georgia	16	16	18	—	yes	3 da.	none	60,207	63,245
Hawaii	16	16	18	18	yes	none	none	9,751	9,673
Idaho	18	16	21	18	yes	3 da.	none	13,105	12,688
Illinois	16	16	18	18	yes	none	none	111,261	111,459
Indiana	17	17[17]	18	18	yes	3 da.	none	56,359	56,075
Iowa	18	16	18	18	yes	3 da.	none	25,643	25,616
Kansas	18	16	21	18	yes	3 da.	none	23,416	23,767
Kentucky	([19])	([19])	18	18	yes	3 da.	none	34,807	32,068
Louisiana	18	16	18	16	yes	none	72 hr.	39,050	37,309
Maine	16	16	18	18	no	5 da.	none	11,345	11,190
Maryland	16[15]	16[15]	16	16	no	48 hr.	none	44,891	44,776
Massachusetts	14–17[12]	12–15[12]	18	18	yes	3 da.	none	40,928	42,103
Michigan	18	16[8]	18	18	yes	3 da.	none	83,193	82,856
Minnesota	18	16	21	18	no	5 da.	none	33,198	32,261
Mississippi	17	15	21	21	yes	3 da.	none	26,450	26,279
Missouri	15[12]	15[12]	18	18	yes	3 da.	none	44,750	50,147
Montana	18	18	18	18	yes	5 da.	none	7,328	7,331
Nebraska	18	16	19	19	yes	2 da.	none	13,386	13,087
Nevada	16	16	18	18	no	none	none	99,722	101,559
New Hampshire	14[12,15]	13[12,15]	18	18	yes[11]	5 da.	none	8,437	8,831
New Jersey	18	16	18	18	yes	72 hr.	none	52,281	53,008

In 1976, Blacks made up 11 percent of the population and totaled 24.2 million. There were also 11.1 million persons of Spanish origin, comprising 5 percent of the population. Persons of Spanish origin included 6.6 million of Mexican origin; 1.8 million of Puerto Rican origin; 0.8 million of Central or South American origin; 0.7 million of Cuban origin; and 1.3 million of other Spanish origin.

The U.S. population has been growing at a slower rate for several years. The past trends in the number of births are gradually changing the country's age structure. Since 1970, the number of children under age 14 has declined by 5.5 million. During the same period, however, the population of age 65 and over has grown by 3 million, or 14.8 percent. Over 10 percent of the population is now 65 or older. The median age of the population has risen from 27.9 years in 1970 to 29.0 in 1976.

Table 1, continued

State	Legal minimum marriage age				Blood test required	Waiting period[1]		Marriages[2]	
	With parental consent[3]		Without parental consent			Before license	After license	1976[4]	1975
	M	F	M	F					
New Mexico	16	16	18	18	yes	none	none	12,393	15,790
New York	16	14[5]	21	18	yes	none	([10])	136,694	142,752
North Carolina	16	16	18	18	yes	none	none	42,548	42,310
North Dakota	18	15	18	18	yes	none	none	5,638	5,993
Ohio	18	16	18	18	yes	5 da.	none	97,929	101,135
Oklahoma	18[17]	16[17]	18	18	yes	none[14]	none	40,677	40,110
Oregon	18	15	21	18	yes	7 da.	none	19,507	19,322
Pennsylvania	16	16	18	18	yes	3 da.	none	88,557	91,665
Rhode Island	18	16[9]	18	18	yes	none	none	6,910	6,695
South Carolina	16	14	18	18	no	24 hr.	none	50,698	50,249
South Dakota	16	16	18	18	yes	none	none	10,755	11,074
Tennessee	16	16	18	18	yes	none[14]	none	53,365	51,530
Texas	14[13]	14[13]	18	18	yes	none	none	156,479	153,154
Utah	16	14	21	18	yes	none	none	14,275	14,905
Vermont	16	16	18	18	yes	none	5 da.[16]	56,474	54,688
Virginia	16	16	18	18	yes	none	none	4,292	4,553
Washington	17	17	18	18	no	3 da.	none	40,684	41,807
West Virginia	18	16	18	18	yes	3 da.	none	17,145	17,041
Wisconsin	16	16	18	18	yes	5 da.	none	35,972	35,886
Wyoming	18[20]	16[20]	18[20]	18[20]	yes	none	none	5,763	5,649

[1] In some states, waiting period may be waived or reduced by court order. [2] By place of occurrence. [3] In most states, persons younger than the age shown may be married by court permission. [4] Provisional figures; data represent marriages reported, marriage intentions filed, or marriage licenses issued. [5] 96 hours if nonresidents. [6] Day of application and day of pickup are included in 5-day waiting period. [7] No exceptions granted under this age. [8] Consent of one parent or guardian necessary for female only. [9] Females 14 to 16 years old must also have consent of judge of Family Court. [10] Marriage may not be solemnized within 10 days from date on which specimen was taken for serological test, and not until 24 hours after issuance of marriage license. Waiting period may be waived by court order. [11] Blood test may be waived by court order. [12] Need court order. [13] Parent must appear in person or provide doctor's affidavit of his or her illness. [14] 3 days if either party is under legal age. [15] If pregnant. [16] After date on which marriage application has been filed with town clerk, excluding date of filing. [17] Males under 18 and females under 15 only if female is pregnant. [18] Blood test for rubella and RH type not required of females over 45 years or found by physician to be incapable of bearing children. [19] No age limit. [20] If under 18 or 16 need court order. [21] Males and females under age of 16 may obtain a license with parental consent and judicial approval.

1. From *Information Please Almanac* 1978. Used with permission of the publisher.

The shifting age structure is also apparent in the 12 percent drop in elementary school enrollment in the years of 1971-77. The total fertility rate in 1976 was 1.76. This means that an estimated 1760 children would be born to every 1,000 women during their lifetime. This rate is well below the natural replacement level of 2.1 children per woman. Because of the large number of women of childbearing age, however, it will still be many years before the United States can attain zero population growth.

Other social changes are having their effect on the number of children born. The number of divorces rose to 1,077,000 in 1976. The number of marriages fell to 2,133,000. The divorce rate per 1,000 population doubled from 2.5 in 1966 to 5.0 in 1976. But the marriage rate has been declining since it peaked at 11.0 in 1972. By 1976 there were 9.9 marriages per 1,000 population.

Table 2[2]

Labor Force Marital Status

Marital Status of Women in the Civilian Labor Force: 1940 to 1976

[Persons 14 years old and over through 1965; 16 years old and over thereafter. As of March, except as indicated. Prior to 1960, excludes Alaska and Hawaii. Figures for 1940 based on complete census revised for comparability with intercensal series. Later data based on Current Population Survey. Beginning 1955, figures not strictly comparable with previous years as a result of introduction into estimating procedure of 1950 census data through 1960, and of 1960 census data beginning 1965. See also *Historical Statistics, Colonial Times of 1970*, series D 49–62]

Year	Female Labor Force (1,000)					Percent Distribution of Female Labor Force			Female Labor Force as Percent of Female Population				
	Total	Single	Married, total	Married, husband present	Widowed or divorced	Single	Married	Widowed or divorced	Total	Single	Married, total	Married, husband present	Widowed or divorced
1940	13,840	6,710	5,040	[1] 4,200	2,090	48.5	36.4	15.1	27.4	48.1	16.7	14.7	32.0
1944, Apr	18,449	7,542	8,433	6,226	2,474	40.9	45.7	13.4	35.0	58.6	25.6	21.7	35.7
1947, Apr	16,323	6,181	7,545	6,676	2,597	37.9	46.2	15.9	29.8	51.2	21.4	20.0	34.6
1950	17,795	5,621	9,273	8,550	2,901	31.6	52.1	16.3	31.4	50.5	24.8	23.8	36.0
1955, Apr	20,154	5,087	11,839	10,423	3,227	25.2	58.7	16.0	33.5	46.4	29.4	27.7	36.0
1960	22,516	5,401	13,485	12,253	3,629	24.0	59.9	16.1	34.8	44.1	31.7	30.5	37.1
1965	25,952	5,912	16,154	14,708	3,886	22.8	62.2	15.0	36.7	40.5	35.7	34.7	35.7
1967	27,545	5,915	17,486	15,908	4,144	21.5	63.5	15.0	39.7	50.7	37.8	36.8	35.9
1968	28,778	6,357	18,234	16,821	4,187	22.1	63.4	14.6	40.7	51.3	39.1	38.3	35.8
1969	29,898	6,501	19,100	17,595	4,297	21.7	63.9	14.4	41.6	51.2	40.4	39.6	35.8
1970	31,233	6,965	19,799	18,377	4,469	22.3	63.4	14.3	42.6	53.0	41.4	40.8	36.2
1971	31,681	7,187	19,986	18,530	4,508	22.7	63.1	14.2	42.5	52.7	41.4	40.8	35.7
1972	32,939	7,477	20,749	19,249	4,713	22.7	63.0	14.3	43.6	54.9	42.1	41.5	37.2
1973	33,904	7,739	21,343	19,821	4,822	22.8	63.0	14.2	44.1	55.8	42.8	42.2	36.7
1974	35,320	8,230	22,009	20,367	5,081	23.3	62.3	14.4	45.2	57.2	43.8	43.0	37.8
1975	36,496	8,433	22,796	21,143	5,266	23.1	62.5	14.4	45.9	56.8	45.0	44.4	37.7
1976	37,817	9,083	23,355	21,554	5,379	24.0	61.8	14.2	46.8	58.9	45.8	45.0	37.3

[1] As of April.

2. U.S. Bureau of the Census, *Statistical Abstract of the United States: 1977.* (98th edition.) Washington, D.C., 1977, p. 391.

More young people are postponing marriage, or deciding not to marry at all. The percentage of single men between 20 and 24 years old increased from 53 percent in 1960 to 62 percent in 1976. Of the women of the age when men and women have traditionally married, 43 percent were still single in 1976 compared to 28 percent in 1960.

As more women have postponed marriage and childbearing, or have become separated and/or divorced, the college enrollment of women 25 to 35 years old has more than doubled, from 409,000 in 1970 to 971,000 in 1976.[3]

Marital status of the labor force

Tables 2, 3, 4, and 5 show the marital status of the labor force participation rates by marital status, age, and sex.

3. From "Changing Population Patterns" by Manuel D. Plotkin in *The World Almanac & Book of Facts,* 1978 Edition; copyright © Newspaper Enterprise Association, Inc., New York, N.Y.; 1977. Used by permission.

Table 3[4]

Labor Force Marital Status

Labor Force Participation Rates, by Marital Status, Age, and Sex: 1960 to 1976

[Percent civilian labor force of noninstitutional population]

Year and Marital Status	Percent Male					Percent Female				
	16–19 years	20–24 years	25–44 years	45–64 years	65 and over	16–19 years	20–24 years	25–44 years	45–64 years	65 and over
1960: Married, spouse present	[1]91.5	97.1	98.7	93.7	36.6	[1]27.2	31.7	33.1	36.0	6.7
Single	[1]42.6	80.3	90.5	80.1	31.2	[1]30.2	77.2	83.2	79.8	24.3
Other [2]	[1]68.8	96.9	94.7	83.2	22.7	[1]43.8	58.0	67.2	60.0	11.4
1965: Married, spouse present	[1]88.0	96.4	98.5	92.6	31.0	[1]30.6	37.1	36.2	39.5	6.7
Single	[1]40.9	75.7	89.0	78.1	23.2	[1]28.8	72.9	82.4	76.1	22.4
Other [2]	[1]77.8	96.6	93.8	80.8	18.7	[1]42.1	59.2	67.2	61.6	10.5
1970: Married, spouse present	92.3	94.7	98.0	91.2	29.9	37.8	47.9	42.7	44.0	7.3
Single	54.6	73.8	87.4	75.7	25.2	44.7	73.0	80.5	73.0	19.7
Other [2]	68.8	90.4	92.3	78.5	18.3	48.5	60.3	67.2	61.9	10.0
1973: Married, spouse present	93.4	95.4	97.6	88.6	24.8	43.5	52.7	46.4	42.9	7.2
Single	58.4	77.6	85.9	70.9	20.8	48.6	72.9	79.6	69.1	16.5
Other [2]	77.8	89.9	92.0	74.4	15.8	44.4	63.0	67.7	60.3	9.0
1974: Married, spouse present	94.4	96.2	97.6	87.7	24.2	44.9	55.3	48.1	43.3	6.8
Single	59.4	78.7	86.0	70.8	20.2	49.9	73.1	80.2	69.2	13.3
Other [2]	72.0	93.6	92.7	74.4	16.1	46.2	65.6	69.0	59.9	8.5
1975: Married, spouse present	92.9	95.3	97.3	86.8	23.3	46.2	57.0	50.0	43.8	7.0
Single	57.9	77.9	86.0	69.9	21.0	49.6	72.5	80.3	68.3	15.8
Other [2]	70.6	88.8	91.1	73.4	15.4	47.6	65.3	68.9	59.0	8.3
1976: Married, spouse present	93.5	95.6	97.2	86.1	21.9	46.9	57.3	52.0	44.3	7.0
Single	58.2	79.1	86.5	68.8	20.7	50.3	73.8	81.4	69.6	15.6
Other [2]	79.2	92.3	91.2	71.5	13.6	49.6	64.4	71.2	58.2	8.3

[1] 14 to 19 years old.   [2] Includes widowed, divorced, and married (spouse absent).

4. U.S. Bureau of the Census, *Statistical Abstract of the United States: 1977.* (98th edition.) Washington, D.C., 1977, p. 391.

Family tasks or functions

The family has many forms. These forms vary according to the hopes, desires, and values of the family members. They also vary according to the abilities, potentials, and capacities of the family members.

The 1970 White House Conference on Children defined the primary tasks or functions of families. These are as follows.

1. to develop their capacities to socialize children

2. to enhance the competence of their members to cope with the demands of other organizations in which they must function

3. to utilize these organizations

4. to provide the satisfactions and a mentally healthy environment intrinsic to the well-being of a family

Table 4[5]

Labor Force, Employment, and Earnings

Employment Status of the Population, by Sex and Race: 1960 to 1977

[Persons 16 years old and over. Monthly averages. Total population and total labor force include Armed Forces. See also *Historical Statistics, Colonial Times to 1970,* series D 11-19 and D 85-86]

Year or Month, Sex, and Race	Total noninstitutional population (1,000)	Total Labor Force		Civilian Labor Force					Not in Labor Force	
		Total (1,000)	Percent of population	Total (1,000)	Employed (1,000)	Unemployed		Employed/population ratio[1]	Total (1,000)	Percent of population
						Total (1,000)	Percent			
Total:										
1960	119,759	72,142	60.2	69,628	65,778	3,852	5.5	54.9	47,617	39.8
1965	129,236	77,178	59.7	74,455	71,088	3,366	4.5	55.0	52,058	40.3
1968	135,562	82,272	60.7	78,737	75,920	2,817	3.6	56.0	53,291	39.3
1969	137,841	84,240	61.1	80,734	77,902	2,832	3.5	56.5	53,602	38.9
1970	140,182	85,903	61.3	82,715	78,627	4,088	4.9	56.1	54,280	38.7
1971	142,596	88,929	61.0	84,113	79,120	4,993	5.9	55.5	55,668	39.0
1972	145,775	88,991	61.0	86,542	81,702	4,840	5.6	56.0	56,785	39.0
1973	148,263	91,040	61.4	88,714	84,409	4,304	4.9	56.9	57,222	38.6
1974	150,827	93,240	61.8	91,011	85,936	5,076	5.6	57.0	57,587	38.2
1975	153,449	94,793	61.8	92,613	84,783	7,830	8.5	55.3	58,655	38.2
1976	156,048	96,917	62.1	94,773	87,485	7,288	7.7	56.1	59,130	37.9
1977, Jan.-Apr.	157,683	97,546	61.9	95,410	87,890	7,520	7.9	55.7	60,137	38.1
Male:										
1960	58,144	48,870	84.0	46,388	43,904	2,486	5.4	75.5	9,274	16.0
1965	62,473	50,946	81.5	48,255	46,340	1,914	4.0	74.2	11,527	18.5
1968	65,345	53,030	81.2	49,533	48,114	1,419	2.9	73.6	12,315	18.8
1969	66,365	53,688	80.9	50,221	48,818	1,403	2.8	73.6	12,677	19.1
1970	67,409	54,343	80.6	51,195	48,960	2,235	4.4	72.6	13,066	19.4
1971	68,512	54,797	80.0	52,021	49,245	2,776	5.3	71.9	13,715	20.0
1972	69,864	55,671	79.7	53,265	50,630	2,635	4.9	72.5	14,193	20.3
1973	71,020	56,479	79.5	54,203	51,963	2,240	4.1	73.2	14,541	20.5
1974	72,253	57,349	79.4	55,186	52,519	2,668	4.8	72.7	14,904	20.6
1975	73,494	57,706	78.5	55,615	51,230	4,385	7.9	69.7	15,788	21.5
1976	74,739	58,397	78.1	56,359	52,391	3,968	7.0	70.1	16,341	21.9
1977, Jan.-Apr.	75,564	58,342	77.2	56,319	52,103	4,216	7.5	70.8	17,222	22.8
Black and other:[2]										
1960	5,595	(NA)	83.0	4,645	4,148	497	10.7	74.1	951	17.0
1965	6,330	5,084	80.3	4,855	4,496	359	7.4	71.0	1,246	19.7
1968	6,755	5,322	78.8	4,979	4,702	277	5.6	69.6	1,434	21.2
1969	6,918	5,404	78.1	5,036	4,770	266	5.3	69.0	1,513	21.9
1970	7,098	5,507	77.6	5,182	4,803	379	7.3	67.7	1,591	22.4
1971	7,286	5,533	75.9	5,220	4,746	474	9.1	65.1	1,753	24.1
1972	7,533	5,630	74.7	5,335	4,861	475	8.9	64.5	1,902	25.2
1973	7,845	5,868	74.8	5,555	5,133	423	7.6	65.4	1,977	25.2
1974	8,107	6,028	74.4	5,700	5,179	521	9.1	63.9	2,079	25.6
1975	8,360	6,077	72.7	5,734	4,947	787	13.7	59.2	2,283	27.3
1976	8,622	6,198	71.9	5,853	5,108	745	12.7	59.2	2,425	28.1
1977, Jan.-Apr.	8,762	6,221	71.0	5,867	5,117	750	12.8	60.9	2,542	29.0
Female:										
1960	61,615	23,272	37.8	23,240	21,874	1,366	5.9	35.5	38,343	62.2
1965	66,763	26,232	39.3	26,200	24,748	1,452	5.5	37.1	40,531	60.7
1968	70,217	29,242	41.6	29,204	27,807	1,397	4.8	39.6	40,976	58.4
1969	71,476	30,551	42.7	30,513	29,084	1,429	4.7	40.7	40,924	57.3
1970	72,774	31,560	43.4	31,520	29,667	1,853	5.9	40.8	41,214	56.6
1971	74,084	32,132	43.4	32,091	29,875	2,217	6.9	40.3	41,952	56.6
1972	75,911	33,320	43.9	33,277	31,072	2,205	6.6	40.9	42,591	56.1
1973	77,242	34,561	44.7	34,510	32,446	2,064	6.0	42.0	42,681	55.3
1974	78,575	35,892	45.7	35,825	33,417	2,408	6.7	42.5	42,683	54.3
1975	79,954	37,087	46.4	36,998	33,553	3,445	9.3	42.0	42,868	53.6

Table 4, continued

Year or Month, Sex, and Race	Total noninstitutional population (1,000)	Total Labor Force		Civilian Labor Force					Not in Labor Force	
		Total (1,000)	Percent of population	Total (1,000)	Employed (1,000)	Unemployed		Employed/population ratio[1]	Total (1,000)	Percent of population
						Total (1,000)	Percent			
Female: *(continued)*										
1976	81,309	38,520	47.4	38,414	35,095	3,320	8.6	43.2	42,789	52.6
1977, Jan.–Apr.	82,119	39,204	47.7	39,092	35,787	3,305	8.5	43.6	42,915	52.3
Black and other:[2]										
1960	6,369	(NA)	48.2	3,069	2,779	290	9.4	43.6	3,300	51.8
1965	7,133	3,467	48.6	3,464	3,147	317	9.2	44.1	3,666	51.4
1968	7,670	3,784	49.3	3,780	3,467	313	8.3	45.2	3,886	50.7
1969	7,877	3,922	49.8	3,918	3,614	304	7.8	45.9	3,955	50.2
1970	8,114	4,019	49.5	4,015	3,642	373	9.3	44.9	4,095	50.5
1971	8,351	4,107	49.2	4,102	3,658	445	10.8	43.8	4,243	50.8
1972	8,736	4,254	48.7	4,249	3,767	482	11.3	43.1	4,481	51.3
1973	9,109	4,476	49.1	4,470	3,999	471	10.5	43.9	4,632	50.9
1974	9,455	4,643	49.1	4,633	4,136	497	10.7	43.7	4,812	50.9
1975	9,766	4,810	49.3	4,795	4,124	671	14.0	42.2	4,956	50.7
1976	10,075	5,062	50.2	5,044	4,356	688	13.6	43.2	5,013	49.8
1977, Jan.–Apr.	10,268	5,093	49.6	5,072	4,387	685	13.5	42.8	5,174	50.4

NA   Not available.   [1] Employed as percent of noninstitutional population.   [2] Other than W..ite.
5. Ibid., p. 388.

Reprinted by permission of Orlando Busino.
From *Saturday Review,* © 1972.

"... or if you don't care to get quite so emotionally involved."

Table 5[6]

Civilian Labor Force Participation Rates,[1] by Marital Status, Age, and Sex, 1957–74

Marital status and year		Females							
		Total	14 to 17 years	18 and 19 years	20 to 24 years	25 to 34 years	35 to 44 years	45 to 64 years	65 years and over
MARRIED, SPOUSE PRESENT	1957	30.1	17.0	29.8	30.9	27.6	36.5	32.4	6.6
	1958	30.7	17.1	30.2	31.7	27.9	36.9	33.5	6.6
	1959	31.2	16.8	30.1	31.4	28.2	36.9	35.0	6.3
	1960	31.9	16.8	30.9	31.7	28.8	37.2	36.0	6.7
	1961	32.5	18.4	31.1	33.0	29.1	37.8	36.9	6.8
	1962	32.8	18.6	33.6	33.6	29.3	38.5	37.4	6.3
	1963	33.4	19.8	33.8	33.3	30.1	39.0	38.2	6.3
	1964	34.1	18.4	32.9	35.9	30.3	39.7	39.2	6.4
	1965	34.9	18.6	34.1	37.1	31.5	40.5	39.5	6.7
	1966	35.9	20.5	37.3	38.9	33.1	41.4	40.3	6.8
	1966[2]	35.9	20.6	37.3	38.9	33.1	41.4	40.3	6.8
	1967	37.3	21.8	38.6	41.5	35.5	42.7	41.3	6.9
	1968	38.2	23.4	40.8	42.8	36.3	44.1	42.0	6.9
	1969	39.5	22.0	41.7	46.4	37.3	45.5	43.2	7.1
	1970	40.5	27.0	40.3	47.9	38.8	46.8	44.0	7.3
	1971	40.6	23.5	41.7	48.4	39.2	47.3	43.7	7.2
	1972	41.2	30.5	44.2	50.1	41.1	47.8	43.4	7.4
	1973	42.3	31.3	46.6	52.7	44.0	49.3	42.9	7.2
	1974	43.3	29.0	48.2	55.3	46.0	50.8	43.3	6.8
SINGLE	1957	50.0	21.3	60.6	76.6	84.4	82.9	76.4	23.7
	1958	48.5	19.7	60.6	76.5	84.2	82.8	77.2	24.1
	1959	47.4	21.0	57.1	75.5	82.9	82.3	77.8	22.3
	1960	48.0	20.9	58.6	77.2	83.4	82.9	79.8	24.3
	1961	46.5	20.2	58.4	75.9	84.1	81.7	76.7	23.0
	1962	44.8	19.3	57.4	74.1	82.3	80.8	76.6	18.5
	1963	44.2	19.0	56.6	73.7	81.9	80.6	76.8	19.3
	1964	44.2	19.8	54.9	74.0	84.2	79.6	76.7	21.7
	1965	44.4	19.9	54.4	72.9	82.9	81.8	76.1	22.4
	1966	45.6	21.9	56.3	73.8	82.2	80.7	76.5	18.8
	1966[2]	55.6	31.1	56.3	73.8	82.2	80.7	76.5	18.8
	1967	55.3	31.5	56.0	72.1	82.2	80.0	74.2	19.4
	1968	55.6	32.1	55.5	73.1	81.8	79.2	74.6	19.1
	1969	56.7	34.2	56.4	72.5	82.4	80.5	75.2	20.2
	1970	56.8	35.3	57.3	73.0	81.4	78.6	73.0	19.7
	1971	56.3	34.9	56.3	72.3	81.5	78.1	72.6	17.8
	1972	57.5	37.0	58.6	72.6	82.5	74.8	70.6	17.2
	1973	58.6	39.6	60.0	72.9	80.8	76.2	69.1	16.5
	1974	59.5	40.9	61.3	73.1	81.3	77.2	69.2	13.3
OTHER[4]	1957	41.3	(³)	46.3	55.8	63.9	72.6	58.8	11.2
	1958	41.6	(³)	44.0	56.9	64.1	72.6	59.5	10.8
	1959	41.6	(³)	51.6	55.2	62.7	71.5	60.0	10.9
	1960	41.6	(³)	47.9	58.0	63.1	70.0	60.0	11.4
	1961	41.7	(³)	46.6	57.5	62.1	69.4	60.7	11.6
	1962	40.6	(³)	45.0	57.1	60.3	67.3	60.8	11.2
	1963	40.9	(³)	47.3	55.3	62.3	69.3	61.2	10.5
	1964	40.6	(³)	43.1	56.6	61.5	67.8	61.7	10.9
	1965	40.7	(³)	44.1	59.2	64.1	69.3	61.6	10.5
	1966	41.3	(³)	54.4	61.1	63.2	70.4	62.5	10.4
	1966[2]	41.3	(³)	54.4	61.1	63.2	70.4	62.5	10.4

In other words, families function if they help their children to become contributing members of society and if the individual members gain support physically and psychologically from each other.

Table 5, continued

Marital status and year		Females							
		Total	14 to 17 years	18 and 19 years	20 to 24 years	25 to 34 years	35 to 44 years	45 to 64 years	65 years and over
OTHER[4] *(continued)*	1967	41.0	(³)	50.0	62.5	64.3	71.7	61.8	10.1
	1968	40.4	(³)	50.9	59.3	63.6	69.7	61.8	10.9
	1969	40.7	(³)	51.6	62.1	64.8	68.8	62.6	10.5
	1970	40.3	(³)	52.1	60.3	64.6	68.8	61.9	10.0
	1971	40.3	(³)	47.1	59.2	62.8	69.3	62.2	9.9
	1972	40.0	(³)	49.5	59.7	64.1	69.3	60.6	9.7
	1973	39.7	27.8	50.0	63.0	65.9	69.5	60.3	9.0
	1974	40.2	(³)	48.1	65.6	69.1	68.9	59.9	8.5

[1] Percent of civilian noninstitutional population in civilian labor force.   [2] Beginning with 1966 data revised to refer to persons 16 years of age and over and persons 16 to 17 years old (instead of 14 to 17) in accordance with change introduced in January 1967.   [3] Percent not shown where base is less than 35,000.   [4] Includes widowed, divorced, and married-spouse absent.

6. U.S., Department of Labor, *Handbook of Labor Statistics: 1975* (Washington, D.C.: Government Printing Office, 1975), p. 40.

Distribution of adult Americans by type of household

There are eight main family forms. J. Ramsey compiled recent Bureau of Labor Statistics and arrived at the pattern of distribution shown in the following table.[7]

Distribution of adult Americans by type of household

Types of households	Percentage of all households
Living in child-free or post childbearing marriages	23%
Other single, separated, divorced or widowed	21%
Living in dual-breadwinner nuclear families	16%
Heading single-parent families	16%
Living in single-breadwinner nuclear families	13%
Living in extended families	6%
Living in experimental families or cohabitating	4%
Living in no wage-earner nuclear families	1%

7. From "Experimental Family Forms—The Family of the Future" by J. Ramsey in *Marriage and Family Review*, January/February 1978. Used by permission of the publishers, The Haworth Press.

Descriptions of family forms

Marvin Sussman in the March/April 1978 issue of *Children Today* has made an appraisal of the strengths and weaknesses of some of the family forms on the previous table.

The dual career family: intact nuclear family consisting of husband, wife and offspring living in a common household where both partners work. (Represents 16 percent of all households.)

Strengths

Competent structure to provide maximal income for maintenance and to achieve quality of life aspirations.

Highly adequate form for effecting goals of gender equality. It provides work options for both marital partners and opportunity to share household tasks and marital responsibilties.

Weaknesses

Dependence on kin and institutional support systems for effective maintenance and functioning.

Developing but still non-institutionalized values and means to harmonize the career activities and ambitions of both partners and the roles concerned with marital relationships and parenting.

The single parent household: with children under age 18. (Represents 16 percent of all households.)

Strengths

Many adults who can function as socialization models for children are potentially available. Adults other than parents may be more effective in teaching and socializing children.

If supported appropriately, the single parent can achieve greater self-expression than a married counterpart; accountability is limited to children.

For a significant number of single-parent families, which result as a consequence of separation and divorce, the removal or absence of a violent parent results in a nurturant and liveable family form.

Weaknesses

Need for support systems for parenting, economic and health maintenance and social relationships—often scarce or unavailable in particular communities.

The insufficiency of finances endemic to this family form often results in higher morbidity and expenditure of third party monies for maintenance and survival. Another consequence of economic deficiency is the pressure for some to remarry in order to obtain such support, with increased probability that the previous marriage experience will be repeated.

For some families, when the single parent is gainfully employed and substitute parents are unavailable or ineffective, the socialization is done by peers, and the behavior of children may be viewed as deviant and delinquent.

The single career family: intact nuclear family consisting of husband, wife and offspring living in a common household where one partner, usually the husband, is the provider. (Represents 13 percent of all households.)

Strengths

Maintains its position as the primary structure for potential socialization of members over the life cycle.

Is the primary unit for taking care of disabled, deviant and dependent members.

Is among the best adapted in terms of fitting the demands of the corporate economic structure.

Weaknesses

Is easily broken, with increasing intervention of organizations and expenditure of monies to maintain individuals of broken marriages and new family forms.

The single breadwinner of the working class is unable to provide adequately for its maintenance. Among the middle classes, there is difficulty in providing an expected quality of life.

The remarried nuclear family: husband, wife and offspring living in a common household. (Represents 11 percent of all households.)

Strengths

Previous marital experiences may result in an increased number (actual incidence unknown) of stable marriages.

Parenting, which may formerly have been the function of a single adult, may be shared with the new partner and his or her older children.

For some, there is improved economic status as a consequence of shared income.

Weaknesses

The difficulties in blending two formerly independent households into one functioning unit may result in extreme psychic stress for some members.

Formations consisting of two large-size families may require substantial economic help, counseling and other supports in order to survive.

Economic and social commitments to individuals of previous marriages may restrict the development of adequate, stable relationships in the new marriage.

The kin family: consisting of bilateral or intergenerational-linked members living in the same household. (Represents six percent of all households.)

Strengths

Maintenance of familial values and transmission of accumulated knowledge and skill are likely occurrences.

Multiple adults are available for socialization and shared household and work responsibilities.

Weaknesses

Demands for geographical mobility are not easily met.

From one perspective, the resistance to changes which threaten the maintenance of this family form can reduce the motivation of individuals to achieve in the society.

Experimental families: individuals in multi-adult households (communes) or cohabitating. (Represents four percent of all households.)

Strengths

In communal forms, a large number of individuals are available to form a support system to meet individual needs, a situation especially important to individuals in transition from one family form to another, such as recently divorced women with small children.

Individuals not ready or unwilling to make a commitment to a long-term partnership can experience economic and social sharing, psychic growth and open communication and interpersonal relationships.

Weaknesses

Few of these forms have developed strategies, techniques or economic bases to sustain their activities or achieve their goals.

In a large number of experimental family forms, role responsibilities are not clearly delineated or articulated, with consequential difficulties in implementing parenting, economic, household and other functions.[8]

Questions

1. What are the functions of the family?

2. What are the forms that the family takes presently?

3. What are some of the strengths of the dual-career family, the single-parent family and the single-career family?

4. Which family type do you know most about? Of the family types that you have experienced which seems most advantageous? What are its advantages?

5. What are the requirements for marriage other than age?

6. Why do the requirements for marriage exist?

7. What are the major changes in population patterns?

8. How do you think the current population changes will affect the culture of the United States?

Further reading

Etzioni, A. "The Family: Is It Obsolete?" *Journal of Current Social Issues,* no. 1 (1977).

Handbook of Labor Statistics 1975. Bulletin 1865. Washington, DC: Superintendent of Documents, U.S. Government Printing Office.

The World Almanac, 1978. New York: Newspaper Enterprise Association for Doubleday & Co., Inc. 1978.

Statistical Abstract of the United States: 1977. 98th Annual Edition. Washington, DC: Bureau of the Census.

Sussman, Marvin. "The Family Today." *Children Today,* March–April 1978.

Ramsey, J. "Experimental Family Forms—The Family of the Future." *Marriage and Family Review,* January/February 1978.

8. From "The Family Today: Is It An Endangered Species?" by Marvin B. Sussman in *Children Today,* March/April 1978, pp. 32–38, 45. Used by permission of the author.

Chapter 21

Marriage and commitment

Commitment is what makes marriage, living together, or any human relationship work. This means commitment to each other, to each other's ideas, ideals, and basic values.

Reprinted by permission of Sidney Harris.
From *American Scientist*, March/April 1975.

"This one writes some fine lyrics, and the other one
has done some beautiful music, but they just don't seem
to hit it off as collaborators."

If a relationship is built only on continuing "as long as we're both happy" then it is doomed for destruction. Every human relationship has its low and troublesome times. However, two persons committed to the continuation of the relationship and realistic about the problems that may arise can create an ongoing relationship.

Staying married

It is easy to marry. Staying married is difficult. The building of a happy marriage is a full-time task. It is a challenge to your individualhood, and your couplehood. The commitment of marriage is a step-by-step process. The marriage partners each need to be persons in their own right. They need to first establish their personhood or individualhood. The identity of self needs to face squarely, "Who am I? What do I stand for? What do I believe? What do I value? What are my goals?" The questions raised in Unit 1 and the answers to those questions establish your personhood or individualhood. Marriage then becomes a union between two well-defined persons, well-known to themselves and to each other.

This union might be diagrammed in the following way:

The marriage has security if each partner is a pillar of strength and contributes those strengths to the maintenance of the marriage. For example, if the wife commits her energy, skills, time, and money to the unity of the marriage and if the husband commits his energy, skills, time, and money to the unity of the marriage then that marriage has strong, sure, stable support.

Partnership

Support for and commitment to the marriage might be viewed as a partnership. In an effective partnership both parties must feel that they are important to each other in achieving their own as well as their common needs and objectives. Marriage is an individual as well as a team effort. Only when a couple is united toward achieving common goals can they hope to achieve their own goals better. If marriage partners focus on their marriage and common values and goals, then they are encouraged to fight the problems they have rather than each other.

A marriage is a union of two unique and independent individuals. A spouse is not a possession. The marriage certificate is not a contract of ownership. Competition has no place in a partnership. It is not a demonstration of how much better one is than someone else. The nature of competition is that one person wins and another loses. When two people are working toward common objectives, what value is gained by proving the other person inferior? To form a strong union, partners must first find their own individual areas of interest and expertise which can give them the personal satisfaction they need. They must also acknowledge, support, and benefit from each other's abilities and positive qualities.

One of the common misconceptions about marriage is that each partner must make personal sacrifices for the other. Such persons are confusing giving up with giving. When you give to a partner you receive some benefits from the act. It may be a personal satisfaction or some other good feeling which the act provides. But when you give up you feel martyred. An attitude of martyrdom is destructive to a marital relationship. Many men and women insist on being self-sacrificial. Then they become resentful toward their spouse because they feel they are missing out on their good times. Examples are, "I used to play golf on Sunday morning, but I don't do that anymore because I feel I should be with my family." Or, "I used to enjoy playing bridge, but I haven't played since we married." These self-sacrificial gestures, which are really attempts to maintain domestic tranquility, build walls between couples. When one partner submits to unreasonable demands that make him or her feel that he or she is giving up some important things, then the self, the partner, and the relationship are being shortchanged. In order to invest fully in a partner, a person must also invest in self. You cannot give to others until you first give to yourself. When personal desires are continually sacrificed to please a spouse, then the person feels cheated and martyred. This is not the kind of person your partner or spouse wants or wants to be responsible for creating.

Relationship states

In the book *Alive and Aware*, Miller, Nunnally, and Wackman discuss four relationship states. These are behaviors that partners, as husband and wife, adopt toward each other. The time intervals for these relationship states vary greatly from a brief moment to perhaps years.

The following diagram depicts these states.[1]

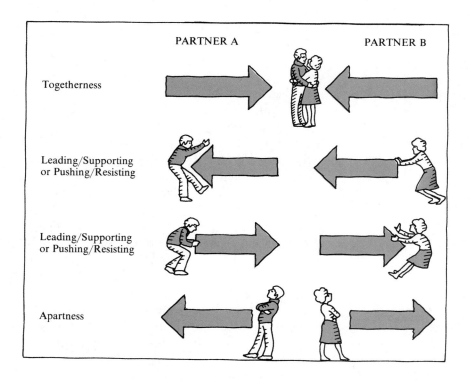

Togetherness. This first relationship state is the state where partners are involved with each other. The focus of this state is caring, sharing, talking seriously about an issue that affects their relationship. The partners in this state might be disagreeing or arguing, but nevertheless they are together and concerned with each other.

Leading/supporting. This second state occurs when one partner takes the lead, choosing to focus his or her energies on some

---

1. Reproduced from p. 16 of ALIVE AND AWARE: HOW TO IMPROVE YOUR RELATIONSHIPS THROUGH BETTER COMMUNICATION by Sherod Miller, Elam W. Nunnally, and Daniel B. Wackman. Minneapolis, Minn.: Interpersonal Communication Programs, Inc., 1975. Used by permission of the publisher.

outside interest or activity. The second partner follows and lends encouragement and support.

Pushing/resisting. This is the third relationship state. This occurs when one partner prods or pressures the second into focusing his or her energy in a certain direction.

Apartness. The fourth state is labeled apartness. Apartness occurs when partners are focusing their involvement and energies away from each other or on different things. A state of apartness can be pleasant and comfortable or upsetting. When the husband and wife pursue separate careers in an encouraging, supportive fashion, apartness is likely to be very fulfilling for each partner.

Each of these relationship states can be rewarding and fulfilling or upsetting and destructive depending upon how it is used. There is no single pattern of relationships which is ideal. Togetherness and apartness, leading and supporting, pushing and resisting all are essential for a growing relationship. Relationships which rotate primarily between the states of togetherness and apartness are typically happy and productive ones. However, to introduce new experiences, new information, and to discover new possibilities, these relationships shift to the leading/supporting and pushing/resisting states.[2]

Communication

Positive communication in marriage is a mutually satisfying way of expressing positive, love-enriching feelings. Communication can lead to understanding, understanding to acceptance, and acceptance to adjustment in marriage. Partners who will not or cannot communicate at all have little opportunity to either improve or even maintain their relationship. Most couples actually increase their communication and therefore their understanding by talking with one another. Most studies show that the more time couples spend in talking to each other, the more likely they are to report a high level of marital satisfaction.

2. Ibid., pp. 13–15, 20.

Couples who would have good communication need to improve both their desire and ability to listen. To listen carefully and objectively, and to listen to their partner's meanings as well as the words.

Dinah Maria Mulock Crails, an English novelist of the nineteenth century, described the best communication environment.

O, the comfort, the inexpressible comfort of feeling safe with a person, having neither to weigh thoughts nor measure words, but pouring them all right out, just as they are, chaff and grain together; certain that a faithful hand will take and sift them,

"Aren't you glad you're a nobody and not a big shot with the media picking on you all the time?"

keep what is worth keeping, and then with the breath of kindness, blow the rest away.

Four styles of communications[3]

Four different ways of talking or styles of communication are described. The examples will show the styles when they are pure. However, in conversation, most people do not use a style in its pure state, but mix the styles.

Style I. Style I is the communication style used in most of our everyday ordinary activities. In this style the person is trying to be

Intentions in Style I.

```
            I
        sociable
        friendly
      conventional
        playful


   II          III

        IV
```

3. Ibid., pp. 174, 181, 189, 202.

pleasant and friendly. He or she is not trying to change anybody or anything. The persons are involved and feel positive about each other. They want to share in acknowledging each other. They may even have a mutual affection for each other but do not say so directly.

Style II. As you can see Style II is different from Style I. In Style I, the individuals are giving simple preferences, chit-chatting, reporting events, telling stories, joking in a friendly way, complimenting on possessions, giving references, personal traits, or biographical data. In Style I, this is done in a normal, relaxed, friendly, tension-free manner.

Intentions in Style II.

However, in Style II diagrammed above, the individuals are trying to change each other. The tone is firm, loud, maybe even harsh. Certainly the voice is emotionally charged. Sometimes one can detect threats or sarcasm. The intentions in Style II do not simply involve keeping things moving smoothly. Style II has a certain outcome in mind. Style II is concerned with questions of right and wrong and what should or should not be done. In everyday conversation, Style II is very common. It is not always unfriendly because it is used to compliment, praise, persuade, or direct. Also it is the style used when one is lecturing, bargaining, selling, or advocating.

Style III.   In Style III the voice is calm, quiet, and a bit hesitant. In Style III one wants to reflect, explore, look at issues. Rather than trying to keep things smooth, as in Style I, or to change and control, as in Style II, one is trying to get a perspective.

Intentions in Style III.

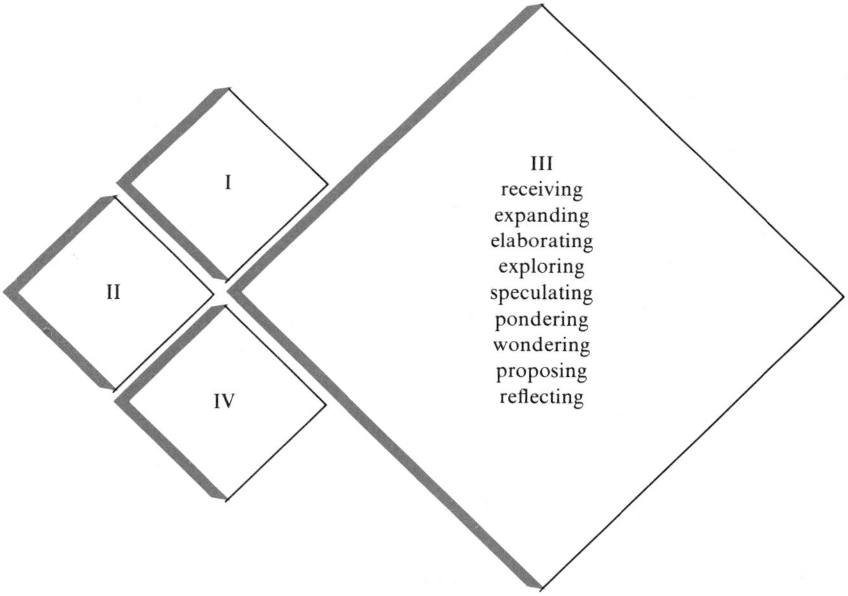

III
receiving
expanding
elaborating
exploring
speculating
pondering
wondering
proposing
reflecting

I

II

IV

Style IV.   In this style there is a commitment to deal completely and methodically with one issue. The partners are communicating with the intentions of valuing both themselves and each other. One partner accepts the other partner's self-awareness. One partner tries to understand the other accurately, not necessarily agreeing, but hearing and accepting the intimate disclosure. Style IV expresses an intention to pursue an issue openly and directly rather than avoiding it.

Intentions in Style IV.

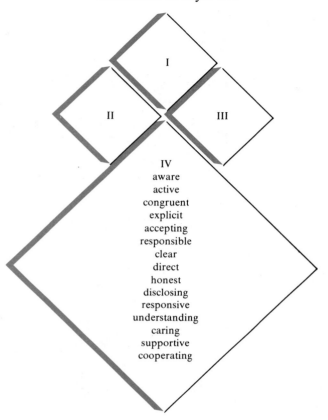

IV
aware
active
congruent
explicit
accepting
responsible
clear
direct
honest
disclosing
responsive
understanding
caring
supportive
cooperating

Intentions and behaviors have been associated with each of the four styles of communication.

Communication in marriage[4]

Communication is important in marriage. There are many styles of communication and states in relationships. They are mingled, not clear-cut. But an awareness of this inevitable incompleteness is itself a contribution to marital adjustment. A commitment to the relationship and an awareness of the challenge of communication should be helpful.

One often hears it said that when a couple have a marital problem, they should talk it over. This is good, to the extent that this implies

4. Ibid., pp. 208, 210.

getting the problem out in the open instead of hiding it. But because of the incompleteness of communication, discussion is not an automatic solution to all problems. There can be hearing without listening. Hearing is merely the perception of sound. Listening is attention to sounds in an effort to gain meaning. When listening the partner opens his or her mind to what is being said through attention, interest, and concern. Listening is an active art. One partner can aid another's speaking or make it more difficult by the way he or she listens. If attention is divided, if the listener is distracted by reading the paper or drumming on the table, the speaker's problem is increased. On the other hand, the speaker cannot expect full attention if he or she tries to talk to the listener when the partner is already occupied. It is not only what is said but how it is said. The listener reacts to both. The content of communication may be resisted because of the tone of voice or attitude of the speaker.

Behaviors Characteristic of Each Style.

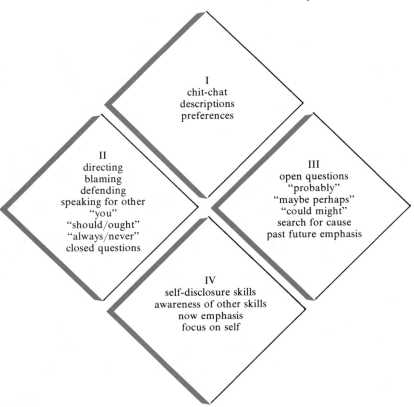

I
chit-chat
descriptions
preferences

II
directing
blaming
defending
speaking for other
"you"
"should/ought"
"always/never"
closed questions

III
open questions
"probably"
"maybe perhaps"
"could might"
search for cause
past future emphasis

IV
self-disclosure skills
awareness of other skills
now emphasis
focus on self

Intentions Associated with Each Style.

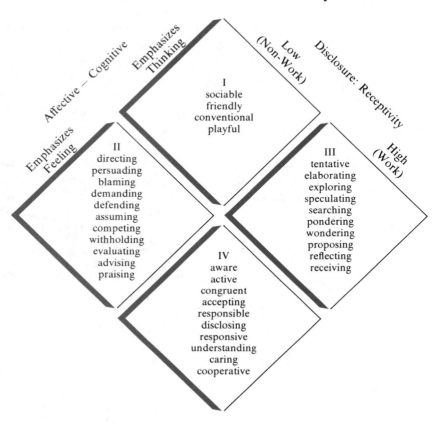

Communication is furthered to the degree that each person is aware of complexes, special sensitivities, fears, values, biases, and points of resistance. Communication is also furthered to the degree that each person is confident of understanding and acceptance rather than judgments and rejection.

When a couple who want their marriage to succeed reach the end of communication and therefore understanding, they must commit an act of faith, and accept differences because of their trust, confidence, and love for each other. Again, marriage is commitment.

Questions

1. What is meant by commitment in marriage?

2. How is marriage security created?

3. How should one's marriage partner be viewed to promote a positive marriage relationship?

4. Give conversation examples for each style of communication.

5. Give a negative and a positive example for each of the four relationship states.

6. Interview couples from different marital periods to see if there are communication growths that they can detect.

7. Do you think growth in communication skills would increase happiness? Why? Why not?

| **Further reading** | Mace, David R. *Getting Ready for Marriage.* Nashville, TN: Abingdon Press, 1972. |

Miller, Sherod; Nunnally, Elam; and Wackman, Daniel. *Alive and Aware: Improving Communications in Relationships.* Minneapolis, MN: Interpersonal Communications Programs, Inc., 1975.

Myers, Gail E., and Myers, Michele. *The Dynamics of Human Communication.* 2d ed. New York: McGraw-Hill, 1975.

Nichols, R. G., and Stevens, L. A. *Are You Listening?* New York: McGraw-Hill, 1957.

Smith, Rebecca M. *Klemer's Marriage and Family Relationships.* New York: Harper & Row, Publishers, Inc., 1975.

Stinnett, Nick, and Walters, James. *Relationships in Marriage and Family.* New York: Macmillan, Inc., 1977.

Wahbroos, Sven. *Family Communication.* New York: Macmillan, Inc., 1974.

Chapter 22

Marriage and role

Role equality depends on one's view of the role to be played. Role satisfaction is tied to role expectation. If marriage partners have conflicting ideas of their individual roles, they will experience dissatisfaction.

Reprinted by permission of Mel Yauk.
From *Good Housekeeping,* © 1974 by The Hearst Corporation.

"I know I could learn housework well enough to do half of it."

The changing male role

There are many factors that have contributed to changing the male role. This change has positive and negative values. The judgment of which is positive and which is negative will be determined by your own personal values, standards, and attitudes. Some factors that have contributed are these.

1. To the extent that women have gained privileges, men have had to change attitudes and expectations. They have suffered considerable loss of self-esteem. For example, the nineteenth amendment to the Constitution, which gave women the vote, altered the male privilege of making and executing the laws and planning the government.

2. The training of the child has been left to the mother and the female teacher because of the daily absence of the father from home and the disappearance of the male teacher from the grade school. The male child has been left with only female models much of the time.

3. Human brawn and brute strength have been replaced by atomic power, electricity, machines, and horsepower.

4. The amount of work a man has to do outside the home has diminished. He has time to share in child care and other domestic tasks. This is especially true if he lives near his work and works regular hours.

5. The disappearance of the servant class has made it necessary for both husband and wife to work at home. The increase in the mechanical servants (dishwashers, garbage disposals, etc.) has made this more acceptable to male interests.

6. The change in our value system toward occupations and interests that were previously considered effeminate such as drama, beauty culture, sculpture, dress designing, interior decorating, and food preparation have made vast differences in career training and acquired skills.

7. The entrance of women into numerous vocations has often reversed the roles of the male and female in the field of parenthood itself. In many families both parents work. One may work during the day while the other works at night. Thus, each parent plays the dual father-mother role during their portion of the day alone with the children.

Men have come to recognize that they can be oppressed by a designated role or traditional view of having to prove themselves as achievers and providers. Men are taking a hard look at the mixed blessedness of being male. They are reassessing their priorities, their ideas about success, their notions of themselves.

Some are turning down overtime, transfers, and promotions in favor of more time at home and a more stable family life. They are getting more involved as fathers, from the prenatal stage onward. They are asserting their rights as fathers in divorce cases. More and more fathers are demanding equality as a parent in custody battles.

Men are venturing to express emotions. They are finding it acceptable to confess fears, even to weep. This shift in male attitudes is most apparent among men in the 20-30 age group who are educated. The majority of older men have modified their views of male-female roles very little. The blue-collar community still sees the man's home as his castle with the wife working to please him and to make ends meet.

A case study on the changing male

I Can Be Open[1]
Newsweek, January 16, 1978

At 22, Bob Amore belongs to a generation still grappling with the transitional roles of the sexes. Like many of his campus contemporaries, he supports most feminist goals as a matter of simple justice. "It seems moronic to me that a woman could be working herself as hard as a man and not get paid as much," he says. And like many young males, he also harbors some primal notions of the rights of men. A girlfriend paying her own way on a date makes him feel "a little less macho," he says. And a girlfriend driving the car is even worse: "I feel like a little kid being driven around by my mother. When I'm driving, I feel like I'm in control. For one thing, I like the idea that I'm *protecting* her."

As a music and acting major at Northwestern University, Amore is the product of two cultures—the traditional one he grew up in and the liberated one that surrounds him at school. Raised in a Roman Catholic family in Brooklyn, N.Y., he senses that he is more conservative on the issues of the women's movement than some of his friends. But he knows he has become more liberal than his father, a teacher. "I used to copy my father's ideas," he recalls. "I can remember thinking, 'Who do these women think they are?' Today, I'm liable to pick up one of their magazines and read through it. I've actually been reading that 'trash' and there are some good things in it. So I've become a lot more open-minded to feminism."

The Upper Hand: Amore's parents divorced when he was a college freshman, and he believes it was due, in part, to his father's being too "overbearing" in the marriage. He is certain he will be more "understanding" toward his own wife when he marries. Yet he is equally convinced of his need to have the upper hand. "I don't think my family would work if I wasn't the head of it in a domineering way," he says. "I think I need it, and I think my wife would have to know I need it." His present girlfriend surely knows: though he doesn't hesitate to do the cooking and cleaning in his own off-campus apartment, when he has dinner at her house, there is not much question about who does the chores. "Oh, I may help her with the dishes," he says, "but in a very chauvinistic way I feel she's the woman and that's her job. Sometimes she likes it, sometimes she hates it."

Amore is aware that his cherished ideas of male and female roles are undergoing a gradual, significant change, but he is still confused. "Intellectually I realize women are taking on different roles but I still like to think of them in a rather traditional sense," he says. "Maybe women really are superior to men, as I heard a psychiatrist say on a TV show. They seem to cope with strain better and they don't need their egos boosted all the time like we do. Guys still need to hang around together, reinforce each other. That hasn't changed from my dad's time."

Breaking the Barrier: The dawning sense of male hangups helped Amore work through an important decision. As a youngster, he explains, he had been enthralled at performances of the American Ballet Theater, and he harbored a secret desire to be a dancer. But although dancing would have helped him advance his acting ambitions, it struck him as being too "feminine." Instead, Amore says, he went in for sports and weight-lifting. "I guess I considered myself more masculine the more I lifted weights. But recently, I broke down the barrier in myself and started practicing ballet. I'd worked through the whole 'queer' stigma. And I realize now that I had more hangups when I lifted weights than now that I'm dancing. I love it. I look better and feel better—though my father still has a problem with it."

In spite of himself and the covenants of his upbringing, Amore finds the new sexual egalitarianism is having its effect on him. He never would have taken up ballet, he says, except that it has become more acceptable for men who are "straight." And his tensions about masculinity have eased up in other ways as well. "Nowadays I'm still not sure of myself about a lot of things," he says. "But at least I can be open. I can pinpoint my problems, even if I don't know what to do." And just being able to admit that uncertainty separates the new male from the old macho.

—David Gelman with *Bureau Reports*

The changing female role

Homemaking used to be the career choice of married women. Today many married women combine this career with another career outside of the home. Some married women plan to work only until their children are born while others combine homemaking, parenting, and a career outside the home. For a number of reasons, 40 per cent of all American mothers work. These women are parents of 26 million children, of whom 6 million are under six years of age.

Some of the factors that have contributed to changing the female role are as follows.

1. To the extent that the man is away from home, the wife must assume the role of a male as well as a female figure in the family.

2. To the extent that the number of single-parent families has increased through divorce, loss of the father by an early death, or unwed parenthood, the woman has had to assume the head of the household position.

3. Women are becoming increasingly better educated. They are capable of wage-earning outside the home and of assuming responsible community positions.

4. The change in our value system allows us to accept career women in medicine, business, law, politics, and other professions formerly closed to women.

5. Women are interested in economic independence and feel the need to use their education to contribute to the world of work.

6. New technological advances have decreased the time needed for home maintenance.

7. New improved birth control means that couples can plan their families and limit the number of children.

8. Society is more accepting of women in the work force and of working mothers.

Why women work

The Gallup Organization conducted a survey of married women between the ages of 18 and 35 to find out why they work and how they feel about their work. This was reported in the April 1978 issue of *Redbook* Magazine,[2] and is given on the next page.

2. From "Women and Their Work" by Morton Hunt. Copyright © 1978 by Morton Hunt. Originally appeared in *Redbook* Magazine. Reprinted by permission of Robert Lescher Literary Agency.

Four out of ten working wives—including those whose husbands earn under $7000—said that the money they earn is less important than the "pleasure," "fulfillment" or "recognition" they get from working.

Two out of three said they'd feel stifled and bored if they didn't work.

Three out of four said they find their present work "very satisfying" or said that it gave them a "sense of identity."

Finally they were asked, if money were no object and child care no problem, would they still want to work? More than four out of five said they would want to work.

For most women as well as men, in addition to the money, work has major psychological and social rewards. Contrary to the accepted myth, wives who work are as committed to their jobs as men are. The marriages of working wives are as good as those of full-time homemakers. Nearly all the mothers among working women feel that holding a good job does their children no harm. These women meet the demands of their complex lives with little outside help, except for child care. Though few have husbands who share household tasks equally, the great majority consider themselves more fortunate than wives who don't work.

However, the full-time homemakers who choose to be homemakers also report contentment. This current survey indicates that women today, working outside the home or as homemakers, have a higher degree of self-esteem than in the 1960s and early 1970s.

When discussing marital relationships, the majority of working wives report certain good effects.

1. more to talk about with their husbands

2. more input into the finances of the family

3. interests other than marriage and family so they are more interesting people

4. a greater sense of self-esteem so less dependent upon the husband for ego-enrichment

The partners are freer to have a more equal relationship as two independent persons rather than one being dependent upon the other.

Marriage roles and the family life cycle

The family life cycle, shown in the following sketches, brings with it changes in roles, conflicting roles, and shifting role expectations.

Clifford Kirkpatrick has made a distinction between three roles provided in our society for the married woman. Each role implies certain privileges and certain obligations.

The wife-and-mother role. The wife-and-mother role is the traditional role of the married woman. It implies privileges of security, the right of support, alimony in case of divorce, respect as a wife and

"Good grief! What have you done with Santa Claus?"

Family-founding

This is the establishing phase. The young couple faces conflicting loyalties between parents and spouse. Husband may feel guilty about neglecting his mother.

Child-bearing

Young husband may feel guilty if his wife is very uncomfortable. He may also feel displaced by a new baby. Wife may be uncertain about her new role and her changing appearance.

Child-rearing

As children grow and develop minds of their own, they normally disobey. However, this may make the parents feel incompetent and anxious about the way they are playing their roles as father and mother. The father, engrossed in earning a living, may feel guilty not spending more time with his wife and children.

mother. It also implies a certain amount of domestic authority, loyalty of husband to the mother of his children, and sentimental gratitude from husband and children. Corresponding obligations include bearing and rearing children, making a home, doing domestic service. It requires being loyal to the economic interests of the husband, accepting a dependent social and economic status, and tolerating a limited range of activities.

The companion role. The companion role is essentially one which fulfills joint psychological needs. The privileges in this role include pleasures shared with the husband, a more romantic emotional response, admiration, respect for the opinions and requirements of the other, shared leisure in social and educational activities, plus chivalrous attention. On the other hand, it implies as obligations the

Child-launching
In this phase children leave the family to establish their own lives away from the family. Mother may feel neglected and misunderstood. She may feel worthless since her childcare duties are over.

The empty nest
The husband and wife have to readjust to having just the two of them in the home. They now have time to have a social life that is geared to their wishes and needs rather than having to consider the children's wishes and needs. They can take more responsibility for life outside their family unit. They need to adjust to living at the retirement income level. They need to consider their role in taking care of themselves and each other physically. They have to prepare for the prospect of the death of either spouse and become widow or widower.

preservation of beauty, the giving of ego and erotic satisfaction of each other, the cultivation of social contacts, staying intellectually alert, and the responsibility for preventing boredom.

The partner role. Finally, the partner role corresponds to a new definition of family relationships. This role includes acceptance as an equal, the privilege of economic independence, equal authority in regard to family finances, equal sharing of domestic duties, equal voice in determining the locality of residence, and equality in regard to social and moral freedom. On the other hand, obligations of this role include renouncing of alimony, except in the case of dependent children, contributing economically in proportion to earning ability, accepting equal responsibility for the support of children. Sharing legal responsibilities of the family, giving up any appeal to chivalry, dismissing special privileges in regard to children, and sharing equal responsibility to maintain the family status by success in a career are obligations.[3]

The three roles are an attempt to make a definite distinction between the kinds of relationships studied. It would seem that a vital marriage might be a combination of some aspects from each of the roles.

The following case study shows role change. Karl and Freda met in college. Karl was majoring in industrial arts. Freda was a medical student. Karl taught industrial arts at a junior high school. Freda was a driving, ambitious doctor, well-liked and respected by her many patients. The tax referendum for the school system did not pass. In order to cut educational expenses, the industrial arts program was cut from the curriculum. Karl was unemployed. The couple had two children. Because of her irregular hours, Freda had always left the routine care of the children up to a baby-sitter and Karl. Freda's practice became more and more demanding. As the children grew, baby-sitters were less competent to handle their growing needs. Karl decided to stay home and take over the maternal role. Because he had been with the children more than Freda and because he was more easygoing, more affectionate, and a willing listener, he was already the emotional center of the household. Today Karl and Freda are a very happy couple who have a delightful family. While such instances are rare and are perhaps not yet fully approved by our culture, they do represent the extreme to which the male role has been modified and can be modified in our day.

Adults want to be children

Marriages are often unhappy because men and women, subconsciously, want to remain children all of their lives. There is no way for an adult to recapture childhood in the world of work. He or she wants to be the happy, selfish, waited-upon child. He or she wants his or her spouse to be the loving parent. A person's home may seem to be his or her castle to the outside world. Inside, it is more often his or her nursery. That is one of the reasons why some marriages are unhappy. Each spouse wants to be the child and wants his or her spouse to be the parent.

The honeymoon is over when she says "Don't expect me to wait on you like your mother!" and when he says, "Look, you are not Daddy's baby girl anymore. Act like a grown woman!" Love in

3. From pp. 168–169 of *The Family: As Process and Institution*, 2d ed., by Clifford Kirkpatrick. Copyright 1963, The Ronald Press Company. Used by permission of John Wiley & Sons, Inc.

marriage seldom lasts unless both husband and wife are willing to behave like mature people. For this is reality. There is no return to childhood, in or out of marriage. The real world of struggle and suffering, of tragedy, of the need to take responsibility and to make hard decisions sooner or later comes into the home. The best chance a married couple have of overcoming their troubles is to face them as adults and as equals.

Deciding on roles

Increased concern over marital roles is normal and natural in a culture that increasingly emphasizes freedom for individuals. Pressures from society, however, often make today's mates feel guilty because of their personal rejection of the traditional patterns of behavior.

Many conditioning factors influence role expectations in marriage. These include early family experiences, cultural sex influences, environmental factors, and group factors such as ethnic and social-class backgrounds.

One major modern-role concern involves the family power structure. Originally, the male was the supreme head of the family. His position has been supported by such influences as religion, law, a belief that man was superior to woman and that woman was naturally more submissive.

There are many frustrations for modern, well-educated wives and their husbands who try to conform to traditional marital roles. Some of these stem from the fact that modern wives lack sufficient training or skills in homemaking, having neglected this side of their education. A deeper appreciation for homemaking, family relations, and child development by both sexes is lacking. In some cases, the professional career of the husband appears to dictate the role of the wife. Often this role is not acceptable to a modern, ambitious woman.

The time to consider these problems, however, is before marriage, not afterward. This challenges each of you to know your chosen mate well enough before marriage so that you have an idea of his or her role expectation as well as your own. This knowledge takes time, maturity, career preparation, and the ability to communicate with another person.

Modern couples cannot return to an agriculture-oriented society. Instead, they must prepare themselves socially, technically, and psychologically for today's life. Biological limitations will always mean that the roles of the sexes will be different. However, when that difference is understood and acceptable to each sex through an appreciation of role expectation in today's society, stronger marriages will emerge.

Questions

1. How is one's role expectation a predictor of one's role satisfaction?

2. How has the male role changed?

3. How are men accepting change in their lives?

4. How has the female role changed?

5. Why do women work? What rewards do they get from work?

6. Why do marital partners look to each other for nurturance? How does this affect their marriage?

7. How is the family life cycle simplified if the couple remains childless?

8. What are the different marital roles?

9. Which sex seems to be changed the most in terms of traditional roles? What are the causes or explanations of this situation?

10. Describe several areas in which the line of demarcation between male and female roles seems to be disappearing.

Further reading

Cullison, Pamela Wilson. "Woman's Rights and the Family: A Commonsense Look." *Better Homes and Gardens,* October 1973.

Bernard, Jessie. *The Future of Marriage.* New York: World Publishing, 1972.

"Human Roles: Examining Choices Through Education." *Illinois Teacher,* no. 5 (1975).

Hunt, Morton. "Women and Their Work." *Redbook Magazine,* April 1978.

Westlake, Helen. "Today's Sex Roles and Developmental Differences in the Male and Female." *Illinois Teacher,* no. 4 (1973).

Yorburg, Betty. *The Changing Family.* New York: Columbia University Press, 1973.

Chapter 23

Marriage and love

Marriage and love are thought of together. What is an ideal marriage? Is it separateness or togetherness? These ideas are worlds apart. Many people become bewildered because each idea seems to offer its own special fulfillment.

Intimacy

Marriage partners are looking for a significant relationship. They do not want the suffocating intimacy that welds two people into one, thereby inhibiting growth. Rather they want intimacy that allows the two to grow. Unfortunately, this is a goal more often sought than gained.

What is this intimacy that so many people want? It is a relationship of trust. It is one in which each partner can feel free to reveal his or her deepest and most hidden emotions. It is one in which each partner feels free to become emotionally sincere, open, and honest, confident that he or she will not be judged or betrayed. It is a relationship of understanding in which one partner doesn't have to keep saying, "Do you know what I mean?" It's a shared perspective of life and a sense of common values and goals. It's a sanctuary from the outside world, a sanctuary that gives rest and then energy to the partners for going out into the world.

Intimacy in which two people reinforce each other and their relationship is rare. But these rare moments can help a couple through a lot of everyday experiences. Such moments also establish a tone for the marriage, a sense that the partners have a caring relationship.

From *Saturday Review*, © 1971.
Reprinted by permission of *Saturday Review* and Barney Tobey.

"The answer is yes. Now move over.
The Jets are on the ten-yard line."

Intimacy is precious, but costly. The price is giving up some personal secret. This giving can bring a couple closer if the gift is given in a spirit of love and choice rather than as a duty and an obligation.

Separate identities

Often couples who have become close to each other begin to wonder if they are losing their separate identities. They may feel insecure about the phrases "we think," "we want," or "we'll see you later." They may wonder about what has happened to the "me" in "we."

When either partner feels that his or her separate identity has been drowned in the relationship, there is rebellion. Generally the partners try to rediscover themselves. Each nurtures private interests, develops his or her own friends, confides less in the other, seeks the self at every turn.

During the times of separation there are moments of tension. The pair may be frightened by the change from the safe, stable situation they knew to one whose outcome is uncertain. But these moments can still be thought of as gifts to the marriage. They are gifts that will keep the marriage from becoming so comfortable that it is dull and predictable. For in a good marriage, as both people grow, they keep revitalizing their relationship.

Conflict

Many people feel conflict between what they owe their partner and what they owe themselves. In relationships between two vital, healthy people, there are bound to be times when the needs of the individual conflict with the needs of the twosome. When people care about their relationships, they realize that what they want calls for sacrifice from the other person. For example, consider the young mother who plans to go back to college full time, the husband who turns to using his spare hours to train for a marathon race, or the spouse whose new job requires a great deal of travel. All need to talk to their partners about why the particular goal is important and what its pursuit will mean to them as a couple and as individuals.

Changes in standards

The standards for what people owe each other have changed. Years ago, if a woman fulfilled her role as homemaker and didn't run around with other men or if a man provided for his family, didn't drink or gamble or beat his wife, the couple stayed together. There was a mutual understanding that each would fulfill the traditional roles. If marriage brought happiness and companionship, the couple considered themselves blessed. If not, that was "God's will." In the musical *Fiddler on the Roof,* the milkman, Tevye, asks his wife, "Do you love me?" "Do I . . . what?" she answers, adding. "For twenty-five years I've washed your clothes, cooked your meals, cleaned your house, given you children, milked the cow. After twenty-five years, why talk about love right now?"

But today people expect more from marriage. Intimacy is what marriage is all about today. Marriage partners often have no idea what their mates will interpret as an intimate act. They need time to talk, to raise questions such as "Can you think of three times when you felt especially close to me?" or "How can I show you that I love you?" Refusing to show how much the other person means to you is one way of putting intimacy into the future. For many people sex is not the rich experience that it could be, partly because people are unsure of themselves and afraid to lose themselves in physical intimacy. Psychoanalyst Erik H. Erikson feels that sexual intimacy cannot exist until each partner has developed a good sense of personal identity and is ready to join this identity with that of the loved one in a committed relationship. On the other side of the conflict between selfhood and intimacy is the creation of a new and larger

Reprinted by permission of Al Ross. From *Saturday Review*, © 1970.

"I like the rhetoric. Give him a dollar, dear."

Reprinted by permission of John Jonik.
From *Saturday Review/World*, © 1974.

"When I think of all those winters we wasted
hibernating in that stupid cave . . . !"

identity in the marriage relationship itself. This identity goes beyond the individual personality each partner has brought to the marriage.

Intimacy is not a prison that locks us away from our individual selves but is an open avenue for finding ourselves and our loved ones. Each couple in love can define their own level of intimacy. Two healthy individuals can be close without the need to be with each other constantly, unable to exist without the other. Both partners can go their separate ways, each proclaiming independence and coming together only for the practical business of food, children, paying bills, and sexual needs.

Somewhere between these extremes lies the ever-changing and growing phenomenon of a mature, healthy, emotional interdependence in which each person loves, values, and nurtures the other and lets the other thrive in his or her own way.

Marital love

Love in a marriage relationship must grow and change with time. When the partners grow, develop, and change for their individual betterment and for the enrichment of the couplehood, we have a positive marital love. Probably the one most important word to describe a positive love is dedication. This is love that is dedicated with determination, dedicated to the partner, to the partner's growth, and to the partnership. Partners who are committed to the growth of the marital relationship concentrate on the many facets of marriage.

Marriage has four main aspects: the bond of love and sex, mutual aid, the struggle for existence, and the desire for children. Each of these aspects changes over the years. But if a couple are dedicated to marriage in principle and are willing to learn to accept and to appreciate the changes, the result can be a dynamic life together.

Modern couples may or may not have children, but whether they do or don't, they expect love and romance to continue throughout their marriages. There is nothing wrong with expecting love, emotional and sexual gratification, security, intellectual companionship, playfulness, intimacy, growth, and stability in marriage, unless we expect too much. It is unrealistic to expect perfection, and self-defeating to be disappointed when a good marriage stops just short of perfection.

Life consists, at best, of a number of deep pleasures and satisfactions interwoven with problems, disappointments, and pain of one sort or another. Nothing is flawless all of the time. Things do go wrong now and then. But so long as the basic structure of the marriage is sound, there is no reason to feel angry or betrayed when difficulties arise. Dedication can stem the tide.

Carl Sandburg describes marital love as honey and salt in the following poem.

Honey and Salt[1]

A bag of tricks—is it?
  And a game smoothies play?
If you're good with a deck of cards
or rolling the bones—that helps?
If you can tell jokes and be a chum
and make an impression—that helps?
When boy meets girl or girl meets boy—
                        what helps?
They all help: be cozy but not too cozy:
be shy, bashful, mysterious, yet only so-so:
then forget everything you ever heard about love
for it's a summer tan and a winter windburn
and it comes as weather comes and you can't change it:
it comes like your face came to you, like your legs came

1. From HONEY AND SALT, copyright © 1963 by Carl Sandburg. Reprinted by permission of Harcourt Brace Jovanovich, Inc.

and the way you walk, talk, hold your head and hands—
and nothing can be done about it—you wait and pray.
      Is there any way of measuring love?
      Yes but not till long afterward
      when the beat of your heart has gone
      many miles, far into the big numbers.
Is the key to love in passion, knowledge, affection?
All three—along with moonlight, roses, groceries,
givings and forgivings, gettings and forgettings,
      keepsakes and room rent,
      pearls of memory along with ham and eggs.
Can love be locked away and kept hid?
      Yes and it gathers dust and mildew
      and shrivels itself in shadows
      unless it learns the sun can help,
      snow, rain, storms can help—
      birds in their one-room family nests
      shaken by winds cruel and crazy—
      they can all help:
      lock not away your love nor keep it hid.
How comes the first sign of love?
      In a chill, in a personal sweat,
      in a you-and-me, us, us two,
      in a couple of answers,
      an amethyst haze on the horizon,
      two dance programs criss-crossed,
      jackknifed initials interwoven,
      five fresh violets lost in sea salt,
      birds flying at single big moments
      in and out a thousand windows,
      a horse, two horses, many horses,
      a silver ring, a brass cry,
      a golden gong going ong ong ong-ng-ng,
      pink doors closing one by one
      to sunset nightsongs along the west,
      shafts and handles of stars,
      folds of moonmist curtains,
      winding and unwinding wisps of fogmist.

How long does love last?
As long as glass bubbles handled with care
or two hot-house orchids in a blizzard
or one solid immovable steel anvil
tempered in sure inexorable welding—
or again love might last as
six snowflakes, six hexagonal snowflakes,
six floating hexagonal flakes of snow
or the oaths between hydrogen and oxygen
      in one cup of spring water
       or the eyes of bucks and does
or two wishes riding on the back of a
      morning wind in winter
or one corner of an ancient tabernacle
held sacred for personal devotions
or dust   yes   dust in a little solemn heap
      played on by changing winds.
      There are sanctuaries
            holding honey and salt.
      There are those who
          spill and spend.
      There are those who
          search and save.
      And love may be a quest
          with silence and content.
      Can you buy love?
Sure   every day with money, clothes, candy,
with promises, flowers, big-talk,
with laughter, sweet-talk, lies,
every day men and women buy love
and take it away and things happen
      and they study about it
      and the longer they look at it
the more it isn't love they bought at all:
      bought love is a guaranteed imitation.

      Can you sell love?
Yes   you can sell it and take the price
      and think it over
      and look again at the price
      and cry and cry to yourself
and wonder who was selling what and why.

Evensong lights floating black night waters,
a lagoon of stars washed in velvet shadows,
a great storm cry from white sea-horses—
     these moments cost beyond all prices.

     Bidden or unbidden? how comes love?
Both bidden and unbidden, a sneak and a shadow,
     a dawn in a doorway throwing a dazzle
     or a sash of light in a blue fog,
a slow blinking of two red lanterns in river mist
or a deep smoke winding one hump of a mountain
and the smoke becomes a smoke known to your own
     twisted individual garments:
the winding of it gets into your walk, your hands,
     your face and eyes.

Questions

1. What is the basic meaning of the term "intimacy"?

2. What is an ideal marriage?

3. How does an intimate relationship change over time?

4. How have the standards for love in marriage changed? How do you feel about the change?

5. Write your personal promise of love.

6. List at least 10 characteristics of love from Sandburg's poem.

Further reading

Attman, I., and Taylor, D. A. *Social Penetration: The Development of Interpersonal Relationships.* New York: Holt, Rinehart & Winston, CBS, Inc., 1973.

Goffman, E. *Encounters.* Indianapolis, IN: The Bobbs-Merrill Co., Inc., 1961.

Grossman, Jack H. *The Business of Living.* Briarcliff Manor, NY: Stein & Day Publishers, 1975.

Lasswell, Marcia, and Lobsenz, Normal. "The Varieties of Intimacy." *McCall's,* June 1976, pp. 50–56.

Sandburg, Carl. *Honey and Salt.* New York: Harcourt Brace Jovanovich, Inc., 1963.

Chapter 24

Marriage and money

Money, in our technical and urban society, has become the measure of value. The "things" that money buys have become status symbols. The worth of a person is measured by his or her securities instead of his or her sincerities.

We are oriented to the future. By the future, we mean tomorrow. Tomorrow we will make the big deal, get the promotion, go to a better job. We search for happiness. When we are pressed for our definition of happiness or how it is achieved, we think usually of income, social status, a beautiful partner, brilliant children, a 24-foot boat, or a fine car.

This may not be a description of you, but it does describe thousands and thousands of people. With these values and goals, people often find themselves in the situations shown by the cartoons. Putting a longer pole on the mail box won't deter the bills, just inconvenience the person who delivers the mail. Having to meet a daily installment often leads people to a loan shark or to full dependence in money management. You should manage money. It should not manage you.

Marriage and the use of money

Money problems are among the most common problems in marriage. There is never enough money to satisfy all desires, and unless couples learn to cooperate in the spending of it, there is trouble.

Our expectations, values, attitudes, family background, training, religious beliefs, and physical environment all affect our use of money.

Reprinted by permission of Joseph Mirachi.
From *Saturday Review,* © 1971.

"Maybe it would help, dear, if you could just think of being stuck in a holding pattern as getting more flying for your money."

Influence on the use of money

Values and expectations. Individual values and expectations in the use of money are important. The occupational demands of the family members dictate some of the items on the budget. For example, a doctor or a college professor may need to buy books or to attend professional meetings at his or her own expense. The salesperson may find it necessary to play golf and to belong to a country club in order to have the proper business contacts. The craftsman, truck driver, or electrician may have to spend a certain amount for union dues. Clothing expenditures are also influenced by the occupations of the family members.

Social pressures. If a family lives among families of like income and interests it is hard to resist the influence of the social group. If all children in the group attend children's theater it is hard to deny the children in the family the same experience. If weekend outings

for couples are a part of the club recreation there is pressure on the couple to participate.

Psychological needs.   Psychological needs often determine the use of money.   For example, a husband and wife may not achieve the recognition they need.   Therefore they entertain frequently in order to compensate and to be accepted in the "right circles."   They may find it necessary to bowl, play poker, belong to a certain club, or join the group in the corner tavern for the same reason.   Some couples satisfy their need for status by being sure that their children are given all the advantages they were denied or could not achieve.

Whether the need is to compensate for insecurity, lack of status, or for some other lack, these attempts to satisfy do affect spending.   It is impossible to indicate all the forms such action may take.   It is important we understand rather than judge a family's idea of its needs.

Just as the family can have a need for security or status, so can the individual.   Individual psychological needs are sometimes met through the use of or the hoarding of money.   The husband who must constantly prove that he is the dominant figure in the family can do so by holding a tight rein on the family's expenditures.   The wife may demand that she control the finances.   She may arbitrarily dole out a small allowance to her husband because she resents his headship in the family.

Life cycle.   The changes in the needs of the family members as the family moves through the life cycle also influence the use of money.   The new family spends more for major appliances, furniture, and other items that make up the foundation for a family.   Whereas the family in the child-rearing stage may spend more for education, medical bills, and insurance.

The optimistic expectations of teenagers about their first home after marriage and the high priority assigned to car ownership can be sources of financial problems for teenagers entering marriage.   Without adequate financial counseling, these expectations and attitudes can become problems for newly married couples.

Financial mistakes

Young married couples, as well as others, need help with financial plans.   Often young couples feel that they do not have enough money to make any difference.   However, a plan for financial security is just as important as are the plans for other goals and values.   Perhaps by studying this list of ten common financial mistakes, couples can better make a financial plan that will be effective.

10 Common Financial Mistakes[1]

Haphazard financial planning isn't limited to inexperienced people or those with modest incomes. Top executives often make blunders in handling their money. Investment authorities identify these common errors:

1. *Failure to set long range objectives.* "Having a financial plan and holding tó it is just as crucial as having a blueprint for building a good house or creating a successful business," says investment counselor David Wendell of David L. Babson & Company, Inc. "In my experience," he adds, "most investors don't set goals and stick with them. Instead, they have collections of securities bought on tips, hearsay advice or casual comment from friends."

2. *Lack of an up-to-date will and estate plan.* Many financially successful people haven't kept their wills updated. The Tax Reform Act of 1976 made so many changes in taxation of estates and gifts that a will drawn more than 18 months ago probably is outmoded.

3. *"Falling in love" with one's investments.* Even the most carefully selected securities can go sour as a result of changing government policies, shifts in consumer preferences, or management upheaval. "At least once a year, go over your stocks and make it a point to sell one that has done poorly," says David Sargent, president of United Business Service. "Continually weeding out deadwood will strengthen your list."

4. *Being too greedy.* An old Wall Street adage says, "A bull or a bear can make money in the market, but a pig rarely can." Conservative advisers suggest selling stock that has had a sharp run-up in price rather than holding on in the hope that it will go even higher.

5. *Neglecting an insurance program.* Inflation has outdated millions of insurance plans. Life insurance policies need to be checked periodically, along with the homeowner's policy.

6. *Failure to recognize that tax shelters have drawbacks as well as advantages.* Many an investor in shelters involving oil-well drilling, cattle raising or risky real-estate ventures has lost more money than was kept out of the hands of the tax collector. "If you undress most tax shelters," says Peter M. Mazonas, a vice president of Bank of America, "you'll find that they make

---

1. Reprinted from *U.S. News & World Report*, April 17, 1978. Copyright 1978 U.S. News & World Report, Inc.

money for the organizers but can't stand on their own two economic feet."

7. *Lack of detailed financial records.* Many individuals don't know exactly what investments they own. It's wise to keep a list in a safe-deposit box, including an inventory of personal possessions such as antiques, paintings, collections of coins, stamps or art objects.

8. *Shying away from paying for professional advice.* Many people with substantial incomes figure they'll save money by managing their personal investments. This may work out for those with broad experience and plenty of spare time. Others may save in the long run by seeking professional help.

9. *Trading or speculating rather than investing.* The temptation to try to buy low and sell high has proved disastrous for millions of unwary individuals. Says Jay Vawter, an executive with the counseling firm of Stein Roe & Farnham: "Owning stocks of well-managed companies, particularly those able to finance future growth internally and pay an increasing dividend to shareholders, is likely to be a far surer path to financial well-being than trying to pin one's hopes on high fliers."

10. *Failure to follow a balanced investment program.* In an era of stock-market volatility and steady inflationary pressures, most money managers say it's wise to have a financial nest egg spread over several investments. Those could include high-grade bonds, quality common stocks with superior growth characteristics, a house or other real estate and a cash reserve for emergencies.

Planning finances

Record keeping, careful planning or budgeting, and knowing how much money one has spent are all important.

Record keeping. Keeping account of what is spent can save money in the long run. From records, receipts, and cancelled checks individuals or families will know what they have spent and how much their life-styles have cost. These records are clues as to ways to control spending and to offer a means of saving. Careful record keeping helps to take the guesswork out of financial management.

Budgeting. A plan for spending is the number one tool for financial management. It should be made before spending is done. Such a plan, along with record keeping can be a big help in making decisions about spending and controlling spending.

In making a budget the individual or family must look at short-term and long-term goals. These goals will influence how the individual's or family's money will be spent. Second, all income must be accounted for. Income will include wages, gifts, interest, bonuses, and any other sources of money available to the individual or family. Third, all expenses must be included. There are two types of expenses, fixed expenses and flexible expenses.

Fixed expenses. These are the expenses for which money has been previously committed. That is, they are the expenses which must be paid. They cannot be changed except with much difficulty. They include rent, taxes, insurance, telephone, electricity, mortgage payments, and other debt payments. For some persons or families such payments may be due weekly, monthly, or two or three times a year. The listing of all fixed expenses is most important in making a budget. They must be taken care of before any other allowances are made.

Flexible expenses. These are expenses which involve items that must be bought at some time, but the time and the cost may vary. Examples of flexible expenses are clothing, home furnishings, recreation, gifts, vacations, and donations. These expenses will change as needs change. Day-to-day living costs such as food, gas and oil for a car, carfare, and dry cleaning or laundry are also flexible. They are necessary but the amount of money spent on them will vary.

How detailed individuals and families choose to make their plans for controlling their spending will vary. The important idea is to make the plans work so that goals and values are satisfied.

A simplified trial budget is outlined below.

1. What is the total income? $_____

2. What are the fixed expenses? $_____

3. What are the flexible expenses? $_____

4. Add items 2 and 3. $_____

5. Subtract item 4 from item 1. $_____

The amount in item 5 is the amount of savings that would be left after all expenses have been taken care of.

Savings help individuals and families to be self-supporting when emergencies come. Purchases can be made without the additional cost of credit. A savings program also allows the money in the savings accounts to earn additional money.

Handling money

Credit.   Credit in any form costs money. When you borrow money, you must pay interest on the money borrowed. Rates may range from 6 to 30 percent and more for the use of cash or installment credit. The most common forms of credit are charge accounts, installment plans, and loans. Charge accounts offer convenience, but they may encourage careless buying. Installment plans and loans differ in the conditions under which they are set up. The buyer should consider very carefully how much extra will be paid for the privilege of an extended payment plan. Contracts must be read very carefully. The advantages and disadvantages of credit are listed below.

Advantages	**Disadvantages**
1. credit increases buying power	1. credit purchases create a debt
2. some appliances may pay for themselves in the length of time required to save the money	2. the fees for the credit increase the cost of the item being purchased
3. necessary items can be had now	3. buying power is restricted while the family pays off the debt

Reprinted by permission of Dave Gerard.
From *Saturday Review*.

"Under our full-security plan you pay one monthly premium and we provide all your needs—insurance, housing, food, clothing, education, entertainment, a new car every three years, and burial service."

Four types of life insurance[2]

Individual insurance is available in a variety of policies to fit a great number of different needs. There are only four basic types of policies, each designed to do a different kind of job. Note that the first two protect for the whole life, and the others have shorter protection periods.

Straight life. Protection lasts for the insured person's lifetime and premiums are payable for life. This is the most flexible type of policy and the least expensive kind of permanent protection.

Limited-payment life. Like straight life, this type offers protection for life with similar flexibility. But premiums are limited to a set number of years. One example is a 20-payment life policy with premiums payable for only 20 years. Another is life paid-up at 65, with premiums ending at that age. The shorter the premium-paying period, the higher the premium for a given

2. From *Policies for Protection* (Washington, D.C.: American Council of Life Insurance, 1978), p. 7. Used by permission.

amount of protection. These policies are often used by professional people who want their insurance completely paid up before retirement.

Endowment. This is a life insurance plan which protects the insured person for a stated number of years; at the end of the period, the full amount of the policy is paid to the policyholder, and the insurance ends. If the insured person should die before the end of the period, the full amount is paid immediately to the beneficiary—the person named to receive the amount.

These three types of policies have level premiums. This means the premium paid each year remains the same, even though the risk of death increases as the policyholder grows older. All three types of policies accumulate a "cash value" whose size can be determined from a table in the policy. The cash value is the sum received should a policyholder decide to give up the insurance protection policy—but, as we shall see later, cash values offer several extremely useful options to the policyholder.

Term. As the name implies, this policy protects for a given term, often five years, and then may be renewed for another term at a higher rate, without a medical examination, if the policy contains a renewal provision. When it is in force, term insurance offers the same protection against death as other policies, but generally has no cash value. When a term ends, so does the protection, and the policy expires. If term policies are renewed for several periods, people often find that the rates become prohibitively high in later years. In any event, term insurance is not generally available past age 65 or 70. (Some term policies protect a person through age 65, and carry a level annual premium as other policies.)

Most term policies can be converted to permanent policies without a medical examination, at the regular rate for the policyholder's age at the time of conversion.

What life insurance provides[3]

Of all the purposes of life insurance, the most important is to provide money for the family if the wage earner dies. To help do this job effectively, policies offer a choice of methods of payments called settlement options. These options are designed to pay an income to the family best suited to their needs.

Here are four settlement options:

3. Ibid., pp. 7–8.

Lump sum. This is the way most policies will be paid unless some other choice is made.

Income for a stated period. Regular monthly payments are made from the proceeds of the policy until the money has all been paid to the beneficiary. Each payment includes interest on the proceeds that are still held by the company. This option is often used to provide a continuing family income while the children are growing up.

Income for life. This guarantees a regular payment for life to the beneficiary. The income also includes interest.

Interest only. The proceeds are left with the insurance company, which makes regular interest payments to the beneficiary. This is often done to create a family fund for emergencies, college expenses, and other future needs. It also gives a family time to decide whether it would prefer another settlement option.

Investing

The purpose of investing money is simple. First, it is a way of allowing your money to work for you. Second, if you do not invest your money in some way it is going to decrease in value due to inflation. For example, you have $100 which you save for one year. At the end of that year, if inflation is running at 10%, your $100 will buy goods worth $90. Another way to think of it, you have taken a 10% pay cut. Economic survival for people depends on keeping pace with the inflationary pattern of the time.

There are three things which one can do with money: (1) *hold it in cash;* (2) *lend it for a return of income in interest;* (3) *make it increase in value.* There is a simple rule of thumb often given by investment experts, called the Rule of 72. This rule says to find out how many years it takes your money to double, just divide 72 by the annual interest rate. If you lend your money at 4 percent, it takes 18 years to double its value. If you invest that same money at 12 percent growth rate, it takes only six years. One must remember, however, that the higher the possible return on any investment, the greater the risk.

Paula Nelson, financial advisor, says that in managing money one should aim for a balance of low-income, low-risk assets and high-risk holdings. On the next page are some forms of investment.[4]

4. Copyright © 1975 by Paula Nelson. From the book *The Joy of Money* by Paula Nelson. Reprinted with permission of Stein and Day Publishers.

1. Standard bank savings account. Low interest, very low-risk.

2. Long-term (time deposit) or investment savings account. Higher rate of interest but you must commit leaving your money on deposit for a certain period, usually 1 to 4 years.

3. United States Savings Bonds. Low interest, but high degree of security.

4. Treasury Bills. Sold in minimum amounts of $10,000, with interest rates higher than those of savings accounts. The interest rates vary. The rates are set on the basis of an auction held each Monday.

5. Treasury Bonds. These bonds are long-term obligations of the U.S. Treasury and are sold at $1,000 minimum. Their life is up to 30 years. Their yield varies as does that of other bonds on the basis of long-term interest rates.

6. Government Agency Bonds. These bonds are issued by such government institutions as the Federal Land Bank. They pay high interest rates (typically ½ percent higher than U.S. Treasury Bonds). They also carry a higher risk since they are not direct government obligations.

7. Certificate of Deposit. These certificates are short-term I.O.U.'s issued by commercial banks. Rates vary from bank to bank. Interest rates on Certificates of Deposit over $100,000 are not fixed by the government. However, they are regulated for amounts under $100,000. A lower interest rate is paid for a $10,000 certificate and a higher rate is paid for a $100,000 certificate, for example.

8. Commercial Paper. Large corporations frequently issue commercial papers to cover their own short-term financial needs. Commercial Paper is usually purchased through a commercial bank. There is a $10,000 minimum investment. Typically, about 1% more in interest is paid on commercial paper than on Treasury Bills.

The test for carrying out any plan for the use of money is in making it work. A plan is a record of decisions to be made about the spending of money. The real decisions are made when the money is actually spent. The value of any plan for spending increases as individuals and families gain experience in making the necessary estimates of cost. The better the estimates are, the better the plan is as a guide to spending and its control.

Because this text deals primarily with relationships, not finances, the list of investment opportunities is by no means comprehensive. For example, tax sheltered investments are not mentioned, because they are usually more advantageous to people who have higher incomes than the majority of young married couples. Questions about tax shelters may arise, however, especially since they play a prominent role in the new Tax Law, the Economic Recovery Tax Act of 1981.

Among the more conservative forms of tax shelter are annuities, individual retirement accounts (IRA), Keogh Plans, and highly rated municipal bonds. All-Savers Certificates, introduced in the new Tax Law, allowed a couple to earn as much as $2000 in interest for one year from these special certificates of deposit as tax-free income, but these were not available after December 31, 1982.

An annuity can be purchased in a lump sum or with regular, smaller payments. Interest rates are modest, but the advantage lies in the fact that no taxes are paid on that interest until such time, in the future, when the interest is withdrawn by the depositor from the account. If this is taken in the form of monthly payments upon retirement of the depositor, the amount of tax may be reduced by the fact that the individual will probably be in a lower tax bracket than he or she was while working.

Some employers have retirement plans that function as annuities. In some qualifying plans, an employee can supplement the regular, contracted contribution to the annuity, when his or her current income exceeds budgeted needs. The additional tax advantage to such supplemental contributions to one's retirement annuity is that neither the supplement nor the interest earned by it are counted as current income. They become taxable only when they are taken out of the account by the depositor.

In the past, employees *not* covered by a qualifying retirement plan could open their own Individual Retirement Account (IRA). Since the new Tax Law, even an employee who *is* covered by a qualifying retirement plan can open an IRA and take as much as $2000 per year (or $2250 if the account includes a non-working spouse) as a deduction on his or her tax return. Taxes on both contributions and interest are deferred until the money is withdrawn from the account. Penalties are substantial if withdrawals occur before age $59\frac{1}{2}$. IRA's are available in many forms. As certificates of deposit, there are ranges of both interest rates and times to maturity. Variable interest rates are also popular. Through brokerage houses and other financial institutions, one can obtain IRA's that include investments in common stocks, bond funds, high grade bonds, gold or silver certificates, mutual funds and others.

Keogh accounts have several features common to IRA's but are available only to self-employed persons, such as doctors, accountants, dentists, lawyers and unincorporated business owners. By the new Tax Law, these individuals will be allowed a maximum deductible annual contribution of $15,000.

Highly rated municipal bonds, those that are considered very safe, pay lower interest rates than are available from many other forms of investment, but they are attractive, nevertheless, to persons in high tax brackets. For example, let us consider a couple who reported a taxable income of $55,000 on their joint federal income tax return, which put them in the "49% tax bracket." They had $20,000 in a certificate of deposit that paid 14% interest, a total of $2800. Because of their tax bracket, they had to pay nearly half of that interest to the Internal Revenue Service. Had they purchased $20,000 worth of municipal bonds that were paying only 9% interest, they could have earned $1800 and paid no federal income tax on it. Thus, they would have been able to keep nearly $400 more, if they had invested in tax-free municipal bonds instead of the certificate of deposit. For a couple with taxable income of $20,000, which would have put them in the "24% tax bracket," obviously, the certificate of deposit would have given a higher yield after taxes than the bonds.

The comparison given above points up the following generalization: For every investor, there is a special set of circumstances; no investment formula fits the needs of all. It is wise, therefore, for the novice to seek financial counseling from experts who can analyze individual cases.

One of the fixed expenses mentioned in this chapter, that of a mortgage payment, includes a form of investment. That portion of the monthly mortgage payment that reduces the outstanding debt is buying equity in the house for the homeowner. In the recent past, the selling prices of homes were increasing faster than the inflation rate, while the returns from many other forms of investments were not keeping up with inflation. When lending institutions have reduced amounts of money to lend, however, interest rates go up. Such a situation exists at the time of this writing, and many young couples, who wish to puchase a home, are told that they do not qualify for a mortgage loan, because the overall cost of buying a home is too high when compared to the couple's income. Presently, lenders are using a rule-of-thumb that says the qualifying buyer should make monthly mortgage payments no higher than one week's income minus debts. Both incomes of a working couple are considered by the lender in judging qualification for a mortgage, a mortgage life insurance is taken on both lives. Problems in meeting payments can arise, if, at some later date, one partner no longer has an income, or there are unanticipated expenses. For example, a house may require correction of structural problems that went undetected before the purchase. Also, in the purchase of condominiums, the buyer should be aware of any additional maintenance fees and what they cover. The buyer should ask, also, whether these fees are fixed or variable, and whether special assessments can be made.

To obtain a conventional mortgage, a couple must make a down-payment of 20% of the sale price and pay interest of 17% of the unpaid balance for a period of 30 years. For example, a couple buys a $75,000 house and pays $15,000 down. They are required to pay a fee of 3% of their $60,000 loan to the lending institution ($1800), and the sum of their title expenses and lawyer's fee is $400. Their monthly payment of $1,000 includes $856 for interest and principal, and $144 for taxes, mortgage life insurance and house insurance. At 17% interest, they gain very little equity in their house, initially; the first month's interest is $850. After $29\frac{1}{2}$ years, all the principal would be paid, and they would have paid nearly $242,000 in interest. The total expenditure for the $75,000 house would be in excess of $319,000.

Currently, there are also mortgages with sliding interest rates. This means that the interest which you pay on your mortgage may be higher some years and lower other years to reflect the change in the interest rate. Therefore, it is important to know the kind of mortgage agreement you are making.

One possibility for purchasing a house at lower interest rates arises if the seller is willing to do the financing. In such a transaction, the seller holds the deed and the buyer makes payments of principal, interest, taxes and insurance according to the agreements in a contract. Interest rates in these agreements are usually about 5 percentage points below the current mortgage rate. Often, such conracts are for terms of only 3 to 5 years after which the buyer must seek a conventional mortgage. The buyer is hoping, of course, that interest rates will be lower at that time. Should it happen that conditions are still such that the buyer cannot qualify for a mortgage, he may lose his equity in the house, because the seller still holds the deed.

F.H.A. loans can be helpful to those who cannot meet the requirement for a down-payment of 20% of the sale price. For such a loan, only 5% of the first $25,000 and 3% of the remainder is required; the maximum loan is $82,500. Interest rates are only a little less than those for conventional mortgages. On F.H.A. loans, the seller pays the points, i.e., the fee charged by the financial institution for making the loan. This can amount to 3-10% of the mortgage amount, so the seller is apt to hold rigidly to his asking price if the buyer is obtaining an F.H.A. loan.

Another form of F.H.A. loan is the graduated payment mortgage, in which the monthly payment increases each year for five years, on the assumption that the buyer's income will also increase. There are many variations of conventional loans, as well. One of these has a variable interest rate; an adjustment is made every three months in accord with different financial indexes. Another allows the buyer to assume the seller's mortgage balance at the same interest rate and the difference at the current interest rate. Both buyer and seller should seek the counsel of experts to be sure that the most viable option is not overlooked.

Questions

1. Define the following terms:

credit	endowment policy	treasury bill
budget	certificate of deposit	commercial paper
straight life policy	term policy	graduated mortgage rate

2. What factors cause money problems in marriage?

3. What affects an individual's use of money?

5. How are differences in the use of money solved?

6. What are some factors that influence investments?

7. Interview an auto salesperson and find out at least three ways by which an automobile may be financed. What would be the sum of all payments on a $7000 auto bought by each plan?

8. What are some common financial mistakes?

Further reading

Allentuck, Andrew J., and Bivens, Gordon E. *Consumer Choice.* New York: Harcourt Brace Jovanovich, Inc., 1977.

Gross, Ruth B. *Money, Money, Money.* New York: Scholastic Book Services, 1976.

McGough, Elizabeth. *Dollars and Sense: The Teenager Consumer's Guide.* New York: William Morrow & Co., Inc. Subsidiary of Scott, Foresman & Co., 1975.

Nelson, Paula. *The Joy of Money.* Briarcliff Manor, NY: Stein & Day Publishers, 1975.

_____. "Make Your Money Work for You." *The Saturday Evening Post,* March, 1978.

"Personal Financial Planning for 1978." *Business Week,* 23 January 1978.

Chapter 25

Marriage and career

No matter who you are or what you do there is always something about your situation that you like and something that you dislike. Many teachers may love teaching but dislike grading. A veterinarian may like her or his work but dislike the billing.

Concerns of marriage and a career

If we are really clear-eyed and thinking in terms of today, we recognize that each one of us has many careers in our lifetime. Some of these careers occur at the same time. For example, one might be a parent, a spouse, a worker and/or professional in a business or school or institution. In addition that person might also be an active member of a volunteer group of hospital workers, fire fighters, or some other group. The multiple-career person has always been a part of life. In the past, a career was defined as a vocational choice for which one trained and received pay. Today we recognize the multiple careers, the changes in careers, and the paid and non-paid career choices that exist.

Men are no longer the only ones who have careers. Women are pursuing a wide range of careers. Homemaking is also currently defined as a career. The idea of a dual or triple or quadruple career is not uncommon for both men and women. The question of what it means to be an adult is really an outline of multiple careers and the progression of task development and accomplishment.

Between the ages of 17 and 33 most young people go through the novice phase of tasks of life. They face four main tasks.

1. to define their dream of adult accomplishment

Drawing by V. Gene Myers. From *Saturday Review*, © 1977 by Saturday Review Magazine Corp. Reprinted by permission.

"You know what I hate?
Picking up those little mice with my feet."

2. to find a mentor to guide them

3. to develop a vocation

4. to open themselves to new intimate relationships

Task development for adults[1]

Dream of adult accomplishment. We talk about someone succeeding beyond his or her wildest dreams. Most of us have a "dream" of the kind of life we want to lead as adults. This "dream" is a vague sense of self-in-the-adult world. A few adults by their early 40's have achieved all or most of what they had set out to do. They feel that they have succeeded and are assured of a happy future. Others, who have fallen short of their "dreams," may come to believe that they have been found wanting. They may believe that their work has no value and that they have no value as persons.

Whatever the nature of the "dream," a person has the task of giving it greater definition and finding ways to live it out. The process of entering adulthood is more lengthy and complex than has usually been imagined.

Many young people develop a conflict between a life direction expressing the "dream" and another that is quite different. A person may be pushed away from the "dream" by parents, by a lack of money or opportunity, or by various aspects of his or her own personality, such as guilt, submission, competitiveness, or special talents. Sometimes a person succeeds in an occupation that holds no interest. This conflict may extend over years. Those who build a life structure around "the dream" in early adulthood have a better chance for personal fulfillment. However, years of struggle may be needed to maintain the commitment and to work toward realizing it.

The novice phase. The beginning or novice phase begins about age 17 and continues until about age 30. There are three periods: the early-adult, the entering adult and the transition. During this novice phase, one is exploring the adult world, developing adult interests and values, and making choices with regard to work, marriage and family. There are other tasks also of importance such as learning to relate to authority and to gain greater authority for self; to form meaningful peer relations with both sexes; relate as an adult to people of different ages; form mature attitudes toward religion, politics, community.

1. From THE SEASONS OF A MAN'S LIFE, by Daniel J. Levinson. Copyright © 1978 by Daniel J. Levinson. Reprinted by permission of Alfred A. Knopf, Inc.

The novice phase may contain concrete achievements, such as winning the Nobel Prize, making the all-star team, or winning an Emmy award. It may take the dramatic form, as a "hero," a great artist, or an intellectual receiving honors. It also may take the form of the excellent craftsperson, the spouse/parent in a particular family, the highly respected citizen of the year, or outstanding community member.

The mentor phase.   The second phase, forming a mentor relationship, is necessary for support and to help with the realization of the "dream."   The mentor is a person who fosters the young adult's development by believing in him or her, sharing the "dream" and giving it support.   The mentor, usually several years older, has great experience and seniority in the chosen world.   This mentoring relationship, a relationship of teacher, advisor, or sponsor, often develops in a work setting.   However, it may also come about informally when the mentor is a friend, neighbor, or relative.   The mentor may become a model.   Models are a major source of development in adulthood.

Developing a vocation.   It is often assumed that by the early 20s a person has made a firm occupational choice and is launched on a well-defined career.   This notion of choosing an occupation is too narrow and superficial.   It is more useful to speak of developing a vocation, a complex process that extends over the novice phase and well into or beyond the mentor phase.   The transformation of interests into occupation is rarely a simple or direct process.

Once an initial choice is made, a person must acquire occupational skills, values, and credentials.   A person needs to develop a differentiated occupational identity and establish for himself or herself a chosen world.

Developing intimate relationships.   The process of forming a marriage and family starts well before the wedding ceremony or the birth of the first child.   As with a person's occupation, marriage and family life go through a formative process.   It takes time for a young person to learn about inner resources and vulnerabilities in relation to the opposite sex.   It takes time to learn about the characteristics of the persons who attract or repel.   It is also a learning process to recognize one's own appealing and objectionable qualities.

A person in early adulthood usually accepts responsibilities and pleasures of parenthood and lives out, in some measure, both the masculine and the feminine aspects of the self.   Under reasonably favorable conditions, being a husband/wife and father/mother contributes to development. It is, in part, a developmental failure when a young person is unable to function adequately in the family. When this occurs on a large scale, it is also a failure of society and might have destructive consequences for that society.

The special person. A person's love relationship with the opposite sex can take many forms and serve many functions. One of the most interesting people in a person's life is the one we call special. The special person is a true mentor. He or she helps to animate the part of the young person's self that contains the "dream." This is a unique relationship that ordinarily includes sexual, romantic, and loving feelings. But the special person is "special" because of the role as helper in making entry into the adult world to shape and live out the "dream." Like the mentor, the special person is a transitional figure. The special person fosters adult aspirations in the young adult while accepting dependency, incompleteness, and the need to accomplish things together. A couple can form a lasting relationship only if it furthers individual and mutual developments. If his sense of her, or her sense of him, stems mainly from his or her wishful projections and not from his or her own desires and efforts, then sooner or later the bubble will burst and both will feel cheated. If either one supports the other's dream and thus loses his or her own dream, then the couple's development will suffer and both will later pay the price.

Their career choice is marriage. In order for this couple to have an ongoing, growing relationship their first career choice must be their marriage, their homemaking, their family. A man's wife may be his special woman or a woman's husband may be her special man. Alternately, they may have a relationship that is loving and supporting but that has little connection with his or her vocational dream. This may often become a source of bitter discontent and conflict even years later in marriage.

This phase of life career, this settling-down phase is filled with positive responses to these questions. "What has been done with my life so far?" "What do I really get from or give my spouse?" The couple should know their values and how these values are reflected in their lives. An appraisal of their talents should find them being used rather than wasted.

Midlife transition. For many people, age 40 to 45, midlife transition is a time of moderate to severe crises. It brings struggle within the self, and between the self and the world. It is hoped that this

"We've got a little tomato juice as an introduction, some warmed-over spaghetti as a second movement, with three hard rolls as a contrapuntal theme leading into a cold asparagus salad crescendo. But what do you want for an encore?"

challenges individuals to be more creative; to create products that have value for self and others, to join in enterprises that advance human welfare, to contribute more fully to coming generations. Paramount to happiness in marriage and career is the "dream" at some point touching reality.

Women and careers

Ninety percent of young women ages 18 to 34 expect to have a career other than homemaking. Whatever one's views of the effects of women's employment on the family, the fact is that it would be difficult, probably impossible, to turn the tide. Recent studies indicate that the likelihood of a wife's working is increased by family economic pressure, by her ability to get a job, by her educational attainment, by labor market environment that provides equal opportunities regardless of sex, and by woman's status in the household.

Working women accumulate seniority, make friends on the job, and increase their standards of living. For many women, economic activity is a major source of ego gratification. When young people, ages 12–17, are interviewed the boys and the girls expect to be gainfully employed. The young people expect to marry and expect to have one or two children. They expect both man and woman to be employed outside the home. They expect both to be responsible for the homemaking tasks. This is quite a change from the expectations of youth just five years ago. Five years ago the young women expected to be employed outside the home but they also expected to be responsible for the homemaking tasks. Now the young men expect to be as responsible for the homemaking tasks as do the young women.

The individual attitude of both husband and wife is of first importance. If they both have a positive attitude toward the wife's employment, they might want to consider these questions.

1. Is the wife's or husband's health such that carrying two jobs will not overtax it?

2. Are the husband and wife willing to share in the household tasks or willing to have the family spend additional money to have these tasks done by outside help?

3. Is the husband's profession the type that needs the full-time help of his wife? Wives of certain professional men, such as business executives, officials in government, members of the clergy, and so on, may be needed as helpers and hostesses for their husbands.

4. Does the wife have special talents or skills which she should use because of a shortage of trained professionals in her field?

5. Does the wife feel she must have employment outside of the home to keep herself emotionally stable?

6. Does the wife or the husband have the ability to manage a job and a home or does the management of the home alone tax her or his abilities to the utmost?

7. How will the two incomes be used? No one can dictate the best arrangement for the couple, but some plan agreeable to both of them must be worked out if friction is to be prevented.

8. Will there be a lack of common friends? There may be a tendency to form two separate groups of friends if husband and wife work in different places.

9. If there is a child or children, how will they be cared for? Is it possible to find a person who will adequately administer to their needs in their mother's and/or father's absence?

Many women are employed outside of the home but are unpaid. The professional club woman who is prominent in various civic, social and community organizations and enterprises is not unemployed just because she is not paid for her work.

Career, marriage, and parenthood

For the working mother, the husband and wife relationship is of considerable psychological significance. The circumstances that lead to the mother's employment, the personalities of husband and wife, and the immediate situation must be considered. Generally, the employment of the wife will mean changes in the traditional roles of husband and wife.

In addition to these role changes, a change in the more subtle aspects of familial relationships occurs when the mother is out of the house during the work periods. The father will probably have more direct contact with his children and more direct responsibility for their physical care. Such contact with the father may be beneficial or detrimental to the children and the father, depending upon both parents' capacity to adapt to the role changes. Mothers who are on the scene all the time differ widely in how they care for their children. When they are away part of the time, whether the child is better off will depend upon the nature of the child's relationship with his or her mother and with the substitute. It is the quality of the relationship between mother and child that is significant, not the amount of time they spend together. There is no relationship between spending a great deal of time with one's child and the amount of affection that will be afforded him or her.

For some women outside employment is such a contrast to the constant strain of child care that, when the day's work is done, they are able to return home refreshed by the joy of seeing their children. They are ready to give of their ingenuity and patience. Many such mothers contribute much more in the short time with their children than they would in a whole day before they started to work. Sometimes mothers who are working outside the home actually spend more time with their children than do those women who are home all day but send their children outside to play without supervision.

Whether the child is better off is a question that cannot be answered with an absolute yes or no. It depends upon the degree to which the substitute parent respects the mother's or father's authority, the similarity between his or her values and those of the mother or father, and the setting in which the care is provided. All will influence the child's relationship with his or her parents. Most important is the feeling that the parents themselves have about the situation.

Dr. Lois Hoffman, reporting on the effects of mothers who work, discussed the findings of a study of 176 white, intact families. In this study, there were 88 working-mother families and 88 non-working-mother families matched on occupation of father, sex of child, and position of the sibling in the family. The overall patterns of the findings suggested that the working mother who likes working is relatively high on positive effect toward the child, uses mild discipline, and tends to avoid inconveniencing the child with household tasks because of her employment. The child is relatively non-aggressive. The working mother who dislikes working, on the other hand, seems less involved with the child altogether and obtains the child's help with many tasks; the child is relatively assertive and hostile.[2]

The effects of the mother's working on delinquent behavior of boys was studied by the Gluecks.[3] In this study, five hundred delinquent boys were compared to a group of non-delinquents. The two groups were similar with respect to intelligence, ethnic background, age, and economic status. The last factor is, of course, crucial when the effects of the mother's working are to be considered. It was found that both groups had about the same proportions of regularly working and non-working mothers; thus, regular work by the mother did not seem to influence the likelihood of delinquent behavior in the son.

Ruth Whitmarsh found in a pilot study that the adolescent daughters of employed mothers had fewer recognized problems than the daughters of full-time homemakers.[4]

The middle-class adolescent girls in this study whose mothers were employed seemed to be particularly well-adjusted in the area of

2. From "Effects of Maternal Employment on the Child" by Lois Wladis Hoffman in *Child Development,* Vol. 32, 1961. © The Society for Research in Child Development, Inc. Used by permission.

3. From "Working Mothers and Deliquency" by S. and E. Glueck in *Mental Hygiene,* Vol. 41 (1957), pp. 327–352. Reprinted by courtesy of the Mental Health Association, 1800 N. Kent Street, Arlington, VA 22209.

4. From "Adjustment Problems of Adolescent Daughters of Employed Mothers" by Ruth Whitmarsh in *Journal of Home Economics,* Vol. 57, No. 3 (March 1965), pp. 201–204. Used by permission of the American Home Economics Association.

home and family life if an absence of personal problems may be used as a criterion of personal adjustment.

Bruno Bettelheim has indicated that he feels that a woman who enjoys her work makes a better mother than one who rejects it.

Since work around the house is now less than interesting, children are the natural target for the young wife's energies. Here at least she feels considerably more sophisticated than her mother. After all she has had extensive schooling, and has perhaps worked briefly at a demanding job, and motherhood has been depicted to her as another tremendous and enlarging experience—the climax, somehow, to what has gone before. Yet in fact the care of an infant forces her to give up most of her old interests, and unless she is fascinated by the minute developments of the baby, she will seldom find that any new and different enrichment has entered her life to replace them.

This impoverishment is particularly acute when she has her first child. Later on, the concerns of her older children may enliven her days while she cares for a newcomer. However, I believe the current trend toward larger middle-class families reflects not merely a greater prosperity but also the needs of the middle-class mother who finds existence empty without small children to care for. Reluctant to return to the outer world—or perhaps lacking confidence in her ability to do so, she must find something to occupy her which seems vital and demanding of her concentration.

But things change once her children are of school age—and even more so in their teens. They certainly need a mother, but they actually need far less of her than she may devote to them. Chauffeuring children around the suburbs, for example, takes time and requires someone who drives a car, but this person need not be a mother. The children themselves would prefer to be free of it and the tight scheduling it imposes. The same goes for arranging the children's social life, which again they would much prefer to do for themselves.

Of course, the professed concern of many mothers is to watch over their children's educational life, and help them with their psychological problems. But in these things, too, the children would often rather be on their own, except for those occasional crises where the parents are needed for support. And sadly enough the modern mother is often in a poor position to give support when her child is doing badly in school or is not very popular and hence feels defeated. Having invested so much emotionally in her child's achievement, her pride suffers at his failure and as likely as not she administers a bawling out when understanding and compassion are needed. Thus she may fail as a mother because her inner needs make her work at it too hard. The children of women who are doing interesting work of their own during the day will often find more sensible and sympathetic mothers to help them with their studies and problems in the evening. On the other hand, the mother who urges her girl on toward intellectual achievement while staying at home herself poses a contradiction which probably is not lost on the girl.[5]

Lee Burchinal, a sociologist, conducted a study of both working and non-working mothers. This study found, in general, that children whose mothers had worked at various times in the children's lives were not different from children whose mothers had not worked. This conclusion was especially important in that it exposed the myth that working mothers categorically did damage to their preschool and early-school-age children. The argument that the psychological or social development of children is disturbed when their mothers work—especially when the children are quite young—simply was not supported in this study.[6]

This research and the attitudes of Dr. Bettelheim are presented as further evidence that maternal employment in and of itself should no longer be used as a "scapegoat" for marital or familial adjustment problems. However, it is not presented to indicate that the thousands upon thousands of mothers who stay at home should leave their chosen position. If the activities of the home, the community, and their children stimulate their minds and satisfactorily fill their days, then this is, of course, the best choice for them.

We also need to recognize that there are many volunteer groups which need the time, talent, and energy of qualified people. The community needs library board members, persons to conduct programs for youth such as the Scouts, the 4-H Clubs, Boys Clubs, Y.W.C.A., Big Brother, Big Sister organizations, and to work in other civic groups. Most churches and hospitals would have more unfinished work if it were not for the activities and contributions of their various women's and men's organizations. Thus, the homemaker, male or female, can certainly stimulate his or her mind as well as contribute to home and community.

5. From "Growing Up Female" by Bruno Bettelheim in *Harper's Magazine,* October 1962. Copyright 1962 by Harper's Magazine, Inc. Used by permission of the author.
6. Lee Burchinal, "Working Mothers: What Effect on Children?" *Iowa Farm Science,* Vol. 17, No. 6 (1962), pp. 9–11.

There is no magic formula to follow when an individual attempts to make a decision concerning marriage and a career. As Dorothy Cotton states:

Being an effective mother (working or not), rearing happy, healthy, responsible children, building a successful marriage—these have always been the most subtle and difficult of all human endeavors.

Those mothers who devote themselves to the care of their families can chalk up as many difficulties with their youngsters as those who do not, and working mothers have their own built-in set of unique problems with their families. No two working mothers are alike. No two stay-at-home mothers are alike. There is simply no "always right" solution to be discovered in any one special prescription for parenthood. Just as staying home will not automatically make a mother "good" neither will going to work automatically make her "bad." One thing is certain: no clear-cut pattern of what a mother should do, or be, exists to fit all mothers.[7]

Questions

1. Why is marriage thought of as a career?

2. Why is homemaking defined as a career?

3. How important is a college education to the girl who hopes to combine marriage and a career?

4. Why do some women choose the dual role of wife and career-girl?

5. What is the most important factor when a wife considers employment outside the home?

6. Write a story of a couple whose situation is such that (a) the wife should work outside the home; (b) the wife should not work outside the home.

7. What factors should a mother consider when she elects to work outside the home?

8. What position does the research reported take in regard to working mothers?

9. How do the attitudes of Bruno Bettelheim agree or disagree with your own attitudes?

7. Copyright 1965 by Dorothy W. Cotton. From the book *The Case of the Working Mother* by Dorothy W. Cotton. Reprinted with permission of Stein and Day Publishers.

10. Boys: Write a paper titled (a) I want my wife to work because . . . or (b) I do not want my wife to work because . . .

11. Girls: Write a paper titled (a) I want to work after marriage because . . . or (b) I do not want to work after marriage because . . .

Further reading

Bettelheim, Bruno. "Growing Up Female." *Harper's Magazine,* October 1962, pp. 120–128.

Kanter, Rosabeth. "Jobs and Families: Impact of Working Roles on Family Life." *Children Today,* no. 2 (1978).

Kohn, Melvin. *Class and Conformity: A Study of Values.* 2d ed. Chicago: University of Chicago Press, 1977.

Lamb, Michael E., ed. *The Role of the Father in Child Development.* New York: John Wiley & Sons, Inc., 1976.

Lynn, David B. *The Father: His Role in Child Development.* Belmont, CA: Wadsworth Publishing Co., Inc., 1974.

Whitmarsh, Ruth. "Adjustment Problems of Adolescent Daughters of Employed Mothers." *Journal of Home Economics,* no. 3 (1965): 201–204.

Chapter 26

Marriage and crises

A crisis is a crucial time, the decisive moment or turning point in a situation. The decisive moments vary according to our experiences and the way we view situations. Crises for some people are humorous situations for other people.

We view with mixed reactions depending upon our experiences and emotions. What is a crisis for you may be just an annoyance for me. On the other hand, the situation which is of major concern to me may go unnoticed by you.

Family crises

There are four main kinds of crises that families face. These are loss of a member, addition of a member, loss of status or of face, and a combination of loss or addition of a member plus loss of status. These crises are defined as follows.

1. Loss of a member may be brought about by death, hospitalization, or separation for business reasons or military service.

2. Addition of a member is characterized by birth, adoption, moving of a relative into a family home, return of a deserter, the remarriage of a parent, or a reunion after a long period of separation.

3. Loss of status or face and a sense of disgrace can be fomented by alcoholism, drug addiction, crime, or delinquency. It can also be brought about by dissension, infidelity, and nonsupport.

4. A combination of loss or addition plus a loss of status is defined by situations such as suicide or homicide, imprisonment, illegitimacy, divorce, desertion, or annulment.

This chapter will not deal with all of the major crises. It will deal with some of those crises that are commonly faced in our culture.

"Today's forecast calls for fire and brimstone"

Reprinted from *The Saturday Evening Post.*
© 1966 The Curtis Publishing Company.
Courtesy of *The Saturday Evening Post* and Orlando Busino.

"I understand this play opened to mixed reviews."

We must remember, however, that what may cause a major crisis in one marriage may not cause a crisis in another.

The first year of marriage is a year of new adjustments for both partners. Depending upon their maturity and temperament, it may be completed without undue stress. On the other hand, these new adjustments may cause serious problems. The largest number of divorces is reported in the first year of marriage, the next largest numbers in the third and fifth years. Adjustment to the role of parent, in addition to that of husband and wife, imposes additional strain. How severe the strain and whether the birth of a child may disrupt the marriage depend upon the couple's marital stability and their readiness for the responsibilities of parenthood.

Loss of a member

Death.   Death is a part of life. It is another life experience. The democracy of death will eventually include us all.

Death can mean different things to different people. Its specific meaning depends on the nature and fortunes of a person's development and his or her cultural setting. To many, death represents a teacher of truths incomprehensible during life. For others, death is a friend who brings an end to pain through peaceful sleep. Still others see it as an adventure, a great, new experience. On the other hand, there are those who see it as the destroyer who is to be fought to the end.

Attitudes toward death are the result of many factors. Some of the more significant ones seem to be the age of the person, his or her religious orientation, psychological maturity, and level of threat. For example, it is apparent that the thought of death may mean one thing at the age of twenty, another at the age of forty, and something

Drawing by Gross.
Reprinted by permission. From *Ladies' Home Journal,* © 1977 LHJ Publishing, Inc.

"The sky fell on me. Do I have a case?"

quite different at the age of eighty. Consider the aspect of the nearness or remoteness of personal death. It is quite possible that a person's perception of the world and his or her attitudes about death might not be quite the same tomorrow as they are today, if, meanwhile he or she has been told that he or she has cancer. Likewise, a person who knows that he or she is suffering from a terminal disease but continues with regular duties and problems is quite unlike the person who is immobilized and awaits death in a hospital bed. The type or kind of person one is may sometimes be more important than the threat of death itself in determining the individual's reaction.

Our life receives one of its principal directions, if not its main one, from what death means to us. The kind of immortality we may seek has an impact on the kind of life we lead. We may seek immortality which is biological, social, or transcendental. Biological immortality is achieved through children. Social immortality is achieved through work accomplishments that testify to our existence and live on in the thoughts of other people. Transcendental immortality is achieved in beliefs that this life is but the precondition for the "true" life which is yet to come.

There is also, of course, the outlook of the Roman poet, Horace, which highlights personal pleasures and gratifications. His philosophy implies that since this life is the only one we have, let's "live it up." Others with a similar view feel that if we do have only this one chance at living, then life must be used to its utmost to give it full value and meaning. Religion is another factor that guides us to live in such a manner as to be judged favorably in the hereafter. Religion also gives direction, value, and meaning to this life.

People ordinarily become conscious of thoughts about death and dying in the following major situations.

1. they personally become seriously ill

2. someone in their immediate family becomes seriously ill or dies

3. friends develop a serious illness or die

4. they join the armed forces or are involved in a war situation

5. they are personally involved in an accident of some consequence

6. disastrous public tragedies are reported in the newspaper or over radio or television

Grief. Grief is the state of pain, discomfort, and often mental and physical impairment that most persons experience after the loss of a loved one. It is marked by the painful feeling of sorrow, loss of appetite and sleep, a sense of excessive fatigue, and a general state of mood depression. While sorrow is the pain and the misery attending the state of grieving, grief itself is an active state of adapting to the loss of a dear one by a special kind of psychological work.

Much can be done to help the mourning person to readapt to life. It seems important to have an opportunity to express the deep emotion that is part of mourning and to have a chance to review the experiences and activities which were previously shared with a lost person. The ceremony is helpful in bringing together friends and relatives to discuss aspects of the lost person's life and to give the mourners a chance to express their feelings without embarrassment. The real work of adaptation, however, usually starts later when the survivors find themselves alone in their efforts to cope with the new situation. Continued friendly contact and more opportunities for talking about the loss are helpful.

A woman younger than her husband is very likely to be left a widow. Only if a wife is five years older than her husband are the odds even against her becoming a widow. If we make allowances for the fact that, as a rule, men are two or more years older than their wives, the conclusion is that many women have to face years of widowhood without a provider or an object of their wholehearted attention.

There are common elements in the experiences of wives and husbands when their spouses die. This does not mean that all share identical reactions to this loss, nor that these reactions will be of the same order or degree of intensity. Much will depend on the specific situation, the nature of the marital relationship, available resources for assistance, and the personality of the spouse.

The initial response to a spouse's death is frequently a kind of numbness or paralysis. The widow or widower is unable to integrate what has happened. The numbness is an expression of the struggle against accepting the finality of the loss. Initially, his or her insulation is a healthy protection against the deep pain and difficult reality.

This numbness ultimately wears off. Reality and pain seep in and a variety of new feelings may appear. There is often physical pain, a tightness in the throat, a choking or empty feeling, and insomnia. Extreme exhaustion and loss of appetite are common physical reactions to loss.

Accompanying these physical reactions is a range of emotional responses.

1. restlessness, with a need for activity that has no purpose

2. inconsistency, with a feeling of being driven in many directions

3. irritability, with no apparent provocation

4. an accompanying sense of resignation, as though nothing mattered

Everything appears distorted. There is often a preoccupation with the image of the husband or wife and a withdrawal from the usual patterns of living. Impatience with other people is common, despite a dread of being alone. A sense of isolation is experienced even among friends and relatives. The widow or widower may accuse self of negligence for not having been a more devoted partner. These may be expressions of a strong sense of guilt and self-pity.

The loss that brings mourning and grieving is most commonly the death of a person important in one's life. However, it may also be the loss of another person who has been jilted or disappointed. It may be the loss of a friend who has moved away. Finally, leaving home and parents at the end of school or leaving one's place of work in order to work in some other location may be followed by grieving and mourning that go under the names of homesickness and promotional depression.

Addition of a member (birth or adoption)

Ordinarily we think about parent-child relationships in terms of the influence of the parents on the child. But a child can also have an effect on the parents. At no time is this impact likely to be greater than at the very beginning of the child's life. Harold Feldman and his co-workers at Cornell University have been studying the behavior and attitudes of married couples before and after the arrival of the first child. In general, they find that childless couples report a higher level of marital satisfaction and talk more with each other about personal feelings and common interests. In contrast, couples with a young child experience fewer stimulating exchanges of ideas, fewer fun times, fewer moments of laughter, and more feelings of resentment. Inasmuch as the couples were matched on age and length of marriage, the differences could not have been due to changes associated with either of these factors. Feldman concludes that the arrival of a child typically brings about a blunting of emotional expression and a lower level of verbal communication between couples.

Such findings bring home the fact that the arrival of a first child involves a period of tension and anxiety for the parents. At the same time, the strain is not without its rewards. The couples in Feldman's research, representing all stages of the family cycle, rated the "first year with an infant" as the most satisfying stage in married life. It was rated superior even to the stage "before the children arrive." The least satisfying period was when children were "gone from home" and next to that, "having teenagers." Clearly child-rearing is filled with both problems and rewards. Wise parents do well to be prepared for the former and let the latter catch them by surprise.

Loss of status or face

Alcoholism is just one of many factors that can cause a feeling of disgrace in any or all of the family members. Whether it be alcoholism, drug addiction, crime, delinquency, or some other cause, the resulting loss of face can have devastating effects on family relationships. Demoralization, because of alcoholism, occurs when the individual exhibits some of the following behaviors.

1. the need to drink before facing certain situations

2. frequent drinking sprees

3. a steady increase in intake

4. solitary drinking

5. early morning drinking

6. Monday morning absenteeism

7. frequent disputes about drinking

8. the occurrence of blackouts

For a drinker, a blackout is not "passing out" but a period of time in which, while remaining otherwise conscious, he or she has a loss of memory. He or she walks, talks, and acts, but does not remember any of his or her words or actions. Such blackouts may be one of the early signs of the more serious forms of alcoholism.

Alcoholism may exist without blackouts, however, and without any of the other accepted symptoms of addictive drinking. Many alcoholics do not go on drinking sprees, do not drink alone, nor drink in the morning. Nor do they miss work on Monday, yet they are considered alcoholics.

In general, persons may be considered to be alcoholics if they continue to drink even though their drinking consistently causes physical illness—headache, gastric distress, or hangover—or consistently causes trouble with wife, husband, employer, or the police.

Among the most demoralizing effects charged against excessive drinking are unhappy marriages, broken homes, impoverished families, and deprived or displaced children. The cost to public and private agencies for support of families ravaged by alcoholism has been said to be millions of dollars a year. The cost in human suffering and loss of status and face cannot be calculated.

It is clear that not only do alcoholics affect their families, but their families also affect the alcoholics and the severity of their illness. Solutions to such tangled relationships usually pose problems that can be resolved only if their biological, psychological, and sociological aspects are placed in balance for each family member.

Research has shown that for people who use alcohol to a significant degree, the lowest incidence of alcoholism is associated with the following habits and attitudes.

1. The children are exposed to alcohol early in life, within a strong family or religious group. Whatever the beverage, it is served in very diluted form and in small quantities, with consequent low blood-alcohol levels.

2. The beverage is considered mainly as a food and usually consumed with meals.

3. Parents present a constant example of moderate drinking.

4. No moral importance is attached to drinking. It is considered neither a virtue nor a sin.

5. Drinking is not viewed as a proof of adulthood or virility.

6. Abstinence is socially acceptable. It is no more rude or ungracious to decline a drink than to decline a piece of bread.

7. Excessive drinking or intoxication is not socially acceptable. It is not considered stylish, comical, or tolerable.

8. Finally and perhaps most important, there is a wide and usually complete agreement among members of the group on what might be called the ground rules of drinking.[1]

Dismemberment plus demoralization

Divorce is just one example of a combined loss of a family member and loss of status.

There are essentially two forms of divorce. One is an absolute legal dissolution of the marriage bond. The other is a judicial separation of man and wife, or termination of cohabitation, without dissolution of the marriage bond.

Although divorce rates are lower in low-income groups, this does not offer a true picture of the amount of family disorganization or marital disharmony existing within these families. The cost of divorce undoubtedly affects the rate of divorce in the low-income group. In many instances where cost is prohibitive and there is a desire on the part of one or both parties to escape their unhappiness, either separation by mutual agreement or desertion by one partner takes place. Permanent desertion has been called "the poor man's divorce." Deserted wives, and wives are more often deserted than husbands, frequently are handicapped both by lack of legal knowledge and by the lack of money to obtain a divorce. Consequently we do not know the extent of desertion, whereas divorce statistics are available for most states and for the country as a whole.

The fact that divorce laws have become more lenient may have some slight bearing on the divorce rate. But marriage and divorce are part of a very complicated and changing cultural pattern. The functions or expectations of marriage are changing, calling for new

1. U.S., National Institute of Mental Health, *Alcohol and Alcoholism*, Public Health Service Publications No. 1640 (Washington, D.C.: Government Printing Office), p. 28.

"It was fun in the beginning. But let's face it, even the most
idyllic relationships lose their glow after forty years."

and untried adjustments. Separation and divorce may seem to many
to be forms of adjustment of conflicting wants and values.

Marriage today, as compared to marriage some fifty years ago, has
as its primary values mutual love and affection, including sexual
satisfaction, equality of the partners, and freedom for personal development and happiness. Anything that disturbs the mutual sympathy and love between husband and wife creates serious tensions.
If happiness is not attained, the marriage is regarded as a failure.
Since marriage for love has become the basic pattern in our country
unhappiness in marriage is often blamed on a faulty choice of mate,
rather than on faulty adjustment between the two partners. Divorce
or separation, with choice of another partner, may be seen as a
possible solution. Essentially, marriage is a vulnerable human relationship composed of the feelings, attitudes, values, behaviors, and
demands that flow back and forth between the partners. Each acts as
both cause and effect within the relationship. The difficulty that
disrupts the relationship lies in destructive interaction between the
two partners. The focus of their difficulty may be in a mother-in-
law, sexual incompatibility, money, and so on, but the basic problem

is the failure of the partners to meet the emotional needs of each other to a satisfactory degree.

Loneliness is probably the most painful fear for both man and woman. Marriage is the most intimate of relationships. It embraces more facets of an individual's personality than do other adult relationships. Loss of this relationship represents a loss of a great number of human satisfactions. Failure in a human relationship, in our culture, carries with it some stigma of shame for the failure and some guilt and question about oneself and one's adequacy. For the woman, there may be loss of adequate support and the necessity, once more, to earn her own living and to help in the support of her children. Usually the woman is responsible for the day-to-day rearing of the children. This imposes a double burden. For she is again faced with the possibility of competing in the marriage market. In addition to loneliness and the lack of home care, a man may face complicated problems in the financial field. It is more expensive to support two households. Should he marry again, he may be faced with supporting two families, neither adequately. If he remains unmarried, his opportunity for building a sustained and satisfying

Reprinted by permission of Edward Frascino.
From *Saturday Review / World,* © 1974.

"Why is it that every time we face reality
it's something unpleasant?"

emotional relationship is limited. His relationship to his children must, of necessity, be piecemeal and unsatisfying. In many instances a man is unfairly treated by the divorce laws.

Facing crises

There is no pat answer to the problem of facing crises, whether they involve one individual or many families. Yet, some help for facing a crisis may come from taking time to consider the following.

1. Try to face and accept the reality of the situation.

2. Try to deal with the emotional upheaval that follows.

3. Try to determine what was good in the past and how it can be used in the present by thinking through needs and wishes, resources and capacities, choices and alternatives.

Questions

1. List some of the crises that a family might have to face.

2. Define crisis in your own terms.

3. What are the main kinds of crises? Does the list you made fit the four categories?

4. What are the two forms of divorce?

5. What are the main causes of divorce?

6. What are the fears of an individual facing divorce?

7. What is your philosophy of death?

8. Do you think that one's philosophy of death influences his or her life? Explain your answer.

9. What influences one's attitudes toward death?

10. What is grief?

11. How would you help a friend adjust to grief?

12. What factors contribute to the demoralizing crises caused by alcohol?

13. Choose a crisis and then analyze how you would face it. Some suggestions of crises are loss of money, loss of father or mother, loss of boyfriend or girlfriend, illegitimate birth, failure in school, lack of a date for the prom, indulgency in drugs, and so on.

The Effects of Alcohol[2]

Almost immediately after it hits the stomach, alcohol is coursing through the bloodstream to the central nervous system, where it starts to slow down, or anaesthetize, brain activity. Though it is a depressant, the initial subjective feeling that it creates is just the opposite, as the barriers of self-control and restraint are lifted and the drinker does or says things that his well-trained, sober self usually forbids. Only later, after a number of drinks, are the motor centers of the brain overtly affected, causing uncertain steps and hand movements.

How quickly the alcohol takes effect depends on many factors. One person may be bombed after a glass, while another stays relatively sober after several. Because alcohol is diluted in the blood, a 200-lb. man can usually tolerate more liquor than a 110-lb. woman. Food also retards absorption of alcohol from the gastrointestinal tract, and a few ounces taken with a meal are less powerful than an equal amount downed an hour before. By the same token, some drinks with food in them—eggnogs made with eggs, milk and cream, for example—have slightly less wallop than straight drinks. The tomato juice in a Bloody Mary or the orange juice in a Screwdriver is not enough to make any appreciable difference.

The total quantity of alcohol in a drink and the rate of consumption determine the alcohol level in the bloodstream. Thus a Scotch and water would pack the same punch as Scotch on the rocks or a Scotch and soda if all three were drunk at the same speed; drinking more slowly gives the system a chance to eliminate some of the alcohol. The mixing of different types—beer, wine, whisky and brandy, for instance—might make a drinker sick, but it would not make him any more drunk than the same alcoholic measure of just one of these drinks.

So far medicine has found no cure for the hangover, although aspirin can alleviate the headache. Despite a plethora of folk cures (none of them really effective), the best policy is to avoid drinking in excess the night before. Actually, no one knows exactly what causes the hangover's unpleasant symptoms of headache, nausea, depression and fatigue, which many drinkers experience at one time or another.

2. From TIME, April 22, 1974, p. 77. Reprinted by permission from TIME, The Weekly Newsmagazine; Copyright Time Inc. 1974.

Some recent research indicates that even social drinking can have both immediate and possible long-range deleterious effects on the body. According to Dr. Peter Stokes, a psychobiologist at Cornell University Medical College, the liver becomes fatty and therefore less efficient after only a few weeks of downing three or four drinks a night. But in the early stages, at least, the condition can be reversed by abstinence. More moderate imbibing—two drinks a night with meals, say—almost certainly does no harm to most people. New studies link drinking to heart-muscle damage and deterioration of the brain. Research by Dr. Ernest Noble of the University of California at Irvine shows that alcohol inhibits the ability of the brain cells to manufacture proteins and ribonucleic acid (RNA), which some researchers believe play a role in learning and memory storage. After 20 or 30 years, says Dr. Noble, two or three drinks a night on an empty stomach may impair a person's learning ability. Both Stokes and Noble cite studies showing premature and irreversible destruction of brain cells after years of heavy drinking.

Such frightening studies of the results of drinking have not yet been accepted throughout the medical profession, but the physical effects on an alcoholic of very heavy drinking are beyond dispute. A pint of whiskey a day, enough to make eight or ten ordinary highballs, provides about 1,200 calories—roughly half the ordinary energy requirement—without any food value. As a result, an alcoholic usually has a weak appetite and often suffers from malnutrition and vitamin deficiency. The slack cannot be taken up by popping vitamin pills; heavy alcohol consumption impairs the body's utilization of vitamins. At the same time, excessive intake of alcohol also affects the production and activity of certain disease-fighting white blood cells, giving the alcoholic a particularly low resistance to bacteria.

Inevitably the alcoholic develops a fatty liver, and his chances of developing cirrhosis, a condition in which liver cells have been replaced by fibrous scar tissue, are at least one in ten. A severely damaged liver cannot adequately manufacture bile, which is necessary for the digestion of fats; as a consequence, the alcoholic often feels weak and suffers from chronic indigestion. This may be made worse by gastritis, which is caused by alcohol irritation of the sensitive linings of the stomach and small intestine. The troubles of a heavy drinker do not end there, and through damage to the central nervous system and hormonal imbalance, alcohol may even cause impotence.

Further reading

Anders, Rebecca. *A Look at Alcoholism.* Minneapolis, MN: Lerner Publications Company, 1977. (An Awareness Book.)

Clinebell, Howard. *Understanding and Counseling the Alcoholic.* Nashville, TN: Abingdon Press, 1976.

Dempsey, David K. *The Way We Die: An Investigation of Death and Dying in America Today.* New York: McGraw-Hill, 1977.

Hornik, Lynn. *You and Your Alcoholic Parent.* Wilton, CT: Association Press, 1973.

Hosier, Helen K. *The Other Side of Divorce.* New York: Hawthorn Books, Inc., 1975.

Hunt, Morton M. *World of the Formerly Married.* New York: McGraw-Hill, 1966.

Ross, E. K. *On Death and Dying.* New York: Macmillan, Inc., 1969.

Wheeler, Michael. *No-Fault Divorce.* Boston: Beacon Press, 1974.

Chapter 27

Marriage and counseling

It's great to ask in-depth questions when they really count, but fighting or constantly quarreling about unimportant points is another matter. Fighting or bickering can become a habit. It is difficult for relationships to succeed with constant bickering.

Failure to communicate

Marriage failure is often related to communication failure. Many marriage counselors find that couples can improve their marriage if they can learn to say what they mean, mean what they say, and learn to appreciate their partner and the views of their partner. Two people may be in the same house and share the same bed, but unless they are tuned in to each other's wavelength, they might as well be miles apart. Living together intimately requires the recognition and expression of real feelings.

What causes couples to fail to express their real feelings? What is communication? Communication is the way we attempt to get through to each other, the process of transmitting feelings, needs, values, hopes, attitudes, dreams, ideas, ideals, and beliefs. It is as vital to a relationship as water is to a fish.

We communicate in many ways. Speech or language is perhaps the main or prime form of communication. It is, however, not the only way. Our facial expression, tone of voice, or word emphasis can alter the same message. Nonverbal symbols and clues such as gestures, touch, silences, facial expressions, vision and hearing are used in giving and receiving messages.

From *Saturday Review/World,* Copyright 1974.
Reprinted by permission of *Saturday Review* and Bernard Schoenbaum.

"It's finally happened—I'm unentertainable!"

There are five major reasons why people fail to make communicative contact or fail to really speak to each other.

1. *False assumptions: We often assume that a person would not want to talk about a particular problem or would not want to make a contribution to a certain conversation or discussion.* We judge others inaccurately because of incorrect first impressions or incomplete information. We often tend to assume things about others without first checking out this impression with them. Acting on a false assumption can cause misunderstandings or keep us from getting to know another person more intimately.

2. *We are not aware of how we come across to others.* We seldom bother to ask for feedback on what we say or do. Some of us have no idea of what our tone of voice communicates to others, how clearly or unclearly we express ourselves, or the mannerisms that may detract from the effectiveness of our communications.

3. *We often fail to listen.* A good listener hears what the other person is saying. A conversation in which the partners are really listening is filled with silence, reflective thought, and consideration to the end of the sentence. We fail to hear the real message or the essence of what the other person is saying if we are preoccupied with preparing our reply, interrupting the other person, or saying "Yes, but" even before the other person is finished speaking.

4. *We fail to communicate if we don't like ourselves.* If we lack confidence or fear rejection and ridicule, we may stop ourselves from making contact with others. When we fear a negative reaction, we avoid certain subjects or keep our hurts and angry feelings to ourselves. These feelings surface later and hamper us in our communications. When we personally lack "OK" feelings, we hesitate to share personal feelings, to trust others, or to be frank and offer constructive criticism.

5. *We often do not communicate in certain areas because our families, friends, communities, and/or society have told us that these things one does not discuss.* We are taught from childhood not to express certain feelings and impulses. Some of us were even taught to deny our feelings. We were prohibited from crying, getting angry, discussing sex, and sometimes even love. By shutting off or by shutting out these emotions, we limit the depth of our relationships with others. Sometimes this inhibition is intensified during courtship and early marriage. The true person is disguised in an effort to favorably impress the other.

"I'll say one thing, Gloria. We cleared the air."

Counseling

Only three states, California, Michigan, and New Jersey, require marriage counselors to be licensed. Consequently some marriage counselors may be phony. This doesn't, however, mean that they all are. It only indicates that one should choose a counselor carefully.

"Is it something I said?"

Use a reference system and feel free to cancel the counseling when it seems pointless.

Families can get help from marriage counselors, non-profit agencies, private therapists, encounter groups, family therapy, sexual dysfunction clinics, and from enrichment of their own lives. A family therapist makes one basic assumption: the family is a dynamic system which affects all of its members and is affected in turn by each member. A change in one member of the family means a change in the others. Therefore, the entire family must be treated. Family therapists help people to reveal their problems. They advise a couple considering divorce, for example, to seek counseling that will help them decide what to do. He or she does not decide for them.

How do a husband and wife save their marriage? The couple must realize that to change a long-term relationship they will have to end their disbelief in each other. They will have to give up blaming each other, their in-laws, the children, even chauvinism and women's lib. They will have to interact as individuals capable of generating their own self-esteem. Each may have to "give up" something and let go of some old, habitual, and destructive behaviors.

A counselor who is treating a sick marriage can neither give advice nor prescribe remedies. A counselor's task is to help a couple "come to grips" with their own problems so they can work them out. The best marriage counseling is, in effect, self-counseling. Marriage is a union. It involves two people each with his and her own background, ideas, attitudes, needs, goals, and dreams. The result is a relationship, with its implications and two people trying to bridge the differences that naturally exist between them.

Self-counseling

Self-counseling is impossible when a conflict has reached a crisis stage. It is impossible when hostility is so deep-seated that any attempt to break through it is instantly short-circuited. It is impossible when a problem is so overwhelming that it paralyzes one's capacity to act.

There are two initial steps in self-counseling. The first is to diagnose or identify marital problems. The second is to learn how to deal with them.

The following four keys may help couples recognize what their problems really are.

The first key. The first key is to establish a "therapeutic environment." A therapeutic environment is setting up a special time and place for the couple to have their discussions. They need to allow enough time for a thorough discussion; they need to prepare for it; and afterward they need to evaluate what was said. Uninterrupted privacy is also necessary.

The second key. The second key is to know as much as you can about each other. History taking, the sharing of biographical data, family background, and previous experiences that still affect the partners are very important. The circumstances of one's background, even trivial or long-forgotten events, can come back to haunt a marriage. To begin to uncover hidden troublemakers the couple should exchange elements in their backgrounds. This means more than just the facts. It means sharing dreams, goals, hopes, fears, things you are proud of or ashamed of, that mark you as an adult and as a marital partner. Consider such topics as: "Tell me about how you spent holidays when you were growing up." "What do you know about how your father and his father got along?" "What are your favorite, or worst, memories of your mother or your father?" "If you could do anything you want, what would you do?" "How do you really feel about the way you look?" "If you could live it over again what would you change about your life?"

The third key. The third key is to acknowledge that a problem does exist and to recognize exactly how and how much each partner contributes to it. Both persons must acknowledge that a conflict exists or that a relationship can be improved before anything positive can occur. Poor listening habits and lack of talking about the situation are usually equally to blame. When one partner is unwilling to complain, unable to express irritation or anger, or reluctant to force an issue, the other can hardly be held responsible if tensions build.

In some cases it takes an emotional earthquake to get a person to admit that something is wrong. A problem may exist for years, yet one partner denies it, or seems oblivious to it, until the other is forced to cry for attention and help. The dramatic gesture is a poor substitute for learning how to listen and to talk about marital conflict.

The fourth key. The fourth key is to identify the real problem that underlies the surface complaints. Listen for and learn to recognize the themes behind the statements you make to each other. Learn to use logical analysis to peel away the layers from these statements— going from the general to the particular, from the obvious to the not so obvious. Probably the easiest way to insure objectivity is to write down your version of the problem. In self-counseling the clearest possible statement about a marital conflict is the firmest basis for diagnosis.

Here, once more are the four keys that may help couples to recognize what their problems really are.

1. Establish a regular time and a private place to serve as your therapeutic environment.

2. Learn about each other's personal and emotional histories.

3. Acknowledge the existence of a marital problem.

4. Share in an accurate diagnosis of the problem.

Quarreling

Constructive arguing may bring a couple closer together, if it helps them see each other's point of view, and makes them more aware of their definite opinions on the particular problem. Such an argument may clear the air and dispel the tension, defining the issues more clearly. It can help the partners see each other as real human beings. It helps to dispel the "halo effect" or the romantic illusion. Their mutual respect and understanding grow because of the outcome of the quarrel.

Guide to Emotional Change[1]

Emotional needs differ at various ages. Here is the response pattern of a group of women asked to evaluate certain statements for their high importance or low importance in their life at the moment.

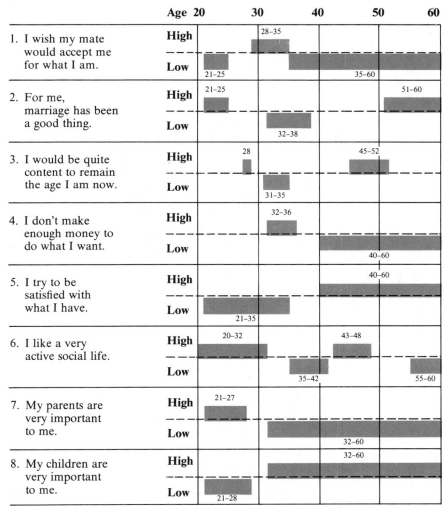

		Age 20	30	40	50	60
1. I wish my mate would accept me for what I am.	High		28–35			
	Low	21–25			35–60	
2. For me, marriage has been a good thing.	High	21–25			51–60	
	Low		32–38			
3. I would be quite content to remain the age I am now.	High		28		45–52	
	Low		31–35			
4. I don't make enough money to do what I want.	High		32–36			
	Low			40–60		
5. I try to be satisfied with what I have.	High			40–60		
	Low	21–35				
6. I like a very active social life.	High	20–32		43–48		
	Low		35–42		55–60	
7. My parents are very important to me.	High	21–27				
	Low		32–60			
8. My children are very important to me.	High		32–60			
	Low	21–28				

Adapted from the results of a five-year study by Dr. Roger L. Gould and colleagues at the UCLA Neuropsychiatric Institute, Los Angeles.

Destructive quarreling widens the gap between a couple. It dissolves in unkind words, hurt feelings, and an attack upon the psychological or physical shortcomings of the partners. The quarrel does not stay on the subject. It deteriorates into name-calling and the belittling of relatives and friends. The subject of the quarrel is lost, but the quarrel leaves deep wounds.

Butterfield, in *Planning for Marriage,* suggests some rules for the prevention of quarreling. He cautions against the problem of rule-following without judgment. With this in mind, the rules are listed here.[2]

1. Be sure you understand the other person's point of view. Many arguments get well along and both contestants are highly over-heated before they discover that they are talking about two different things.

2. Look for all possible points of agreement.

3. Do not start an argument you ought not to win. It is possible to win an argument and lose a marriage.

4. Avoid all forms of pressure tactics, such as (a) shouting the other person down, (b) using force or striking the other person, (c) being completely silent and denying the other person the satisfaction of a decent reply, (d) "pulling one's rank" on the other person, (e) withholding one's physical love.

5. Consider alternatives.

6. Be hopeful.

Few arguments are so important that they demand an immediate and complete solution on the spot. Many an argument at night is tangled with fatigue and the emotional stresses of the day. Tomorrow morning the issues may be crystal clear or they may seem insignificant and even childish.

The stages of adult development[3]

Most experts agree that the majority of us change in similar ways while progressing through fairly definable life stages as adults.

1. Getting into the adult world (ages 20–28). "Establishing an adult identity—that is, coming *to feel* like an adult—is the main theme of the first years of the 20's," says Dr. Gould, who

2. Oliver M. Butterfield, *Planning for Marriage* (Princeton, N.J.: D. Van Nostrand Co., 1956), pp. 111–119.
3. Excerpted from "Your Five Emotional Stages of Life" by Rona and Laurence Cherry. Reprinted from the April 1976 issue of *Family Circle* Magazine. © 1976 THE FAMILY CIRCLE, INC. All rights reserved. Used by permission.

has studied more than 700 individuals ranging in age from 20 to 65. "Usually during those years, most young people have already moved away from home, either to attend school or to live in apartments of their own. At first, however, most simply substitute friends for family, depending on roommates or close friends for the kind of emotional support they once looked for from their parents."

But soon most young people develop a new kind of self-reliance. At the University of California at San Francisco, a team of researchers headed by Dr. Marjorie Fiske Lowenthal found that at this time "there is a growing awareness of new worlds to conquer and the energy and enthusiasm with which to try it."

At every life stage there are two possible roads, one leading toward stagnation and the other toward growth. In the 20's the road to stagnation leads to what some call "the Peter-Pan Syndrome." It describes young adults who are afraid to grow up, who prefer to remain the still-babied members of overprotective families.

The road to growth on the other hand, takes most young people toward marriage.

For most, the first year of marriage is described as almost euphoric. "If you are tuned into yourself, you can really start to find out a great deal about yourself," says Dr. Laura Singer, president of Save a Marriage, Inc. "You explore what the boundaries of the other person are, get to know how you fit in with those boundaries and what they evoke in you."

But the glowing optimism of the 20's has its dangers. "In this period," says Dr. Gould, "your conscious expectations when you go into a marriage may be realistic, but your unconscious expectations often are not."

2. Starting to question (ages 29–34). "In the early and middle 20's, people are busy making things come true," says Dr. Gould. "Their energies are deployed in certain directions—getting married, starting a family, getting a firm foothold in a career. You want to get to the point where you can say to your parents, at least in your own mind: 'Look—I can do it.' But after you've made enough things come true, you begin to ask questions you didn't dare ask before—and these questions seem to cluster around the age of 30."

This questioning makes the whole period from 29 to 34 a time of increased reflection. People often seem to wonder about where exactly in life they're going. Some try to reassure themselves by becoming acquisitive—buying more and more furniture, a new house, new cars—in order to convince themselves they've arrived. But often the questioning leads to positive internal changes. "You definitely see people allowing themselves an opportunity to try on new behaviors," said one New York psychologist.

Growing children now offer the chance for positive inner change. "You can re-experience yourself and your own childhood in a different way, from a different position," says Dr. Singer. Problems not solved in your own growing up can now be seen in a new light. For those who feel their own childhood to have been in some way lacking, this can be very therapeutic.

This period of increased reflection precedes and blends into the adult life stage, when greatest inner change occurs.

3. Mid-life (ages 35–43). "Here many people feel a little scared—more than a little confused," says Dr. David E. Morrison, a Topeka, Kansas, psychiatrist who has studied more than 2,000 people in their mid-life. Yet this period is not necessarily a bad one.

"People who pass through this stage successfully often find a new depth inside themselves," says Dr. Thayer Greene, psychoanalyst who conducts workshops on marriage and relationships in New York. "Maybe they were concentrating on the outside of things. But suddenly there's a new meaning and richness to their lives."

During this period, the sense of time's passing frequently becomes acute. Death—only an unpleasant rumor to most people till now—suddenly seems real and is, to some, frighteningly personal as a friend, a neighbor, a parent dies. The feeling is heightened by the growing up of children—who usually pass through puberty around this time—evoking disturbing memories of their own adolescence.

Researchers have found that people in mid-life fall into three groups, each different in the way it handles the inner changes of this stage.

"By far the greatest group accepts them and isn't disturbed by them," says Dr. Gould. "Some women go back to school to take courses; others go back to work or aim for a new kind of job. New interests emerge."

A second group, much smaller, lives this transition out in a very flamboyant way. Psychologists term it "the Gauguin complex," after the painter who around this age abruptly abandoned his way of life in France to start a new one on a South Pacific island.

Sudden divorces or dramatic changes in life-style may take place. Some women seem outwardly the same and yet start to fantasize obsessively about new relationships with men very different from their husband. Says Dr. Greene, "When a woman starts to fantasize about this kind of dream figure, he may soon—coincidentally—turn up in her life, something Jung called 'synchronicity.' " Women may at this time break up their homes and disappear in search of new experiences and partners. "Unfortunately," says Dr. Greene, "nine times out of 10 they carry their problems with them. Until a woman can resolve these problems, she goes from one relationship to another—and yet finds each one winds up in the same way. She should understand that what she is really restless for is not a new man but finding her own soul, a relationship to her own individuality."

The third group simply ignores inner change and rigidly sticks to old patterns, tastes and thoughts; a few women now dress and even act like their teenage daughters. Sometimes they may even try to keep their children in a childlike state of dependency to help maintain their illusion that things are still the same. "That's failing this period and failing it miserably," says Dr. Morrison. "The result is people who are dried up and stale inside—luckily, they're rare."

4. Rediscovering (ages 44–55). By the time many couples reach the late 40's their children have already left home. Suddenly, for the first time in decades, husband and wife find themselves together in an empty house. For a few women whose lives have been lopsidedly centered on their children, this can be a rather lonely and unhappy time of grieving over an "empty nest"—at least till they can find new activities.

For women, an important physical change—the menopause—also occurs during this period. Contrary to myth, however, "the change of life" causes very little disruption in the lives of most women. A study conducted by the University of Chicago's Committee on Human Development found, in fact, that most women were in retrospect, rather grateful for it. "New sexual opportunities open up for the couple," says Dr. Gould. "Of course, some may have trouble with this; but if they can break through that, they can have a new flowering of sexuality."

Occasionally couples may find that when their children leave home there is little holding them together–then marriages of 25 years or more can break apart. One solution most psychologists definitely consider unhealthy is for husband and wife to try to patch things together by developing a so-called Mom-and-Dad Marriage. "The children are all gone," says Dr. Greene, "but the husband and wife are still calling each other Mom and Dad. It's as if they've gotten jammed into labeled containers and can't get out and become individuals again. They're just too scared to admit change."

Another, healthier way is for the couple to grow as individuals. "You find lots of people are much happier," says Dr. Ethel Shanas, professor of sociology at the University of Illinois at Chicago Circle. "They don't have to worry about their kids— they're on their own."

Couples often move closer together. Dr. John Clausen, a professor of sociology at the University of California at Berkeley, finds that husbands and wives increase their joint activity. "Most women get a new zest from having a measure of freedom and independence from household responsibilities that hasn't been theirs since the early years of marriage."

One 52-year-old businessman remarks: "For a while it was touch and go for us after the kids left." He and his wife constantly quarreled, seriously considered divorce. "Finally we decided we had to let go of some old ways of being dependent on each other. In a way it's been a painful experience, this growing apart in different ways while staying together. But it can be done."

5. Growth toward wisdom (age 56 and beyond). Warren J. Gadpaille, M.D., points out in his book, *The Cycles of Sex:* "These are peak years of productive and creative endeavor." But in this period, people do move toward the crisis of retirement and the possible loss of a mate of a lifetime. By age 65, 20% of husbands and 50% of wives will have lost their mates. Divorce is also increasingly frequent at this period—and there may be problems of health, chronic illness or depression.

Whatever the external realities, the individual is now often thrown back upon his or her own resources. Though some women at this life stage do seem to be more preoccupied with themselves and material possessions, many more seem to achieve a kind of tranquility unknown in their earlier years. In his studies of people past middle age, Dr. Gould discovered that most were "unrushed by the sense of urgency that accompanied the 20's and 30's. They were more eager to have human experiences, such as sharing the joys and confusions of everyday life, rather than searching for the glamour and glitter and power."

Most people now have the pleasure of seeing their grandchildren growing up as well—and, without the responsibility of parenthood, may enjoy them more than they were able to enjoy their own children.

And as for widowhood, Dr. Helene Z. Lopata at Loyola University, Chicago, found that after the initial period of bereavement most widows were able to adapt to their lives quite well. In fact, of the more than 300 widows she studied (all 50 years of age or older), the majority described themselves as being more independent and active since their husbands died—even though each reported herself as having had a happy marriage and as missing her husband very much. Over half, in fact, even felt that they had changed for the better as a result of widowhood. "Growth is something that goes on all our lives," says Dr. Jane H. Wheelwright, a San Francisco analyst who herself is 70. "There are always new facets of ourselves to discover."

Coping with inner change[4]

Can you actually prepare yourself for the various life stages? Almost without exception, yes. "Preparation is both possible and advisable," says Dr. Layne Longfellow of Menninger Clinic. "If we know what is coming, we can relax in the face of it and approach it objectively and constructively." But how?

One way is to realize you change inside whether you want to or not. Don't blame external circumstances and other people for the inner uncertainty that growing independence and integration as an individual may bring. Don't cling to "the way things were." Instead, adjust your own changing needs to changing circumstances.

Learn to understand your adjusting emotions and goals. Many times marriages falter because people insist they want more than their relationship has to offer.

Try to regard your present age as a good one. Consider the benefits you enjoy now and understand that the values of the moment are not necessarily those of the past or of your future.

Increase involvement in new studies, hobbies and community activities. The healthy personality increasingly needs less while giving others more.

4. Ibid.

Share your feelings with your spouse and let him or her share feelings with you. If he or she is concerned about his or her job and you are both worried about the children's leaving home, it's important to talk about the changes you both face.

Remember that drastic solutions should be carefully weighed. "Husbands and wives come to me and say they want to bail out of their marriages," says Dr. Mitchell. "The question I always ask is: Bail out of what? You can bail out of a marriage easily enough but not out of a life-style. We know reasonably well that if you divorce and remarry, you'll probably marry the same kind of person again and have the same kind of problems. I know very few cases where divorce and remarriage have been the right answer—and I know of no case where divorce in order to marry someone else worked. In fact, one of the few concrete pieces of advice I give a couple is: If you're having an affair, don't marry the man or woman you've been having an affair with. It won't work."

Be prepared for changes to come. "I've noticed that it is those events that we don't anticipate that will knock us off balance," says Dr. Jane H. Wheelwright, "and it's the people who hang back and don't dare to look ahead who will get hurt. If you are prepared, and if you can maintain a constant commitment to change and the possibility of growth, no matter what part of life you should be in, you'll do fine."

Questions

1. How might one overcome the bickering habit? What are some things that you bicker about with your parents, your brothers and sisters, and your friends?

2. In what three states is a license required for marriage counseling?

3. Explain the concept that if one family member is troubled the whole family is troubled.

4. List and explain the four keys to self-counseling.

5. Write up an example of a constructive quarrel.

6. Interview people in each of the five emotional stages of life.

Further reading

Cherry, Rona, and Cherry, Laurence. "Your Five Emotional Stages of Life: How to Deal with Them." *Family Circle,* April 1976, pp. 87–94.

Kennedy, Eugene. *On Becoming a Counselor: A Basic Guide for Non-Professional Counselors.* New York: Crossroad Books, 1977.

Krumboltz, J. D., and Thorensen, C. E. *Counseling Methods.* New York: Holt, Rinehart & Winston, CBS, Inc., 1976.

Lasswell, Marcia, and Lakerz, Norman. *No-Fault Marriage.* New York: Doubleday & Co., Inc., 1977.

Mahoney, Stanley C. *Art of Helping People Effectively.* Wilton, CT: Association Press, 1967.

Satir, Virginia. *Conjoint Family Therapy.* Palo Alto, CA: Science & Behavior Books, 1975.

Skoglund, Elizabeth. *Can I Talk to You?* Glendale, CA: Regal Books, 1977, p. 8.

UNIT **4**

Understanding Parenthood

Chapter 28

Reproduction

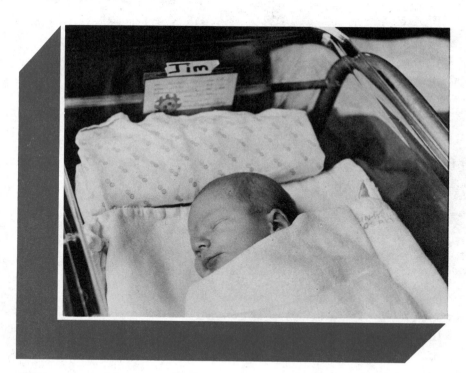

Being born is one of the greatest events in our lives. Birth and the birth process are miracles to behold. Children are helped to understand reproduction by observing the reproductive process as their pets reproduce their young.

332

However, the transfer from animal reproduction to human reproduction is not made unless children feel free to ask questions at different times during their own development.

Children learn about reproduction in steps just as they learn to talk, read, and give their names and addresses. Adults expect the latter to be a long-term learning process. But many times they give education about sex and knowledge about reproduction in one formal talk, movie or special assembly. Education about sex needs to be a continuing process just as in the learning of other concepts. It should begin in infancy and continue on through marriage and parenthood. Because of the importance of the parents' relationship during pregnancy, the need for parents to understand reproduction and pregnancy, and because knowledge of the reproductive system is basic to male-female relations, this chapter is included.

Reproductive organs

In order to understand better the process of reproduction, one needs to be able to name and to define the functions of the reproductive organs. The male reproductive organs consist of the testes, the prostate gland, the urethra, and the penis. The female reproductive system consists of the ovaries, the Fallopian tubes, the uterus, the vagina, and the breasts. These organs compose the reproductive systems that produce the gametes (mature sex cells) which unite to form a new individual. Our human race goes on because human bodies have systems which enable two cells, the sperm from the man and the ovum from the woman, to unite, form a new life, and bring it into the world.

"You wash, I'll dry."

A female gamete, or ovum (ova is the plural form of this word), commonly called an egg, is globular and about 1/100 to 1/200 of an inch in diameter. Sperms (spermatozoa), or male gametes, are extremely minute and are shaped roughly like tadpoles. Each sperm has an oval head approximately 1/5000 of an inch long, a middle section, and a comparatively long tail, making the total length about 1/500 inch. Ova cannot move by their own power. Sperms, on the other hand, are able to propel themselves by lashing their tails in very much the same way a tadpole swims. They can move approximately an inch in five or six minutes.

Sperms are produced in minute tubes within the testes (testicles), two oval-shaped organs suspended in the scrotum. The immature sperms pass from the tubules in each testis into the corresponding epididymis and from there into the vas deferens. During sexual stimulation, the spongy interior of the penis becomes engorged with blood, causing the organ to increase both in size and in rigidity (erection) and enabling it to enter the vagina. At the climax of sexual excitement, sperms are mixed with the secretions of several glands including the seminal vesicles and the prostate gland. The whitish, viscous mixture (called semen or seminal fluid) passes, as a result of muscular contraction through the urethra and out of the male body.

Seminal fluid is ejaculated or discharged during sexual intercourse. It may also be discharged as a result of self-stimulation. Periodically it is discharged spontaneously during sleep (called seminal emissions or nocturnal emissions) when there has been no sexual excitement.

Sperms are produced in great numbers. In a single ejaculation of seminal fluid (about one teaspoonful) there are normally 200 to 300 million sperms. Once discharged into the vagina the sperms tend to move in all directions.

Ova are produced in the ovaries, two almond-shaped organs situated on either side of the uterus. The ovaries are 1 to 2 inches long and in life are reddish gray in color. The formation of ova in the ovaries begins in prenatal life. Many ova degenerate during the life of a woman and new ova are produced. Ova mature one at a time in response to certain hormones which are produced by the anterior lobe of the pituitary gland. During the maturing process, the ovum migrates toward the surface of the ovary. There it becomes surrounded by a fluid which eventually bulges out the surface tissue of the ovary forming a bubble about the size of half a small cherry. This is called the Graafian follicle. This follicle then ruptures or breaks and the ovum is discharged. The release of the ovum is called ovulation. In the normal, mature woman it occurs once in approximately twenty-eight days.

After the ovum leaves the ovary, its life is subject to as much conjecture as is the life of sperms. There is no direct connection between ovaries and Fallopian tubes. The ends of the tubes, in close conjunction with the ovaries, divide into fingerlike projections (fimbriae) which, at the time of ovulation, are activated to come into even closer contact than usual with the ovary. Both fimbriae and the interior surface of the tubes are lined with tiny hairlike protuberances (cilia), which have the capacity to move with a whiplike motion. They move more vigorously toward the uterus than toward the ovaries on the return stroke. Thus a current is set up and the ovum, which has been released, starts its trip toward the uterus. The ovum is moved along by the cilia, much as a ball might roll over a carpet if the fibers could move so as to push the ball. The ovum takes from three to seven days to move from the ovary through the Fallopian tubes into the uterus.

Fertilization is the union of one sperm with the ovum. It occurs in the Fallopian tube. Of all the sperms that enter the vagina, only a very small number ever reach the ovum. Only one sperm is involved in the fertilization process. The zygote (the fertilized egg) is the beginning of a new individual.

Each gamete (mature sex cell) has twenty-three chromosomes. Chromosomes are tiny bodies composed of genes. The genes are determiners of hereditary traits. Thus, when a sperm meets the ovum, its head penetrates the latter's outer wall and fuses with the nucleus of the egg, establishing the twenty-three pairs (or 46) chromosomes. The tail of the sperm drops off. When one sperm has penetrated the ovum, all other sperms are repelled. At the time of fertilization, the new individual's sex and hereditary traits are determined. Conception occurs in human beings only after insemination which occurs normally during sexual intercourse.

The development of the human embryo

After fertilization has taken place, the zygote (the united sperm and ovum) continues its movement through the Fallopian tube to the uterus. Before it reaches the uterus, it has already begun to divide, first into two cells, then four, eight, sixteen, thirty-two, and so on. This early stage of cell division does not cause any increase in size. For a period of time the zygote remains free in the uterus. After several days, it embeds itself in the wall of the uterus, which, through the action of certain hormones, has been prepared for this implantation. Nidation is the term used for the process of implantation.

The stages of the development of the human embryo are pictured and described below and on pages 337–339. The photographs were taken the same distance from the specimens to help you get an orientation to the size at the various stages of growth. No attempt is made to describe all of the physiology. This discussion is included to help you better understand the stages and their importance to the developing individual. The photographs are of the specimens of the human fetuses on display at the Museum of Science and Industry, Chicago, Illinois.

Approximate Age—6 weeks

The embryo is less than 1.25 centimeters (½ inch) long at the end of the first six weeks. The heart and brain are among the first organs to form.

Approximate Age—9 weeks

At two months, the embryo is about 3.13 centimeters (1¼ inches) long. The organs have continued to develop and have assumed their permanent functions. Tiny budlike projections that will form the limbs are noticeable, but fingers and toes are not yet completely formed. The face has begun to look human. Genital organs have appeared. The male genital organs are developed first. In a female, the organs are developed more slowly. However, if the embryo is aborted at this stage and carefully examined, its sex can be determined.

Approximate Age—10 weeks

Approximate Age—12 weeks

The embryo is now called a fetus. The fetus at three months weighs about 28.35 grams (1 ounce) and is less than 7.5 centimeters (3 inches) long. Arms, legs, hands, fingers, toes, and ears are formed. Nails have begun to develop. The fetus appears human but has a head that is very large in proportion to the rest of the body. Vocal cords are formed. Teeth have begun to develop in sockets in the jawbones.

Approximate Age—15 weeks

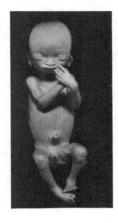

Approximate Age—18 weeks

At four and one-half months, the fetus is 15 to 20 centimeters (6 to 8 inches) long or about one-half its length at birth. It weighs 141.75 to 170.1 grams (5 to 6 ounces). One can hear the heartbeat through a stethoscope. Eyebrows and eyelashes have appeared. The skin is reddish and somewhat transparent. However, the skin ridges, which will make foot and fingerprints possible, have already formed.

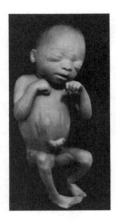

Approximate Age—20 weeks

At five months fetal movements may be clearly felt by the mother. Head hair has appeared. Nails are well formed. The fetus weighs nearly 454 grams (1 pound) and is 20 to 30 centimeters (8 to 12 inches) long. Vernix caseosa covers the surface of the body. This vernix caseosa is a mixture of fatty secretion and dead skin cells which forms a cheesy covering. If born at this time, the fetus usually cannot survive except for a few moments. The fetus may live for a few hours if born at six months. It weighs 908 grams (2 pounds) and is about 35 centimeters (14 inches) tall.

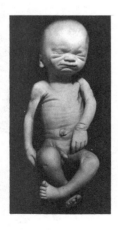

Approximate Age—27 weeks

The fetus measures about 37.5 centimeters (15 inches) in length and weighs approximately 1.2 kilograms (2½ pounds) after seven months. If born at this time, it has perhaps a one in ten chance of survival. The widespread notion that infants born at the seventh month are more likely to survive than those born at the eighth month is quite incorrect.

Approximate Age—31 weeks

As if to improve its appearance before making its debut into the world, the fetus uses the last two months for growing and filling out. With good care infants born at the end of the eighth month have better than even chances of survival, possibly as high as two chances out of three.

The full term fetus weighs, on the average, about 3.2 kilograms (7 pounds) if a girl and 3.5 kilograms (7½ pounds) if a boy; its length is approximately 50 centimeters (20 inches). Its skin is now its natural color and thickly coated with the cheesy vernix. The fine down hair which previously covered its body has largely disappeared. The fingernails are firm and protrude beyond the ends of the fingers. The breasts in both boys and girls are often firm and protruding due to the fact that the same substance which causes the mother's breasts to enlarge during pregnancy passes through the placenta and stimulates development of fetal breasts. This enlargement disappears within a few days of the birth.

Pregnancy

The length of pregnancy varies greatly. It may range between such wide extremes as 240 days and 300 days and yet be normal in every respect. The average duration, counting from the time of conception, is nine and a half lunar months; that is, thirty-eight weeks or 266 days. Counting from the first day of the last menstrual period, its average length is ten lunar months or forty weeks or 280 days. These average figures mean very little, however. It would appear that some children require a longer time, others a shorter time in the uterus for full development. The usual method of predicting the time of birth is to count back three calendar months from the first day of the last menstrual period and add seven days. This would give a rough estimate. For example, if the last period began on April 14, we would count back three months to January 14, and add seven days. Thus the baby's birth would be around January 21.

Being pregnant is a natural and normal condition. A pregnant woman should consider herself capable of doing her daily tasks and recreation the same as before becoming pregnant. However, she should not become overtired nor assume strenuous new activity to which she is unaccustomed.

A well-balanced diet is always important for the well-being of an individual. The diet during pregnancy should provide foods from the four major food groups. The quantity of food eaten should remain the same as before pregnancy, provided that that quantity was adequate for the body build and activity. However, the diet should optimally contain increased amounts of protein, vitamins, and mineral salts, especially calcium, in order to feed the developing fetus. This can and should be done without increasing the caloric intake. If the pregnant woman has a big appetite, the only certain recommendation to meet this situation is self-restraint. She should eat only three meals a day and avoid snacks, especially those composed of fatty foods and sweets.

During the first three and one-half months of pregnancy the weight is usually stationary. There may even be a slight loss. During the latter two-thirds of the period of pregnancy, there is a steady gain. The average increase in weight during pregnancy is twenty-four pounds. The main part of this weight increase is understandable.

Baby	31.78 kilograms (7 pounds)
Amniotic fluid	6.81 kilograms (1½ pounds)
Afterbirth (placenta)	4.54 kilograms (1 pound)
Increase in weight of uterus	9.08 kilograms (2 pounds)
Increase in weight of breasts	6.81 kilograms (1½ pounds)
Increase in blood	4.54 kilograms (1 pound)
	63.56 kilograms (14 pounds)

The remaining 4.54 kilograms (10 pounds) represent general accumulation of fat and the increased amount of fluid which tissues tend to retain at this time. Gains between 8.1 to 11 kilograms (20 and 24 pounds) are natural and in keeping with good health. An increase in weight of 14 kilograms (30 pounds) or more is undesirable on several counts. First, these extra pounds represent unnecessary weight for the muscles of the legs and back to carry about. This suddenly imposed strain is a common cause of backache and pain in the legs. Second, many complications of pregnancy and labor are associated with excessive increases in weight. Third, added fat is likely to be permanent unless removed by dieting.

Emotions affecting pregnancy

An emotionally well-adjusted woman does not suffer excessively from the nausea and cramps which are said to be typical of pregnancy. This does not mean that pregnancy will not have its difficult moments. But rather it reminds us that the way the woman reacts to these disturbances will depend upon her emotional makeup. Some people have difficulty taking even minor physical upsets in stride. The well-adjusted person may use these minor disturbances for all they are worth. Since illness in our culture is an acceptable excuse, there is a tendency for some people to use illness for emotional gains. It is not uncommon for many women to do this during their pregnancies. Because the physical burden of pregnancy is theirs alone, many women will act as though special privileges are in order. Little do they realize that their own deep misgivings about wanting to be a mother are forcing them to retreat into illness.

When a person is getting what he or she wants, the satisfactions enjoyed have a beneficial effect on his or her health. A woman who eagerly awaits the birth of her child, may develop a glow and beauty greater than she ever enjoyed before. In such cases, her enthusiasm for the child she is going to bear is enough to remove the strain, anxiety, and doubt which normally affect her appearance. On the other hand, the woman who has an overprotective attitude toward her child even before birth can focus this tendency on herself by pampering. This focus may limit her activities and cause much self-concern. The growth of this anxiety may enhance the difficulties of the pregnancy and affect her appearance. Instead of developing a warm and enthusiastic glow, such a mother-to-be may seem harried.

The husband can play a leading role in helping his wife make a good emotional adjustment to pregnancy. His task is simply to reinforce the desire for children. He must be enthusiastic, relaxed, and reassuring about the pregnancy. As plans for parenthood are discussed, his attitude should express the conviction of faith in their joint ability to meet any problems successfully. It is during the pregnancy that the parent-child relationship is conceived.

Questions

1. Name and define the function of the reproductive organs in each sex.

2. When does the embryo emerge into a fetus? What developments make it appropriate to change the name?

3. Define the following terms:

gametes	embryo	fetus
fertilization	zygote	semen
ova	sperm	

4. If a child is born prematurely, which month gives it the best chance for survival?

5. What is the average length of pregnancy?

6. What is the main part of the weight increase during pregnancy?

7. Why should a pregnant woman be conscious of diet and calories?

8. How do emotions affect pregnancy?

9. What is the role of the husband during pregnancy?

Further reading

Bourne, Gordon, and Danforth, David. *Pregnancy.* New York: Harper & Row, Publishers, Inc., 1975.

Gruenberg, Sidonie M. *The Wonderful Story of How You Were Born.* rev. ed. New York: Doubleday & Co., Inc., 1970.

Lipke, Jean C. *Pregnancy.* Minneapolis, MN: Lerner Publications Company, 1971.

Novak, Edmund R., and Jones, Georgeanna S., ed. *Textbook of Gynaecology.* 9th ed. Baltimore MD: The Williams & Wilkins Company, 1975.

Patterson, Robert. *Pregnancy Primer.* Nashville, TN: Aurora Publishers, Inc., 1974.

Chapter 29

Responsible parenthood

Children need to be born to parents who are willing to rear them to adulthood, not to parents who are only willing to beget them. Children need to be born to parents who want them.

"Let me get this straight . . . neither one of you wants custody of the children?"

The basic principle that underlies the importance of planning for children is the simple statement that everyone has a psychological "breaking point." Efficient and comfortable functioning of families cannot exist when that breaking point is passed for any member. Families are subject to many different kinds of stresses. Each family feels them differently. The way a family reacts depends upon the personalities in the family, their reactions to each other, their physical conditions, their financial resources, and their emotional stability.

If the world were large enough to provide food for an unlimited population and everyone could get a sufficient share, and if everyone could manage a large household, we wouldn't have to be concerned if all women produced all the children they could in the ages from thirteen to fifty. This however, is not the case. Most families have to plan how many mouths can be fed, how many bodies can be clothed, and how many can be sheltered. In the more developed societies, there must be the additional consideration of how many can be educated to meet the demands of modern industrial societies. Seeing children inadequately fed, improperly clothed, and shelterless is certainly an enormous stress on parents.

For parents affected by poverty and famine and unable to control their economic situation, it would seem wise to limit the number of children with whom they must share their inadequate resources. If family size could be controlled, fewer children would die before maturity, and the health of survivors would be better. Parents could provide more adequately because their own health would be better as a result of getting a larger share of the family's food supply.

In the privileged countries, the issues may be less acute physically and conditions of starvation or disease may be less threatening. However, in these countries, the fact that parents may be unable to supply the necessary education adds another type of strain. Also parents may not be able to supply the emotional or psychological needs required in a large family.

Raising a family successfully requires a certain level of emotional maturity. Not all persons are emotionally and intellectually prepared, or have the needed management skills. The parents may be able to manage a family of two or three or four children but might break under the strain of trying to manage a home of six or more. Many mothers and fathers realize that they are approaching their breaking points but may not know how to limit the number of children. Thus they are more or less forced into stress situations. Furthermore, the care and training any parents can supply their children must be fractioned each time another child is added. Parental care appears to be related to the mental health of the offspring and to the development of their talents.

In short, planning is important so that individuals will not find themselves in situations of severe stress. Children will have healthful places in which to be nurtured and to mature. Populations will not need to kill others in order to have enough space and food to survive and to live in reasonable security and comfort.

Terms

The regulation of the number of offspring, the time at which they are born, and the period between pregnancies is the process of planning for children.

Contraception or prevenception means to prevent conception, that is, to prevent the meeting of egg and sperm. This may be accomplished with a mechanical barrier until egg and sperm are no longer able to unite, by using chemicals to inactivate the sperm, by using hormone drugs that prevent the normal release of the ovum, or by engaging in coitus only at certain times when the sperm and egg are least likely to unite. In any case, the end result is the same. Namely, sperm and egg do not unite to produce a new individual.

Ideally, a contraceptive method allows a couple to have children when they want them. It allows them to plan for the number of children they want and can care for. Children are spaced to permit the woman to maintain good health and to give birth to healthy babies. In short, contraception, or prevenception, allows parenthood by choice rather than parenthood by chance.

The same natural processes that imbue people with reproductive powers also imbue them with intelligence. They must use this intelligence to improve their lot and that of their children on this increasingly restricted and crowded planet. Planning for children, by whatever means the individual married couple is able to accept, is becoming an important part of the use of intelligently controlled and applied knowledge for human betterment.

This matter is one to be handled by doctors on the basis of individual examination and needs. It is not something to be dealt with in a general discussion. No two couples are identical as to physiology, principles, attitudes, or goals.

Decisions about planning for children

Parenthood should be dignified and voluntary rather than the blind acceptance of biological chance. The marriage partners should learn to appreciate each other as individuals with joint family goals. Students of human development have explored the factors contributing to personality growth. They have emphasized the child's need for a home environment that has emotional security and affection, one free from conflict. Children absorb the attitudes, aspirations, joys, anxieties, and tensions they feel in their homes. They will tend to give out what they receive. If they are raised in emotionally secure homes, they will tend to be emotionally secure children. If they are raised in homes which lack happiness and have little emotional security, they may in time tend to be unhappy and insecure. Further, as studies of adjustment in marriage show, there is at least an unconscious tendency for the individuals to repeat in their own marriages the major characteristics they found in their parental families.

The important question, then, is whether or not a couple can provide such an atmosphere of affection and security. The couple certainly cannot supply it for a child until they have supplied it for each other. If there are serious maladjustments in their relationship, it is likely that these will be reflected in any children they may have. If they themselves are well-adjusted, and there are no hereditary or physical obstacles to parenthood, there seems no reason to doubt their suitability as parents. The decision to have or not to have children cannot always be arrived at in the first year of marriage. Adjustment in marriage is the result of a process that requires both time and effort. Some couples adjust well to each other in marriage but have personalities and values that are not compatible with the demands of child-rearing. The value of children lies not in their economic contribution to their parents. Rather it lies in the enriched living that children bring to their parents and that which the parents bring to their children.

The decision to have children is not a simple one. In the first place, a couple needs time in which to make the necessary postwedding adjustments. Those who must face the adjustments required by pregnancy at the same time that they face the adjustments required by the first years of living together are much handicapped in attempting either.

A couple is ready to have a child only when both really want it and have faced all the adjustments in their relationships which will result from its coming. For all but the most affluent, child-rearing involves sacrifices of time, freedom, money, and aspirations. It is worthwhile, certainly, but it demands the giving up of many things. Unless both husband and wife are ready to make these sacrifices, and want to make them, many difficulties are sure to come. When, for example, the wife is very anxious to have a child and the husband agrees only because he thinks it will make his wife happy, there is no way of predicting how he will receive his child. Or a child's presence may stimulate affection permanently, which is all to the good. It may bring affection which is temporary and later changes to resentment, to the detriment of the father-child relationship. It may arouse resentment immediately. Both of the situations just described can only mean insecurity for the child and strained relationships for the parents of the child.

There is no wisdom in deciding to have a child in order to hold a marriage together. The wife, or husband, or both, who believe that affections can thus be restored, or that a child can be "the moral equivalent" of other unfulfilled needs of the marriage, is expecting more from a child's presence than seems wise. Children can cement husband-wife relationships and enrich the lives of both, but only when these relationships are good to begin with and the child is wanted.

Pro and con. The facts of planning for children must be presented and reviewed objectively. Indeed, each married couple should consider seriously both the positive and the negative aspects of planning for their children.

The decision of whether and when to have a baby rests directly with the parents themselves. This is a different kind of responsibility from that of simply letting a pregnancy "happen." Indeed, it may be a difficult decision for some couples who find it difficult to agree even on trivial things.

However, such planning gives the young couple the needed time for adjustment to each other. Most young couples must mature as husband and wife before they can attain the basic prerequisites of parenthood. However, the time required for working out initial marital adjustments varies with each couple, so that it is impossible to generalize.

Economic considerations. Planning is also warranted by economic considerations today. Most people now need more education than their forebears had, not only because technology requires greater skills but because marriage itself demands a higher standard of living. Furthermore, a wife may very well choose to work. She may wish to explore her interests and apply her education in the world of work, so that she can better understand her own potential.

Couples need money in order to raise children. Finances must be a limiting factor in planning to have children, but usually they need not be an eliminating factor. Financial difficulties are less often real than fancied. In one sense, who can ever afford to have children? For example, is it valid for a couple to say they cannot afford a child because they need a new car? Standards of living change. Couples who rationalize that they cannot afford to have children now may find that their standard of living increases every year. After a few years they may still contend that they are unable to afford children. In postponing children for financial reasons, there is a possibility that the period of postponement may never end.

Preparation for responsibility of having a child. By planning their family, the couple can better prepare themselves for parenthood and the responsibilities of parenthood. The techniques of good parents do not come naturally. Too many people learn too late that they should not have avoided courses in child development and child psychology that might have better prepared them for understanding and training their own children. Furthermore, except for those few couples who have been adequately prepared, parenthood is one of the most serious crises of young married life. The haphazard experiences in child care that some young people get within their own families are of questionable value. The oldest child in a larger group is frequently given some responsibility for the care of the younger ones. However, this experience seldom gives insight into proper child-care methods. In fact, many adults who have had this experience frequently may be worse off than if they had had no experience at all.

Some people have little desire for children of their own. For them, parenthood would result probably only in despair and frustration. Such people should probably avoid having any children. A marriage with no children may be better adjusted than a marriage with unwanted children. Interest in children and the desire to have additional offspring seem to diminish as the family increases. Numerous studies indicate that after the first two or three children are born, parents wish for fewer than they had first estimated as their ideal family size.

Today's young couples want children as much or more than ever, but they want them at the time and in the number that seems best for total family happiness.

Questions

1. What are the reasons for planning for children?

2. What are the terms used in discussing planning for children?

3. What decisions should a couple make before deciding to have children?

4. Dick and Pat are feeling bored with each other and their life together. They think that if they could have a baby, life would become more interesting. What would be your advice? Upon what do you base your answer?

5. What responsibilities do parents have toward children today?

6. Why is planning for children important in privileged countries?

Further reading

Becker, Howard, and Hill, Reuben. *Family, Marriage, and Parenthood.* Lexington, MA: D. C. Heath & Company, 1955.

Bossard, James H. *Parent and Child: Studies in Family Behavior.* Philadelphia: University of Pennsylvania Press, 1953.

Clayton, R. C. *Family, Marriage, and Social Change.* Lexington, MA: D. C. Heath & Company, 1975.

Dreikurs, Rudolph. *The Challenge of Marriage.* New York: Hawthorn Books, Inc., 1946.

Kephart, William M. *Family, Society and the Individual.* 4th ed. Boston: Houghton Mifflin Company, 1977.

Chapter 30

Childlessness

Much is said and written about the effects of childlessness upon couples. In our culture, children are highly valued. Their pictures appear on the Christmas greetings of the family. Family activities are centered around the children and their needs.

Happy Holidays

The López Family
(Julio, Elena, Rosa, Teresa and Baby Carlos)

Without doubt, children, when they are wanted, enrich marriage and a couple's life together. When they are not wanted, both parents and children are likely to suffer. The effects of being without children depend upon the personalities of the couple, their attitudes, desires, hopes, and interests. No broad statement to the effect that childlessness warps the personality of a marriage is warranted. In the case of some couples it does. In that of others, it does not.

Unfortunately, there are persons who develop feelings of inferiority when they find that they must be involuntarily childless because of some physiological problem. There is no logical reason for feeling inferior because of low fertility anymore than there is for feeling inferior because one has brown eyes, small feet, large ears, high blood pressure, or any other physical condition over which one has no control.

Physical causes of sterility

The physical causes of sterility in women include the following.

1. absence, defect, or disease of the ovaries

2. failure of the ovaries to develop normal ova

3. blockage of the tubes so that the ova fail to reach the womb or uterus

4. absence, defect, or disease of the uterus, precluding nourishment and development of a fertilized ovum

5. blockage of the cervix or entrance to the uterus which prevents the sperm from reaching the ovum

6. absence, defect, or disease of the vagina sufficient to destroy the sperm, or block their entrance into the uterus

The physical causes of sterility in men include the following.

1. absence, defect, or disease of the testes

2. absence or blockage, due to defect or disease, of the minute tubes that carry the sperm from the testes to the penis

3. blockage, due to defect or disease, of the urethra through which sperm must pass into the vagina

In both men and women, diseases or deficiencies involving the whole body may cause or contribute to sterility. Severe vitamin deficiencies, for example, endocrine or hormonal disorders, or such conditions as malnutrition or tuberculosis can be responsible.

The most common physical cause of sterility, of course, is failure of sexual partners to have intercourse at a time when impregnation can occur. The reasons may be psychological, but physical action is involved.

Psychological causes of sterility

The psychological causes of sterility are many and debatable. Consider, for example, why one partner, or both, consciously or unconsciously avoids sexual intercourse. Reasons range from conscious aversion to the partner, to deeply unconscious fear or guilt about sex, pregnancy or parenthood. There are women whose sexual desire is greatest close to or during menstruation, when impregnation is least likely to occur. Such a situation might indicate a wish for sexual gratification without conception. Spasm of the Fallopian tubes precluding pregnancy can occur in women who nevertheless enjoy frequent sexual intercourse. Comparable emotional conflicts in men can cause avoidance or bad timing in intercourse. Two common forms of sterility in men and women, whether from physical or psychological causes, are impotence and frigidity. Impotence of a man is the incapacity for sexual intercourse. Frigidity in a woman is an abnormal aversion to sexual intercourse.

Incidence of sterility

It used to be assumed that a marriage without children was due to the wife. Some people still have this attitude. Some authorities state, however, that in 30 to 50 percent of such marriages, the cause can be traced to the husband. Others assert that the ratio is about fifty-fifty. Evaluation of a sterile marriage must include both husband and wife.

In considering sterility according to various groups, it is again useful to distinguish fecundity from fertility, that is, the possibility of having children from actually having them. It is estimated that fecundity is about the same the world over. Healthy couples anywhere would have an average of ten or eleven chldren if they were sexually active without contraception throughout the childbearing period of life. This does not vary significantly with race, class, or creed.

Factors that influence fertility, that is, the actual number of offspring, are those that determine the frequency of sexual intercourse, early or late marriage, the use of contraceptive plans or devices, and the health of the marital partners. Age is the most important factor in the frequency of sexual intercourse. The chances of pregnancy fall off rapidly after the age of thirty. Statistically, the period of greatest fertility is under twenty, with the period between twenty and twenty-five a close second. Some authorities believe that the length of marriage before impregnation is attempted may be an even more important factor than age. In any event, the longer a married couple postpones trying to have children, the less is their chance of having them, or at least, having as many as they desire.

Psychological effects of sterility. There are many psychological effects of sterility. Some couples are easily and happily reconciled to being childless. Others react with varying degrees of regret, resignation, and sorrowful acceptance. Still others suffer moderate to severe feelings of social stigma, inferiority, or deprivation. A given person sometimes feels guilty or ashamed because of the conscious or unconscious assumption, perhaps mistaken, that the present infertility is his or her fault. The "fault" is often regarded as a punishment for childhood masturbation, premarital sex relations, or marital infidelity. The sense of guilt or worry often obscures the medical problem. Perhaps just as often there are silent, or not so silent, suspicions of the marital partner. There may be consequent added strains within the marriage.

Social effects of sterility. Social effects of sterility vary with the culture. If regarded as a stigma, it can lead to withdrawal and isolation. Sterility remains a reason for divorce in some parts of the world.

Treatments for sterility

A premarital medical examination may reveal the possibility of sterility. It may also show if there are physical conditions or emotional conflicts that will make pregnancy difficult or impossible. The prospective husband and wife should face and deal with these circumstances as soon as possible. The most beneficial result may be educational. Complete and accurate knowledge about sexual intercourse and conception will often foster positive and confident attitudes that lessen the chances of sterility.

Sterility sometimes disappears when a couple face the problem and decide to do something about it. It is common for pregnancy to occur following an adoption or the decision to adopt. In such cases, of course, psychological factors have been the important ones preventing conception.

Of all couples coming to sterility clinics, from 25 to 35 percent eventually become fertile. In one study of one hundred couples, the causes of sterility were physical in about 40 percent of the cases, psychological in about 30 percent, and a mixture in about 30 percent. Of the total, 27 percent achieved pregnancy—80 percent of these within one year, and 100 percent within four years. It is, from this analysis, worth seeking treatment. In some cases the cure is spontaneous. In others, there will be no cure. Whatever the outcome, it is best to face the problem and then make decisions based on the diagnostic facts rather than on suppositions and concerns.

Adoption

Adoption is the voluntary act of taking a child of other parents as one's own child. The number of adoptions over the past decades may be due to a variety of factors. First, the great value placed on children in our society has given rise to the feeling that a childless couple is incomplete as a family unit. Second, changed social attitudes have made adoption more acceptable. It is associated with greater frankness and enjoyment now than formerly.

Qualities in prospective adoptive parents. In selecting adoptive homes for children under their care, agencies today give the greatest weight to those personal qualities that make for "capacity for parenthood." As a general rule, there must be the capacity for warm, mature love for a child as an individual in his or her own right by each parent and by both as a unit. There must also be a compatible, stable marriage. These are accepted as the mental health prerequisites for any adoption, whatever the age of the adopted child. In addition, adoption agencies give high priority to the applicants' adaptability, flexibility, and ability to cope with the unpredictable situations of life.

Agencies do not look for some single personality stereotype or perfect person among adoptive applicants. They know there are multiple patterns and styles of life through which basically positive human experience may be lived. Similarly, aside from protecting the child against foreseeable extreme economic deprivation, children are placed with adoptive parents who come from various financial backgrounds. Their social and educational backgrounds also may vary.

Eligibility requirements as to the couple's religion vary among different denominational, nonsectarian, and tax-supported agencies. The agencies in turn are subject to widely differing laws and their interpretations in various parts of the country. According to the Child Welfare League of America "the natural mother has the right to determine the religion in which she wishes her child to be reared. Further, placement of children should not be restricted, in general, to homes with formal church affiliations." These principles differ, in certain respects, however, from those held by the Roman Catholic agencies whose statement, also included in the published "Standards," regards the religious status of the adoptive couple as "the weightiest, although not the sole element . . . among the several important factors . . . in successful adoption."

Besides the basic characteristics for all parents which are important to a child's healthy growth and development, and which agencies seek for children they place, there are some psychological qualifications specific to adoptive parenthood. Perhaps the most important of these relates to the couple's ability to successfully transfer their desire from the biologically conceived child they wanted to the adopted child. The wish to adopt is rooted in the reproductive drive with its associated parental feelings. If adoptive parents cannot transfer their feelings to the adopted child comfortably and completely, with minimal persistent anxiety and conflict, this does not detract from their worthwhileness as people. Nor does it mean maladjustment. But it does jeopardize the mental health outcome of the adoption. Such adoptions should not take place since the parent-child relationships, and hence the child's development, will suffer. Various unresolved emotional problems around their inability to bear children may prevent a couple's full acceptance of adoption as a good experience for the child and for themselves. The child may, for example, represent a constant proof of painful defeat and deficiency.

Age limits. There is more leeway about age limits in the placement of older children. Often older couples may decide to adopt a child after their own children are grown and have left home. These placements are with older parents who are experienced and know what to expect. In general, they can be more relaxed in dealing with the special problems that older children may bring to the new adjustment. Also, because their self-confidence as parents has been already established, they can tolerate actions with more understanding. They need not take personally such typical reactions of older children as provocative misbehavior to test the reliability of parental love. Because they are not dependent on the adopted child for their parental fulfillment, they have less need to overtax a child with expectations beyond his or her capacity. This avoids a source of mutual unhappiness. Many deeply satisfying relationships are experienced by these older couples and the older children who choose to adopt each other.

Couples who have already adopted one or two babies may be considered ineligible for more, according to the current policies of most agencies. This limitation, however, does not apply to the hard-to-place children with special needs. That is, it does not apply to children of mixed racial background, older children, brothers and sisters placed together, and handicapped children.

On the whole, agencies feel that adoptive parents should be about the same age as the biological parents. If a childless couple well into middle age, for example, were to adopt an infant, no matter how good their other qualities as potential parents, their relationship with the child would be at a disadvantage in several ways. There would likely be some lack of rapport because of the spread of years between the child and themselves. This deficiency could increase with time as attitudes, interests, and approaches to life changed. Also, such a couple has gone past the time when the necessary energy and endurance for taking care of a young child are usually available, without overexertion. This might impair the child-parent interactions. Furthermore, a couple's good adjustment to childlessness, evolved over the years as a "twosome," might be thrown off balance by the change from "twosome," to "threesome." This could happen even though originally their lives might have been happier with children. Older childless couples are likely to have become "set in their ways," without the desirable degree of flexibility needed for coping with a young child. They may, therefore, lose patience with the child too quickly. They may tend to impose too many restrictions before the child is able to control his or her behavior.

The factor of age also has a bearing on the adoptive parents' life expectancy in relation to the age of the child they adopt. Authorized agencies try to protect the children they place against risks of losing their parents for a second time through death or illness. They require, therefore, that applicants be examined by their own doctor, or a doctor working with the agency. The doctor submits a report of the applicants' medical histories and the findings of the examination.

The adoption agency

Adopting parents should arrange for the adoption through a first-rate child-placement agency. It is unwise to deal directly with the child's true parents or with a third person who is inexperienced. It leaves the way open for blackmail or for the true parents to change their minds. They may try to get their child back. The law stands in the way of this but the cost and unpleasantness of the lawsuits could ruin the happiness of the family and the security of the child. To protect the child, the good adoption agency keeps the two sets of parents involved in the adoption from knowing each other. It keeps them from ever making any kind of trouble for each other.

Fees.   Practices vary among agencies with respect to charging fees for services to adoptive applicants. Ability to pay is not regarded as a proper criterion of applicant acceptability. It should in no way affect the choice of the most suitable home for each child. A good many agencies never charge a fee. Others have a sliding scale based on ability to pay in relation to income. Others have a set fee which can be reduced or waived when indicated. For couples who can afford it, the payment of a fee lets them share the responsibility for the cost of the agency service. This payment is welcomed as a kind of equivalent for the medical and hospital expenses of natural childbirth. All agencies are nonprofit, however. Their expenses far exceed whatever may be collected as fees. Independent adoptions, however, may involve great expense. Of course, the sky is the limit for blackmarket "baby sales."

Inquiries as to agencies in any particular community or area may be directed to the State Department of Public Welfare through its Child Welfare Division. This department in most states has responsibility for the license, standards, and supervision of adoption services by public and voluntary agencies.

Announcement of adoption

Parents should from the beginning let the fact that the child is adopted come openly into their conversations with each other, with the child, and with acquaintances. This allows the child to ask questions as he or she grows and begins to understand. If the parents make great efforts to hide the child's origin, the child may sense that his or her identity and the adoption is something to be ashamed of or to hide.

Attempts are no longer made to keep adoption a secret. In fact, the custom of announcing the birth of a baby is practiced by adoptive parents who often send out announcements of the arrival of an adopted child. Cultural attitudes toward adoption are changing for the better. Agency selection of an adoptive couple may be regarded as a socially valued tribute to their qualities as parents. By the same token, the adopted child is no longer pictured as a homeless waif, at the mercy of anyone who will provide food and shelter. Rather, the child is recognized as privileged. The parents were particularly eager to assume the responsibilities of parenthood. They were chosen by an exacting agency for their child-rearing abilities.

The adopted child will not, of course, be without the problems and conflicts in his or her relationships with others. However, having been adopted need not make him or her any more vulnerable to such difficulties.

The fact that a person has been adopted may, at times, be used as a screen for various unacceptable feelings that arise in human relationships. Children or adults who were adopted, like everyone else, share the general range of human feelings. Clearly, however, they should be judged on the basis of their own good qualities, rather than on the basis of life circumstances that were beyond their control.

Questions

1. Define the following terms:
   sterility   impotence   frigidity
   fertility   fecundity   adoption

2. What are the effects of childlessness?

3. What are the physical causes of sterility?

4. What are the main psychological causes of sterility in men? in women?

5. Who is responsible for a childless marriage?

6. What are the factors that influence fertility?

7. Why do people adopt children?

8. What is the main characteristic that an adoption agency searches for in a couple?

9. What psychological qualifications must adoptive parents have?

10. Are adoption agencies concerned with age? Why or why not?

11. Why is it important to check the agency before adopting a child?

12. How should the family announce the adoption of a child?

13. Should one tell a child that he or she is adopted? Why? Why not?

Further reading

Kirkendall, Lester. *Sex Adjustments of Young Men.* Wilmington, NC: McGrath Publishing Company (formerly Consortium Books), 1970.

McNamara, Joan. *Adoption Advisor.* New York: Hawthorn Books, Inc., 1976.

Raymond, Louise. *Adoption and After.* New York: Harper & Row, Publishers, Inc., 1974.

Weininger, Otto. *Sex and Character.* New York: AMS Press, Inc., 1975.

Westlake, Helen Gum. *Children: A Study in Individual Behavior.* Lexington, MA: Ginn and Company, 1977.

Chapter 31

A birthright

Everyone should have the right to be well-born. "Well-born" does not mean that one should be born with money. The golden birthright provides the greatest chance for each baby to develop his or her potential both physically and psychologically.

"Strontium 90."

A birthright includes being born to parents who want a baby. It is being born to a household that has love and trust to share with a new life. It is being born to parents who realize the basic needs of a new life. These are the birthrights that this chapter will discuss.

Prenatal care

The most important and most crucial time for a baby is in the first ninety days of pregnancy. His or her birthright needs to be considered from the time the ovum and the sperm unite. The earliest stages of pregnancy are the most dangerous ones for the baby. Often this is the time when the mother doesn't even realize that she is pregnant. During these very early weeks the baby's principal organs are formed. For better or for worse, all of the parts for the new human being are present in the baby.

Pregnancy does not begin when the first menstrual period is missed. It begins about two important weeks before. Therefore, it is possible for a woman to be pregnant without knowing it. The importance that is attached to this fact is that a woman should begin taking care of the couple's baby as soon as the couple are married.

More and more doctors are treating all married women as if they were pregnant, at least during the last two-thirds of the menstrual cycle. Everything they do should take into consideration the baby-that-might-be. Because, if that baby really is, he or she is in the most crucial weeks of his or her life. Remember, by the end of the third month, the baby is completely formed. He or she has a brain. He or she has a heart that beats. The baby is either off to a good start, or he or she isn't.

Preparation. Parents-to-be can do some practical things to help insure a healthy, happy baby. First they should bear in mind that it is dangerous to marry a close relative. To do so increases the risk of adding to the errors in heredity.

Family Circus

THE FAMILY CIRCUS by Bil Keane, reprinted courtesy of The Register and Tribune Syndicate.

1-8
© 1976. The Register and Tribune Syndicate, Inc.

"Mommy, what year was PJ invented?"

The newly married couple should choose a family doctor. Both husband and wife should realize that in the event of pregnancy, prenatal care is extremely important. If there is a family history of defects or if there are complications such as Rh incompatibility, the doctor would be alerted. The husband and wife should know their Rh blood group. In addition, medical help should be readily available to avoid a premature birth because premature babies are more prone to defects.

Use of drugs. Every mother should be sure to tell her doctor if she thinks she is pregnant. She should take only the medicines he prescribes. Self-dosing from the medicine chest is dangerous. Some drugs can harm unborn babies. "Pep-pills," tranquilizers, sleeping pills, and pain killers are all medicines. Their effect on an embryo early in pregnancy might be disastrous.

Dr. Virginia Apgar discusses some of these drugs as follows. She writes.[1]

> In the possibly harmful category are many of the tranquilizers that some people take casually. Reserpine (Serpasil) has been shown in animal experiments to increase infant mortality. When rats are given meprobamate (Miltown, Equanil), their offspring are slow learners.
>
> There are some drugs that are even more definitely in the potentially harmful category. They are *known* to have caused damage or even death to unborn babies at least on rare occasions. Iodides, which are commonly used in cough medicines, can produce goiters in babies before they are born. These babies whose thyroids get mixed up may also be mentally retarded. The long-acting sulfa drugs prescribed for some stubborn infections can produce nerve deafness in the unborn child. We also know that the embryo cannot excrete tetracycline. If this common antibiotic is given to the mother, it is deposited in the bones of the baby, where it may slow down growth. It can also cause discoloration of his or her teeth. Chloramphicol, another antibiotic, can cause jaundice and possible brain damage. Excessive amounts of vitamin K can have the same effect, and excessive vitamin D may cause bone damage.

1. From "New Ways to Save Your Unborn Child" by Virginia Apgar in *Ladies' Home Journal*, August 1966. Copyright 1966 LHJ Publishing, Inc., formerly Downe Publishing, Inc. Reprinted with permission.

Of course, we must also recognize that alcohol and marijuana are drugs. Use of either is very dangerous to the unborn child. Excessive use can cause mental retardation as well as birth defects. Alcohol abuse restricts food intake. The unborn child is starved of needed nutrients. It is not uncommon for a child born to an alcoholic mother to have congenital alcoholism at birth.

Virus diseases. Certain virus diseases such as rubella (German measles) can cause birth defects. The pregnant mother should make every effort to avoid contact with these diseases.

X-rays. Abdominal X-rays should be avoided during early weeks of pregnancy. Doctors usually prescribe X-rays of the abdomen only in the first ten days after the beginning of the menstrual period.

Smoking. Excessive smoking during pregnancy should be avoided. This practice is associated with subnormal birth weight. Recent studies indicate that the more cigarettes a mother smokes during her pregnancy, the less her baby will weigh. The average weight loss is half a pound. For the baby under five pounds this half pound is very important because it relates to survival.

Age. Age should be considered. Many studies have been made about the age of the mother and its relation to the well-being of the baby. Although no absolute statements can be made, the following possibilities are reported.

1. The best childbearing years seem to be in the 25 to 34 age bracket.
2. Teenage mothers run a somewhat greater risk of having premature babies and babies who may be retarded.
3. Mothers over 35 also run more risk of having defective offspring.

Spacing. Spacing is important. When babies are only a year apart, there are more complications of pregnancy, more premature babies. More babies do not live. On the average, a full two years between babies seems to be needed to produce the healthiest children.

Diet. Diet affects growth. It is important for girls to acquire proper eating habits early in life. These habits are necessary to their own good health and to that of their children. Because the diet of teenagers is so crucial, one must impress this upon teenagers, particularly upon girls who are from 13 to 19 years of age. This is vital to their health and that of their future children. Yet this is just the time when food fads instead of balanced meals may be the main interest.

The pregnant woman should have a diet that contains increased amounts of protein, vitamins, and mineral salts, especially calcium, in order to feed the developing fetus. A deficient diet may cause a poorly developed baby or a premature birth. There is the consequent danger to the baby's physical and mental health.

Finally, there comes a time when the question is not when one should have a baby, but if. According to some studies, the risk of mental retardation for the third and fourth child is greater than for the first and second. With the fifth pregnancy, that risk doubles. With six or more children, even though a mother is still under 35, the risk is three to five times as great.

In fact the idea of a houseful of healthy, strong children has been attacked as a myth in a number of recent studies. One study shows that the larger the family, the smaller the children in height, weight, and chest circumference. The larger the family, the lower the scores received by the children on memory and I.Q. tests. This general tendency was not influenced by the educational level of the family. One investigator, Dr. Wagner H. Bridger of New York, says that he finds the most vigorous children come from small families with a large span of time between births.

In short, medically speaking, there is an ideal time to have babies and an ideal time to stop.

Symptoms of pregnancy

The physical symptoms of pregnancy are, of course, noticed by the woman. The husband should also be aware of these physical symptoms. The wife needs his understanding and acceptance during this change in their lives. The end of menstruation is the earliest and one of the most important symptoms of pregnancy. However, not until the date of the expected period has been passed by ten days or more can one rely on this symptom. The breasts become larger, firmer, and more tender. A sensation of stretching fullness accompanied by tingling both in the breasts and nipples often develops. In many instances a feeling of throbbing is also felt. Frequent urination is an early symptom. This is due to the fact that the growing uterus stretches the base of the bladder. A sensation results identical with that felt when the bladder wall is stretched with urine. Nausea is of no diagnostic value because many women suffer no nausea. When this "morning sickness" occurs it usually appears about two weeks after the first missed menstrual period. However, this is a symptom of many other conditions, such as ordinary indigestion. All of these symptoms together are a basis for assuming that conception has taken place.

The effect of pregnancy on the marriage relationship

Pregnancy can be a rewarding experience if the marital partners support each other in facing the developments and the challenges of their new roles. Many jokes and cartoons picture the husband during the pregnancy and the delivery as an awkward nuisance. This portrayal is humorous, but not necessarily accurate. A sympathetic and loving husband is of first importance to the pregnant wife. She has an increased need for love and attention. She turns to her husband for increased demonstrations of affection. She wants to be reassured that even with her changing appearance she is still acceptable and lovable in his eyes. Besides turning to their husbands, some women also turn to their mothers. Some women who are pregnant prefer their mothers to their husbands. This may be due to the woman's realization that what she wants is the nurturing love that she received from her mother. She may want this rather than the erotic love she associates with her husband. Moreover, as she prepares for the maternal role, she identifies with her mother. She usually feels a closer bond to her mother than she has felt in the past.

This situation need not cause any problem, since both husband and mother are apt to understand and accept their new roles. Occasionally, if the previous relationship between the woman and her family has been disturbed, the mother may resent the extra demands upon her affection. She may reject her daughter. The husband may feel jealous because he sees himself being passed over by his wife. The increased dependence of the woman on her mother may also lead to difficulties after the baby's birth. The grandmother may be tempted to play too central a role in the baby's care. She may feel rejected when the daughter's dependence upon her changes. After the birth, the daughter may suddenly wish to be independent and take care of her child herself.

The husband and wife should realize that pregnancy, especially the first pregnancy can complicate their relationship. They should plan jointly for the coming baby and for their future roles as parents. On the other hand, psychological changes in the expectant mother interfere with her previous relationship with her husband. The close link between the partners begins to open up to include the baby, at first in fantasy, later in actuality. The changes have a maturing effect on both husband and wife, as individuals and as a couple. At the beginning of pregnancy, the partners achieve a greater intimacy. They have a feeling that their love for each other has been concretely consummated. Later on they progress to the even higher stage of satisfaction. They share a joint responsibility for bringing a new life into the world.

Mood changes. It is common for the mood of the woman to change during pregnancy. Some women feel better during pregnancy than at any other time. Others feel unusually depressed. Sudden unexplainable mood changes are not uncommon, even in women who usually are emotionally stable.

These mood changes are not related to whether the woman wanted to become pregnant. Physicians believe that they are influenced both by the biochemical changes, especially the changes in hormones and by the psychological reactions to pregnancy. These involve preparing for the coming baby and for assuming the mother's role. Some of the common changes observed are a tendency to become angry easily, to laugh and cry easily, and to change mood with little reason to do so.

Introversion and passivity are the chief characteristic emotional changes of pregnancy. These changes usually begin during the second or third month. They gradually increase in intensity, reaching a peak around the seventh or eighth month. The woman previously may have been active and outgoing. As wife and mother she has had the role of nurturance and of giving. She may gradually or suddenly become turned in on herself, feel passive and lazy. She may want to be cared for instead of caring for others. The emphasis is on the increased need for demonstrations of love and affection.

Changes in sexual desire and performance occur in many women at various phases of pregnancy. Some women have increased desire. Others do not. A decrease of sexual desire is common toward the middle of pregnancy.

These changes, as mentioned above, may possibly be due to changes in the pregnant woman's hormones. They are more likely, however, to be due to psychological factors. Sexual desire in the wife may previously have been impaired by fear of pregnancy, which is now removed. Or feelings of doubt about her femininity may have been a factor now reduced because conception has proved that she is fertile. In some cultures, women proudly exhibit the external signs of their pregnancies. Men regard these as signs of beauty. In these cultures, the woman's awareness of the physical changes of pregnancy may stimulate her sexual desire. In other cultures, women feel less beautiful during pregnancy. Sexual desire may be inhibited by feelings of shame or modesty. Or there may be fear that their husbands will turn away from them. Sexual desire and performance may also be inhibited by the unfounded fear that intercourse will harm the fetus by pressure on the abdomen or by trauma to the uterus.

The danger signals in pregnancy

Good care is important for both mother and child.[2] At the first hint of pregnancy, the couple should visit their doctor. Only the doctor's careful examination can reassure the couple that the pregnancy is progressing normally. Sometimes, between visits to the doctor, the expectant mother may notice changes in her condition which the doctor should be aware of at once. Often these findings observed by the mother-to-be are of no significance. However, the doctor should be notified without delay so that he or she may make an examination and evaluate the importance of the report. The following symptoms demand immediate report to the doctor.

1. vaginal bleeding, no matter how slight

2. swelling of the face or fingers

3. severe, continuous headache

4. dimness or blurring of vision

5. pain in the abdomen

6. persistent vomiting

7. chills and fever

8. sudden escape of water from the vagina

These symptoms sound formidable. However, their significance depends entirely on the circumstances under which they occur. Even the development of several of them may be quite normal and not necessarily a cause for concern. In the main, however, these symptoms deserve special attention because they often are warning signs of the three most common complications of pregnancy, namely miscarriage, toxemia, and pyelitis.

2. Copyright 1940, 1947, © 1957 by Nicholson J. Eastman. Copyright © 1963, 1970 by Nicholson J. Eastman and Loretta R. Eastman. Copyright © 1977 by Elizabeth E. Miller and Thomas B. Eastman. From EASTMAN'S EXPECTANT MOTHERHOOD, 6th revised edition, by Keith P. Russell, M.D., by permission of Little, Brown and Co.

A miscarriage or abortion is the premature expulsion of the fetus. The natural miscarriage or abortion is when nature expels a defective embryo. Miscarriage can also occur from some types of infection, certain diseases (such as syphilis), vitamin deficiency, glandular dysfunction, accident, poisoning, or anything that causes the death of the fetus. It is also thought that psychological factors, such as severe emotional shock, can cause natural miscarriage.

Natural miscarriages, it is estimated, end about one in every ten pregnancies. The second and third months are the most dangerous in terms of the possibility of a miscarriage. These miscarriages are nature's way of extinguishing an embryo which is imperfect. Since imperfectly formed embryos are almost always aborted early in pregnancy, the likelihood of a full-term child's being defective is only 5 out of every 100 births.

Toxemia (blood poisoning) is exhibited by an increase in blood pressure, albumin in the urine, swelling of the face and fingers, and increased weight. Toxemia is detrimental to the mother and baby.

Pyelitis is an inflammation of the ureter, the funnel-like portion of the kidney which conveys the urine from the kidney to the tube leading to the bladder. When the flow of urine through the kidney, pelvis, and ureter is not brisk, stagnation is prone to ensue with consequent inflammation. The characteristic symptoms of pyelitis are chills, fever, and pain in one thigh or the other, most frequently the right.

Attitudes

It is important to develop positive attitudes about childbirth and the child's birthright. Birth is a physical and emotional crisis for baby, mother, father, and family. The mother's emotions and her experience of pain during labor are determined to some extent by what she has been taught to expect. Education of the parents for childbirth can be a very positive influence.

Labor, the work which the mother does in giving birth, consists of three stages. The first stage, the opening of the cervix, is accomplished by muscles which are not under voluntary control. The confident, secure mother can probably help the process by relaxing. The second stage, pushing the baby out, is partially involuntary and partially controllable by the mother. Education and a positive attitude can prepare the mother to help herself and her baby. The third stage, a brief process, is the expelling of the placenta. The duration of labor varies considerably with each pregnancy. But the average length of time is seven hours for the first baby and four hours for additional offspring.

Directly connected with the mother's fear or confidence, tension or relaxation, pain or easiness in giving birth, is her confidence in herself and the help she is receiving.

The crowning emotional experience is, of course, the joy of receiving the baby, the result of the mother's labor and the love between the new parents. The child's birthright is to be born to parents who want and welcome him or her and who appreciate the child as a person in his or her own right.

Questions

1. What is the golden birthright?

2. What is the most crucial and important time in the life of a baby?

3. When should a married couple start considering their child's birthright?

4. What practical things can a couple do to help ensure a healthy, happy baby?

5. What should be considered in the spacing of children? In the age of the mother?

6. What are the symptoms of pregnancy?

7. How does pregnancy affect the marriage relationship?

8. What are some of the basic needs of the mother-to-be?

9. What are some of the duties of the father-to-be?

10. What are some of the psychological and sexual changes that may take place in pregnancy?

11. What are some of the danger signals during the pregnancy?

12. Write an attitude analysis about parenthood.

Further reading

Apgar, Virginia. "New Ways to Save Your Unborn Child." *Ladies' Home Journal,* August 1966, p. 46.

Duvall, Evelyn Millis. *Marriage and Family Development.* 5th ed. Philadelphia, PA: J. B. Lippincott Company, 1977.

Walters, C. Etta. *Mother-infant Interaction.* New York: Human Sciences Press, Inc., 1976.

Westlake, Helen Gum. *Children: A Study in Individual Behavior.* Lexington, MA: Ginn and Company, 1977.

Chapter 32

Babies' needs

Babies do not need a spotless home or an expert in formula measuring and bath temperature testing. These things are easy to do reasonably well. Babies, however, do need persons who appreciate them, give them security, and encourage them to develop.

"I'm getting worried about Mom. That's the third time she's painted herself into a corner this week."

Understanding baby

Babies are not unconscious little organisms that simply eat and sleep. They are seeking, reacting human beings with a capacity to learn. They have ability to be deeply influenced for good or ill. Babies want and need to be securely held. They want to be played with and talked to right from the start. Fortunately, most mothers quite naturally hold their babies, play with them, and talk to them. They enjoy these activities. Scientists are finding new proof that these actions are a vital part of mothering. Mothering is defined here as tender, loving care. It is as important coming from fathers as from mothers.

Sight and hearing. Newborn babies can see and are interested in what they see. For example, infants under five days old will stare longer at a patterned surface than at a plain one because it is more stimulating. By the end of the third week of life, babies smile "social smiles," in response to human voices. An investigator who studied babies' smiles states that babies will sometimes smile at the sound of a bird whistle or a rattle. However, the human voice is the sound that brings the most smiles.

Touch. A baby's sense of touch and temperature is even better developed than his or her sight and hearing. The sense of comfort and well-being is made much easier when the baby is held and

There is in life no blessing like affection and adoration.

fondled. Studies of children who do not get much holding or cuddling show that such children do not sleep or eat well. Being held and fondled in infancy helps a baby learn to relate to other persons.

One of the first things babies have to learn is that their parents are separate from them. Each has to learn there is a "me" and a "not-me." There is warmth, comfort, and food that goes away and returns. Playing peek-a-boo helps the baby realize mother or daddy disappears and then reappears.

Anxiety. At about eight weeks of age, babies are old enough to start worrying. Scientists think that at this age the sight and hearing of infants have become keen enough so that they know one person from another. The baby suddenly realizes that there is more than one "not-me." Are all the "not-me's" warm and loving? He or she isn't sure. If a stranger picks him or her up, the baby is likely to cry. Psychologists call this reaction "stranger anxiety."

Somewhat later, babies develop another worry, "separation anxiety." From six months to eighteen months is a crucial period during which the babies are really afraid of losing their parents or the person with whom they have had the closest contact. Perhaps it is at this time that the baby has really identified his or her parent or caretaker as the most important "not-me" in his or her life. Babies understand that they would have a difficult time without parents or the persons who care for them. If anything happens to make babies believe that they have lost their parents, they may suffer a mental depression severe enough to have an effect throughout life. Psychologists now recommend that children not be adopted into strange homes or moved from one foster home to another during this period. For example, if couples wish to adopt children who are in this age span, they should be encouraged to wait until the children have passed through this stage. It is important to emphasize the need for calming the separation anxiety in babies from six to eighteen months. The parent who is going through some emotional problem may increase this anxiety in the baby if he or she is absent either physically or psychologically. This is a period when parents particularly need the reassurance of each other. The knowledge that the marriage is sound gives security to the child.

Security. Security and stimulation are the two gifts that babies continue to need. As they begin to babble and coo, they need verbal responses from their parents. They learn that human beings like to make sounds to each other. There is a pattern of give-and-take in making sounds. Children must learn that pattern before they can begin to learn that sounds have meanings. A baby who has never been talked to never learns to talk. When a baby is encouraged to reach for a rattle, he or she is learning. One recent study has shown that babies who have had this kind of coaching learn to grasp objects six weeks sooner than do babies who are not as well-handled. When babies are held in a standing position, they are being stimulated to learn to stand and walk.

Attitudes toward food. The attitudes that babies develop toward food are also learned. These attitudes may affect their lifelong physical well-being. Experts in nutrition view the United States as a nation of overweight people. They say that the trouble goes back to infancy. Pediatricians (children's doctors) tell parents that a healthy baby gains about seven ounces a week. Some parents consider it a personal triumph if they can make their babies gain eight or ten ounces a week. But the year-old baby dimpled with fat should no longer be cause for maternal pride. Experts now know that the overweight babies have been victimized in several ways. They have been force-fed. Consequently they have lost their innate ability to know when they are full and are ready to stop eating. They have been trained to overeat.

Overweight babies have probably learned to accept food as a substitute for emotional satisfaction. Every time they cry or fret, their parents pop a bottle of milk or some other food into their mouths. Yet children may be crying or fretting because they are lonely or bored. Food, a bottle, or a pacifier should not take the place of holding and cuddling.

Of course, babies who do not gain at a normal rate are in trouble, too. Pediatricians call this condition "failure to thrive." It is a signal to look for the source of trouble. It may be trouble not solved by merely juggling the feeding formula. Such babies may have malformations of the heart or of the digestive tract that can be corrected by surgery. Or they may have metabolic disorders that require prompt treatment.

Inborn errors of metabolism. There is an increasing alertness to the inborn errors of metabolism. In a recent study of 2,000 mentally-retarded children, it was shown that 21 percent of them suffered metabolic disorders. Two of these disorders, phenylketonuria (PKU) and galactosemia can be detected by testing in the first few weeks of life. The child with PKU cannot metabolize one of the common amino acids in protein. The child with galactosemia has a deficiency of an enzyme needed to convert galactose, milk sugar, into glucose. Children with either of these disorders need special diets and medical care if they are to develop normally.

Evaluating the development of a baby

Regular medical, including developmental, observation of a baby under one year of age should be performed at monthly intervals in order to evaluate his or her progress. Babies develop at their own individual rates. Each baby who is healthy has his or her own developmental pattern. It is unfair to compare one baby with other babies of the same age except in a very general way. A baby's growth and development should be monitored. A baby should progress steadily from stage to stage in accordance with his or her own growth pattern. In addition to the developmental observations, visits to the pediatrician or family doctor provide opportunities to immunize the baby against diseases such as poliomyelitis (infantile paralysis), whooping cough, diphtheria, tetanus (lock jaw), measles, and smallpox.

Physical growth. The basic evaluations of physical growth are noted in the baby's weight gain and growth in length. The baby will usually triple his or her birth weight in the first year. He or she will grow to one and one-half times his or her birth length. Regular measurements of the growth of the head are made during physical examinations. This is an indirect measurement of the growth and development of the brain.

Further evaluations of the growth and development of the brain and central nervous system are made by observing behavior and testing reflexes. Observations of the time of responsive smiling, control of head movements, eye and hand coordination, sitting, crawling, standing, walking, and social responsiveness are all helpful in checking the baby's general progress. Observations which have been recorded systematically by observers of child development are guides in knowing what to expect. More detailed studies can be made if needed. These more systematic observations must be done by professionally trained workers. They are familiar with the circumstances under which the tests should be conducted and the proper interpretation of the results.

Lines of communication in infancy

The number of bodily contacts of the infant with his or her parents and others who care for him or her runs into thousands. To pick up an infant, hold, feed, bathe, and play with him or her mean far more than just physical manipulation. Each time there is a special communication between the adult and the infant. An interpersonal relationship is established.

The adult brings to these interpersonal relationships his or her own emotions, moods, and mannerisms. Physical contact is the most successful means of gaining emotional intimacy with a child. This is provided if the adult has the capacity for such intimacy.

Many, perhaps most, of the experiences that occur in an infant's contacts with people early in life are infused with feeling. The child has much at stake. He or she is desperately hungry, for example, even though well fed only a few hours before. Emotion is bound to come into play when something a child is eager for is supplied or withheld. Even when physical needs are cared for, the child is pleased to have company. He or she is disappointed when the company leaves. Meanwhile, many of the child's own undertakings are accompanied by eagerness or annoyance. With emotional overtones he or she cries, coos, trills, smiles, gurgles, yawns, sighs, and belches.

As all of this occurs, the adult who is with the infant is communicating something from within as he or she deals with the child. With older children, what the adults say or do may clearly show that they have a human touch. Or the adults may show that they are unsure of themselves, or that they are plodding through their jobs without enthusiasm.

Emotional ties with parents. However, when a baby is quite young there are subtler interchanges that take place. There is an emotional linkage involving emotional communion between the baby and other significant people (mother, father, or nurse or someone else). This emotional linkage is called empathy. Communication exists between the child and the significant adult through empathy before the child is old enough to notice expressions of emotion, such as smiling, or a worried look. Empathy lasts throughout life. But the time of its greatest importance is in later infancy and early childhood. This is perhaps from the age of six months to twenty-seven months.

Building toward
positive future
parenthood.

Emotional communication between an adult and an infant is shown by many signs. There are studies which indicate that babies in the care of a parent who is obviously anxious cries more than the baby of a parent who is not so obviously anxious. Such studies support the view that a parent's emotional state affects a child. However, to make a conclusive test, it would be necessary to study not only the characteristics of parents but also those of their children. Some babies are more serene or cry more than others regardless of who is caring for them. The idea that there are subtle communications between babies and adults agrees with observations in everyday life. It appears that babies are definitely more fretful or are more at ease with some people than with others. Hospital workers have held, for example, that some nurses seem to have a soothing effect on babies. The same babies tend to fuss and cry when in the care of other nurses. The actions of a nurse who likes children and welcomes them into her arms may differ from those of another well-trained nurse. These differences are noticeable to a baby even though the actions may be too subtle to be measured.

A study found that major benefits came to young children when their mothers were helped to be more understanding and at ease with themselves. Then they were freer to handle wisely the rearing of their children. This necessity for self-understanding, being at ease, and having a kind of inner freedom places the emphasis on the parent as a person. It underscores the position that self-knowledge and a healthy attitude of self-acceptance are more basic to the parent's role than a set of practical rules. It is more basic than an intellectual notion of whether a parent should be strict or lenient, permissive, or authoritarian. Self-understanding is as important for parenthood as for individual acceptance as discussed in Unit 1.

Feeding practices and child behavior

Changes in practices. Advice to parents about the feeding of infants shifts drastically. In the past, for example, most advice-giving articles recommended strict feeding schedules. This is in contrast to the present recommendations for self-regulatory or on-demand feeding. Recommendations have been based upon differing viewpoints concerning the effects of feeding methods on a child's behavior and personality development. Careful studies of feeding practices have found that breast versus bottle feeding has no apparent effect on such behaviors as aggression, dependency, feeding problems, thumb-sucking, bed wetting, or disturbance over toilet training. Researchers are not in complete agreement. But some find the mothers who breast feed feel no warmer toward their children nor no more competent in child care, nor happier about having children. In the past, parents with more education tended to prefer bottle feeding for their children. In recent years, this group has moved toward a preference for breast feeding. Those with lesser education are giving it up. From a clinical viewpoint, breast feeding, when possible, would seem preferable inasmuch as it provides a food uniquely suited for the infant under comfortable feeding conditions.

Flexible feeding schedules. Although most parents now follow a rather permissive feeding schedule for their babies, about one-fifth still schedule feedings rather rigidly. These parents tend to be somewhat more anxious about child care. But the fact that their babies are fed on a rigid schedule does not seem to affect the development of the children's personalities. The occurrence of feeding problems similarly is unrelated to scheduled versus on-demand feeding practices.

Observations suggest that breast feeding and a flexible or rigid handling of the feeding schedule are not the important factors. The parent's attitude toward the child as expressed in the feeding situation is more important than any one isolated factor in the manner of feeding. Similar overt procedures in feeding can have psychologically different meanings, depending on the attitude of the parent. Again, these observations underscore the importance of self-knowledge, self-acceptance, and self-confidence on the part of the parent. Feeding then becomes one of the warm experiences of a total parent-baby relationship.

Maternal behavior and dependency in children

Children show their dependency in their attempts to secure the presence and nurturance of other persons. The degree of dependence is estimated by how hard children try to obtain the company and attention of someone else, usually their mothers. Children use many different modes of dependent behavior. These include crying, following, cuddling, smiling, talking, showing accomplishments, shouting, and asking for help. Dependent behavior has been classified into five types.

1. seeking help

2. seeking physical contact

3. seeking closeness

4. seeking attention

5. seeking recognition

As children grow, their dependent behavior changes in its relation to mutuality. Dependent on others for company and nurturance, they can give as they accept. Dependent in the beginning on his or her mother or father, a child comes to depend upon other family members. This dependency then expands to include peers, teachers, and other adults. He or she eventually depends on a husband or wife and, perhaps, finally on children.

Mother's behavior and children's independence. Many studies have dealt with the effects of a mother's behavior on dependence in children. The availability of the mother has a bearing on the young child's seeking contact. Two- and three-year-old boys sought more affectionate contact with their female nursery school teachers when they, the children, came from large families where children were spaced close together. There is some agreement that frustration and punishment in infancy and preschool years are associated with dependency in the preschool period. Evidence comes from studies which correlated mothers' feeding practices and discipline practices with later behavior in their children. Preschool children's dependency tended to be greater if their mothers used withdrawal of love to

No affection is so purely angelic as the love of a father to a daughter.

discipline them, showed signs of rejection, punished parent-directed aggression, and were demonstrative with affection. There is agreement that maternal rejection is associated with dependency in children. Research suggests that frustration and punishment in early childhood may affect adult dependency behavior.

Overprotection also has been related to child dependency. Very indulgent, protective mothers tended to have children who expressed their dependency in negative, aggressive ways. Dominating, protective mothers' children tended to be passive and submissive in their dependency. A certain amount of protection and nurturance is essential for a child's existence and health. Parents are faced with many decisions as to how to give their children enough response, help, contact, proximity, attention, recognition, and encouragement toward independent effort without forcing or dominating them.[1]

Characteristics of babyhood

Newborn. The newborn baby's activity is related to the state of his or her stomach. He or she needs frequent feedings and usually settles on a 3 to 4 hour schedule. His or her sense of taste gives a positive response to mild and sweet solutions. However, sour, bitter, or strongly salty tastes receive a negative response. The newborn appears to be relatively insensitive to pain. It is hard to determine how soon or how much an infant feels pain as compared to an adult. But it is true that an adult's pain is frequently more intense because of past experiences. If pain stimulation could be stripped of tensions and fears that grow out of past experiences, many agonies experienced by older people would probably be less severe.

It is interesting to observe how the infant's apparent insensibility to certain pains is seen in medical practice. Circumcisions performed without anesthetic upon a child under two weeks of age and other forms of surgical treatment do not usually cause signs of acute suffering as one would expect if an older person were to have similar treatment. However, one cannot be certain that the absence of outward signs denotes a similar absence of feeling.

For infants, crying is one of their most important accomplishments. Crying, for young children, has a vastly complex set of functions and meanings. Through crying, children express their needs, wants, discomfort, and in time, desire for company, wish to be noticed, hurts and bruises, annoyances, impatience, and grief. Crying

1. From "Some Maternal Influences on Children's Personality and Character" by J. C. Finney, from *Genetic Psychology Monographs,* Vol. 63, 1961, pp. 199–278. Used by permission of Journal Press.

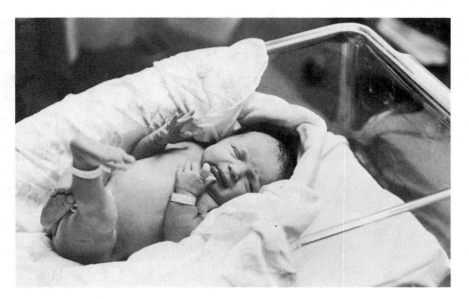

A new born baby is a blank page on which can be written his/her history.

becomes not merely a sign of distress but also a kind of self-assertion. Crying serves children as a means of calling their friends to their side. Very early in life, although not intentionally at first, crying becomes a weapon which children can use as a protest against those who ignore, neglect, or abuse them.

At birth, babies do not show clear-cut patterns of fear and anger. These patterns are learned. The learning starts immediately. Individual babies differ widely in their maturity at birth. The differences in maturity vary as much as the differences in personalities. Some babies are mobile and active. Others are placid and quiet.

Six months old.   By six months, babies discriminate between familiar persons and strangers. They are very conscious of strange places and faces. They recognize their parent's voice and want to join if they hear talking in an adjacent room. They may be able to sit alone. When they are placed on the floor, their knees go into a creeping position. If they are held erect, they can stand firmly with help. Their eyes and hands are beginning to function together. They are able to reach for toys and grasp them. Moreover, they reach a block or a toy promptly on sight. Babies of this age like to bang toys. They also enjoy throwing toys on the floor and looking after them when they have fallen from a high chair or from parent's lap. They inspect all objects and may put them into their mouths. Children, however, vary in their need to mouth objects.

Curiosity in children shows their appetite for knowledge.

Nine months old. By nine months, a child stands alone by pulling himself or herself up with the help of furniture and the sides of the crib. He or she enjoys motor activity such as sitting and playing, creeping, leaning far forward, and standing upright after he or she has pulled himself or herself up. He or she enjoys playing with toys which can be pulled about because he or she can now grasp things by their handles, pluck a string, and give it a tug.

The chief pleasure in eating is in yourself.

The nine-month-olds are very social beings. They respond to demonstrations and teaching. They learn nursery tricks like pat-a-cake and bye-bye. They can say "mamma," "papa," "dada," or make other articulate sounds. Making lip noises and vocalizing at a high pitch are part of their daily enjoyment. Playing in the bath, high chair, play pen, or crib is a delightful pastime. Individuality is beginning to take form. The young child is becoming more discriminating. He or she notices small variations in sight and sound and is more sensitive to surroundings. There is also the beginning of a show of temper that may be either a means of resistance or of communication.

One year old. One-year-old children are learning to walk. They are seldom quiet when awake. They have a variable appetite and begin to show signs of definite food likes and dislikes. They can use a spoon. They want to feed themselves. Sometimes they play at meals and enjoy feeling different food textures. They have learned to drop objects on purpose. They enjoy seeing the way different foods land. They listen to words and try to imitate. However, most of their talk is still gibberish. Their social status in the family is good because they are actors and show-offs. They respond to music. They also laugh at strange and different sounds made by others. They make friends very quickly. Usually one-year-olds designate their friends by bringing them some of their toys to play with or by

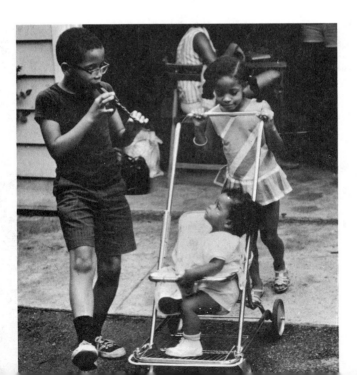

Happiness and companionship are the atmosphere in which all good affections grow.

asking them to read a book to them. They are too young to play with other children but enjoy playing around others. Children who are one year old are capable of showing fear, anger, affection, jealousy, anxiety, and sympathy.

Fifteen months old. At fifteen months, children discard creeping for toddling. Walking is a favorite activity. Usually, while walking, a child carries things in either hand. This age doesn't settle down in any one place for long. They seem to feel a need to exercise their newly formed powers almost to excess. Emptying the wastepaper basket and overturning it many times are among the realm of endless activities. This mobility calls for close supervision from others. This age is a very demanding one. They usually want to be at their mothers' heels, not cooped up in playpen or crib. They also want to be held up so they can see what mother is doing.

Eighteen months old. By eighteen months, children have gained general body control. They can walk upstairs with help, climb into an adult's chair, seat themselves on a child's chair, and move with a hurried gait. Pushing chairs around, throwing balls, and pulling wheeled toys as they walk are enjoyable feats. They can point to pictures they recognize. They can recognize photographs of the family members. They distinguish between "you and me" and are capable of proclaiming "mine." They enjoy errands of fetching and

It is a profound mistake to think that everything has been discovered.

Independence is united to the idea of dignity and virtue.

carrying. Their vocabulary may be about ten words. They gesture to enhance understanding.

The above descriptions are based on average children. Some children will perform at an older level of achievement. Others will perform at a younger level. Some children mature faster than others. Within this growth sequence there are spurts of growth and periods of quiescence. Each individual is unique in his or her pattern and rate of development. Each individual also differs from every other individual in his or her inherent potentialities. Therefore, each child should be treated as an individual. He or she should be given the most effective environment possible to grow toward his or her fullest potential.

Questions

1. What are the basic psychological needs of a new baby?

2. Define "mothering." Must children have their natural mother with them to be well-mothered?

3. What is the degree of sensory development in very young babies?

4. What is the importance of being held and fondled in infancy?

5. When babies begin to worry, what do they worry about?

6. What is separation anxiety? How should one cope with it?

7. What are the two most important gifts that a baby continues to need all through life?

8. How do one's attitudes toward food in babyhood affect his or her life?

9. Describe one of the inborn errors of metabolism in babies.

10. How is the development of a baby judged?

11. How does an infant communicate?

12. What is empathy? How is empathy shown?

13. What are the most important factors in the feeding practices of children?

14. How does the behavior of the parents affect the dependency in the children?

15. If children develop at their own individual rate of growth, why is it important to study the average characteristics of each age?

Further reading

Hurlock, Elizabeth. *Child Growth and Development.* New York: McGraw-Hill, 1970.

Ilg, F. L., and Ames, L. B. *Child Behavior.* New York: Harper & Row, Publishers, Inc., 1972.

Jersild, Arthur T. et al. *Child Psychology.* 7th ed. Englewood Cliffs, NJ: Prentice-Hall, Inc., 1975.

Smart, Mollie S., and Smart, Russell C. *Children: Development and Relationships.* 3rd ed. New York: Macmillan, Inc., 1977.

Westlake, Helen Gum. *Children: A Study in Individual Behavior.* Lexington, MA: Ginn and Company, 1977.

Whiting, J. W. M., and Child, I. L. *Child Training and Personality: A Cross Cultural Study.* New Haven, CT: Yale University Press, 1962.

Chapter 33

Ages and stages

The great joy of the ages and stages of children is that the active two-year-old becomes the contented three-year-old. Parents should not be too concerned nor too smug. With time, each stage, enjoyable or unenjoyable, moves on to a new phase of development.

Family Circus

THE FAMILY CIRCUS by Bil Keane, reprinted courtesy of The Register and Tribune Syndicate.

2-23
Copyright 1978.
The Register and
Tribune Syndicate, Inc.

"Daddy, your sideburns are nice and neat,
but your backburn is getting long."

The toddler

The child between sixteen months and three years is a toddler. The toddler is moving rapidly away from babyhood and into childhood. The central theme of development during toddlerhood is becoming aware of self as a person among other people and wanting to do things for self. This is evident in the mastery of his or her own body, in walking, climbing, jumping, and in controlling muscles. It is in the mastery of objects. The toddler typically wants to push his or her stroller instead of riding in it. He or she wants to put on and remove his or her own clothes. This is the case even though he or she is not very adept at doing so. In social relationships the toddler learns language, begins to refuse parental commands, requests, and offers of help.

Autonomy.   Autonomy is defined as a self-governing state that has no outside control.   During toddlerhood, the push toward autonomy is begun.   However, it is by no means absolute and continuous.   At first the child swings between dependence and independence.   This pattern of behavior will persist in various ways well into adolescence.   The toddler, out on a walk, may plunge off in pursuit of a squirrel, or dash into an empty building.   The toddler may stop short, return to mother and want to be carried.   He or she may strike out on his or her own to explore the wonders of a large department store.   Then burst into tears when he or she finds that the hand he or she is reaching for is that of a stranger.   When trying some new feat such as jumping from a step, he or she will make a great show of boldness but still cling tightly to an adult's hand.   These toddlers are only beginning to try themselves out.   It will take time before they can shift their emotional base from parents to contemporaries.   Finally, they may have a secure hold on a sense of their own identity.

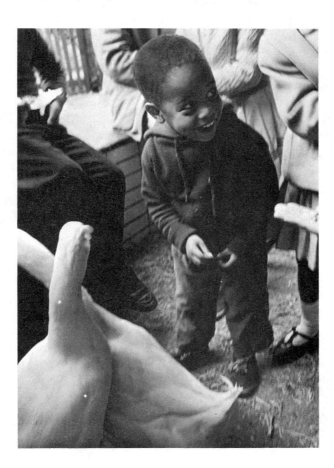

Experience is a good school.

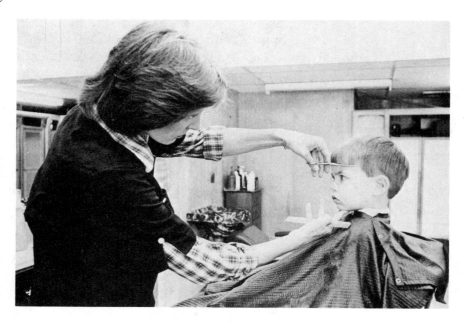

Should I cry? Or should I be quiet and brave?

This self-governing state which is called the sense of autonomy has in it the control of impulses, thus it has the development of conscience. As children take over the wishes and demands of parents and accept them as their own, they are developing a conscience. When conscience isn't strong enough, impulses take over. For example, children say, "no, no," but go ahead and do what they are tempted to do if their parents aren't there to help.

At times the child's conscience becomes so strong that he or she can't stand the guilt feelings. Then he or she chooses ways to relieve these feelings and to control impulses. Four of these ways are described below.

1. *He or she blames someone else.* Sometimes the child adopts a make-believe friend, sister, or brother. When food is spilled, toys scattered or an object broken, he or she blames this imaginary friend.

2. *He or she attacks the person that is causing frustration.* This can result in real guilt feelings if the child is allowed to attack his or her parent. The child desperately needs the parent to love him or her. He or she would usually worry about losing the parent's love if he or she attacks. One way for the parent to handle this situation would be to say, "I know you want to hit me but I can't let you do that. Here, hit your punching clown."

3. *He or she shames self.* Most children shame themselves to control their impulses. They hate this feeling of shame which they heap on themselves. When an adult adds to this load by shaming a child it can be very damaging. An "I am bad, I am unworthy" feeling can result. The feeling can result in extreme shyness.

4. *The child becomes disgusted or loathes an impulse.* Disgust and loathing can be related to any impulse such as climbing, getting hands dirty, or playing with food. When the child feels that the impulse is bad, he or she can't stand any expression of it. This often carries over into adult life. A child that was trained to be fastidious in play may become the adult who cannot make pies because the rolling of the dough is too messy. Finger painting frees some children from a disgust of getting dirty or messy.

Some children who have guilty feelings use fantasy. These fantasies are often extreme and ridiculous. For example, a child becomes angry with his or her parent. He or she feels guilty because of the anger and worries about losing parental love. The child can momentarily wish that the parent would get hurt. Then, upon looking for the parent, the child becomes frantic if he or she can't find the parent immediately.

When the conscience is developing, children start to take responsibility for their environment. Instead of just reacting to circumstances, they have come to feel responsible for the circumstances. The trouble is that they start out feeling totally responsible for what happens to them and for the external factors in their lives. Only gradually do they sort out what they are responsible for from all that they feel responsible for.

Impulses. When children are tired, hungry, or ill, they usually cannot control their impulses. They need kind, firm help. We should remember that most adults can't control themselves either under these circumstances. To help the child, the parent can say, "I know you can't decide for yourself right now, so I am going to help you."

Impulses are much stronger in some children than in others. Those with strong impulses are harder to help and are harder on parents. Progress is made when there is free energy available. If children are too frustrated, they haven't energy to learn new things. Speech is acquired during this time. If a child acquires a hostile conscience, it is harder for him or her to start talking. This compounds the situation because delayed speech prevents children from getting rid of feelings. It is important to remember that a child's orientation is "a tooth for a tooth."

Instinctual drives. Love and aggression are two of the instinctual drives that are operating in the young child. This is a difficult time for young children because they want both parental love and autonomy at the same time. Parents who give the impression that if children control their drives and impulses, they will be loved, make it difficult for children to solve the conflict between love and aggression. Children should have love, regardless of behavior. Parents can give this by saying, "I don't like what you are doing, but I like you." In other words, parents can dislike the act, but not the children. Children see praise as a form of love.

These drives function during toilet training. Children get satisfaction when they know that when they can delay or inhibit impulses, they receive both parent's love and control of self. In toilet training, the parent is asking the child to give up the pleasure of eliminating where and how he or she wants to. Before the child can do this, he or she needs to have voluntary control of sphincter (about 18 months) and anal muscles (about 10 months). In toilet training, the parent should give the child plenty of time to gain control and to take major responsibility for himself or herself. Some children who experience pleasant feelings with the operating of anus and sphincter muscles will enjoy eliminating. They are the children who like to go behind chairs or in the closet to sit and and enjoy it. Urine and feces are a part of the child. Disgust with them can give a young child the feeling that part of him or her is bad. Organs of elimination and of sex are so related that confusion and feelings of badness can spread to sex organs. Severe toilet training often results in damaging feelings about sex.

Freedom of choice. As toddlers develop their sense of autonomy, they need to be given opportunities for a free choice. This free choice should be given gradually. It should also be a well-guided experience. For example, the toddler may have a choice between two or three alternatives. After a nap, he or she may choose from among three or four playsuits. He or she may choose to have a drink of water or milk. The child should have an opportunity to make some independent decisions. This gives him or her an identity with self as a person and an opportunity to be in charge of his or her impulses. However, these free choices need to be ones that the child can successfully manage. If instead of a free choice, he or she has to perform to the letter of parental or adult decisions, the child may develop a feeling that there is only one way to perform. This may create compulsive behavior.

Every noble acquisition
is attended with its risks
. . . especially at three.

Once the first crucial developmental conflict has, in principle, been solved, babies know themselves as distinct from other persons and from objects. When they have learned much about their immediate surroundings, they will begin to feel themselves as persons in their own right. They feel capable of acting on their own impulses and purposes. They can choose between opposing suggestion and command. They feel that they can follow directions and influence what happens to them. They feel capable of doing these things rather than being dependent on the dictates of other people and of circumstances. The feelings of adequacy and of well-being in later life depend upon the development and maintenance of a sense of autonomy. Feelings of self-worth and of counting for something in this world are essential aspects of healthy personality at any age. For the good of the child and for the world, we need the balance of love and aggression to be tipped in favor of love.

Early childhood

Early childhood is usually thought of as the ages of three, four, and five years. This is the time for plans and ideas. This is the age that wakes up before you do and decides that this is the day for scrambled eggs. They scramble all over the kitchen. This is the age to ask questions, observe, and make believe. Children at this age need to try things out. All they ask is the material they need to work with and the time to carry out their ideas in play.

The child's large muscles are developing rapidly. He or she needs opportunities to run, climb, slide, and jump so that he or she can gain control over these muscles and develop coordination. However, motor skills are developing unevenly. The child may perform extremely well in one skill and very poorly in another.

Speech.   At three the child will probably speak in sentences and use words as tools of thought such as, "I don't like this hat" or "My doll is hungry." The next year, he or she asks many questions, recognizes the relationship between things, and displays an active tendency to state an idea and to generalize from it. A four-year-old child may say as many as 1500 to 2500 words.

At five, children usually talk without infantile speech. They can tell a long story and frequently do. Often they talk so much that their mothers find it a trial when they are trying to do something else. When children are at this age, their mothers may wonder whether the gift of speech is such a blessing after all! There is evidence of a close relationship between language and intelligence.

With what do they identify?

Studies show that bright children generally talk earlier and develop more mature vocabularies than children of lesser intelligence. And girls, generally, are ahead of boys in language development, up to maturity. However, environment plays a role in this development.

Social interactions. Friendly contacts between children become more pronounced between the ages of three and five. During these years, children form their first friendships, generally, but not exclusively, with others of their own sex. Friendship patterns change greatly with age. Between the ages of three and four, the number of friends increases. After this age, the primary change is in the closeness of attachment to a few particular children.

A socially oriented and responsive preschool child seeks out companions and has a variety of contacts with them. In the course of learning the modes of social interaction, such a child has both satisfying and frustrating experiences. Consequently, he or she exhibits social responses that seem to be contradictory. For example, preschool friends who have played together in their own neighborhood are more likely to argue with each other in school than with children who are new acquaintances. Highly aggressive nursery school children are also most sympathetic with their classmates, responding most readily to their distresses. The child who grabs a toy from a playmate at one moment may rush to comfort a crying, unhappy child the next.

Popular children and leaders can be distinguished during early childhood. Some children are continually being sought out as playmates. Others are consistently avoided. Some youngsters assume a dominant role, while others are usually passive followers.

The average child of this age, in a social situation, is involved in some sort of conflict every few minutes. Boys tend to be in more conflicts and make more attacks. Girls tend to argue more. These sex differences are more pronounced among the older children of this age group. Perhaps this reflects their more firmly established sex-typing of behavior.

In general, the interactions of these youngsters are more characteristically cooperative and friendly than unfriendly, hostile, or competitive. Even the most highly aggressive three- to five-year-old children actually make more friendly than aggressive responses. Aggressiveness, incidentally, tends to be a fairly stable characteristic. The frequency of a child's conflicts during this age is a reliable indicator of his or her proneness to conflict in school.

Competitiveness appears as early as the ages of three or four, according to the findings of one study. Pairs of children were given a

Popular leaders can be distinguished on the playground.

pile of blocks and each one was asked to compete to build something prettier or bigger than his or her companions could build. Those between the ages of four and six competed with considerable intensity. They grabbed materials from each other, disregarded the other children's feelings and intentions, and refused to give help or materials. By this age, competitive motives are strong enough to produce improvement in performance when a child is competing with someone else. As children advance in age, they become acutely aware of the culture's attitudes toward, and consistent rewards for, competition. Hence, they adopt competitive values and motivations.

Boys seem to compete more than girls. Lower-middle-class children are more competitive than the upper-middle-class children. Highly competitive children often come from democratic, freedom-giving homes. But they are likely to have histories of conflicts with brothers and sisters. During this preschool period, competition and aggression appear to be relatively independent. That is, the most competitive children are not ordinarily the most aggressive. Among older children and adults, these motives are likely to be more closely associated.

Middle childhood

The years from six to twelve compose the period of middle childhood. These are the years when it matters so much for youngsters to be good at something. Much of their real sense of know-how grows on the play fields. This is the age for collections, hobbies, enthusiasms, gang loyalty, sloppiness, and noise. These young people are busy with secret clubs and social organizations.

Identification with peers. In one sense, the peer-group affiliation of these middle years, the immersion of being a child, looks like a detour on the road to maturity. It, however, is a necessary and valuable stage in the process of finding one's own identity. During the preschool years, the child has acquired a first identity from his or

Peer pressure or pleasure?

her parents. This is an identity that is, in effect, an identification. Now, with this foundation, the child is ready to begin the quest for independent existence. As a child has grown in stature, he or she has been able to see parents more realistically. He or she knows their weaknesses and imperfections, and realizes, although still dimly that he or she has to find stability in self. This "detour," then, is an essential moving away from the parents so that a genuine and separate identity can be formed. But the new identity toward which the school child is moving differs from that of the preschool child in more than independence. Most significantly, he or she is becoming less egocentric and more detached from his or her own viewpoint. The school child is more aware of self in objective terms, according to the labels that society attaches to him or her: male or female, age six to twelve, poor or rich, and so forth.

The gang, too, has its set of labels by which it knows the child and he or she knows self. The gang is quick to seize on any idiosyncrasy of appearance, manner, skill, or whatever. Thereafter they treat the child in terms of this trait. The stereotype by which the gang identifies the child is often expressed in a nickname: "Skinny," "Fatso," "Four-eyes," "Mouse," "Dopey," "Limpy." This total frankness, especially of boys, often startles adults. Most children wear their nicknames proudly as a badge of their belonging. Any recognition is better than being ignored. Even the outcast or scapegoat would rather have the gang persecute than ignore him or her. Even the label "Stinky" means that he or she has an identity in the eyes of others. Now, the child's view of self comes not only out of a feeling

Friends forever.

of being loved and accepted by the family, but also from a sense of adequacy and competence that he or she can do what is asked. The child knows that he or she has a role to play. All this further implies that he or she is becoming capable of criticizing and viewing self and achievements through the eyes of others and according to their standards.

The developmental danger of the gang age lies in the failure of the child to go on to relative independence of the group and their standards. Some children who meet persistent rejection by the group may feel isolated and unworthy. Failing to find group acceptance and group support, they return to an identification with adults. It is worth noting that the "good boy" or the "good girl," who may appear to adults as a model for childhood, may be missing out on an important childhood experience and heading for trouble. Such a child's detachment from his or her peer group may be made worse by adult acceptance. The child gets to be known as a "goody-goody," "Mama's boy," or "teacher's pet."

Other children run the risk of so complete an identification with the group that they acquire little ability to think for themselves without depending on group opinion. They feel threatened and disoriented if obliged to take a stand without knowing the "right" way to think. It is, of course, perfectly normal to experience some discomfort and anxiety when one does not know or is in conflict with the standards of the group. The child who has a mature identity knows his or her own opinions. Thus, the child can identify with them confidently, even in opposition to the group.

At this age, a child must make an idea his or her own before accepting it. He or she will not take it merely on adult say-so. Most adults sound foolish to the school-age children they try to influence. They should, however, continue to discuss their notions of conduct and morals, because children continue to identify with the important adults in their lives even as they resist. Children may seem deliberately deaf to parental lectures. They may, also, seem casually deaf to conversations directed over their heads. However, even when they apparently are not listening, they are hearing and learning a variety of facts, opinions, and attitudes.

Early adolescence

The next stages are early adolescence, later adolescence, and young adulthood. Since these are discussed in the first three units, we shall omit them here. Remember, early adolescence is a time when the sense of identity is beginning. Young people are wondering: "Who am I really?" This age goes to extremes at times, particularly in words. The early adolescent has big ideas and very sensitive feelings. They are saying: "I want to like myself." "I want others to like me." "I want to be like others." "I want to like others." The early adolescent needs patience and a sense of confidence from others. The adults in the lives of adolescents should keep all of their requests, demands, and reminders to a minimum. But when discipline is necessary they should stand by their decisions and hold firm.

Changing needs

Since part of the ages and stages are in Unit 1, we shall briefly sketch how needs change with growth. The significant people in the infant's life are the members of his or her immediate family, especially his or her mother. In social contacts, the infant prefers either solitude or one or two people at a time. He or she requires nurturing care. The response to this care is as a receiving, amoral person.

A companion not a playmate nor an adversary.

Interaction with others. Significant people for the preschool child are two or three playmates and family. The preschooler will play beside a friend, but not with him or her. This is called parallel play. The preschooler requires constant supervision. His or her response

to others is one of exchanging. "I'll let you use my airplane if I can play with your car." His or her character type is expedient.

School children need their families and many companions. They enjoy group games and active play. They require guidance. If the guidance is properly given these children are sharing and conforming individuals.

The adolescent needs many friends of his or her own age. It is important for him or her to have contact with boy-girl activities. The adolescent needs encouragement in independence. When received he or she is a very accommodating person.

A wide variety of significant people is required by the adult. He or she needs affirmation through interdependence and many forms of contact. When these needs are satisfied, he or she is a very cooperative person.

Questions

1. What is the central theme of development during childhood?

2. What are the characteristics of a toddler?

3. What is autonomy?

4. How does a child develop a conscience?

5. How does a child relieve guilt feelings?

6. What is the function of fantasy in the development of a child?

7. Impulses are stronger in some children than in others. How should one handle a child with strong impulses?

8. How can one help the child solve the conflict between love and aggression?

9. How do the instinctual drives of love and aggression function during toilet training?

10. What are the characteristics of early childhood?

11. What effect does competitiveness have on early childhood?

12. In middle childhood, the developmental emphasis is on achievement. How is it accomplished? What kinds of achievements are important?

13. How does the child in the 6–12 age span view his or her parents?

14. What are the developmental dangers of the gang age?

15. What are the characteristics of the early adolescent?

Further reading

Bernstein, B. "Language and Social Class." *British Journal of Sociology* 2 (1960): 271–276.

Jersild, Arthur T. *Child Psychology.* 7th ed. Englewood Cliffs, NJ: Prentice-Hall, Inc., 1975.

McCandless, B. R. *Children and Adolescents: Behavior and Development.* 3rd ed. New York: Holt, Rinehart & Winston, CBS, Inc., 1977.

Smart, Mollie S., and Smart, Russell C. *Children: Development and Relationships.* 3rd ed. New York: Macmillan, Inc., 1977.

Spock, Benjamin. *Baby and Child Care.* rev. ed. New York: Pocket Books, Division of Simon & Schuster, Inc., 1977.

Templin, Mildred C. *Certain Language Skills in Children.* Minneapolis: University of Minnesota Press, 1975.

Westlake, Helen Gum. *Children: A Study in Individual Behavior.* Lexington, MA: Ginn and Company, 1977.

Chapter 34

Children's fears

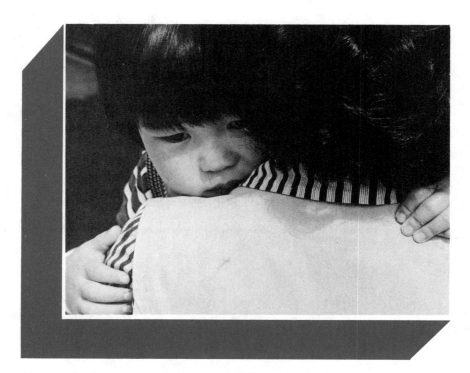

A new baby can cause a child to feel displaced in her or his parents' hearts and home.   A new baby or a new experience, whether it be school or swallowing gargle, can contribute to the fears and anxieties of childhood.

Reprinted by permission of Sidney Harris.
From *Saturday Review/World,* © 1974.

"You mene I've bin spending this whol term
with a defektiv reeding machin?"

Definitions of fear and anxiety

The task of coping with anxieties and fears is a part of the daily job of all children. This task continues into adulthood. *Fear is an emotional reaction to an external danger, real or imagined.* We feel helpless or inadequate. It is a painful feeling consisting of certain physiological changes. It is the awareness of these changes and the particular mental sensations that give to fear its special quality.

Anxiety, like fear, is an emotional reaction to danger. The emotional reaction, the painful feeling, is the same as in fear. The difference is in the nature of the danger. In fear, the danger is external and known. *In anxiety, the danger is internal. It is usually unknown or unconscious.*

The amount of fear we experience at any given time depends on the nature of the danger and our ability to meet it. The fear may be mild, met with alertness, heightened awareness, and sharpened perception. It may be moderate, met with rapid heartbeat, perspiring, and weakness. Or it may be severe, met with panic and disorganization of thought and behavior. Unless the fear paralyzes us, we try to act to reduce it. This may range from the primitive instinctive fight or flight action to more complex planned attempts to avoid, control, master, modify, or otherwise cope with the danger.

Anxiety, the internal danger, is thought to develop from fears that, as children, we could not express. As children, we may have had

---

DENNIS THE MENACE

"QUICK! Where's the top to the corn-popper?"

certain sexual and aggressive impulses, wishes, thoughts, and feelings that we were afraid to express. Correctly or not we may have had the impression that their expression would result in our being deserted, unloved, or punished. In order to lessen our fear, we automatically used an internal action similar to fleeing an external danger. Both the dangerous impulse and the assumed threat became unconscious and the fear disappeared.

Subsequently, however, if either the unconscious impulse or the unconscious threat returns with sufficient intensity, the old danger returns. We experience anxiety as a response to it. The cause is clear in fear. Anxiety has a quality of indefiniteness and a lack of object inasmuch as its cause is internal and unconscious. Fear signals a danger in the external world. Anxiety signals a danger in the inner world of the person, a danger of which he or she is unaware.

1 "Help! Swallowed the gargle!"

2 "Mom, help!"

3 "I swallowed the gargle, help!"

4 "Glug! Swallowed the gargle, Mom!"

5 "Help! I . . ."

"I've been thinking things over.
I'm afraid we're people."

Causes of fear

In the first months of life, infants react to outer stimuli, such as loud noises. They react to inner stimuli, such as hunger, with many emotional spells that are assumed to be painful. As time passes, they learn that certain stimuli or situations will bring on a painful state of physiological tension. They learn to fear and avoid such stimuli. Hunger is difficult to avoid. However, children learn that they suffer more often from hunger pangs in the absence of their parents than in their presence. Thus, this physiological tension is translated into a fear of parental absence. The child fears that if his or her parent is not present, hunger will become unbearable.

These are the beginnings of what we fear in adulthood. From being unaware of most external dangers, as in infancy, we come to know what is dangerous in the physical world. In the psychological realm, matters are more complicated. Each development stage has its own major fear. We proceed from the fear of the parent's absence, to the fear of the withdrawal of parent's loving care, to the fear of the withdrawal of love, to the fear of physical injury, to the fear of punishment. Finally we proceed to the fear of our own conscience.

Development of fear

Age in Years: 1–1½
Fear: separation from parent
Possible Aids:

1. Children from infancy who have been around different people and who have been allowed to develop independence and outgoingness are less apt to develop such fears.

2. Let the child gradually get used to the person who is going to take care of him or her. If parent reappears after a short period, the child is reassured that she or he will always come back.

3. If the parent acts hesitant or guilty every time she or he leaves, if the parent hurries into the child's room at night, parental anxiety reinforces the child's fear that there is great danger in being apart.

4. To avoid a two-year-old child's fear, be careful about drastic changes.

Age in Years: 2
Fear: terrified of going to bed
Possible Aids:

1. The child may be afraid of parental disapproval if he or she wets or soils the bed. The child may feel that if he or she wets, the parent won't love him or her so much and will therefore be more likely to go away.

2. Reassure the frightened 2-year-old by sitting by his or her bed as he or she goes to sleep.

3. Do not be overprotective.

Age in Years: 3–4
Fear: the dark
Possible Aids:

1. Try to reassure the child by words and by your manner.

2. Don't make fun of the child or try to argue him or her out of the fear.

3. Avoid scary movies or TV programs and cruel fairy tales.

4. Never threaten a child with bogeymen or police officers or the devil.

5. Arrange a full, outgoing life with other children every day. The more a child is absorbed in games and plans, the less he or she will worry about his or her inner fears.

Age in Years: 3–4
Fear: death
Possible Aids:

1. Realize that questions about death are apt to come up at this age. Make the explanation casual and suggest that death is a natural part of life.

2. Remember to hug, smile at, and reassure the child that you are going to be together for years and years yet.

Age in Years: 3–4
Fear: dogs
Possible Aid:

Don't drag the child to a dog to reassure him or her. The more he or she is pulled, the more the child is made to feel that he or she must pull away.

Age in Years: 3–4
Fear: becoming a cripple or being physically different
Possible Aids:

1. A child of this age wants to know the reason for everything. He or she worries easily, and applies dangers to self. Give the child opportunities to see that his or her body is similar to the bodies of children who are the same sex and age.

2. Give the child reasons for the crippled people he or she may meet.

Age in Years: 3–4–5
Fear: of sex differences
Possible Aids:

1. Normal children between 2½ and 3½ years of age are likely to wonder about things like bodily differences. If they aren't given

an explanation when they first get curious, they're apt to come to worrisome conclusions.

2. Children should be made to feel comfortable about their sex differences, about their questions, and interest in handling the genitals.

3. Explain in a matter-of-fact manner that boys differ from girls, men differ from women, girls differ from women, and boys differ from men. If they feel your acceptance of their questions, they will ask many and thus dispel their worry.

Age in Years: 6–11
Fear: loss of status in peer group
Possible Aids:

1. Adults should not kiss children of this age in public or treat them in an infantile way around their peers.

2. It is important for such children to dress, talk, and play like the other average children in the neighborhood. It is important that they have the same allowance and privileges.

Age in Years: 6–11
Fear: going to school
Possible Aid:

This often happens after a child has been absent for a few days because of an illness or accident, especially if the illness or the accident happened at school. If a child is freely allowed to stay home, his or her dread of returning to school usually gets stronger. It is increased by the fear that he or she is behind in the school work. It usually works best for the parents to be very firm about getting the child back to school promptly. They should not be dissuaded by physical complaints or try to get the doctor to excuse the child.

Avoidance of fears in children

Parents often develop unnecessary fears in their children by behaving in a frightening manner with threats that reinforce the child's ordinary fears. They may react to danger with panic or denial and be unduly harsh in their punishment. The future health of a child depends not only on the presence and severity of early fears but also on the child's resolution of these fears. If the resolution is a poor one, he or she may become anxious. If it is successful, he or she will become courageous, not timid.

Some fears are necessary for normal development. A child must learn what is dangerous. He or she must also develop a conscience. Nor can one avoid unnecessary fears even in the best parent-child relationship. They seem to be a part of becoming civilized, resulting from the conflict between the child's feelings of love and hate, between the child's impulses, and parental control, and reality, and between the child's impulses and his or her conscience.

It is impossible to know everything about how children should be reared in order to avoid unnecessary fears. However, many simple fears can be subdued with reassurance and explanation. Sometimes fear expresses itself as something else, such as apathy, avoidance, or stubbornness. It is important to recognize and understand the underlying fear in order to help the child. If discipline is too lax, it will not help a child learn to tolerate small but increasing amounts of frustration and fear. If the discipline is too strict, it may lead to excessive fear in connection with learning controls.

Influences of fear upon a child

It is important here to distinguish between what may be termed "healthy" fears and "morbid" fears. Children need to learn early that some situations are dangerous and should be avoided. They must be aware of the fact that they may be hurt if they touch a hot stove, step out into the middle of traffic, or put themselves into any other danger-producing situation. This is the development of reasonable caution. It is not accompanied by inner or overt symptoms of the fear emotion. Children also need to learn to behave so that they do not harm someone else. Emotionalized fear results when or if a child finds himself or herself in a dangerous situation which may be real or imagined but can produce hurt and he or she can do nothing about it. Morbid fears are irrational fears. They usually have little or no basis in fact. But they can cause considerable suffering on the part of the child. Because of the irrational nature of the fears, it is difficult for a child to express what he or she fears and to ask help from concerned adults. Adults are likely to make light of the statements of fear because of their irrational nature. Shadows, dragons, monsters, or bogeymen are seen as objects of laughter rather than concern.

The following list explains the way that children react to healthy fears and morbid fears:

Rational responses to fears	Irrational responses to fears
Flight	Contrariness
Illness	Nightmares
Caution	Daydreams
Reduced Activity	Overaggressive Behavior
Stepped-up Activity	Psychosomatic Illness
Bragging	Withdrawal
Lying	

Most children have many ways to cope with both rational and irrational fears. Some children who experience rational fears during an activity that could be harmful will simply put much effort into learning to avoid the danger, without having to leave the activity itself. For example, some children learn to master swimming or a jittery pony instead of having to develop anxious avoidances of such activities altogether. For some others, the most reasonable way out is simply a readiness to ask for help around the danger area. For still others, the emotional tie to a beloved person present at the time of danger or the exposure to a "secure" and accepting group atmosphere may be all that is needed. This allows children to cope with fears which might have kept them from entering the activity.

For fear with real danger and for irrational fears or anxieties from within, most children manage to use the defense mechanism of displacement and dramatic play, talking, or daydreams as ways to lessen their fear. Clinging to fantasies of power, force, indestructibility or omniscience, or acting out terrifying play behavior or bravado, they cope happily with what otherwise might become a state of panic or an anxiety attack.

Development revisited

In order to understand anxiety, guilt feelings, and fears both rational and irrational, we must keep in mind the developmental phases. When the development of the child is hindered or threatened, fears, guilt feelings, and anxieties can result.

Early psychoanalytic theory of the development of personality came about through the study of adults' recall of their childhood. But it led to many investigations with infants and children as subjects in the areas of feeding, toilet training, identification, dependency, and the growth of conscience and guilt feelings.

INFLUENCES OF FEAR UPON A CHILD

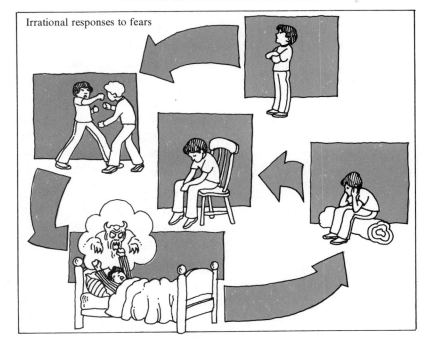

Irrational responses to fears

or

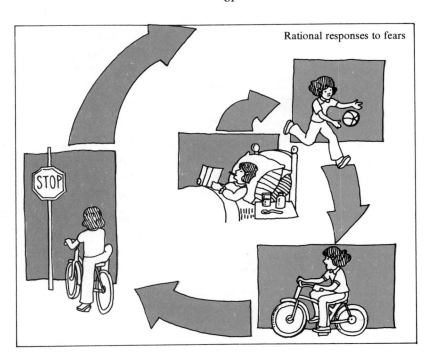

Rational responses to fears

After much research, Erikson suggested eight successive periods of development.[1] Each with its "psychosocial crises" to be resolved by the child before he or she can move to the next level.

1. *Learning trust versus mistrust.* During infancy, the child who is loved and nurtured becomes basically secure and optimistic. The child who is unloved becomes insecure and mistrustful.

2. *Learning autonomy versus shame.* The learning of bowel control is the prototype of many social lessons during the ages one to four, during which the child may develop either feelings of pride in accomplishment and self-control, or feelings of shame.

3. *Learning initiative versus guilt.* During the preschool years, the child learns to develop his social skills with other children, to cooperate, and to lead as well as to follow. The child not able to do this feels guilty, clings to adults, and does not develop play skills and imagination.

4. *Learning industry versus inferiority.* The school child learns the techniques of self-discipline, more formal rules of living in his peer group, and the satisfaction of accomplishment. Failing to do this, the school child feels inadequate and inferior.

5. *Learning identity versus identity confusion.* During adolescence, a mature perspective of time and a sense of achievement develop in the successful person. Although most adolescents probably experiment with minor delinquency, are rebellious, and have feelings of self-doubt, the maturing young adult gradually learns, by trial and error, a stable social role. At this stage, the growing and developing youth looks for models to inspire and for ideals to guide him or her.

6. *Learning intimacy versus isolation.* A successful basis for marriage and lasting friendships depends upon the development of the ability to experience real intimacy. The avoidance of such experiences may lead to isolation.

7. *Learning generativity versus self-absorption.* The successful adult lives productively, in his family as well as in his lifework. If the individual is unable to do this, he or she may become overly self-absorbed.

8. *Learning personality integration versus despair.* The mature adult, having successfully passed the earlier stages, develops in-

1. Erik H. Erikson, *Childhood and Society*, 2d ed. (New York: W. W. Norton and Co., 1963).

dependence and security. The adult who remains at conflict on one or more of the lower levels is chronically dissatisfied and never at peace with himself.

The successful growth of an individual through each of the above periods of development would eliminate many anxieties and fears. It is important to remember two generalizations. They are these.

1. When an individual experiences satisfaction from the results of a particular pattern of behavior, he or she is likely to incorporate that pattern into his or her behavior.

2. To the extent that an individual's developmental needs are met as they occur, he or she is free to move toward full potential. If the basic needs of children are met, one can be unafraid in the handling of their fears.

Questions

1. Define fear and anxiety. Give an example of each.

2. The statements below depict either healthy or morbid fears. Indicate which is described.

   a. "I am afraid of snakes because their appearance surprises me."

   b. "I wish my brother were dead."

   c. "When there is thunder and lightning outside, my heart beats rapidly and the palms of my hands sweat."

   d. "When mother sits and reads, she is really wishing I'd go away."

   e. "If I don't say anything, my father won't spank me."

3. What are the causes of fear in infants?

4. If you were a nursery school teacher, how would you help a two-year-old child overcome his or her fear of separation?

5. Why is a two-year-old child often terrified of going to bed?

6. Johnny is three years old. He wants a light on in his room while he goes to sleep. If you were his parent, what would you do about this request?

7. Della's grandfather died. Della is four years old. Her grandfather was someone very special to her. For the last two weeks

since his death, she has been playing funeral with her dolls and teddy bears. If you were her parent, how would you handle this? Is this a healthy activity for Della?

8. Children worry about the natural differences between boys and girls. When children ask a question about physical differences they are asking it as they would any question. Thus they need an honest, direct, reassuring answer. How would you answer little Johnny who while watching his baby sister being diapered asks why she has no penis?

9. How would you deal with a four-year-old girl who became worried when she found out that the genitals of boys were different from her own genitals?

10. How do parents develop unnecessary fears in their children?

11. Why are some fears necessary?

12. Why is it important to recognize the way that a child is coping with a specific fear?

13. What kinds of fears might develop if the first three developmental stages designated by Erikson are not successfully mastered?

Further reading

Erikson, Erik H. *Childhood and Society.* 2d ed. New York: W. W. Norton & Co., Inc., 1963.

———. *Identity and the Life Cycle: Selected Papers.* New York: International Universities Press, 1967.

Ilg, F. L., and Ames, L. B. *Child Behavior.* New York: Harper & Row, Publishers, Inc., 1972.

McCandless, Boyd R. *Adolescents: Behavior and Development.* New York: Holt, Rinehart & Winston, CBS, Inc., 1970.

Shindelus, Mary, and Durkin, Mary. *People in Families.* Reading, MA: Addison-Wesley Publishing Co., Inc., 1972.

Simpson, George. *People in Families.* Cleveland, OH: World Publishing Company, 1966. p. 121.

Smart, Mollie S., and Smart, Russell C. *Children: Development and Relationships.* 3rd ed. New York: Macmillan, Inc., 1977.

Westlake, Helen Gum. *Children: A Study in Individual Behavior.* Lexington, MA: Ginn and Company, 1977.

Chapter 35

Discipline

The person who is disciplining is often turned off by a question or joke by the one who is being disciplined. In fact, some children learn very early how to break a disciplinary mood or how to skirt the subject which is under discussion.

"And if he gives you any trouble, just give us a call."

To discipline is to train, to educate, or to bring under control. Educationally and psychologically, discipline is social control within a group. It includes all the forces that mold attitudes and inspire conduct.

Children of all ages need to know the limits of their behavior. Children need to feel that their parents will help them control themselves. Children want parents to be firm and to help them become reasonable and thoughtful people. However, parents must be consistent and fair in their discipline. The parental mood should not influence the rules of discipline for a particular child. Parents should feel free to discipline their children while they are still feeling friendly toward them. For example, if a child wants to continue playing ball after his or her parents are exhausted, they should not hesitate to say pleasantly but precisely, "We're tired of playing ball. We're going to read the newspaper now. You can read one of your books."

When a child is being rude, perhaps because he or she is jealous or frustrated, one should promptly stop him or her and insist upon politeness. Children know when they have displeased or have broken a rule. They expect to be corrected. They are more secure if they are disciplined. Their conscience is cleared. But at the same time, children should be helped to understand that we all get cross sometimes. All people sometimes become angry at those they love best. Children should know that in spite of their angry feelings or their hostile actions they are still loved. It is only their behavior that is unacceptable. This realization helps a child get over his or her anger and keeps him or her from feeling too guilty or frightened because of it. It is helpful to make a distinction between hostile feelings and hostile actions.

Effects of various kinds of discipline

The behavior of the child is a function of the balance between parental support and parental discipline. This general principle is further complicated by the different effects of various types of discipline. For example, several investigators have shown that so-called "psychological" techniques of discipline, such as reasoning, appealing to guilt, showing disappointment, are more effective in bringing about desired social behavior than more direct methods,

" . . . and the flashlight!"

such as physical punishment, scolding, or threats. In fact, a number of studies indicate that the more children are spanked for being aggressive, the more aggressive they will be. However, one must be careful about jumping to conclusions from such findings. For researchers have not pinned down the direction of the relationship. Is it spanking that causes the aggressiveness, or the aggressiveness that brings on the spanking? Moreover, there are indications that a reliance on psychological techniques of discipline to the exclusion of more direct methods, such as spanking, may result in an "over-socialized" child lacking in spontaneity and initiative.

Such considerations may help to explain the differences in behavior seen in children of different sexes and from different social class levels. Psychological techniques of discipline, for instance, are more likely to be used with girls than with boys. They are more frequently used in middle-class families than in working-class ones. It is also a well-established fact that girls are generally more obedient, cooperative, and better socialized than boys at comparable age levels.

Systematic differences are seen not only in the techniques used, but also in the occasions when they are applied. For example, working-class parents tend to punish children more for the consequence of their action than for the underlying motive. The reverse holds true for middle-class parents. Much work remains to be done, however, in exploring the relations between parental techniques of discipline, the occasions on which they are used, and the values in the name of which they are carried out. Lastly, the effect of all these factors on the child's behavior must be considered. In the meantime, the clearest lesson one can draw from available research is that use of any one type of discipline alone is likely to have undesirable effects. This holds regardless of whether it is physical punishment, reasoning, or withdrawal of parental companionship.

Discipline and dependence

Biological as well as cultural and direct experimental factors cause dependence. Babies come into the world in a condition of biological helplessness. They would soon die if their parents did not care for them. Babies perform, at first, few purposeful skeletal body movements except sucking and those associated with excretion. Even these seem relatively unconditioned. A baby's physical dependence upon the parents for food and care generates a related emotional dependence which at first is focused on the mother. This is especially true in American culture based upon a small family unit. It may be contrasted with the more diffusely directed dependence in some other cultures.

In our culture, the mother (or substitute) is usually the one most concerned in the development of the basic socialization of the child. As the baby grows through infancy, he or she gradually begins to recognize his or her mother as a separate person. The baby realizes his or her dependence upon the mother and comes to take refuge in her in time of trouble. The mother gives solace and a sense of security. The father, too, serves to protect the child from the hazards and insecurities of a large and unknown world. If children's security is threatened, as by separation from parents or their failure to respond to needs, children may become disturbed in a variety of ways. It is mostly through dependence upon and trust in the parents that it is possible for children to grow and to adapt themselves to the world's requirements. Some degree of dependence is, therefore, essential in normal development.

Degrees of dependency. Overdependency may result from the failure, unwillingness, or inability of parents to promote their child's growth. The degree of dependence is conditioned by early affectionate relations with the parents, early training, and discipline. It is also conditioned by the parents' wisdom in permitting the exercise of initiative, creativeness, and imagination consistent with the child's abilities. Parents who need to dominate may use their children as objects to express their own need for superiority by controlling their children too much. On the other hand, failure to provide loving discipline may leave a child insecure and anxious. Children growing up in a healthy family environment make the transition from dependence to independence gradually.

Probably the best philosophy is one which recognizes that childhood with its varying degrees of dependence and independence is a significant and important time of life. The child's expression of growing independence need not be accepted as final. It is important that a child be given the opportunity to grow. But at the same time, the child should recognize that the insights he or she gains as a child will be enlarged as he or she grows up. This process of widening horizons need never end in his or her life.

Dependence can be normal or abnormal. The kind of dependence is determined by biological factors such as sex and physical patterns, customs of child rearing, and attitudes and practices of education and training. The child's dependence upon a parent is conditioned by the parents' capacity for fostering growth, recognizing normal changes in dependence needs, and giving loving support and discipline. When children are deeply dependent upon the parents in an emotional relationship and yet feel unwanted, unloved, and rejected, they will suffer anxiety. They may react to this in many ways. They may become permanently embittered, hostile, or fearful. They may never be able to achieve independent status. They may cling to a parent or parent substitute even as adults.

Abnormal dependency in adult life may be prevented by helping a child to learn gradually to assume responsibility and independence. These measures should be taken from birth. In the early years, children depend upon their parents and should be allowed to satisfy their need to be secure. Some anxiety is inevitable for biological and for sociological reasons. However, in a loving, disciplined family, children are usually able to build adequate defenses. Children need growing space so that they can become persons uniquely aware of their capacity for self-determination. Children will show spontaneously their desires toward independence. If given the opportunity, they will take responsibility and be creative in terms of ability at each stage of growth. If parents are able and willing to give up control gradually their child will develop into a normal adult. Unfortunately, some parents are not sufficiently secure. They impose their own will and deny their child room to grow. They become frightened if the child's behavior threatens them. They blame rather than support their child in his or her problems.

Development of independence. The process of becoming a more and more independent person is slow and gradual. It continues from birth through adulthood. Children need discipline. Then they need the gradual release from discipline as well as the parents' help and encouragement in this process. Persons who have grown up in this way are better prepared to face the inevitable changes from early adulthood to old age.

Discipline and aggression

Aggression refers to the total energy spent in activity trying to satisfy instinctual, or inborn, drives. In human beings, we prefer to speak of drives. In lower animals, aggression is seen as a way of dealing with instincts. The psychiatric meaning of aggression refers to the forceful attacking action that can be physical, verbal, symbolic, or a combination of all three.

Development of aggression. There are aggressions that develop slowly and are in keeping with day-to-day problems and frustrations. This happens particularly during the growing phases of human development. These aggressions may be reactions to too much discipline or to too little. When there are excessive prohibitions, young children may feel a need to mobilize constantly increasing amounts of aggressive energy to cope with their frustrations. Where there is a lack of discipline, children may feel that they are being left on their own too much. They then become anxious. This anxiety can stimulate aggressions in order to provoke their elders into giving them more protection and guidance. Such aggressions are expressions of children's sense of insecurity.

Aggressions may be rational or irrational. Rational aggressions are most often a response to actual situations. Most often they are justifiable. The irrational aggressions usually result from some mental attitude that compels a person to act aggressively.

Essentially, aggressions are caused by frustration or interference with a natural development of the instinctual drives. Since a person, from the beginning, encounters checks on his or her instinctual drives, frustration is ever present. The amount of frustration, the capacity to tolerate it, the degree of parental support, and others' support, all contribute to the degree of aggressive feelings.

Discipline and punishment

Unfortunately, many people equate discipline with punishment. Discipline, however, should be a scheme for regulating children's behavior. It should teach children self-control through reward and punishment, and help them to internalize moral standards.

Sex differences and punishment. From several studies about punishment as experienced by children, it was found that there are important sex differences as to who gives and who receives punishment. Fathers punish more than mothers, especially where boys are concerned. Fathers use physical punishment more than mothers, especially with boys. Boys receive more physical punishment. Girls receive more verbal punishment.

When children distinguish between the power of their parents, they tend to see the father as more powerful. They report that punishment, particularly physical punishment, is more often given by the father. They see their mothers as nurturant, helpful, and lenient. It is not surprising, therefore, that children more often like their mothers better than their fathers.

Kinds of punishment. Important elements in punishment are the way in which it is given and the way in which it is received. Most parents agree that they have to impose punishment on their children. But they also agree that one has to give thought to what punishment is best. Many agree that there is a time for physical punishment, but that taking away privileges or restricting freedom are often more effective.

The discipline which tries to use children's internal forces to get them to comply seems to foster understanding and adoption of appropriate behavior. Using children's internal forces means appealing to their need for affection, their self-esteem, and concern for others. Psychological or love-oriented discipline uses children's affectionate relationship with their parents. The importance of loving children and letting them know it cannot be stressed too strongly. Physical force and other forms of direct power of parent over child promote a moral orientation based on fear of detection and punishment.

Discipline and life

One of the most needed lessons for adulthood for achievement, happiness, and growth toward maturity is the lesson of discipline. People must discipline their behavior in terms of their conduct and actions toward others.

Importance of discipline. Discipline is important in all of life. For example, one must use self-discipline in eating to avoid being overweight. To practice a vocation successfully demands the strictest kind of discipline. For the artist, life is always a discipline. No discipline is without pain. This is true even of dancing, which, of all the arts, is the most associated in people's minds with pleasure.

Self-discipline does not really end with the self. Throughout history peoples and nations thought they were self-disciplined. But they could not control themselves in their actions toward other peoples and nations. Struggle for power over others which leads to inhumanity and war is evident in every day's newspapers, whether the articles focus on street crimes or war crimes.

Discipline should be guidance in personal, national, and international growth. Young people should try to discipline themselves in areas such as school work, responsibilities at home, and relationships with their peers. Persons in vocations should try to discipline themselves in doing the best and most creative work they can. Leaders in government should discipline themselves in dealing intelligently with world crises. This means using intelligence, sensitivity, and peaceful alternatives rather than weapons and armed might in times of stress. In all of these cases, there should be a consistency between words and actions. Peoples and nations should mean what they say. If these types of discipline could be basic in personal and national transactions, many acts of aggression would not be committed.

Questions

1. What is discipline?

2. What is the value of discipline to children?

3. What are the psychological techniques of discipline? What are the physical techniques of discipline? What are the advantages and disadvantages of each type?

4. How does discipline differ among the social classes?

5. Should one rely on any one type of discipline? If so, why? If not why not?

6. What causes overdependency?

7. How is dependence related to the type of discipline?

8. What is aggression?

9. What is the relationship between aggression and discipline?

10. Should discipline be equated to punishment? How are they alike? How are they different?

11. What type of discipline seems to foster the greatest degree of understanding in the child?

12. What are some of the individual and social advantages of self-discipline? What might be some of the disadvantages?

Further reading

Combs, Arthur W. *Perceiving, Behaving, Becoming.* Washington, DC: National Education Association. Association for Supervision and Curriculum Development, 1962.

Cressy, Byron. *Discipline and Children.* Glendale, CA: Regal Books, 1977.

Gardner, L. P. "An Analysis of Children's Attitudes Toward Fathers." *Journal of Genetic Psychology* 70 (1947): 3-28.

Ginott, Haim G. *Between Parent and Child.* New York: Macmillan, Inc., 1973.

Hymes, James L., Jr. *Behavior and Misbehavior: A Teacher's Guide to Action.* Englewood Cliffs, NJ: Prentice-Hall, Inc., 1978.

Kagan, J. "The Child's Perception of the Parent." *Journal of Abnormal Social Psychology* 53 (1956): 257-258.

Rasmussen, Margaret. *Discipline.* Bulletin No. 99. Washington, DC: Association for Childhood Education International, 1957.

Rosen, B. C. "Social Class and the Child's Perception of the Parent." *Child Development* 35 (1964): 1147-1153.

Walker, Nigel. *Behavior and Misbehavior: Explanations and Non-explanations.* New York: Basic Books, Inc., Publishers, 1977.

Westlake, Helen Gum. *Children: A Study in Individual Behavior.* Lexington, MA: Ginn and Company, 1977.

Chapter 36

For all of us

It is ironic that nations devote so much expertise and resources on an intercontinental missile system while famine, disease, illiteracy, inequality, and poverty continue to be world-wide problems.

"What do you think, Professor? Is it a laser, a maser,
a quasar, or just a little ray of hope for all mankind?"

If we could shift our priorities from learning how to destroy toward greater understanding and mutual respect, our uncertainty about our lives might be lessened. If much more of our intelligence, devotion to research, and technological knowledge are applied to the problems of understanding ourselves, we might see breakthroughs which would light and inspire our whole idea of the future.

All over the world, more and more people seem to be unsure about where they stand, what they expect, and above all, what they should believe. This uncertainty shows up in individuals as alienation and identity crises. This same uncertainty expresses itself in society, in delinquency, alcoholism, drug addiction, child abuse, husband or wife abuse, and other forms of violence.

Yet, with all of the uncertainty as to priorities, position, and meaning in life, people have been and continue to be reluctant to look at their own relationships. They have tended instead to charge their failures to "human nature." It seems that they have often found it easier to assume that "human nature" is a force which cannot be controlled or improved. They have often found it easier to hide behind "human nature" instead of trying to adjust to technological and social change.

Fear of change is, no doubt, in all of us. But it most afflicts those who fear that any change must lead to loss of wealth and status. When this fear becomes excessive, one may, if one has political power, do away with civil rights and the rule of law. The argument is used that one does away with rights and rules only to keep them. If such a person would say, "I do this because I am afraid," there would be hope. When he or she says, "I do this because I am good and I know best," it becomes hopeless.

One of the main reasons for rapid change is technological development. This development is producing constant change in our physical environment and social relationships. Our inability to adjust with sufficient speed and success causes personal and social confusion. This new technology requires that we make new appraisals. We must adjust to changing institutions and behaviors. We find this difficult to do. Indeed, we have often found that just as we try to change to meet the technological development, technology advances further. The new adjustment is already obsolete and meaningless.

Technology has brought people into more frequent and intimate contact with others whose discipline, values, and relationships differ widely. This has tended to rob us of a complacency in our rightness and in the universal applicability of our particular way of life.

Medical technology, in particular, is possibly one of the causes of our difficulties. It not only preserves lives, but it lengthens them. Youth and age confront each other more often and dramatically than ever before. Major advances in heart and other organ transplants are requiring us to rethink our moral standards as well as the questions, "What is life? What is death?"

Does this suggest that we should try to restrain our technological development? Of course not. The weight of history is totally against such an action. Ever since people began using tools, there has been steady advancement in technical knowledge and skill. Yet, what is lacking is the accompanying progress of intelligence and greater sensitivity in using this technological power.

We must face fast-moving technological growth as a basic fact in human societies. Narrow views which include too simple ideologies and the adoption of unchangeable ways are not appropriate. Whether one is optimistic or pessimistic, bold or cautious, as our position is reviewed today, it suggests that this age requires us to respond realistically and creatively lest our technological gains destroy our sense of the worth of living. People must keep their intelligence and sensitivity in front of technological developments, not miles behind. People are no longer the victims of life. They are the masters, and this may be the ultimate danger.

People have the biological capacity to use their intelligence and sensitivity to adjust to and keep pace with technology. Taking the long view, people have many very real assets for the task of flexible adaptation. First, people have relatively few behaviors that are genetically specific. As seen in Unit 1, they are capable of changing themselves if they seriously and conscientiously attempt to do so. Second, a person, as discussed in Unit 4, has a long infancy, during which he or she is capable of much learning. One does not have to look further than the exploratory behavior of young children to find that the urge to learn is inherent in people. The eagerness young children show in exploring new objects and in trying out new skills seems proof enough. Pre-adolescents, however, with their endless questions about how things work, and adolescents, with their discussions of sex and the meaning of life, provide even more evidence. At whatever level of development one looks, people show a burning curiosity, a tremendous urge to know. Third (and perhaps more magnificently), people have an incredible capacity for symbolizing. People are still in the state of mind where the traditional attitudes born of past wants and conflicts influence them more than the many largely unexploited opportunities of the hopeful present. The note of hope and idealism in the world is tremendous. But it tends to be drowned out by qualification, compromise, and cynicism. We must continue to have hope until it overpowers fear, cynicism, and reaction. We must gain enough confidence in ourselves and in others to turn ideals and potentiality into reality.

[1] One thing I know deep out of my time: youth when lighted and alive and given a sporting chance is strong for struggle and not afraid of any toils or punishments or dangers or deaths.

What shall be the course of society and civilization across the next hundred years?

1. Excerpt from ALWAYS THE YOUNG STRANGERS, copyright, 1952, 1953, by Carl Sandburg. Reprinted by permission of Harcourt Brace Jovanovich, Inc.

For the answers read if you can the strange and baffling eyes of youth.

Yes, for the answers, read, if you can, the strange and baffling eyes of youth.

Yet, consider also the following words of Mark Twain.[2]

> Every man is in his own person the whole human race, with not a detail lacking. I am the whole human race without a detail lacking. I have studied the human race with diligence and strong interest all these years in my own person; in myself I find in big or little proportion every quality and every defect that is findable in the mass of the race. I knew I should not find in any philosophy a single thought which has not passed through the heads of millions and millions of men before I was born; I knew I should not find a single original thought in my philosophy, and I knew I could not furnish one to the world myself, if I had five centuries to invent it in. Nietzsche published his book, and was at once pronounced crazy by the world—by a world which included tens of bright, sane men who believed exactly as Nietzsche believed but concealed the fact and scoffed at Nietzsche. What a coward every man is and how surely he will find it out if he will just let other people alone and sit down and examine himself. The human race is a race of cowards; and I am not only marching in that procession but carrying a banner.

We cannot avoid change or choices. We can only assume responsibility for our decisions and hope that they are made with intelligence and thoughtfulness. We must make every effort to see that we are educated in breadth and depth, both intelligently and socially. Social structures must exist. However, this does not mean that such structures can never be changed.

Questions

1. Why have people been reluctant to work at a study and investigation of their own relationships?

2. What are some of the main reasons for rapid changes?

3. How do people react to change?

2. Prefatory note "September 4, 1907" by Mark Twain in MARK TWAIN IN ERUPTION, edited by Bernard DeVoto. Copyright 1940 by The Mark Twain Company. Reprinted by permission of Harper & Row, Publishers, Inc.

4. What are the assets that people have for the task of adapting to change?

5. What are some examples of compromise and cynicism that you see in your personal world or the world at large today?

6. Mark Twain said, "Every man is in his own person the whole human race, with not a detail lacking." What does this mean to you? Write an essay titled "I Am the Whole Human Race" or "The Human Race: A Race of Cowards."

7. How might we gain enough confidence in ourselves and in each other to turn our ideals and our potentiality into reality?

Further reading

Ardrey, Robert. *Territorial Imperative.* New York: Dell Publishers, 1977.

Kagan, J., and Moss, H.A. *Birth of Maturity: A Study in Psychological Development.* New York: John Wiley and Sons, 1962.

Sandburg, Carl. *Always the Young Strangers.* New York: Harcourt, Brace and World, 1953.

Thurber, James. *Thurber Country.* New York: Simon and Schuster, Inc., 1960.

"A leaf has its own fascination moved by wind or colored by fall. But when it floats above your hands, slick in the water, a leaf has a special wonder."

The Christian Science Monitor.

Index

FGH   0854
Printed in the United States of America

PICTURE CREDITS

Illustrators: Mary Reilly/Designworks pp. 7, 10, 241, 242, 243, 244, 245, 246; George Ulrich pp. 31, 35, 49, 66, 191, 195, 203, 236, 238, 256, 257, 279, 351, 355, 415.

Photographers: Jeff Albertson/Stock, Boston pp. vi–1; David Austen/Stock, Boston p. 405; Fredrik Bodin p. 176; Andrew Brilliant/Picture Cube p. 53; John D. Burns, Jr./D.P.I. p. 387; Jon Chase p. 399; Bobbi Carrey p. 389; Betsy Cole p. 199; Garbor Demjen/Stock, Boston p. 407; A. Devaney p. 116; T. C. Fitzgerald/Picture Cube p. 429; Mimi Forsyth/Monkmeyer p. 299; Rich Friedman/Picture Cube p. 130; Ewing Galloway p. 384; George Gardner p. 220; Charles Gatewood p. 42; Jim Harrison/Stock, Boston pp. 77, 372; Ellis Herwig/Stock, Boston pp. 184, 210; Ken Heyman pp. 150, 350, 435; J. R. Holland/Stock, Boston p. 332; Bohdan Hrynewych pp. 128–129, 199, 314, 330–331, 378; E. P. Jones p. 108; George Knight p. 398; Susan Lapides p. 14; George W. Martin/D.P.I. p. 385; Terry McCoy p. 186; Peter Menzel/Stock, Boston p. 343; Henry Monroe/D.P.I. pp. 391, 395; Major Morris p. 384; Marjorie Pickens pp. 374, 396, 400; H. Armstrong Roberts p. 386; Eric Roth/Picture Cube pp. 26, 87; John Running/Stock, Boston p. 102; Sybil Shelton/Monkmeyer p. 163; Ruth Silverman/Stock, Boston p. 419; Frank Siteman pp. 2, 63, 218-9, 261; Rose Skytta p. 248; Frank Staub/Picture Cube p. 99; Peter Vandermark/Stock, Boston pp. 141, 235, 270; Dan Walsh/Picture Cube p. 392; Donald G. Westlake pp. 156-7, 337–339; Leo deWys, Inc. p. 381.

BCDEFGH   087654
Printed in the United States of America